SECOND LANGUAGE ACQUISITION

Routledge Applied Linguistics is a series of comprehensive resource books, providing students and researchers with the support they need for advanced study in the core areas of English language and Applied Linguistics.

Each book in the series guides readers through three main sections, enabling them to explore and develop major themes within the discipline:

- Section A, Introduction, establishes the key terms and concepts and extends readers' techniques of analysis through practical application.
- Section B, Extension, brings together influential articles, sets them in context, and discusses their contribution to the field.
- Section C, Exploration, builds on knowledge gained in the first two sections, setting thoughtful tasks around further illustrative material. This enables readers to engage more actively with the subject matter and encourages them to develop their own research responses.

Throughout the book, topics are revisited, extended, interwoven and deconstructed, with the readers' understanding strengthened by tasks and follow-up questions.

Second Language Acquisition:

- introduces the key areas in the field, including: multilingualism, the role of teaching, the mental processing of multiple languages, and patterns of growth and decline
- explores the key theories and debates and elucidates areas of controversy
- gathers together influential readings from key names in the discipline, including: Vivian Cook, Eric Kellerman, Merrill Swain, Sharon Lapkin, Alison Mackey, Robert Gardner and Nina Spada.

Written by experienced teachers and researchers in the field, *Second Language Acquisition* is an essential resource for students and researchers of Applied Linguistics.

Kees de Bot is Chair of Applied Linguistics at the University of Groningen. **Wander Lowie** and **Marjolijn Verspoor** are lecturers in the Department of English and the Department of Applied Linguistics at the University of Groningen.

ROUTLEDGE APPLIED LINGUISTICS

SERIES EDITORS

Christopher N. Candlin is Senior Research Professor in the Department of Linguistics at Macquarie University, Australia. At Macquarie, he established and was Executive Director of the National Centre for English Language Teaching & Research (NCELTR) and first Director of the Centre for Language in Social Life (CLSL). He has written or edited over 150 publications and from 2004 will co-edit the new *Journal of Applied Linguistics*. From 1996 to 2002 he was President of the International Association of Applied Linguistics (AILA). He has acted as a consultant in more than 35 countries and as external faculty assessor in 36 universities.

Ronald Carter is Professor of Modern English Language in the School of English Studies at the University of Nottingham. He has published extensively in the fields of applied linguistics, literary studies and language in education. He has given consultancies in the field of English language education, mainly in conjunction with The British Council, in over thirty countries worldwide. He was recently elected a fellow of the British Academy of Social Sciences and is currently chair of the British Association of Applied Linguistics (BAAL).

TITLES IN THE SERIES

Intercultural Communication: An advanced resource book
Adrian Holliday, Martin Hyde and John Kullman, Canterbury Christ Church University College, UK

Translation: An advanced resource book
Basil Hatim, Heriot-Watt University, UK and The American University of Sharjah, UAE and Jeremy Munday, University of Surrey, Guildford, UK

Grammar and Context: An advanced resource book
Ann Hewings, Open University, UK and Martin Hewings, University of Birmingham, UK

Second Language Acquisition: An advanced resource book
Kees de Bot, Wander Lowie and Marjolijn Verspoor, University of Groningen, Netherlands

Second Language Acquisition

An advanced resource book

Kees de Bot, Wander Lowie
and Marjolijn Verspoor

Routledge
Taylor & Francis Group

LONDON AND NEW YORK

First published 2005
by Routledge
2 Park Square, Milton Park, Abingdon, Oxon OX14 4RN

Simultaneously published in the USA and Canada
by Routledge
270 Madison Ave, New York, NY 10016

Routledge is an imprint of the Taylor & Francis Group

Designed and typeset in Akzidenz, Minion and Novarese
by Keystroke, Jacaranda Lodge, Wolverhampton
Printed and bound in Great Britain
by TJ International Ltd, Padstow, Cornwall

British Library Cataloguing in Publication Data
A catalogue record for this book is available from the British Library

Library of Congress Cataloging in Publication Data
De Bot, Kees.
    Second language acquisition : an advanced resource book /
Kees de Bot, Wander Lowie, Marjolijn Verspoor.
      p. cm. – (Routledge applied linguistics)
      Includes bibliographical references and index.
      1. Second language acquisition. I. Lowie, Wander, 1959–
II. Verspoor, Marjolijn. III. Title. IV. Series.
P118.2.D395 2005
418–dc22
                                           2004021210

ISBN 0–415–33869–7 (hbk)
ISBN 0–415–33870–0 (pbk)

Contents

Contents cross-referenced

Section C: Exploration

Series editors' preface

This series provides a comprehensive guide to a number of key areas in the field of applied linguistics. Applied linguistics is a rich, vibrant, diverse and essentially interdisciplinary field. It is now more important than ever that books in the field provide up-to-date maps of ever-changing territory.

The books in this series are designed to give key insights into core areas of applied linguistics. The design of the books ensures, through key readings, that the history and development of a subject is recognised while, through key questions and tasks, integrating understandings of the topics, concepts and practices that make up its essentially interdisciplinary fabric. The pedagogic structure of each book ensures that readers are given opportunities to think, discuss, engage in tasks, draw on their own experience, reflect, research and to read and critically re-read key documents.

Each book has three main sections, each made up of seven units:

A   An **Introduction** section: key terms and concepts are introduced, along with introductory activities and reflective tasks, designed to establish key understandings, terminology, techniques of analysis and the skills appropriate to the theme and the discipline.

B   An **Extension** section: selected core readings are introduced (usually edited from the original) from existing books and articles, together with annotations and commentary, where appropriate. Each reading is introduced, annotated and commented on in the context of the whole book, and research/follow-up questions and tasks are added to enable fuller understanding of both theory and practice. In some cases, readings are short and synoptic and incorporated within a more general exposition.

C   An **Exploration** section: further samples and illustrative materials are provided with an emphasis, where appropriate, on more open-ended, student-centred activities and tasks, designed to support readers and users in undertaking their own locally relevant research projects. Tasks are designed for work in groups or for individuals working on their own.

The books also contain an index, which provides a guide to the main terms used in the book, and a detailed, thematically organised further reading section, which lays the ground for further work in the discipline. There is also a detailed reference section.

The target audience for the series is upper undergraduates and postgraduates on language, applied linguistics and communication studies programmes as well as teachers and researchers in professional development and distance learning programmes. High-quality applied research resources are also much needed for teachers of EFL/ESL and foreign language students at higher education colleges and universities worldwide. The books in the Routledge Applied Linguistics series are aimed at the individual reader, the student in a group and at teachers building courses and seminar programmes.

We hope that the books in this series meet these needs and continue to provide support over many years.

The Editors

Professor Christopher N. Candlin and Professor Ronald Carter are the series editors. Both have extensive experience of publishing titles in the fields relevant to this series. Between them they have written and edited over one hundred books and two hundred academic papers in the broad field of applied linguistics. Chris Candlin was president of AILA (International Association for Applied Linguistics) from 1996 to 2002 and Ron Carter is Chair of BAAL (British Association for Applied Linguistics) from 2003 to 2006.

Professor Christopher N. Candlin
Senior Research Professor
Department of Linguistics
Division of Linguistics and Psychology
Macquarie University
Sydney NSW 2109
Australia

and

Professor of Applied Linguistics
Faculty of Education and Language Studies
The Open University
Walton Hall
Milton Keynes MK7 6AA
UK

Professor Ronald Carter
School of English Studies
University of Nottingham
Nottingham NG7 2RD
UK

Acknowledgements

We are grateful to the copyright holders for permission to reproduce extracts from the following books and journal articles. While every effort has been made to contact owners of copyright material which is reproduced in this book, we have not always been successful. In the event of a copyright query, please contact the publishers.

Cook, V. (1995). Multi-competence and the learning of many languages. *Language, Culture and Curriculum*, *8*, 93–98. Reprinted by permission of Multilingual Matters.

Hansen, L. and Chen, Y.-L. (2002). What counts in the acquisition and attrition of numeral classifiers? *JALT Journal 23*, 90–110. Reprinted by permission of the authors.

Pallier, C., Dehaene, S., Poline, J. B. *et al.* (2003). Brain imaging of language plasticity in adopted adults: Can a second language replace the first? *Cerebral Cortex, 13*, 155–161. Reprinted by permission of Oxford University Press.

Corder, S. P. (1967). The significance of learners' errors. *International Review of Applied Linguistics in Language Teaching*, *5*, 161–169. Reprinted by permission of Mouton de Gruyter and Nick Corder.

Kellerman, E. (2000). What fruit can tell us about lexicosemantic transfer: a non-structural dimension to learners' perceptions of linguistic relations. In C. Muñoz (Ed.) *Segundas lenguas. Adquisición en el aula*. Barcelona: Ariel. Reprinted by permission of the author, publisher and volume editor.

Gregg, K. R. (1984). Krashen's Monitor and Occam's Razor. *Applied Linguistics*, *5*, 79–100. Reprinted by permission of Oxford University Press.

Kroll J. F. and Stewart E. (1994). Category interference in translation and picture naming – evidence for assymetric connections between bilingual memory representations. *Journal of Memory and Language, 33*, 149–174. Reprinted by permission of Elsevier.

Kroll J. F. and Dijkstra, T. (2002). The bilingual lexicon. In R. Kaplan (Ed.), *The Oxford handbook of applied linguistics* (pp. 301–321). Oxford: Oxford University Press. Reprinted by permission of Oxford University Press. Copyright © 2002 Oxford University Press, Inc.

Swain, M. and Lapkin, S. (1995). Problems in output and the cognitive processes they generate: A step towards second language learning. *Applied Linguistics, 16*, 371–391. Reprinted by permission of Oxford University Press.

Gass, S., Mackey, A. and Pica, T. (1998). The role of input and interaction in second language acquisition – Introduction to the special issue. *Modern Language Journal*, *82*, 299–307. Reprinted by permission of Blackwell Publishing.

Bongaerts, T. (1999). Ultimate attainment in L2 pronunciation: the case of very advanced late L2 learners. In D. Birdsong (Ed.), *Second language acquisition and the critical period hypothesis* (pp. 133–159). Mahwah, NJ: Erlbaum. Reprinted by permission of Lawrence Erlbaum Publishers.

Sparks, R. L. and Ganschow, L. (1991). Foreign language learning differences: Affective or native aptitude differences? *Modern Language Journal*, *75*, 3–16. Reprinted by permission of Blackwell Publishing.

Gardner, R. C., Tremblay, P. F. and Masgoret, A.-M. (1997). Towards a full model of second language learning: an empirical investigation. *Modern Language Journal*, *81*, 344–362. Reprinted by permission of Blackwell Publishing.

Spada, N. (1997). Form-focussed instruction and second language acquisition. *Language Teaching*, *30*, 73–87. Reproduced by permission of Cambridge University Press and the author.

Mackey, A. (1999). Input, interaction and second language development: an empirical study of question formation in ESL. *Studies in Second Language Acquisition*, *21*, 557–587. Reproduced by permission of Cambridge University Press and the author.

Dörnyei, Z. (2001). *Teaching and researching motivation*. Harlow: Longman. Reprinted by permission of Pearson Education. Copyright © 2001 Pearson Education Limited.

Savard, J.-G. and Richard J. (1970). *Les indices d'utilité du vocabulaire fondamental français*. Québec: Les Presses d'Université Laval. Reproduced by permission of Les Presses d'Université Laval.

Van Dijk, M. (2003). *Child language cuts capers. Variability and ambiguity in early child development*. University of Groningen. Reproduced by kind permission of the author.

MacWhinney, B. (1997). Second language acquisition and the competition model. In A. de Groot and J. Kroll (Eds), *Tutorials in bilingualism: Psycholinguistic perspectives* (pp. 113–142). Mahwah, NJ: Erlbaum. Reproducedy by permission of Lawrence Erlbaum Publishers.

How to use this book

As with all books in the Routledge Applied Linguistics Series, this book consists of three sections: an Introduction, an Extension and an Exploration. In the Introduction (Section A) we introduce key terms and concepts, including introductory activities and reflective tasks aimed at awareness raising and generation of interest in the reader. The main aim is to establish key understandings of the main themes in the field of second language acquisition (SLA).

In the Extension (Section B) we present core readings on the various topics dealt with in Section A. The aim is to present the reader with some core readings from existing books and articles, most of them edited to improve clarity. All readings include pre-reading, while-reading and post-reading tasks that should help the reader to come to a better understanding of the texts.

In the Exploration (Section C), we present assignments with an emphasis on open-ended, student-centred activities and tasks in the form of small-size projects designed to enhance the readers' understanding of the main issues discussed. The tasks and projects are designed in such a way that students can work through them and apply them in their own contexts. Most tasks can be done individually, though we believe that they have more to offer when performed in groups.

Each section starts with an introduction. Section A starts with a short introduction to the field and highlights the main topics. In the introduction to Section B we give some information on how to read the SLA texts, pointing out some of the pitfalls in reading scientific materials. We encourage the readers to be critical in what they read and not to take anything for granted. We will provide them with some insights into the textual characteristics of publications in this field. The introduction to Section C aims at providing the reader with some knowledge and skills to complete the tasks and projects in this section. It deals very briefly with some statistical issues, but we do not assume any statistical skills or knowledge.

Like all books in this Series, the target audience is upper undergraduates and post-graduates on language, applied linguistics and communication studies programmes as well as teachers and researchers in the field of language teaching. Although there is no specific language focus, many of the examples are English based, simply because this is the language our intended international readership has in common.

There are basically two ways to use this book. The first is to go through Section A first, and then on to Sections B and C. The advantage is that after reading Section A, the students will have acquired some knowledge about the issues discussed in the later sections. Some of the tasks in sections B and C are based on this approach because they refer to theories and concepts that are discussed in Section A. The other approach is to go through the first parts of each of the sections together, so first A1, B1 and C1, then A2, B2, C2 and so on. The advantage of that approach is that the issues presented in Section A are developed more deeply through the combination of theory, readings and tasks. In the first trial of this book in the MA in Applied Linguistics programme at the University of Groningen, we took this approach and it seemed to work quite well.

Finally, we want to point out that the present book is not just a restatement of what others have written on this topic. We have tried to re-conceptualise some of the basic issues in SLA by linking them to a theory that has its origins in the hard sciences and mathematics: Dynamic Systems Theory. We have tried to stay away from the mathematics as much as possible and to link some theoretical notions to aspects of SLA. This is clearly an on-going project that is not quite finished with this book. On the contrary, readers are invited to make their own judgement with respect to the relevance of this theory for language learning and teaching.

SECTION A
Introduction

Unit A1
Defining the field

The field of Second Language Acquisition (SLA) research focuses on how languages are learned. Even though a great deal of research has been conducted on this topic over the last two decades, we are still far from understanding all the details of that process. Many books and articles have been written on many different aspects of SLA, more than can be reported on in any single textbook. Therefore, every book on SLA has to restrict itself in the choice of topics discussed.

The focus of this particular book will be the dynamic aspects of SLA. To make our point clear, we will make use of Dynamic Systems Theory (DST), which will be explained in detail in Unit A2. For SLA, in short, this implies that a person's knowledge of a language (first, second, third and so on) is never stable and keeps developing when used. When not used, there is stagnation and ultimately a loss of skills. This continuous growth and loss is influenced by a whole range of factors: not only the type and amount of contact with a language, but also individual factors such as age, attitude, motivation, intelligence, and earlier learning experience are important.

Another important point is that these factors all interact and therefore it is impossible to tease away the exact effect of any one of these factors in isolation. What we do know through large-scale studies is what effect these factors may have in general. However, we can never predict exactly how any particular factor will affect any particular learner, not only because it is impossible to know exactly all factors involved and how much exactly each of these factors might influence language development but especially because these factors interact with each other. In addition, an individual's knowledge of a language is never completely stable and may vary from day to day.

Finally, it is the amount of variation in the knowledge that can tell us much about the learning process. Usually, there is a great deal of variation in a specific language aspect while it is being reorganised and learned. For instance, a learner of German as a second language may for some time have a system with only two gender distinctions – *der* for masculine and *die* for feminine – and later on find out that there is also a *das* for neutral. While his German system may have shown a continuous development in the acquisition of the masculine and feminine gender markings, it will be completely reorganised to include the new markings for neutral and it will take some time again for the gender markings to become stable in his language.

 Task A1.1

➤ To become aware of the complexity of the interaction of different factors, compare the following five acquisitional settings and try to find factors that are the same and factors that are different for these settings. Try to distinguish factors relating to the system to be learned, the setting of acquisition, and the language learner.

A. A young child (age 2) learning German as a first language in Germany
B. A young Turkish child (age 5) learning German as a second language in Germany
C. A Finnish boy (age 13) learning German as a foreign language in Finnish secondary education
D. An educated Danish elderly person (age 63) learning German as a foreign language through a self-study computer program
E. An uneducated Chilean woman (age 32) learning German without formal instruction through working as cleaning lady in a hotel

It may help you to organise the different factors on three levels:

➤ the relation between the first and second language;

➤ the setting in which the second language is learned and the amount and kind of input in the language;

➤ the language learner's individual characteristics such as aptitude (including intelligence and L1 ability), age, attitude and motivation.

BASIC ISSUES IN SLA

In the SLA literature of the last 20 years or so, a few basic issues have been addressed in many different ways within different theoretical frameworks and from different points of view. Often these issues are presented as involving binary choices; however, they usually refer to a continuum in settings or ways of acquisition. Here we will give a brief overview of relevant issues, most of which will be discussed in more detail in the units to come.

Monolingualism, bilingualism and multilingualism

In this book we will often speak of someone's first language (L1) or second language (L2), and in the experiments we report on the subjects are often classified as 'monolingual' or 'bilingual'. In this section, however, we want to make clear that these terms may oversimplify actual situations. When do we label a person as bilingual or multilingual? In the past, there were two extreme positions, both of which are now seen as untenable. One is that only people who grow up in two languages are 'real' bilinguals because they have a full command of those languages. The other extreme is that any knowledge of another language will make you a bilingual. So if you can read Hebrew characters, you are a bilingual in Hebrew and your first language. Clearly, the definition should be somewhere between those two extremes.

Task A1.2

➤ To show you how difficult it is to define 'full command', take a good monolingual dictionary in your first language. Start at page 146 and read the entries. Write down every word you don't know. How many pages did you turn before you reached 20 unknown words? By counting the total number of words, you can get an idea of the percentage of the total number of words you do and do not know.

The problem is that it is not clear what a full command of a language is. The point of Task A1.2 is to show that native speakers may not have a 'full' command of their L1. No one knows all the words of a language. If that is true for one language, how can anyone ever have 'a full command' of more than one language? Because it is impossible to define 'full' command of a language, a strict definition of bilingualism is untenable.

A related question is whether pure monolinguals really exist. Most speakers can speak more than one variety of their language. Some speak more than one dialect, but almost all speakers have a range of different styles and registers at their disposal. Depending on the situation, a different set of words and grammatical conventions may be used. For example, when talking to an old friend, a person is likely to use a different register and style from when she is speaking to a high-ranking diplomat. From a psycholinguistic perspective, it is very difficult to indicate how registers of a single language can be distinguished from different languages in an individual. In terms of processing, there are no differences whether someone speaks two different languages or two different varieties of the same language, so it is only at a socio-linguistic level that we can talk about differences in range and status between a language and a variety.

From Unit A2 it will become clear that the exact definitions of monolingualism, bilingualism and multilingualism are not that relevant for us because we claim that all the knowledge of different languages and varieties that an individual knows are part of one dynamic system, and the state of that system at any one time very much depends on the degree of recent input and active use of any of the languages or varieties.

First, second and third language

Just as the definitions of monolingualism versus bilingualism are problematic, so are the definitions of L1 and L2. In countries such as England and France, many children are socialised in a variety of the standard language, and it seems clear what their first language is. But the majority of the world population is multilingual, and for many people it is not really clear what constitutes their first, second or third language. Children may learn one or two other languages at school, and later in life they may even learn and use again another language to such an extent that the first foreign language is no longer used and fades away. How 'second' and 'third' should be distinguished in such cases is unclear. Some linguists order languages in terms of level of proficiency, others in the order of the time of acquisition, but neither of these distinctions applies to children who have two or more languages from birth. In such cases first, second or third can be defined only in terms of settings of use.

In many migrant settings, the first language of a migrant family changes status through time. Parents may keep their first language as the means of communication at home, but their children may increasingly start using the language of the larger environment to communicate among themselves and with their parents and even grandparents. In such settings, the first language loses its special status and becomes the second or third language for the younger generation.

 Task A1.3

➤ If you have friends or relatives who have grown up in a setting where more than one language was used, ask them what they consider their first language and why they consider this as their first language.

Task A1.3 and the brief examples have shown how difficult it is to define a first, second or third language. Moreover, these rankings may change over time and may be influenced by environmental factors. In this book, we will use the term second language to refer to any new target language to be learned, unless there is a need to differentiate between target languages.

Second language acquisition and foreign language acquisition

Just as it is difficult to define a first, second or third language in such a way that it applies to all cases, it is often difficult to distinguish between the terms *second* and *foreign* language learning.

According to the traditional definition, second language acquisition typically takes place in a setting in which the language to be learned is the language spoken in the local community. Therefore, a Farsi speaker learning English in England is generally defined as a second language learner. In some definitions of second language acquisition, the acquisition needs also to take place in a non-instructed setting.

Foreign language acquisition takes place in a setting in which the language to be learned is not the language spoken in the local community. So the learning of Polish by a Hungarian adult in Hungary would be an example of foreign language acquisition. In most cases, foreign language acquisition takes place in a setting with formal language instruction.

In this book, we will use the term SLA to refer to both types of acquisition because we assume that the underlying process is essentially the same. Where necessary, though, we will make use of the distinction between a second and a foreign language, as was done in Task A1.1.

Task A1.4

➤ To show you the problem of defining the L1 and L2, consider the following: A child with normal hearing is born into a family in which both parents are deaf and use sign language as their main language. Is the acquisition of spoken language by a hearing child of such deaf parents an example of a second or foreign language acquisition?

Acquisition versus learning

A particularly tricky but also controversial distinction is the one between *acquisition* and *learning*. Krashen and Terrell (1983) defined 'acquisition' as the product of a 'subconscious' process, very similar to the one children use in learning their first language, and learning as the product of formal teaching, which results in 'conscious' knowledge about the language, but the distinction cannot be as simple as that.

Schmidt (1990: 134) has pointed out that the term 'subconscious' may be misleading, and that it is not used in a technical sense here as in consciousness research, where it would imply totally 'without awareness', an unlikely proposition. In a non-technical sense, the term could mean 'not being aware of having noticed something', which would be related to subliminal learning, a way of learning that takes place, for example, while listening to a tape while sleeping. Apparently, there is some evidence that people may pick up subliminal signals that they already know, but there is no evidence as yet that new information may be picked up in such a manner. Subliminal language learning is therefore considered extremely unlikely. In consciousness research, it is commonly accepted that some level of attention is required to be able to notice something, and that noticing is crucial in obtaining new information or uptake.

Probably, Krashen and Terrell (1983) used the term 'subconscious' in another non-technical sense, namely as the inability to explain what one knows. In other words, learners may use language forms correctly without being able to say exactly why the forms are the way they are. Defined as such, acquisition is seen as a natural process of growth of knowledge and skills in a language without a level of meta-knowledge about the language, while learning is seen as an artificial process in which the 'rules' of a language are focussed on. Krashen claimed that learning the rules could not lead to an automatic use of language as in acquisition. In Unit A3, the Krashen hypotheses are discussed in more detail, and in Unit A5 we will point out that there are indeed two different mental processes involved in acquisition and learning, but that this does not mean that they cannot interact. Learning could be the carrying out of activities that enhance the growth of knowledge, but not all learning necessarily leads to acquisition.

Input versus intake

Related to the notion of 'consciousness' discussed above is the distinction between input and intake. 'Input' is everything around us we may perceive with our senses, and 'uptake' or 'intake' is what we pay attention to and notice. Some level of attention is required to be able to notice something, and that noticing is crucial in obtaining new information. For example, there is a lot of information in our environment, but what we use of all that information depends on our needs and interests. We may not be interested in the colour of our neighbour's eyes, but for someone else, or even for ourselves at another moment in time, it may become a very relevant piece of information. And at that point, we will notice.

The same is true for language learning. There is little doubt that input is the main source of information for learning (see Unit A5), but not all input becomes intake, which is necessary for learning. It is not particularly easy to know under what conditions input is actually used for learning. From experiments in consciousness, we do know that unexpected events often capture attention. In addition, expectations are important determinants of perceptibility and noticeability, so it is plausible that instruction may have an awareness-raising effect, increasing the likelihood of noticing features in input through the establishment of expectation and comprehending. For intake, at least some minimal level of processing needs to take place. There must be some awareness of new information that is relevant for the learning system to incorporate. Intake may refer to information that strengthens existing knowledge, or it may fill a gap in knowledge that was noticed by the learner before.

Task A1.5

➤ Listen to a news broadcast in one of your foreign languages. Try to understand what is said, but also monitor yourself while listening. What do you do: are you listening in a similar manner all the time or are you going through waves of noise and understanding? Do you notice when the input becomes intake?

Implicit versus explicit learning

Very much related to the acquisition versus learning distinction is the debate on implicit versus explicit learning: the difference between the two is captured well by R. Ellis (1994: 2), who uses the phrase 'unconscious operation' in yet another sense, namely whether general principles in language can be induced without really being able to formulate an understanding of them.

> Some things we just come to be able to do, like walking, recognizing happiness in others, knowing that *th* is more common than *tg* in written English, or making simple utterances in our native language. We have little insight into the nature of the processing involved – we learn to do them implicitly like swallows learn to fly. Other of our abilities depend on our knowing *how* to do them, like multiplication, playing chess, speaking pig Latin, or using a computer programming language. We learn these abilities explicitly like aircraft designers learn aerodynamics.

> Implicit learning is acquisition of knowledge about the underlying structure of a complex stimulus environment by a process that takes place naturally, simply and without conscious operations. Explicit learning is a more conscious operation where the individual makes and tests hypotheses in a search for structure. Knowledge attainments can thus take place implicitly (a non-conscious and automatic abstraction of the structural nature of the material arrived at from experience of instances), explicitly through selective learning (the learner searching for information and building then testing hypotheses), or, because we can communicate using language, explicitly via given rules (assimilation of a rule following explicit instruction.

According to Schmidt (1990) the implicit learning issue is the most difficult to resolve. On the one hand, there is evidence for it, but there is also evidence that conscious understanding helps in the acquisition process.

> There is not much evidence on which to base an evaluation of the question of implicit rule acquisition in second language learning. There is evidence that giving learners explicit rules helped in an experimental study (Van Baalen, 1983), and the results of larger scale studies also slightly favor an explicit focus on grammar (Chaudron, 1988). At the most general level, studies of the global role of instruction in second language learning indicate that it is facilitative, but such studies do not say whether such effects are due to increased learner understanding as a result of instruction, or increased salience of forms leading to awareness only at the level of noticing.
>
> (Schmidt, 1990: 146)

In Unit A7, we will see that there is indeed quite a lot of evidence that instruction has a positive effect on learning. Looking at Schmidt's question from a dynamic perspective, we can assume that any kind of input – both a great deal of meaningful input and explicit instruction – will interact and affect the system. However, we may never know precisely how.

Incidental versus intentional learning

Another related and much debated distinction in the SLA literature is the one on incidental versus intentional learning. A prime example of intentional learning is learning words from a bilingual list in a decontextualised manner. Learning words by reading and inferring meanings from context is usually seen as incidental learning.

However, a clear distinction between incidental and intentional learning is difficult to formulate. Most of the work on this has focused on lexical knowledge. For example, when a person reads for pleasure and doesn't bother to look up a word he or she doesn't know in a dictionary, but a few pages later realises what that word means, then incidental learning is said to have taken place. If a teacher instructs a student to take a text and read it and find out the meanings of unknown words, then it becomes an intentional learning activity.

According to Schmidt (1990), the incidental versus intentional learning question is related to whether noticing is required and, if so, whether such noticing is automatic or requires attention. Apparently, incidental learning without 'paying attention' is both possible and effective, but only when the demands of a task focus attention on what is to be learned. However, paying attention is probably facilitative, and may be necessary if adult learners are to acquire grammatical conventions that are difficult to discern such as the difference between 'he'd' meaning 'he had' or 'he would'.

> What learners notice is constrained by a number of factors, but incidental learning is certainly possible when task demands focus attention on

relevant features of the input. . . . Incidental learning in another sense, picking up target language forms from input when they do not carry information crucial to the task, appears unlikely for adults. Paying attention to language form is hypothesized to be facilitative in all cases, and may be necessary for adult acquisition of redundant grammatical features. In general, the relation between attention and awareness provides a link to the study of individual differences in language learning, as well as to consideration of their role of instruction in making formal features of the target language more salient and facilitating input encoding.

(Schmidt, 1990: 49)

The point is that an L2 learner who is rather fluent in the L2 may pay attention only to a message as a whole rather than to any particular forms of the language with which the message is expressed. In such a case, it is likely that he will learn something new from the information provided by the message, but it is unlikely that he will learn anything new about the forms of the language. If, on the other hand, he has to pay some attention to a particular form to understand the message, then it is likely that he will learn something about that form.

Even though the incidental versus intentional learning issue will not be focussed on again separately in this book, it is very much related to the role of instruction in SLA, the topic of Unit A7.

Task A1.6

➤ We are learning all the time, simply because we interact with our environment and we cannot stop ourselves from interacting. We only realise how much information we encounter and partly take up when we pay attention to that. Here's a rather difficult exercise: try to think of what you learned today. What did you learn that was new? What particular language forms did you learn that were new? For instance, are there any words in this unit that you didn't know before? Did you learn them implicitly or explicitly? Intentionally or incidentally? Did you infer them from the context? Do you know the colour of the eyes of the person who sits next to you?

Instructed versus non-instructed SLA

Neither the distinction nor the interaction between instructed and non-instructed SLA is completely clear either. In many settings, acquisition takes place through a mix of instructed and non-instructed learning.

On the one hand, some languages are learned mainly through education. For example, when a person learns Swedish in Ireland, there is little chance for him to meet Swedish people and find a Swedish setting in which he can pick up the language. His main source of contact and input is the institute or school, but he may also 'pick up' some of the language through reading on his own.

On the other hand, some languages are learned mainly through informal interaction. Many migrants throughout the world move into a setting in which they have to learn the local language on their own in order to survive. In many such settings there is no formal system of education to learn that language, so people have to pick up the language from what they hear and see in their environment. However, it is possible that a migrant follows some language courses in a community centre or he may be told what he is saying incorrectly through interaction with another speaker.

The English language is typically a language that is acquired in a setting in which there is a combination of instructed and non-instructed SLA. An example of such a situation is Norway, where English is taught at school and English is very prominently present in many parts of society. There are many English-language programmes on TV, computer software is only partly available in Norwegian, and in higher education, industry and trade English is emerging as the dominant language.

 Task A1.7

➤ In a project on the acquisition of English, Dutch adolescents were asked to indicate what percentage of their English they had acquired through school, through the media (TV, radio, computer) or through other sources. The scores ranged between 35% and 60% for school, and 70% and 30 % for media. Take one of your foreign languages and try to indicate for that language what your percentages would be for school, media and other sources. Ask some friends or colleagues to do the same and compare your percentages with theirs and try to explain the differences.

CONCLUDING REMARKS

The basic issues touched upon so far in this unit will come back directly or indirectly in the units to come. The book is organised as follows: Section A consists of a set of introductory units on six topics, Section B provides a set of extension units containing excerpts of scholarly articles related to the topics presented in Section A. Finally, Section C provides a set of exploration units, again on the same topics as in sections A and B, but containing ideas for small-scale research projects for students and tutors.

The topics will be discussed in the following order. In Unit A2, we will introduce Dynamic Systems Theory (DST), which will serve as the theoretical basis for the way SLA is presented in the remainder of the book. In Unit A3 we present a brief historical overview of the way other general theories have affected SLA research and explain in what way DST is different or compatible with these theories. Unit A4 focuses on the presence of more than one language in our mind and on the processing of these multiple languages in psycholinguistic terms. Unit A5 concentrates on how an individual's language system develops and Unit A6 on learners' characteristics that may play a role in this development. Unit A7 aims at translating many of the issues discussed into issues relating to the role of instruction. We do not claim that all the theoretical insights we present can easily be turned into practice, but we certainly do believe that teaching has to be inspired and enriched by findings from research in SLA.

Unit A2
Dynamic aspects of SLA

In many studies on SLA, the learner's language development is pictured as a more or less linear development from zero to near-native, in gradual consecutive steps, as if the L2 slowly and neatly develops next to the L1, which is so engrained that it will influence the development of the L2. However, it has been shown that when people learn an L2, the development is not straightforward, with lots of variation especially just before a certain construction becomes more stable. Also, the L1 of a learner may be affected by the L2.

Our aim in this book is to show how the development of more than one language in an individual takes place and what factors have an impact on that process. Obviously, the number of factors that play a role is enormous, and only a part of that complexity can be captured. To be able to present these factors, they are discussed separately in the units to come, but, in reality, these factors interact continuously in intricate ways in each individual language learner.

To provide a framework that shows how this interaction takes place, we will look at SLA and multilingualism from a specific perspective: Dynamic Systems Theory (DST). Originally developed in the field of biology, this theory seeks to clarify systems that seem to be chaotic and self-organising, and it has now found applications in many other disciplines, including first language acquisition and more recently in SLA. After a brief introduction to DST, this unit will give examples of how DST may apply to language, language development and SLA. We will also argue that 'forgetting' is as much part of a dynamic system as 'acquiring'.

DYNAMIC SYSTEMS THEORY

First, we need to define what a system is. Imagine there are all kinds of systems in the world. Some of the most obvious ones are the weather, the economy of a country, and traffic. The two main properties of dynamic systems are that all variables interact and that this continuous interaction keeps changing the system as a whole over time. The following two quotes define what a system is and what its main characteristics are.

A system [...] is more than just a collection of variables or observables we have isolated from the rest of the world. It is a system primarily because the variables mutually interact. That is, each variable affects all the other variables contained in the system and thus also affects itself. This is a property we may call complete connectedness and it is the default property of any system. The principal distinctive property – compared to a constant – is that it changes over time. Consequently, mutual interaction among variables implies that they influence and co-determine each other's changes over time. In this sense, a system is by definition, a dynamic system and so we define a dynamic system as a set of variables that mutually affect each other's changes over time.

(Van Geert, 1994a: 50)

Another quote that makes the dynamic aspects and change over time clear is by Briggs and Peat, two of the founders of DST.

Complex systems – both chaotic and orderly ones – are ultimately unanalysable, irreducible into parts, because the parts are constantly being folded into each other by iterations and feedback. Therefore, it is an illusion to speak of isolating a single interaction between two particles and to claim that the interaction can go backward in time. Any interaction takes place in the larger system and the system as a whole is constantly changing, bifurcating, iterating. So the system and all its 'parts' have a direction in time.

(Briggs and Peat, 1989: 147–148)

Task A2.1

➤ 'Systems' sounds rather abstract. However, we are constantly faced with complex systems wherever we look. Below are some examples. Try to explain why they can be analysed as dynamic systems in terms of the two main properties of systems discussed above – interconnectedness of different factors and continual change: your family, your university, and your government.

NESTING OF COMPLEX SYSTEMS

The following quote, also by Briggs and Peat (1989), makes clear that complex systems may be 'nested'. In other words, smaller systems are part of greater systems.

Every complex system is a changing part of a greater whole, a nesting or larger wholes leading eventually to the most complex dynamical system of all, the system that ultimately encompassed whatever we mean by order and chaos – the universe itself.

(Briggs and Peat, 1989: 147–148)

How does this idea of 'nested systems' apply to a language and L2 acquisition? Any language is a complex system in its own right with variation at any moment in time and continuous change. At any particular moment in time, there is a great deal of variation among dialects in a particular language, registers, and also in individual speakers, who will never use the exact same utterances two days in a row in conversation. This inherent variation in a language at one particular moment in time and external forces cause a language to change over time. For example, one language (such as English nowadays) may become so influential that other languages adopt words and expressions from it; within a 'language', some dialect may become more prestigious and be 'imitated' by speakers of other dialects, some event may cause the invention of a new word, some individual may come up with a new expression that gets accepted by many speakers, and so on. Of course, a language as a whole – with pronunciation, vocabulary and grammar as its sub-systems – is a rather large system and many of the little changes never take a lasting hold, but as the history of any language shows, big changes do take place in all three areas, albeit very slowly. As the field of sociolinguistics has shown us, it is impossible to pinpoint exactly what causes such changes, but usually the change results from a complex interaction between internal and external factors.

Within the larger system of a language there are many sub-systems. One kind of subsystem is the language system of an individual, which can also be considered as a dynamic system in its own right, which changes over time due to a complex interaction of a wide range of factors. Of course, when a young child is in the process of learning his first language, the changes are very rapid and noticeable. But even an adult L1 changes over time. Any time an individual reads, interacts with another speaker, writes, and so on, his language may change as a result of that. Many of these changes are too small to be noticed, but if such a speaker moves to another part of a country her pronunciation may change quite a bit, or when she gets interested in a different field of study, her vocabulary might change. When she moves back to her original place of residence the 'strange' pronunciation features may disappear again and when she stops reading in that particular field of interest, she may forget the words she once used every day.

As far as language is concerned, we can detect a whole system of nested systems: there is language in general, consisting of separate languages, dialects of varieties spoken by groups of people, and within these language systems we can see sub-systems such as the phonemic, lexical and grammar systems. Then each individual has his own language system, which may contain different sub-systems, such as different languages, varieties, registers, each again with its own phonemic, lexical and grammar systems.

 Task A2.2

➤ When listening to speech in a second language, what sub-systems can you think of that will play a role?

ATTRACTOR STATES

What we have seen so far is that in a complex system all the components are directly or indirectly connected: it is constantly changing and self-organising. But even though there is a great deal of variation and changes over time, there are times of more or less inherent stability. A time when there is a profusion of internal variation is usually a sign that the system is in the process of changing rapidly, but a time of little internal variation is a sign that the system is relatively stable. In such a case, only stronger external forces will change the system to any great extent. States of less variation are called 'attractor states'. A non-linguistic example of an attractor state is a pendulum of a clock swinging. At first, the clock is 'wound up' and the pendulum gets pushed. After a few seconds of great internal variation, the pendulum will find its natural path, which depends on its length and the amount of friction it receives. The pendulum will then swing in this natural path for a while until some external force – such as the clock's internal mechanism or someone's hand – stops it. Usually the complete stop is preceded again by a great deal of internal variation, as the pendulum will not stop abruptly. The following quote shows how such an attractor state applies to human action and cognition.

> Many configurations in action and cognition, and in development, that act like permanent programs or structures are stable attractors whose stability limits may indeed be shifted under appropriate circumstances. That is to say, many mental constructs and movement configurations, object permanence and walking for example, are attractors of such strength and stability that only the most severe perturbations can disrupt them. They look as though they are wired in.
>
> (Thelen and Smith, 1994: 61)

In L1 language development, too, attractor states can be recognised. For example, we know that a child's acquisition of one of the sub-systems of a language, e.g. the formation of the past tense, goes through various stages, each of which is an attractor state in itself. The child may first learn that the past tense of *get* is *got* and use *got* for quite a while. Then she may see that most past tenses are formed by adding *–ed* to verbs and by analogy she may add *–ed* to *get* and may say *getted* or even *gotted*. Then a while later again, she may discover that even though most verbs add *–ed*, some verbs do not, and she may use the irregular form *got* correctly again. Eventually, all past forms are used correctly and we may say that the sub-system of past tense formation is in an 'attractor' state that is unlikely to change much again.

It is also well known in SLA that for many L2 learners many sub-systems become stabilised before they have reached the target forms, especially in pronunciation (see Unit A6). Such a stabilised 'incorrect' form is called a sign of 'fossilisation'; Selinker (1972) describes 'fossilisation' as follows:

> Fossilizable linguistic phenomena are linguistic items, rules and sub-systems which speakers of a particular NL [native language] will tend to

keep in their IL [interlanguage] relative to a particular TL [target language], no matter what the age of the learner or amount of explanation and instruction he receives in the TL.

(Selinker, 1972: 36)

As R. Ellis (1994: 353) indicates, fossilised forms may sometimes disappear only to come back later on. He refers to this as 'back sliding'. Fossilisation in this sense is a perfect example of an 'attractor state' in DST: a state that the system tends to prefer over other states and that can only be overcome through strong forces. So far it is unclear which forces might be lacking to prevent 'fossilisation' from occurring, but it is generally assumed that no single variable can explain it. In addition to contrasts and similarities between L1 and L2, R. Ellis (1994: 354) lists a number of individual differences, which will be discussed in Unit A6, such as the age of learning, the lack of desire to acculturate in a new society by migrants, the need to communicate before sufficient linguistic means have been acquired, the lack of learning opportunity, or the lack of adequate feedback in the learning process.

 Task A2.3

➤ Some examples of constructions (in pronunciation or grammar) that tend to become fossilised in English as an L2 (depending on the L1 of the learners), even for advanced learners are (1) the incorrect use of the article and (2) the mispronunciation of the *th* sound. Try to think of some examples for your own L2 for speakers with the same L1.

VARIATION AND STATISTICS

In the section above, the example about L1 learning has shown that before a child learns to use all past tense formations correctly, she may go through a time of 'confusion', resulting in quite a bit of variation in correct and incorrect forms used during a relatively short time. It is assumed in DST that such a profusion of variation precedes a moment of change in development from one stage to the other. In most development studies, however, which usually look for a general pattern that may apply to many individuals, the usual statistical methods average out the variation. Van Dijk (2003), who has looked at the L1 development of young children, explains that in such traditional research 'variability' is seen as 'noise' and 'error' (which will be explained in more detail after the quotation below). Quoting Thelen and Smith (1994), Van Dijk makes clear that because 'variability' is actually needed to develop further, it should be considered as part of normal development of a child and therefore also worthy of study.

Dynamic systems theory aims at explaining two levels of development with the same principles (Thelen and Smith, 1994). The first level is the view from above, or the 'grand sweep' of development. At this perspective, we see global structure, similarities across subjects. For instance, when infants learn how to walk, they perform roughly the same behavior. The second level of development takes a view from below. From there, we observe the messy details: behavior that is variable, fluid, and highly context dependent. We see for instance that not all infants use the same strategies when learning how to walk and show large variability across time. This variability is viewed as an important internal developmental characteristic and not of something externally added to the process of development (such as noise). The theory radically rejects the automatic retreat to the error hypothesis and claims that variability bears important information about the nature of the developmental process. Dynamic systems theory stresses the importance of the context in which the behavior is displayed. Development takes place in real time and is considered highly context dependent. Therefore, it can be compared with an evolutionary process, which is also mindless and opportunistic. Thelen and Smith agree with the classical Darwinian emphasis on variability as the source of new forms. They state: 'we believe that in development, as in evolution, change consists of successive make-do solutions that work, given abilities, goals and history of the organisms at the time.' (Thelen and Smith, 1994: 144)

Variability is considered to be the result of the systems' flexibility and adaptability to the environment. From a dynamic systems angle, variability has been viewed as both the source of development and the indicator of a specific moment in the developmental process, namely in the presence of a developmental transition.

(Van Dijk, 2003: 129)

Task A2.4

➤ Can you remember when your L2 (or someone else's) showed a great deal of variability at a certain point in time? Can you think of some 'make-do' solutions you used in your using and learning your L2?

To clarify what Van Dijk (2003) calls 'noise' and 'error', we need to look at how data are usually gathered and interpreted. Suppose a researcher wants to find out the level of language proficiency in a group of students. She will typically use tests to find those patterns, but she knows tests can never be totally adequate to measure the concept she wants to find out more about because language proficiency is enormously complex. So by using tests, she knows she can capture only a part of what she wants to capture. Therefore, when she interprets the data, she has to keep in mind that the inadequacy of the test itself may cause some variation among some students who may actually have the same level of proficiency. Therefore, the score may also depend on factors other than the ones intended. Such unwanted variation is called the 'measurement error'. What a researcher usually really wants to know is the 'true' level of proficiency of one individual at a particular moment in time.

In testing circles it is generally accepted that researchers can learn more about the 'true score' by looking at what individuals have in common and where they vary. By eliminating the variance, they arrive at what they have in common and can then arrive at a 'true score'. In other words, in most statistical techniques looking at the 'grand sweep of things', 'variance' is regarded as a source of 'noise'.

Of course, these traditional statistical analyses provide a practical way to ascertain someone's approximate level of proficiency and they are very useful in discovering the global picture of development, i.e. the general patterns that emerge when we test large numbers of individuals. However, to see how one particular person actually develops, we may also overlook some very interesting information if we ignore variance. Following the ideas on DST outlined above, researchers like Thelen and Smith, and Van Geert have started looking at variation in one individual over time not as a source of noise, but as a source of information on the process of development. In DST variability, discontinuity and change are inherent properties of systems and tell us something about the state of the system and changes taking place in the system. In this line of research, data typically come from individual case studies with lots of measurements over a short period of time, because such data are suitable for finding variability. In this view, a great deal of variation is a sign that the system is in the process of changing.

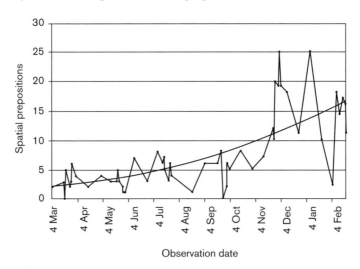

Figure A2.1 Raw data of Heleen's spatial prepositions, including a polynomial trend line (2 degrees)

Source: Van Dijk, 2003: 44

Figure A2.1 taken from an article by Van Geert and Van Dijk (2002) serves to illustrate this variation. The graph shows how many spatial prepositions (like 'in' or 'under') a little girl, Heleen, used in total within a set amount of language utterances. In the course of a year, 55 measures were taken when she was between the age of 18 months and 30 months. On the one hand, the clean up-going curve, obtained with a traditional statistical method showing averages, shows the general development in the use of prepositions, and it is clear that slowly but surely the girl uses more spatial prepositions. The strong zigzag pattern showing the actual 'raw' data, however, shows that this development is not very smooth at all, and especially in the last four months there is a much greater degree of variation in consecutive weeks than before.

We assume that when the development of one individual learning an L2 is traced in detail over a longer period, similar patterns of variability will show up; however, so far, no such detailed studies have been conducted.

Task A2.5

➤ When you look back at the figure depicting Heleen's development in using spatial prepositions, during which months does her spatial preposition system seem to be in an attractor stage? (Note: only one attractor stage can be clearly identified.)

In SLA similar phenomena have been observed. A learner may go through quite some variability, often referred to as 'free variation', in the use of a certain construction before it stabilises, either in the correct target L2 form or in some 'incorrect' interlanguage form. Ellis (1985) defines free variation as two or more forms that perform the same language function within one particular context. For example, one of his subjects uttered 'No look at my card' and 'Don't look my card' within the same game of bingo. Another learner produced sentences like 'there church' or 'there's church' within similar contexts. R. Ellis (1994: 136–137) concludes that such instances of free variation are quite conspicuous in his own data and in several detailed studies.

> A general finding of these studies is that free variation occurs during an early stage of development and then disappears as learners develop better organized L systems, a view first put forward by Gatbonton (1978). According to her gradual diffusion model, there are two broad stages of L2 development: an 'acquisition phase' and a 'replacement phase'. In the former, the learner first uses one form in a variety of situations and contexts, and then introduces another form, which is used in free variation with the first in all contexts. In the replacement phase, each form is restricted to its own contexts through the gradual elimination of the other in first one context and then another.

CONSTANT REORGANISATION

Several of the issues raised above will come back in the units in this book. Here we want to start from the basic assumption that there is a language system in every language user and that that system has all the characteristics of a dynamic system: it is complex, the components are all directly or indirectly interconnected, it is constantly changing, and it is self-organising. As Herdina and Jessner (2002) have argued, from a DST perspective the distinction between SLA and multilingual processing more or less disappears: the system is reacting to external input and its entire organisation, including the L1, changes with new input. It reorganises itself constantly in order to find equilibrium, but even then it does not come to a complete standstill.

The notion of a language as a dynamic system that changes continually even though it develops relatively stable 'attractor states' conflicts with the idea of an individual ever reaching an 'end state', a state that signals the end of development, which is a notion commonly referred to in SLA studies from a Universal Grammar (UG) perspective (see Unit A3). The inadequacy of the 'end state' concept is also evident in research on attrition, which has shown that aspects that had seemed to be firmly established were actually lost due to no use or lack of activation.

INTERACTING SYSTEMS

If the different languages that an individual knows are part of one dynamic system, then one would expect that the two languages would interact. And indeed, many studies have shown that when an individual learns an L2, both his L1 and L2 can be affected. At the beginning stages of learning the L2, changes in the L1 may be hardly noticeable, but the changes in the L2 can be very noticeable. New L2 ways of pronouncing phonemes, words, expressions, and types of sentence structures are added every day. At later stages of L2 learning, the L2 may stabilise and the changes may be less noticeable. In Unit A3, we will give a brief history of the development of SLA research and give examples of how the L1 may affect the L2, a common area of interest in SLA research.

 Task A2.6

> Did you ever have the experience of words from your L2 popping up when you were trying to speak your L1? For instance, has this occurred during a longer stay abroad where you spoke the L2 mainly? Was it words, or grammatical constructions, or L2 pronunciation of L1 words?

One of the consequences of looking at SLA as a dynamic system is that the first language of the learner is part of the system too, and interacts with other parts.

This means that the L1 may become affected by learning the L2. As illustrated with two studies below, one dealing with a slowed down speed of processing in L1 and the other with an effect on L1 parsing, even a relatively low level of proficiency in an L2 may influence the L1. In the last section we argue that 'forgetting an L1' is also evidence that the different language systems interact. If an individual lives in the L2 country for a while and has no opportunity to speak the L1 anymore, the L1 may become affected significantly by the L2. The speaker may no longer be able to retrieve his L1 words and expressions and use L2 words and expressions instead.

SPEED OF PROCESSING

One of the few studies that have looked at the impact of bilingualism on processing in the dominant L1 is the one by Ransdell and Fischler (1987). They compared monolingual speakers of English with bilinguals with English as their L1 and a variety of L2s on the speed with which they could name different objects.

Ransdell and Fischler's (1987) subjects were tested in English only on four different tasks: word list recognition, lexical decision, object naming and free recall of list-learned words. No differences in levels of accuracy were found between the monolingual and bilingual groups, but there was a difference in speed of processing, both in the word recognition task and in the lexical decision task. No differences were found for the naming and recall tasks. They conclude that 'it seems likely . . . that there are cognitive as well as cultural benefits of being multilingual that outweigh the processing speed disadvantage seen in the present tasks' (Ransdell and Fischler, 1987: 403). Interestingly the two groups did not differ on a more real world test like the Scholastic Aptitude Test (SAT), which includes speeded comprehension. So the speed differences found may only be relevant in the specific laboratory conditions they were tested in and need not have an impact on more real-life activities. However, it does show that L1 processing may be influenced by an L2.

Task A2.7

> Suppose you are a business person who has to negotiate in your L2 with a native speaker of that language. Do you think a non-native negotiator is at a disadvantage compared to a native negotiator mainly because it takes him or her longer to find the right words?

L2 INFLUENCE ON PARSING IN L1

The impact of bilingualism and multilingualism is not restricted to speed of processing. Also the cross-linguistic interaction between different languages is dynamic and related to use and input. An example of research showing this nicely is Dussias's (2001) study of parsing in bilinguals. She presents data on one specific aspect of bilingual processing: parsing of sentences in comprehension. In her research, she compares various theories on parsing by looking at data from early and late Spanish–English/English–Spanish bilinguals and monolingual speakers of both languages. The following type of sentence was used in the study:

> Peter fell in love with the sister of the psychologist who studied in California.

The same sentence was also used in a slightly adapted Spanish translation:

> Pedro se enamoró de la hija del psicólogo que estudio en California.

Subjects had to answer the question 'Who studied in California?'. When presented with the English set of items, English monolinguals show an overwhelming preference for 'the psychologist', which is called 'the low attachment option'. Spanish monolinguals on the other hand have a clear preference for 'the sister', which is called 'the high attachment option'. Dussias was interested in seeing what happens when Spanish speakers acquire English: will that have an impact on the processing of English too, or are those systems completely separated? She compared early bilinguals, speakers who acquired Spanish as a second language at an early age, and late bilinguals. The late bilinguals showed a pattern similar to the Spanish monolinguals, with the early bilinguals preferring the low attachment option, though to a significantly lesser degree. So the early bilinguals showed a pattern in their Spanish that is more like English. Their preference appeared to be closely related to their pattern of language dominance: most of the bilinguals were English dominant and showed the low attachment preference. For the early bilinguals the difference between the Spanish and the English conditions was very small, suggesting both the influence of Spanish when processing English and vice versa. These findings suggest that in the early stages of acquisition, strategies of L1 are used in processing L2. At later stages L2-based strategies tend to dominate L1-based strategies. Strategy use appears to be influenced by frequency of input in either L1 or L2: the early bilinguals seem to have 'lost' their high attachment in Spanish due to extensive exposure to (English) low attachment sentences. Dussias (2001) concludes that an exposure-based theory, in which processing decisions in comprehension reflect construction frequencies in the environment, best explains her data.

 Task A2.8

➤ You may try to find out how high and low attachment as in the Dussias study works for your language when it is not English or Spanish. Are there similar constructions, and if so what is the preferred parsing?

➤ If you have ever been in an English-speaking setting for more than half a year or so, do you have the feeling that your L1 system is influenced by English? If not, ask a friend or colleague about his or her experience.

Such data show that the line between growth and decline is difficult to draw, and that even the first language may be influenced by a continued use of another language, which is also in a constant state of flux, depending on patterns of use.

LEARNING AND FORGETTING

In research on SLA there has traditionally been much interest in theories of learning. Much less interest is shown in theories of forgetting. This is in a way peculiar, since learning and forgetting are closely related. Language skills and linguistic knowledge are not special if it comes to storage and retrieval from memory. There is a simple rule: information that is not retrieved regularly will become less accessible and ultimately sink beyond reach. So everything we learn is in constant danger of being forgotten. There are huge individual differences, but the general trend is clear: non-use leads to loss. However, attrition is not an on/off phenomenon. Non-use leads to a gradual decline in retrievability, which sets off slowly but after some time falls more steeply. In language use all sorts of information have to be accessed at an incredible speed, and loss of speed has a major impact on processes of language production and perception (Schmid and De Bot, 2003). So even if knowledge is not really forgotten, retrieval becomes more difficult and slower, which has an impact on the proficiency in that language. When the language is used more frequently again, retrieval will become easier and faster again. Because the use of particular languages is likely to vary over time, so will levels of proficiency due to use and non-use. This means both the L1 and L2 are in a constant state of flux, depending on the degree of exposure to those languages. This also implies that research on language attrition should be considered as an integral part of the process of SLA.

Task A2.9

➤ Paul Meara, an applied linguist from Swansea, refers to the reactivation of a seemingly forgotten language as the 'Boulogne Ferry effect'. This refers to the experience of British travellers who took the ferry to Boulogne in France across the English Channel in the old days before the Euro-tunnel was built. Once they arrived in France and they saw the French signs and heard French spoken on the street, all of a sudden large parts of their skills in French seemed to re-emerge while they thought they had forgotten it all. Did you ever have this experience? Can you describe a particular situation in which you remembered seemingly forgotten items in an L2?

CONCLUDING REMARKS

In this unit we have tried to explain some of the basic aspects of Dynamic Systems Theory, a theory that we think is very relevant to our understanding of the process of SLA and the organisation of the multilingual system. Its main characteristics are that all parts of the system are interconnected, that the system is constantly changing either through external input or through internal reorganisation, and that growth and decline of knowledge are normal characteristics of a system. Development is discontinuous and 'jumps' from one attractor state to the next. In the units that follow, we will gradually develop this theory further and show how it applies to many aspects of SLA.

Unit A3
Historical perspectives

In Units A1 and A2 we have suggested that second language acquisition could be regarded as a dynamic process. In the first part of this unit, we will briefly discuss other theories that have looked at language in general and language acquisition in a different manner. We will make clear that theory formation itself can be regarded as a dynamic process, too. A theory in one field, such as philosophy, psychology or general linguistics, may influence a theory in another field such as applied linguistics, and vice versa and cause theories to develop in new, usually unpredictable, directions. Also findings in first language acquisition have influenced the directions of SLA research. In the second part of this unit, we will present a brief history of SLA research, and we will look in particular at how the influence of L1 on L2 has been regarded and applied to teaching an L2. At the end we will show how these findings can be interpreted within a DST framework.

INTERACTING THEORIES

To be able to understand the directions that SLA research has taken, it is necessary to understand two important positions in twentieth-century linguistic theory first: 'empiricism' versus 'mentalism'.

At the end of the nineteenth century and at the beginning of the twentieth century, there was a great deal of interest in the USA in recording Indian languages that were rapidly dying out. To discover the structures of these languages, as much 'empirical evidence' as possible needed to be collected for analysis. But first it had to be made clear what phenomena to look at. Ferdinand de Saussure, an early-twentieth-century Swiss linguist, made a useful distinction between 'parole' (the raw linguistic data) and 'langue' (the underlying, more theoretical system).

Task A3.1

➤ To see how difficult it may be to work directly with the with 'langue/parole' distinction, try to work out what should be regarded as features of 'langue' in the following excerpt (from Clark, 1996):

The symbols mean the following: a comma indicates the end of a tone unit; a period, a brief pause; text between asterisks, overlapping text; and double parentheses, the speech was almost inaudible to the transcriber.

June: ah, what ((are you)) now, *where*
Darryl: *yes* forty-nine Skipton Place
June: forty-one
Darryl: nine.nine
June: forty-nine, Skipton Place
Darryl: W one.
June: Skipton Place, W one ((so)) Mr D Challam
Darryl: yes
June: forty-nine Skipton Place, W one,
Darryl: yes
June: right oh.

A useful technique in analysing the raw data (parole) and finding the general patterns (langue) was to see how elements were distributed. For example, personal pronouns could be used systematically to replace nouns. This type of linguistic approach is generally referred to as 'structuralism'. It was the linguist Leonard Bloomfield (1933) who systematised these analytic techniques even more and published them in 1933 in his influential book *Language*. One of his main concerns was that the general description of a language should be scientific, and to him only an analysis based on 'real data' could be considered scientific. This type of general approach towards linguistic data has been labelled 'empiricism'.

Parallel to these developments in linguistics, there were developments in the field of psychology, or to be exact, in learning theory. Influenced by the writings of Ivan Pavlov, a nineteenth-century Russian scientist, John Watson, and Edward Thorndike (both early twentieth-century American scientists), B. F. Skinner (1957) published a famous book called *Verbal behaviour* in 1957. In the behaviourist tradition, learning is seen as the product of teaching: conditioning and habit formation. The most famous example of 'conditioning' is the Pavlov dog experiment. Because dogs had been taught to associate a bell with food, dogs were 'conditioned' to salivate when hearing the bell. Learning was thus seen as making a series of connections, called stimulus–response bonds. When more complex learning was involved, the teaching was done in smaller successive separate steps, referred to as 'shaping'. Learning in general, but also learning of a language, was thus seen as pure habit formation.

 Task A3.2

➤ Assume you believe in 'conditioning' as a way to learn and you have to teach someone to say, 'My name is X and I am from X' in an L2. How would you go about teaching this phrase? Would you teach individual sounds or words first, or would you teach the whole phrase at one time? If possible, try your 'method' out on someone. Does it work?

In 1959, Chomsky, who took a 'mentalist' position to linguistics closely related to Platonic and Socratic philosophy, wrote a very critical review of Skinner's book *Verbal behavior*. The mentalist school, in contrast to the behaviourist school, values subjective data as for example gained by introspection. Chomsky argued that language could not be explained by just looking at observable facts, and assuming learners learned patterns from them because such observable data were inadequate and incomplete as evidence. When people speak, they often use incomplete sentences and produce truncated sentences, false starts and corrections. Also, some constructions 'look alike' but are quite different in underlying structure when examined more closely. One of his most famous examples is the pair of constructions 'John is easy to please' versus 'John is eager to please'. On the surface (and in the structuralist tradition) these sentences would be treated as the same, but when these sentences are 'transformed', the difference in meaning becomes apparent. It makes sense to say 'It is easy to please John' but not 'It is eager to please John.' In other words, 'John is easy to please' means that it is easy for someone else to please John, but in 'John is eager to please', it is John who does the pleasing. Using examples like these, Chomsky argued that language could not be analysed by looking purely at observable data but needed to take into account data that could not be observed. For example, the sentence 'It is eager to please John' would never be observed as it does not belong to the normal repertoire of the English language. His argument, therefore, was that the way to understand language was not to examine 'performance', which is similar to the Saussurian notion of 'parole', but to discover the speaker's underlying 'competence', the equivalent of 'langue'. In the same vein, he argued that children could never learn their first language purely by habit formation. His main argument was that children can learn a language very adequately even if the 'input' they have received from their caretakers is far from perfect. Another argument is that children and people in general may produce sentences they have never heard before. Pure conditioning and habit formation could never account for this rapid acquisition of or creativity in language. Chomsky concludes that in order to learn a language, children must be biologically programmed to learn a language. This special ability is referred to as the *Language Acquisition Device* (LAD), which is thought to contain all and only the principles of languages that all languages have in common. These universal principles constrain the types of structures that are possible. One such principle might be that all languages have verbs. But clearly there are also differences between languages, such as putting a determiner before or after a noun. Through the input, the child discovers which of the two choices his language permits. This common underlying grammar of all languages is referred to as 'Universal Grammar' (UG). For the child to learn a language he needs access only to samples of a natural langue, however imperfect, and these samples serve as a trigger to activate the device.

Task A3.3

➤ What do you think? For a child, is learning a language similar to any other type of learning, such as learning to categorise (e.g. recognise his mother's face, learning that a cup holds liquid, learning that some things are edible and others are not, and so on) and developing motor skills (such as learning to walk or to build with blocks). Or does learning language involve a totally separate set of abilities? If so, what do you think they might be?

Larsen-Freeman (1997) – who was one of the first to point out the usefulness of DST to SLA – points out that even though she does not wholly adhere to the idea of LAD and UG as described above, there may very well be universal principles and constraints on the type of constructions used in languages. She argues that these principles may be 'initial conditions' that constrain all human languages. Nonetheless, unlike in Chomskyan UG, these principles do not depend on clear 'yes' versus 'no' choices (called 'parametric choices') but on general tendencies (called 'fields of attraction') that languages may exhibit.

 Task A3.4

➤ Can you think of some features in word order, producing sounds, forming form/meaning relationships, and so on that many languages may have in common?

Complex nonlinear systems exhibit sensitive dependence on their initial conditions, and language is no exception. We might call UG the initial condition of human language – it contains certain substantive universal principles that apply to constrain the shape of human languages. For instance, there are a small number of archetypal or core phonological patterns that apply to all languages, e.g. almost all languages have voicing assimilation of obstruents. (...) However, languages also differ. In English, the voiced consonant assimilates to the voiceless, whereas in Spanish and Russian, the first consonant assimilates to the second regardless of the voicing feature (Mohanan, 1992). To explain interlinguistic differences like this in a manner consistent with the view being proposed in this article, Mohanan posits UG 'fields of attraction' that permit infinite variation in a finite grammar space. Fields of attraction are by nature gradient, unlike parametric choices, which are generally seen to be discrete. The strength each field exerts on a particular language differs thus allowing for interlinguistic variation. For any given language, the fields of attraction will define the state that the system is attracted to, i.e. its most natural or unmarked state. Because of them, the changes a language undergoes leave its basic shape intact. Therefore, anything borrowed into the language will be adapted to conform to the permissible phonological sequences and sometimes to the morphosyntactic constraints as well (e.g. *aisukuriimu* of Japanese and *Le Drugstore* of French, borrowed from English).

(Larsen-Freeman, 1997: 149–150)

So what Larsen-Freeman is basically saying here is that UG defines the beginning or initial state of the grammatical system and that rules that follow UG tend to be attractors in the developing system: the system is less likely to settle for a rule that does not follow UG than one that does. At the same time languages have become different from each other, and the rules of the language interact with the more general universal rules. The most unmarked state is then the state that applies for many languages and the marked state the one that applies to only a few.

Even though Chomskyan thinking has been very dominant over the last 50 years or so in linguistics, the majority of linguists in the world do not (or no longer) work exclusively within this paradigm. However, until recent findings in cognitive science became better known, it has been difficult to challenge the basic premises on which the Chomskyan argument is based.

Connectionism (cf. Elman *et al.*, 1996) is a movement in cognitive science that seeks to explain human intellectual abilities by using computer simulations of neural networks. Experiments on models of this kind have shown that neural networks can learn such skills as recognising a face, reading, and discovering simple grammatical structures. They can also learn to extend these simple structures into more complex ones. Thus, a computer can learn to generalise from what it has been exposed to. In consequence, connectionists claim that language learning can be explained in terms of learning in general, so no special language learning module is needed, and children can learn a language from the input they receive because they can generalise beyond what they have actually been exposed to. Various simulation experiments have been carried out to see how in a connectionist network input and output are related. The main finding was that the developing connectionist networks develop remarkably similarly to naturally developing systems in children. Interestingly, the output of the system appeared to show more variation when it was about to reach a point where it reorganised itself significantly. This is where connectionism is especially compatible with Dynamic Systems Theory, which also looks at self-organising systems that change due to interaction between its components and interaction with the environment.

Empirical evidence for the human ability to generalise comes from cognitive psychologists such as Gentner and Medina (1998), who have shown by means of experiments that children learn to 'generalise' by means of analogy. After they have become aware of the similarities between two or more things, they can 'generalise' this knowledge to new situations. As far as language acquisition is concerned, a connectionist approach would entail that the rules of a language are not part of the child's initial mindset, but 'emerge' by means of general learning processes such as the ability to generalise and recognise patterns in similar things. Language acquisition is seen as the result of some very well-developed mechanisms in perception and organisation that help the child to acquire fundamental aspects of the language very quickly. As Marchman (1997) shows in her overview of research on early acquisition, very young children show an amazing awareness of characteristics of their first language. For example, 7.5 months old infants are able to distinguish words they have heard before from words not presented earlier, even after very brief exposures. Also the specific sounds of the first language are distinguished from sounds not found in that language after a few months. So rather than a very crude general learning device, emergentists assume the existence of very sensitive and specialised perceptual and learning mechanisms that are particularly tuned to learning relevant aspects of language at that age. 'An emergentist alternative argues that language acquisition gets off the ground due to a set of general capacities for perceiving and processing speech information in the context of a powerful learning mechanism which abstracts and simultaneously stores information about the regularities inherent in the input at a variety of levels' (Marchman, 1997: 295).

★ Task A3.5

➤ Even though you are not a child, and the input below is written rather than spoken, you might like to test your own generalising ability by analysing the small corpus below. Isolate the morphemes in the sentences and state the meaning or syntactic function of each one. Also try to explain how you have reasoned to come to your solution.

(1)	ʔáañi ʔañ číkpan	'I am working'
(2)	míḍ ʔo hígay	'He is running'
(3)	ʔáapim ʔam číkpan	'You (plural) are working'
(4)	číkpan ʔo hígam	'They are working'
(5)	ʔáapi ʔap míḍ	'You (singular) are running'
(6)	číkpan ʔač ʔáačim	'We are working'
(7)	hígay ʔo míḍ	'He is running'
(8)	číkpan ʔañ	'I am working'
(9)	hígam ʔo číkpan	'They are working'
(10)	ʔáačim ʔač číkpan	'We are working'

(Langacker, 1972: 61)

Tomasello (2000) summarises several studies in which children's linguistic input and output is meticulously followed and argues convincingly that the child learns the rules from the input. One study in which one child was followed very closely for six weeks shows that it takes quite a bit of time before a child uses constructions creatively. First a child will use the same set phrases he has heard, such as 'Where's daddy?', 'Thank you', 'There you go', 'I want bottle' a lot. Tomasello argues that the child first repeats and learns a whole adult utterance. The creativity and emerging complexity occurs slowly when the child appears to recognise a pattern in his own utterance repertoire and replaces one item in the set phrase, such as 'I want tissue' instead of 'I want bottle'. A construction with an open slot such as 'I want X', Tomasello calls an utterance schema. He concludes his article as follows:

The general picture that emerges from my application of the usage-based view to problems of language acquisition is this: When young children have something they want to say, they sometimes have a set expression available and so they simply retrieve that expression from their stored linguistic schemas and items that they have previously mastered (either in their own production or in their comprehension of other speakers) and then 'cut and paste' them together as necessary for the communicative situation at hand – what I have called 'usage-based syntactic operations'. Perhaps the first choice in this creative process is an utterance schema which can be used to structure the communicative act as a whole, with other items being filled in or added on to this foundation. It is important that in doing their cutting and pasting, children coordinate not just the linguistic forms involved but also the conventional communicative functions of these forms – as otherwise they would be speaking creative nonsense. It is also important that the linguistic structures being cut and pasted in these acts of linguistic communication are a variegated lot, including everything from single words to abstract categories to partial abstract utterance or phrasal schemas.

(Tomasello, 2000: 77)

In a way, developments in linguistic theory seem to have made a full circle. Tomasello, who looks at the 'parole' or 'performance' of children and their care-takers, is, like Bloomfield, an empiricist in that he insists on real data to draw conclusions from. He also shows that Skinner was partially correct in saying that children repeat and imitate adults' utterances; however, what is different is that, like Chomsky, he tries to account for the creativity and emerging complexity in a child's language. The main difference between a UG and usage-based approach is that the former is a top-down and the latter a bottom-up approach as far as grammar is concerned. A UG approach postulates that the child already knows the general rules of language, which s/he progressively refines and applies to his/her own language, and a usage-based approach assumes that the child has a general learning mechanism that enables him/her to recognise patterns in utterances and build rules for his/her own language.

Task A3.6

➤ Which of the language acquisition approaches mentioned above appeals to you the most? Do you think that humans have a learning device that is dedicated to language only or do you feel that there is a more general learning ability that also applies to language? Can you give arguments for this opinion?

SLA RESEARCH AND PARADIGMS

The changes in theoretical thinking sketched above have influenced approaches to SLA. Behaviourism and structuralism were strongly related to an approach called 'contrastive analysis', the best-known paradigm for studying FL/SL learning and organising its teaching in the 1950s and 1960s. When Chomskyan thinking came into vogue, the interest in contrasting the L1 and L2 declined because it was believed that the process of L2 acquisition was very similar to the process of L1 acquisition, which takes place without explicit attention to language forms.

FROM CONTRASTIVE ANALYSIS TO CROSS-LINGUISTIC INFLUENCE

Because in the 1950s and 1960s language learning was viewed as the result of habit formation, it seemed likely that a person who had learned one language would revert to those habits when learning a second language and that these 'old habits' would be helpful if they were similar to the L2 habits, but would interfere with correct learning if they were different. To be able to determine which 'old habits' might give rise to interference, the structures of the two languages were systematically compared within a structuralist paradigm. Early Contrastive Analysis proponents claimed that the Contrastive Analysis Hypothesis (CAH) could accurately predict most of the errors made in the L2. There was little doubt that the learner's L1 influences the learning of L2, but researchers also found that not all errors predicted by the CAH were actually made. Moreover, quite a few errors that L2 learners make seemed to be unrelated to their L1, and L2 learners with different first languages often made similar errors. By the early 1970s, strong reservations about the CAH and CA in general were voiced, not only because the hypothesis did not live up to its expectations, but even more so because the two theories – behaviourism and structuralism – on which it was based had become outmoded and discredited.

The paradigm proposed as a replacement for Contrastive Analysis was Error Analysis (EA). (See article by Corder, 1967 in Unit B3). According to this theory, it could not be denied that the first language did have an influence on the L2, but rather than taking the L1 as starting point to predict L2 errors, the language that the L2 learner produced, the learner's 'Interlanguage' (IL), a term coined by Selinker (1972), became the starting point for analysis. Some of the errors that the L2 learner made could be traced back to 'cross-linguistic influence' (a term used by Kellerman and Sharwood Smith (1986) to show that the influence could go from L1 to L2 and vice versa) or to 'language transfer' (a term used by Gass and Selinker (1983) which gives emphasis to the influence of L1 on L2), and other errors could not. Another notion was that not only errors are transferred (negative transfer) from L1 to L2 but also things that were similar between L1 and L2 can be helpful in acquiring the L2 (positive transfer). In this vein, Kellerman (1979) also showed that there are constraints on positive transfer. (See Kellerman's article in Unit B3). The fact that many errors do occur in a learner's L2, traceable to the L1 or not, is very much in line with thinking in terms of Dynamic Systems Theory. As was mentioned in Unit A2, and as is argued by Larsen-Freeman (1997) in Unit A7, errors and a great deal of variability are part of an individual's learning process.

Task A3.7

➤ In the following five sentences, each with a clear IL error, two are clearly related to the L1, the others are not. With a common-sense approach, try to explain what may have caused the L2 learner to make the errors (all taken from James, 1998: 147).

Can I *become* (rather than get; from German *bekommen*) a beefsteak.
He wanted to *cancel* (rather than *conceal*) his guilt.
I think Senhor is *constipated* (rather than *caught a cold* from Portuguese *constipado*).
It was a *genius* (rather than *genuine*) diamond.
She listened to his *speak* (rather than *speech*).

At one point, EA developed two totally different goals. On the one hand, applied linguists such as Corder and James were interested in the errors for pedagogical reasons. By addressing those errors clearly influenced by the L1, the applied linguist could improve the teaching process. On the other hand, applied linguists such Gass and Selinker wanted to study the learner's Interlanguage in its own right, not so much to discover ways to teach but to discover in a more abstract manner how language is learned. Clearly influenced by the dominant linguistic thought of the time, much of this kind of SLA research has gone into finding evidence for supporting UG, finding the general principles of UG, or inquiring whether adults had access to UG the way children do. Related to this is the discussion on the existence of a 'critical period' for language learning, the assumption being that the Language Acquisition Device would only be active during a given period of time. We will come back to this discussion in Unit A6.

IS L2 ACQUISITION LIKE L1 ACQUISITION?

In the 1980s the interest in the influence of the first language on the second and vice versa became overshadowed by new insights into the acquisition process of a second language. Krashen, who felt that the process of second language acquisition was not that different from first language acquisition, argued that people do not learn a language by talking 'about' it (i.e. studying the rules of grammar), but by experiencing enough meaningful input and communication within that language.

Krashen, who had a background in neuro-psychology, managed to bring different strands from various fields together into one overarching approach. He took components from various fields – first language acquisition, developmental studies, neuro-psychology and so on – and forged them into a model for SLA without, however, advancing a strictly coherent theoretical basis for the model. Krashen's work gave a very strong impetus not only to the 'communicative approach' in second language teaching (see Unit A6) but also to SLA research, much of which concerned itself with proving or disproving the five theoretical hypotheses Krashen advanced. These are listed below.

■ The Acquisition versus Learning Hypothesis: Here, Krashen and Terrell (1983) make a distinction between acquisition and learning, a distinction that is at the basis of the other hypotheses. Acquisition is the product of a subconscious process, very similar to the one children use in acquiring their first language. The term learning, used here in a very specific sense, is the product of formal teaching and results in conscious knowledge about the language.

■ The Monitor Hypothesis: According to Krashen and Terrell (1983), it is nearly impossible for people to use consciously learned knowledge when they speak naturally. At most, the learning system performs the role of the 'monitor' or the 'editor', which may help plan, edit and correct speech, but only when the second language learner has sufficient time, consciously focuses on form or thinks about correctness, and knows the rule.

■ The Natural Order Hypothesis: The Natural Order hypothesis is based on findings (cited in Krashen, 1987) that suggest that the acquisition of grammatical structures in a second language follows a predictable 'natural order'. No matter how old the learner is, how much input he has received, how he has 'learned' or 'acquired' the L2, or what his first language background is, some grammatical structures are acquired early while others late. Even though there was individual variation, the similarities among the learners were very strong.

■ The Input Hypothesis: If the learner does not acquire a language by consciously studying the grammar of a language, how does he acquire it? According to the Input hypothesis (Krashen, 1985: 100), the learner improves and progresses along the 'natural order' when he receives second language 'input' that is one step beyond his/her current stage of linguistic competence. For example, if a learner is at a stage 'i', then acquisition takes place when he is exposed to 'Comprehensible Input' that belongs to level 'i + 1'. Because not all learners are at the same level of linguistic competence at the same time, Krashen suggests that natural communicative input is the key to designing a syllabus, ensuring in this way that each learner will receive some 'i + 1' input that is appropriate for his current stage of linguistic competence.

■ The Affective Filter Hypothesis: According to the Affective Filter hypothesis, a number of 'affective variables' such as motivation, self-confidence and low anxiety can play a facilitative role in successful second language acquisition. Low motivation, low self-esteem, and anxiety, on the other hand, can work together to 'raise' an affective filter and form a 'mental block' that prevents comprehensible input from being used for acquisition. In other words, when the filter is 'up' it hinders language acquisition. However, even though positive affect is necessary, it is not sufficient on its own for acquisition to take place.

Although there is now strong evidence that Krashen's distinctions and hypotheses cannot all be maintained as originally formulated (see, for example, the basic issues in Unit A1 and the Gregg, 1984 article in Unit B3), there is no doubt that his insights have given a strong impetus to fundamental issues in current SLA research: the nature of a natural order, the role of input, implicit versus explicit learning, incidental versus intentional learning, the role of teaching formal aspects of a language, and the impact of psychological factors in language learning, many of which were mentioned in Unit A1 and some of which will be discussed in more detail in subsequent units.

Task A3.8

➤ In the section called 'Basic issues' in Unit A1, findings in consciousness research were quoted, explaining that 'awareness' and 'noticing' are prerequisites for 'intake' and that 'understanding' may facilitate learning. How do these findings relate to Krashen's hypotheses? What would DST have to say about the last sentence in the paragraph describing the Natural Order Hypotheses?

Some of Krashen's hypotheses are compatible with DST, others partially, and others not in their extreme forms. In a Dynamic System, we know different factors interact, but we can never be sure how they interact. Compatible with DST is the heavy emphasis on input, the idea that the learner needs to be exposed to things he does not know yet in order to progress, and the notion of an affective filter that may inhibit one's ability to take in new information. Partially compatible is the notion that acquisition is different from learning, but within DST any external factor, including formal teaching, would be assumed to affect the system, and indeed, as many studies have shown (see Unit A6), formal learning has proven to have positive effects on SLA. Also the monitor hypothesis is partially compatible. There is indeed a difference between automatic and monitored processing (see Unit A5), but that is not to say that they cannot take place simultaneously and/or consecutively in one speech event or that enough practice in monitored processing affects automatic processing. Least compatible with DST, however, would be Krashen's strong version of the natural order hypothesis because there are too many different factors – the actual input, the learner's L1, age, intelligence, setting of learning, motivation and so on – that interact to allow us to predict exactly how a learner's IL will develop. As Larsen-Freeman (1976) has shown, frequency of input can predict quite accurately the acquisition of English morphemes in L2 development.

CONCLUDING REMARKS

In this unit, we have looked at developments over the last 50 years or so in general theory formation – especially empiricism and mentalism – and how these have influenced SLA research and teaching. We argued that connectionism and emergentism may also explicate the way a language is learned. As in the other theories, connectionism and emergentism depend to a great degree on input. Only when children have become very familiar with a few similar constructions will they generalise from these to new ones. In the process, children make errors and may overgeneralise. As far as L2 acquisition is concerned, L2 learners' errors were first seen as bad habits caused by incorrect transfer from L1 to L2 that had to be avoided as much as possible. Later these errors were seen either as a way to conceive of appropriate teaching methods or as a way to discover UG principles. From a Dynamic Systems point of view, where the L1 and l2 are just two of the many different variables of the same system, it is more than obvious that there is cross-linguistic influence. Indeed, in some cases it might be helpful to point out differences between languages to avoid certain errors. Moreover, the degree of variability in errors is interesting in that they may show that the learner's system has reached an attractor state (called 'fossilisation') or precedes a development to mastering a particular construction (called 'attainment'). In the 1980s, Krashen's hypotheses caused SLA research to seek new directions. As we indicated, these hypotheses are partially compatible with a DST approach, but a DST approach would not claim that 'learning' is of little use in 'acquisition' because in a dynamic system any force will affect the system.

Unit A4
The multilingual mind

If we want to understand how people acquire or learn a second language, we need to know how information – especially in different languages – is processed in the human brain. New techniques, like brain scans and the use of electrodes to investigate brain activity (ERP) have shed some new light on language processing. Not surprisingly, the most important insight so far is that language processing is a complex interaction of a wide range of factors. It is not possible to look into a person's brain to see what happens, but even if we could, we would probably never really know how all the different factors interact. However, because we want to understand what the different factors are that affect multilingual processing, we have to depend on metaphors and models of language processing that can subsequently be tested.

In this unit, we will start with a familiar, general processing model (Levelt, 1993) and work towards a dynamic model of the multilingual lexicon. Then we will briefly explain what the implications are of this model for SLA.

A GENERAL LANGUAGE PROCESSING MODEL

When a person speaks many different 'steps' are involved. When a person wants to express an idea, she has to find words for that idea, put those words in a well-formed sentence, pronounce the words in the right order, and in doing so she has to co-ordinate thousands of tiny little muscles. To explain this complexity of interacting events in speech processing, Levelt's Speaking blueprint (Levelt, 1993; Levelt, 1989) has become the most complete and accepted one for a monolingual speaker. According to this model (see Figure A4.1), the production of speech takes place in three relatively distinct stages: the Conceptualiser, the Formulator and the Articulator.

Task A4.1

> Even though you are not familiar with the model yet, can you think of how the different steps are ordered? For example, when you want to say something, do you first form a concept and then find a word, or do you first find the word?

Once you have found words, how and at what stage are they put in the right order? At what point do you begin to actually pronounce each word? – after you have mentally constructed a whole sentence or as each word or series of words that belong together have been formed?

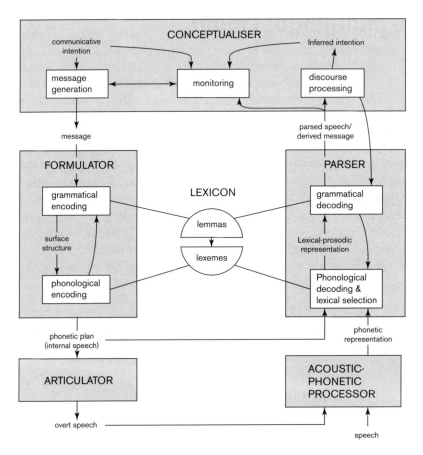

Figure A4.1 Schematic representation of the processing components for the comprehension and production of spoken language

Source: After Levelt, 1993

The starting point of speech production is the Conceptualiser, which generates a 'preverbal' message and contains meaning intentions that have to be put into words and sentences in the next two stages. This preverbal message contains a number of conceptual characteristics, which lead to the selection of a set of lexical items called 'lemmas' in the Formulator. A 'lemma' can be seen as the 'word to represent a concept'. In addition to representing a concept and containing semantic information, each lemma contains all kinds of other information – most importantly, how this word combines with other ones. In other words, is it a noun or a verb, and if it is a verb, what type of complement does it take? Or, is this word formal enough (register), or is this word appropriate in this context (pragmatic information)? Once the appropriate lemmas have been selected, they have to be combined into a well-formed sentence. This process is called 'grammatical encoding', which Levelt describes as 'solving a set of simultaneous equations' (1993: 4). Grammatical encoding results in a surface structure of a sentence in which all the properties of all the lemmas selected are satisfied.

However, the surface structure has not yet been specified for its phonological characteristics. This is taken care of in the next stage, 'phonological encoding', where the phonological information associated with the selected lemmas is matched to phonologically encoded word frames. This procedure takes place in two steps: first an empty skeleton, a 'metrical frame' is generated, which is then filled with the segmental content retrieved from the lexicon. The segmental content is stored in the lexeme related to a particular lemma.

To summarise, the lexicon in Levelt's model consists of two separate elements: the lemma, which contains conceptual, semantic, syntactic and pragmatic information, and the lexeme, which is the phonological form associated with the lemma. It is important to realise that an entry in the lexicon can be a single word (*school*), a compound word (*high school*), and a fixed expression (*go to school, graduate from high school*), an idiom (*to be of the old school* = 'to have an old-fashioned or traditional opinion') or any other group of words that are stored as a conventional unit.

Levelt's model (in which speech comprehension can broadly be regarded to involve the same steps as production, but in reversed order) is widely used as a general framework of language processing and is corroborated by many experimental data. One source of evidence for the separation of a lemma and a lexeme, for example, is observations made about speech errors. Most word-finding problems can now be interpreted as the difficulty of finding the lexeme belonging to a particular lemma. In tip-of-the-tongue phenomena speakers commonly do know the number of syllables and the stress pattern of a word, but fail to fill in that skeleton with segmental information. This is exactly what the model predicts.

However, in spite of its wide recognition, Levelt's model also has its problems. One of the strong points of the model is its strict modularity: once information has left one stage, it cannot return to that stage. In this way both the speed of language processing and the errors that speakers produce can be accounted for. The disadvantage of this starting point is that although the model allows for corrections by starting at the beginning again (making a loop), the lack of a direct feedback mechanism makes it more difficult to account for the transitions between the stages. How, for instance, can exactly the right words be selected from the lexicon when the Conceptualiser has no knowledge of which lemmas the lexicon contains? Many solutions have been proposed to this question and other questions about the model, but even though these lead to interesting discussions, they go beyond the scope of this book. Nonetheless, the model still stands and the least we can say is that it serves as an excellent starting point for shaping our thoughts about language processing in general and the lexicon in particular, as we will show next.

TOWARDS A DYNAMIC MODEL OF THE MULTILINGUAL MENTAL LEXICON

Levelt's model is geared towards monolingual speakers and so the question remains how it can account for processing by a multilingual speaker. Attempts have been made to adjust Levelt's model for the multilingual speaker. For example, De Bot (1992) argues that the Conceptualiser is most likely to be language-independent, whereas the Formulator is the most likely candidate to be language-dependent because it contains information about grammar. However, selection of the words from the right language requires the inclusion of language-related information in the preverbal message (De Bot, 2002). As the lexicon plays a central role in language processing, we will discuss these and other matters from the perspective of the multilingual mental lexicon.

For our purposes, three questions are most relevant concerning the multilingual mental lexicon:

1   Is lexical information stored in one big lexicon containing all the words of all the languages, or are there separate lexicons for different languages?
2   Can languages be switched on or off to achieve accurate processing?
3   And if so, how can languages be kept apart in speech production?

 Task A4.2

> ➤   Intuitively, what do you think are the possible answers to these questions? What do you feel is the most likely answer to each of these questions?

ONE BIG LEXICON OR SEPARATE LEXICONS FOR DIFFERENT LANGUAGES?

As with to what we said about language processing in general, the discussions about the mental lexicon are largely based on models and metaphors. The answers to the questions above are largely dependent on the model or the metaphor referred to. Early models were commonly based on the *spatial* metaphor, in which lexicons or parts of lexicons are assumed to be located in separate places. Recent models are mostly based on connectionist models consisting of networks, in which each entry may be connected to one or many other entries, similar to what we know about neural networks. Almost all models today are based on this principle, combined with a reference to the *activation metaphor*. This metaphor entails that entries in the lexicon may vary in their degree of activation. Activation may increase as the result of some event (for instance after coming across a certain word) and will decrease in the course of time. Figure A4.2 graphically represents the three metaphors: the spatial metaphor, the connectionist metaphor and the activation metaphor.

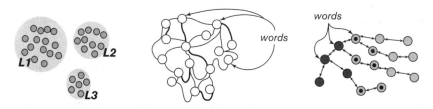

Figure A4.2 Three types of lexical representation: separate lexicons for each language; a network of words; activation spreading through a network

By looking at the development of these different models, we will try to make clear why the spreading-activation model seems to be the most appropriate one for our purposes. One of the earliest and most frequently quoted sources on the different possibilities of storage in the multilingual brain is Weinreich (1953). The central assumption in Weinreich's approach is that concepts and words are stored separately. With this assumption in mind, Weinreich argued that there are three different ways in which the multilingual lexicon could possibly be organised (see Figure A4.3): as a *compound*, as a *co-ordinate* and as a *subordinate* one. In a compound organisation, it is assumed that there is one common concept with a different word in each language. In a co-ordinate organisation, there is a complete separation between the different languages: each word in each language has its own concept. In a subordinate organisation, there is just one set of concepts, but the items in the second language can only be reached via the items in the first language: there are no direct connections between the concepts and the words in the second language.

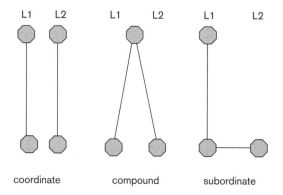

Figure A4.3 Three possible types of representation, proposed by Weinreich (1953)

Task A4.3

➤ Even though Weinreich may not have thought about different organisations of the bilingual lexicon at different moments in the development of an L2 learner, current thinking does not exclude that idea. What do you think is the most logical development that goes along with increasing proficiency: from compound to subordinate or the other way around? Think of some good reasons for your assumption.

In the past few decades, numerous other proposals have been made about the organisation of the multilingual mental lexicon, many of which are very similar to the types brought forward by Weinreich. The most important progress was made by formulating new possible combinations, by putting the combinations in new frameworks, and by empirically testing these combinations. In a range of experiments, researchers have attempted to find evidence for the different types of organisation. An experimental task that very obviously follows from Weinreich's spatial metaphor is the translation task: in an experimental setting in which response times can be measured, learners with different levels of proficiency are asked to translate words from L1 to L2 and from L2 to L1. For instance, in their article included in Unit B4, Kroll and Stewart (1994), found that translation from L1 to L2 is considerably slower than translation from L2 to L1, especially at lower levels of proficiency. This is interpreted as evidence that L1 lexical access runs through the concept, whereas L2 lexical access runs through the L1 entry. The underlying assumption in these models, then, is that there is one common conceptual system, but that there are independent lexicons for the words in each language. With regard to the way L2 learners develop their multilingual mental lexicon, these studies indicate a change from an initially subordinate organisation towards a compound organisation at later stages.

However, other studies investigating the multilingual lexicon demonstrate that Weinreich's spatial model seems to oversimplify matters. In particular, the assumption that there are separate lexicons for the different languages has become difficult to maintain. Several reaction-time experiments have shown that the selection of words in one language may conjure up words from another language. For instance, Beauvillain and Grainger (1987) showed that even in a completely French context, providing the word *four* ('oven') had a facilitating effect on the recognition of the subsequent word *five*. (We will return to this point when we discuss the possibility of a language switch, below.) Furthermore, apart from the speaker's level of proficiency, other factors, such as the semantic characteristics of a word (e.g. whether the word is *abstract* or *concrete*) and the degree of similarity of words in the different languages also tend to affect response times in experiments. Moreover, the traditional views of the mental lexicon are essentially static. We must realise that the lexicon is constantly changing due to the influence of a wide range of interrelated factors. Several of these factors have been investigated in empirical studies. Among other things, it has been shown that the lexicons of entire languages are not stored in one particular way or in one place. For concrete words a direct link between an L1 and L2 word and the concept may be more likely than for abstract words; the intervention of L1 words in the storage and retrieval of L2 words may be stronger for words that are very similar between the languages (cognates) than for words that are dissimilar; and the type of organisation may change with developing proficiency. In other words, there is a clear need for a more dynamic model that can take into account all these different factors, some of which are continuously changing. In view of this observation, the activation metaphor seems to be the most attractive alternative, as the level of activation can continuously change for each individual lexical item.

CAN LANGUAGES BE SWITCHED ON AND OFF?

The second question, whether separate languages (or language *subsets*) can be switched on or off, has an equally long history of answers. An influential proposal was that of Green (1986), who proposed three states in which languages can be at a certain moment in time: selected, active and dormant. The language that is used at a certain moment is the *selected* language; languages that, at that particular moment, play a role in the background are labelled *active*; languages that do not play a role at that moment are *dormant*. The assumption of the middlemost level – that of the active language – is required by the observation that when speaking a particular language, a speaker may use words from another language, either because that word is more appropriate or because the speaker cannot immediately find the word in the selected language. This *code-switching* is very common, and models of lexical processing must be able to account for this phenomenon.

Task A4.4

➤ Have you ever experienced 'confusing' your L1 and L2, for example by being able to think of an appropriate L2 word while speaking your L1 or the other way round? Can you think of any particular instances when this has happened? Do you have any idea what might cause it?

When multilingual listeners are confronted with utterances in any of the languages they know, they will not limit their search for words to one language only. This has been called non-selective access. Selective access would mean that only one language is addressed at a time. Experimental evidence on multilingual processing points to *non-selective lexical access*, rather than *selective access*. A method of investigation that is commonly used for this purpose is the lexical decision task (LDT) with *priming*. In LDTs, the participants are shown strings of letters on a computer screen and are asked to say whether that string is an existing word in a specified language. The subject's response time is measured. In a priming condition, the words on the screen are preceded by another word, the *prime*. By varying the prime and the context of the experiment, reaction time differences can be measured between, for instance, a cross-linguistic priming condition (with prime *blanc* and target *white*) and a control condition (*grand – white*). These experiments show clear cross-linguistic priming effects that cannot be accounted for when one of the languages is switched off. Also, other types of evidence are found to support non-selective access. One of these is the so-called 'neighbourhood' effect: longer response times are found for words that have many neighbours, i.e. words such as *word*, *work*, *worm*, *warm*, and so on that are very similar in form to many other words. This effect is not limited to neighbours within one language, but also occurs across languages.

The observation that lexical items can affect the activation of other lexical items, even across languages, is the basis of the BIA (Bilingual Interactive Activation) model of lexical processing. In this model, all lexical items are part of the same network. As lexical items are connected through this network, the activation of one lexical item may interactively affect the level of activation of all the lexical items it is attached to. Multilingual interactive activation may occur as a result of overlap in meaning, overlap in form or any other characteristic lexical items may have in common. From this perspective, code switching and cross-linguistic priming effects can logically be accounted for. A speaker may come up with a lexical item from another language simply because that item has a much higher level of activation, for instance resulting from its higher frequency.

Language development can also be viewed from this perspective: at lower levels of proficiency, L2 items may generally have a lower level of activation due to lower frequencies and less interaction, as the network of this language subset will be relatively small. At higher levels of development, the lexical connections within the L2 network will have become stronger.

SELECTING THE RIGHT LANGUAGE

Our discussion so far has pointed to a single lexical network for all languages, based on the BIA (Bilingual Interactive Activation) model of lexical processing, and has excluded the possibility of switching languages off. However, this still leaves the question of how speakers are able to keep their languages apart. Although code switching is a common phenomenon, speakers generally manage to speak only one language at a time. There is some evidence (Van Hell and Dijkstra, 2002) that a default level of activation is required for the selection of a lexical element. So it is not enough to have encountered a word once superficially to make it accessible in use. For elements from another language to be selected, they need to have a level of activation above the default level.

A helpful concept in our understanding of lexical storage is the idea of language *subsets*. Most researchers today will agree that there is one lexical repository, but that the individual items in the lexicon are tagged for (among many other things) the language to which they belong, grouping them functionally into language subsets. Subsets are groups of lexical items that are clustered due to some shared characteristic. The shared characteristic may, for instance, be a register (formal, informal, etc.) or a language. Moreover, in a multidimensional view of the lexicon, one and the same word can be a member of several subsets; for instance, the word *perceive* will be part of the subset of [English], but may at the same time be part of subsets like [Formal], [Verbs], [Abstract], etc. (see Figure A4.4)

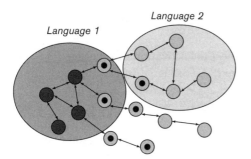

Figure A4.4 Representation of subsets in a lexical network

It is likely that the activation level of entire language subsets may be increased or decreased. Even though experimental evidence for this possibility is still limited, we will work with this assumption in mind. If this is the case, then it must be assumed that at some stage in language processing a choice is made for the language to be used and that language selection must occur at the lemma stage before it is matched with a lexeme. We will return to Levelt's blueprint to make this clear.

As we have seen, a crucial step in the formation of several models, including Levelt's, has been the introduction of *lemmas*, which mediate between the concepts and the words. Lemmas not only contain semantic and syntactic information but also all other information associated with the use of that lemma, such as how to use it pragmatically correctly. To accommodate multilingual processing, several authors (De Bot, 2002; De Bot, 2003; Lowie, 2000; Woutersen, 1997) have proposed adding a 'language node' to the lemma. In other words, in addition to semantic, syntactic and pragmatic information, the lemma is specified for language, and in the process of lemma selection, the language information will be one of the lexical concepts that determine the selection of the best matching lemmas.

Figure A4.5, which is a detailed projection of 'the lexicon' in a general processing model, makes clear how the semantic, syntactic, pragmatic and language information (small circles with information on the right) may be part of the lemma (bigger circle in the middle) and the lexeme (squares on the left). This representation should be seen within the activation metaphor. The links (the arrows in the figures above) can be seen as flows of interactive activation that go in both directions; from the lexical concepts to the lemmas and vice versa. For example, the Dutch lexeme 'eerlijk' ('honest') is associated with information about its meaning, it syntactic category, its language, but also its English counterparts and vice versa.

The model shows that the lexicon can be seen as a dynamic system in its own right because it constantly changes, influenced by external and internal forces, and self-organises. All the possible information associated with a lemma and the degree of activation of a lexeme depend on the input and output a speaker has experienced to a greater or lesser degree not only in his entire life, but also in very recent times. Suppose a Dutch speaker is trying to describe someone else in English and she is trying to find a word for the concept 'honest' ('eerlijk'), various ways of retrieving

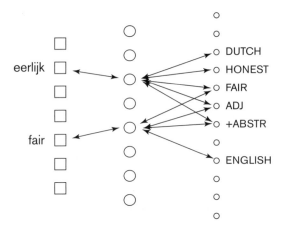

Figure A4.5 A dynamic model of the multilingual mental lexicon. This version is abbreviated for the different types of information associated with the lemma: the syntactic, semantic and language information must be assumed to have different sources, but are represented at the same level

the word are possible. Depending on how relatively often the Dutch and English words have been activated, not only in her entire life, but especially in most recent times, she might directly think first of the word in English or in Dutch. The more fluent speaker who has heard enough English in recent times will probably find the lexeme 'honest' directly. If she is not very fluent or has not used English much in recent times, she may think of the word in Dutch first. Then, she might also have a problem deciding whether she should use 'honest' or 'fair', each of which has different conceptual representations that partially overlap in Dutch. She may think of the word 'fair' first and then through association come up with the word 'honest'. To summarise, this model accounts not only for many different phenomena such as code-switching, different effects at different levels of proficiency, and the effect of priming, but also for the fact that people can keep their languages apart.

The language node will help control processing for language by activating a particular language subset and inhibiting others, but this does not necessarily exclude the possibility that words from other languages are activated during processing, as the following 'ping-pong' metaphor illustrates:

> Activation, and in particular inhibition will never be like an on/off switch. It is more like holding down ping-pong balls in a bucket filled with water: With your hands you can hold down most of the balls, but occasionally one or two will escape and jump to the surface. Likewise, complete suppression of a language, in particular one with a high level of activation may be impossible. Therefore, interference of the stronger language into the weaker language is more likely than interference from the weaker in the stronger. There is ample evidence for this from research on e.g. Dutch

migrants in the US and Australia, who when interviewed in Dutch had all sorts of problems suppressing their English, the language they usually spoke, but hardly any when speaking English.

(De Bot 2004: 26–27)

Task A4.5

➤ Try to draw a dynamic model of the mental lexicon (see Figure A4.5) with two entries from your own L1 and L2. The example in the figure has given information on only a few nodes (e.g. Dutch, adjective, abstract, and so on). Try to think of more information that might be connected to the entries. For ideas you may want to consult information on lemmas in the first section of this unit.

A DYNAMIC MODEL OF THE MULTILINGUAL MENTAL LEXICON AND ITS IMPLICATIONS FOR SLA

If the dynamic model of the multilingual mental lexicon is correct, it will have certain implications for SLA. The key words are 'association' and 'activation'. The words that are heard, seen or used most often are the words that are most easily accessed again and will have the most associations with other information such as how it is used. Words that are heard, seen or used the least will be the more difficult to retrieve. This would explain that it is just as easy to 'forget' words, even in an L1, as it is to 'acquire' them. It would also explain how one can be fluent in an L2 when talking with a friend about a common interest but have difficulty understanding a radio programme about a less known topic.

Task A4.6

➤ Can you think of particular ways, methods or strategies that have helped you learn L2 words? What implications would the model as presented in this unit have for learning vocabulary?

For L2 learners, this model implies that for different levels of proficiency there are different ways that are effective to acquire new words in the L2. Even though lots of input in the target language is a prerequisite for improving fluency, at early stages it may be necessary to go through the L1 to build enough vocabulary to be able to read items in the target language.

The literature on effective and efficient vocabulary acquisition generally points to the necessity of 'association' and 'activation' with the terms *elaboration* and *rehearsal* (Hulstijn, 2000). Elaboration means that a maximum number of associations is made in relation to a lexical item; the word should be seen in several different contexts and the learner should pay explicit attention to all characteristics of a word, from orthography and prosody to the word's syntactic and semantic features. Besides elaboration, rehearsal is required to make access to the lexical item more automatic. The best results will be achieved when rehearsal takes place with increasing time intervals, from minutes up to about one month.

Elaboration, or the linking of new information to existing knowledge, makes perfect sense when the lexicon is regarded as a network in which all lexical items may be linked. Rehearsal will increase the level of activation of lexical items. Since the level of activation will decrease over time, it is important not to allow the level of activation to drop beyond a threshold level. If a lexical item is reactivated before the activation level has dropped, the increase is more effective. (Some more detail about such principles as they apply to vocabulary acquisition can be found in Unit A5 in the section about building a knowledge system.)

CONCLUDING REMARKS

In this unit, we started with Levelt's general speech processing model and then we focussed on the mental lexicon. By showing the development of different models of the mental lexicon and pointing out empirical evidence that either supported the models or not, we argued in favour of an interactive activation model that has a language node in the conceptual representation of the lemma. The mental lexicon as presented by this model is a dynamic system in its own right in that it is subject to a great number of internal and external factors, is chaotic, not predictable, self-organising, and always subject to change. The implications for the learning of another language are that a great deal of input and reactivation in the target language is necessary for the learner to be able to 'remember' words.

Unit A5
The developing system

In the previous unit on the multilingual mind, we proposed a dynamic model of the multilingual lexicon in which the degree of activation and numbers of associations between entries determine the state of the lexicon at any moment in time. The lexicon – lemmas with all kinds of conceptual, semantic, syntactic and pragmatic information with their corresponding lexemes – is only one aspect of the information speakers may have. Speakers may also have emotions that correspond with certain concepts, and they may possess concepts for which there is no lemma.

Still, if lemmas contain as much information as proposed by the different models of the lexicon, and if they interact as much as the network models suggest and are affected by activation as the activation metaphor suggests, then we can see the dynamic model of the multilingual lexicon as a micro-system of a larger dynamic learning system. This view still leaves us with several questions: how does information become activated, how do associations between pieces of information become strengthened, and how does new information become assimilated in the system?

All language-learning theories will affirm the importance of input, but especially connectionist and emergentist approaches are based on the assumption that learning is primarily driven by input. It is important to realise that input is variable and so is the learner. Here too, a wide range of interacting factors continuously affects the system. Any type of input in any context may differentially affect the individual learner at different moments. That is why it will be very difficult to make generalisations about the role of input in second language acquisition. In spite of this reservation, we will attempt to draw conclusions based on research into the role of input and learning.

In this unit we will first discuss the general relationship between input and learning and how such learning works. We will look at how concepts, words and eventually sentences are learned, how they can be accommodated in a knowledge network, and how this knowledge system can develop optimally. In the first part of the unit, we imply that most of the learning is automatic and implicit. However, in both L1 and L2 learning there are moments when rules are explicitly stated. In the second part of this unit we will address the way implicit and explicit knowledge are related.

LEARNING MECHANISMS

The first question that needs to be addressed is what language learning really is. In line with theories of developmental psychology, we argue that learning is essentially a matter of assimilation and accommodation: a repeated perception will be noticed and will become established into the system by linking it to already existing information. In other words, learning is making new connections that remain.

From concept to words

 Task A5.1

➤ Imagine a very young child who is discovering that the word 'puppy' refers to one particular species of animates. Can you think of the situations and events the child has to experience before he understands to a degree of certainty which concept the word 'puppy' refers to? How would the child learn to limit the reference to dogs?

To understand the basics of learning in a DST approach, we need to go back to how infants learn very basic things early in life. For example, learning through perception takes place because the system already meets certain conditions. According to Edelman (1989) humans and other animate beings are endowed with 'very general biases that are the heritage of natural selection'; these are called 'values' (Thelen and Smith, 1994: 185). One 'value' is that humans tend to keep moving objects in view. Another may be that humans tend to grasp objects for feeding or exploration or tend to categorise objects and sounds. For the acquisition of knowledge, the simultaneous interaction of different values, which become correlated, is crucial. For example, imagine a young child, who has not yet learned the word 'ball', moving his head to follow a round thing going through the air and hearing the sound 'ball' uttered by his caretaker. The different activities, following the moving object with his eyes, which coincides with the muscular activity that goes with turning the head, which coincides with perceiving a round thing and which coincides with hearing the sound 'ball', form a pattern of connected systems that can be further developed. So seeing a ball moving in the air and hearing the word 'ball' leads to learning through the interaction of three activities: following the object (visual), moving the head (gestural) and hearing the word (auditory). The category of 'ball' is not the moving of the head nor the visually following it, nor the sound sequences in themselves, but the mapping of these activities onto each other. Then other co-occurring activities may become part of the complex of ball. Note that there is no other storage than the registration of co-occurrences, the history of a correlation of events. Eventually, the child realises that the sound 'ball' stands for a concept of 'ball' with all the relevant associations that the child may have experienced up to that time: it is a thing, it is round, it can move, it can hurt a bit if it hits you, it can have different colours and sizes, some squeak, people play with it, and so on. The child will no longer have to see the real object to interpret the symbolic sense of the word 'ball'. Once the child has learned enough concrete concepts and their words in this manner, the child can learn new and abstract concepts through his language and culture.

Task A5.2

➤ Suppose you have been exposed to the new English (nonsense) word 'trank' and have no idea what it means and are then successively exposed to the following sentences. While trying to understand its meaning, what connections would you make? Try to read each sentence separately and think about the meaning before moving to the next sentence. Try to make all your thinking explicit.

(All the sentences below have been taken from the *New York Times* and a rather common, frequent word has been replaced by 'trank'.)

1   At first, some NASA officials were uneasy about leaving the station unmanned for spacewalks, but Russia said the walk to be done this week was **trank** to maintain some outside scientific experiments and to examine the exterior of the station.

2   Both, he suggests in this short, elegant collection of essays, are **trank** in today's messy world.

3   Copper-nickel alloys, carbon steel and other compounds that are efficient in transferring heat, and are thus **trank** elements of many processing and climate-control systems, are also the first to corrode when water hits them.

4   McDonald's fought off a lawsuit from two teenagers who accused the company of failing to provide **trank** information about health risks associated with its meals.

5   Mr. Bornstein argues that social entrepreneurs are **trank** because governments 'appear increasingly impotent in the face of concentrated corporate power'.

6   Taste, and add more pepper or soy sauce if you like and salt if **trank**. Serve immediately.

7   The problem is not only logistics, but also security: no one can guarantee the safety of the thousands of polling places that would be **trank** for millions of Iraqi voters.

8   While they say they want to protect traditional matrimony, many are not yet convinced that an amendment is **trank**.

In general terms, the learning process as described above can be applied to the L2 learner. Of course, the big difference is that the L2 learner has already developed concepts in the L1 and words to refer to that concept. So, for example, when learning the word for the concept 'ball' in an L2, the L2 learner does not have to be exposed to many co-occurring activities to grasp the concept of ball because he has already learned the concept. The association between the concept and the L2 word may then go through the L1 (cf. Weinreich's subordinate system in Unit A4). At first, the learner may assume that there is full overlap between the conceptual representations of the L1 and L2 word, but because in many cases there is no direct translation between an L1 word and an L2 word, he will come to realise that the conceptual representations of the L1 and L2 words are different. It will therefore take a number of co-occurring activities (i.e. different contexts in which the L2 word is used) to fully grasp the meaning and use of the new L2 word.

Learning rules from input

The child does not hear just isolated words. In many cases, caretakers will use whole utterances with a particular meaning, such as 'Look at the ball!'. In Unit A3 we discussed how within an emergentist view children acquire their first sentences. At first they use whole utterances quite often exactly as they have heard them, such as 'Where's daddy?' Only after they seem to recognise some pattern do they substitute one word or so, such as 'Where's the ball?' The eventual language the child learns is much more complex, and the question is how the child learns to recognise and apply all the rules of a language. One theory very much compatible with the spreading activation model, connectionism, DST, and emergentism that tries to account for the acquisition of this complexity in both L1 and L2 is the Competition Model, developed by Bates and MacWhinney. According to Bates and MacWhinney (1981), complex language processing may result from the interaction of some basic simple rules which are inferred from the input.

The Competition Model is based on the assumption that there is a direct mapping between the form and meaning of an expression. For example, the sound of /kæt/ is associated with the whole concept of 'cat', involving the connection of one set of nodes to another, including connections to the words that usually precede and follow it. Also with sentences there is a form–meaning mapping. Often sentences 'reflect' real world events in a straightforward manner. For example, in an event there is usually an agent, someone performing an action, an action, and often an 'undergoer' of that action. These events are described rather similarly in most languages. Usually the most salient entity, the one performing the action, is put at the beginning, the action in the middle and the undergoer at the end of a sentence. By far the majority of the languages in the world express such an event with Subject–Verb–Object (SVO) order as in 'Dan hit the ball', but there are also some that use SOV or OVS word order ('Dan the ball hit' or 'The ball hit Dan'). However, among the SVO languages, there are differences. There are differences in how free the word order is (English has a rather strict word order), most languages make many distinctions in subject–verb agreement (but English marks only for third person singular), some languages use case marking (English does not for nouns) to show whether a noun is subject or object, and so on. In sum, in many languages there are several 'cues' to show whether a noun is subject. Relevant cues can be preverbal positioning, agreement with the verb, case marking, the use of the article 'the' and semantic information like animate/inanimate. In different languages, the cues have different weights. For example, preverbal position is very strong in English, but not in German because the case marking also shows whether an entity is a subject or not. Also subject–verb agreement is a good cue in most languages. Compare the following sentences:

English: The boy sees the man.
German: Der Junge sieht den Mann.

In English, if you turned the order around as in 'The man sees the boy', 'the man' would be considered subject, but in German 'Den Mann sieht der Junge' still means 'The boy sees the man', because of the case markings on the articles. 'Der' is masculine subject, and 'den' is masculine object.

One of the functions that have been studied in a large number of studies using the Competition Model is on such types of cues to agent identification, i.e. what cues or information is used to interpret a part of an utterance as the agent. There is rarely a direct one-to-one mapping of functions and forms, so a limited number of forms can be used to express various functions. These cues have different strengths of weights, so some cues carry more weight than other cues. Therefore, the part of the sentence that agrees in number with the verb in Dutch is very likely to be interpreted as the agent. However, there are several cues, and these may be in competition. In Dutch the agent tends to be positioned preverbally so a sentence like 'De man zien de jongens' ('The man see the boys') is complex because two cues for agency are in competition: agreement points to 'de jongens' as the agents, while preverbal position suggests that 'de man' is the agent. (Such a sentence is rare and might be used if the boys had been mentioned before and 'de man' were given some emphasis.) Through coalitions of cues such more complex functions can be expressed. In language acquisition, learners gradually develop a feeling for the role of such cues in the language to be learnt. They do this on the basis of the frequency of occurrence of such cues and their saliency in the input. 'Cue-validity' is the term used to refer to the weight of different cues. Languages differ in the strengths of different cues and the learner needs to develop a feeling for the competing weights in the new language. In the following extract, an example of L2 grammar learning shows how difficult it may be to get a feel for cues that do not exist in the L1.

> In grammar, the weights connecting functions to clusters of forms must be retuned during second language acquisition. In some cases, the second language requires the learner to seek out entirely new conceptual or discourse distinctions that were ignored in the first language, but which are now obligatory grammatical contrasts in the new language. A prime example of this type of restructuring might be the foreigner's attempts to pick up the category structure underlying the two major verbal conjugations of Hungarian. Every time a speaker of Hungarian uses a verb, he must

decide whether it should be conjugated as transitive or intransitive. Making this choice is not a simple matter. The intransitive conjugation is used not only when the verb is intransitive, but also when the direct object is modified by an indefinite article or by no article at all, when it is in the first or second person, when the head of the relative clause is the object within the relative clause, when the direct object is quantified by words, such as *each*, *no*, and so on. For example, the intransitive conjugation is used when a Hungarian says *John runs*, *John eats an apple*, *John eats your apple*, and *John eats no apple*. On the other hand, the transitive conjugation is used when the object is definite, when it is modified by a third person possessive suffix, when it is possessed by a third person nominal phrase, and so on. Thus, the transitive, or 'definite' conjugation, is used when the Hungarian wants to say *John eats the apple* or *John eats Bill's apple*, whereas the intransitive is used when saying *John eats an apple*. There are some 13 conditions that, taken together, control the choice between the transitive and intransitive conjugations (MacWhinney, 1989). There is no single principle that can be used to group these 13 conditions. Instead, transitivity, definiteness, and referential disambiguation all figure in as factors in making this choice. This way of grouping together aspects of transitivity, definiteness, and possession is extremely foreign to most non-Hungarians. Not surprisingly, L2 learners of Hungarian have a terrible time marking this distinction; errors in choice of the conjugation of the verb are the surest syntactic cue that the learner is not a native Hungarian.

In order to acquire this new category, the L2 learner begins by attempting to transfer from L1. To some degree this can work. The learner attempts to identify the Hungarian intransitive with the English intransitive. However, the fact that many sentences, with objects, also take the intransitive, if the objects are somehow indefinite, tends to block the simple application of this conceptual structure. In the end, no simple transfer will succeed and the learner is resigned to picking up the pieces of this new category one by one and restructuring them into a working system. [Here is an area in which attempts at formal linguistic analysis on the learner's part only make matters worse.] If the learner had proceeded like a Hungarian child, he would have learned the conjugations by generalizing from a rich database of collocations and phrases. The adult needs to amplify this case-based approach to learning with a way of focusing on contrastive structures in which cues are competing. For the adult, such focusing on particularly difficult parts of a grammatical system increases the efficiency of acquisition.

(MacWhinney, 1997: 128–129)

There is a considerable body of research on the application of the Competition model in SLA. Though the model can thus far only explain fairly simple function–form mappings, it nicely illustrates how frequency of occurrence of such mappings lead to the development of a system of cues used to interpret sentences in L1 and L2.

BUILDING A KNOWLEDGE SYSTEM

So far in this unit we have tried to show how important real language input is for the learner to acquire language. But of course if the learner just heard words and sentences without really understanding their intention or meaning and were just to repeat them, no learning beyond the ability to utter words and phrases would take place. According to Vygotsky, children first need these words and phrases for concepts and understand their meaning, but then in turn this language can help develop further learning.

Van Geert (1998) argues that two mechanisms proposed by some of the founding fathers of developmental psychology, Piaget and Vygotsky, can be used to explain this change and development. He argues that bringing together their classic notions and DST will lead to a new synthesis. Piaget has argued that development is a process of equilibration between internal knowledge and input. He distinguishes two mechanisms: 'assimilation', which is 'the integration of external elements into evolving or completed structures of an organism' (Piaget, 1970: 706–707), and 'accommodation', which is 'any modification of an assimilatory scheme or structure by the elements it assimilates'. Or to put it differently, assimilation is a conservative force aiming at keeping the system close to its present form by incorporating the new input, while accommodation is a progressive force aiming at changing the system through input. However, assimilation should not be viewed here as a purely absorbing mechanism. Assimilation of new input may lead to more automatisation of an activity and an increase in mastery, which in turn implies a decrease in error and an increase in generalisation, which in turn may apply to a wider range of activities. An example could be the way a child learns to draw simple figures over and over again. Through such practice, the hand–eye coordination will improve, which may be useful for many activities other than drawing figures.

Task A5.3

➤ An analogous example of more automatisation of an activity and an increase in mastery which leads to a decrease in error and increase in generalisation in L2 learning is the following:

> Many L2 learners of English have difficulty producing and keeping apart the initial sounds of *sea* and *she*. By intensively practising and finally mastering the production of a sentence such as 'She sells the sea shells on the sea shore', the learner can pronounce these sounds better in other situations.

Try to think of a similar example in your own L2 that you have trouble with (e.g. French: 'Un chasseur sachant chaser sans son chien n'est pas un bon chasseur.' Dutch: 'De kat krabt de krullen van de trap') and practise it intensively for a few days. Eventually, see if the practice helps decrease errors and increase generalisation to other contexts.

To make clear how information may be assimilated, Anderson's theory of semantic networks, explained in the following excerpt, is helpful. The excerpt explains how L2 vocabulary learning takes place. The notion of 'accommodation' is quite similar to the notion of 'semantisation' because both are concerned with bringing new information into the system, and the notion of 'assimilation' can be related to 'consolidation' because both are concerned with incorporating the new knowledge into the system. Below, it is argued that strengthening the links between the new information to the system as a whole helps to incorporate the new knowledge.

The process of vocabulary acquisition can be simplified down into recursive stages that are usually referred to as 'semantization' and 'consolidation' (cf. Beheydt, 1987; Mondria, 1996). At the first stage, the formal characteristics of a word are matched with semantic content. At the second stage, a newly acquired word is incorporated in the learner's permanent memory. These two stages are strongly interrelated. If a word is not adequately semanticized, consolidation cannot take place. In terms of the mental lexicon, a new lemma is created for a newly encountered word.

For the consolidation stage in vocabulary learning, Anderson's influential theory of semantic networks has great explanatory power (Anderson & Reder, 1979; Anderson, 1983: 197–208; Anderson, 1990). The basic assumption of this theory is that all of an individual's declarative knowledge is represented in the shape of a network consisting of nodes (cognitive entities) and paths (relations among these nodes). New propositions cue the retrieval of related prior knowledge and are acquired when they are stored with related units in the knowledge network as a result of productions (acquisition procedures). The new propositions and the prior knowledge may also stimulate the student's generation of other new propositions. All new propositions, both those presented by the environment and those generated by the learners themselves, are stored close to the related prior knowledge that was activated during learning. Within this network a great number of 'retrieval paths' are possible, but the more retrieval paths are linked to a particular unit of information, the better the recall of information will be. If activation of a certain retrieval path fails, information can be reconstructed by an alternative retrieval path (Anderson, 1976; 1983). The process of the learner producing information in addition to the information to be learned – which can be in the form of an inference, a continuation, an example, an image or anything else that serves to connect information – is called 'elaboration'.

It is obvious that elaboration is particularly relevant for the second stage of vocabulary acquisition: consolidation. The more active processing and association is involved during this stage, the more elaboration takes place, the more likely it is that a word is retained in the lexicon. After an extensive review of studies in this field, Hulstijn concludes that 'they all agree that processing new lexical information more elaborately will lead to higher retention than by processing new lexical information less elaborately.'

(Verspoor and Lowie, 2003: 551)

Task A5.4

➤ Try to apply the above explanation of semantisation and consolidation to your own experience with the nonsense word 'trank' in Task A5.2. What else would be necessary for you to retain the word for a long time and use it productively? (By the way, have you discovered which real English word 'trank' has replaced? It starts with an *n*, has nine letters, and ends with a *y*.)

According to DST, a system continuously changes as it interacts with its environment. However, there are moments of equilibrium (attractor states) and moments of great variation, which are moments in which the system is changing more rapidly and developing, either through interaction with the environment or through internal reorganisation of the system. Development is therefore the move from one equilibrium to the next due to such forces. Learning then is the move into the direction of a target equilibrium, and loss (which is also a form of development) is a move away from that. The target in a language can be defined at various levels; it can be the learning of all the different meanings of a particular word or the formation of a complex sentence in another language.

Van Geert (1998) argues that Piaget's concepts of assimilation and accommodation are closely related to Vygotsky's 'zone of proximal development' (ZPD). ZPD is defined as 'the difference between the child's developmental level as determined by independent problem solving and the higher level of potential development as determined through problem solving under adult guidance or in collaboration with more capable peers' (Vygotsky, 1978: 85). In other words, the 'actual developmental level' refers to what a child can perform independently and the 'zone of proximal development' includes those functions and activities that a child or a learner can perform only with the assistance of someone else. The person assisting could be an adult (parent, teacher, caretaker, language instructor) or another peer who has already mastered that particular function. To make clear how Piaget's 'accommodation' can be related to Vygotsky's 'ZPD', van Geert states: 'In so far as accommodation is a source of novelty and new information, new must always be close to old, that is within the postulated reaction norm' (1998: 637). In other words, accommodation takes place when new information is within the learner's ZPD.

As far as L2 vocabulary learning is concerned, we can provide the following fictitious example. To be able to read a text on his own without too much trouble, a learner needs to know at least 90% of the words in the text. Thus, the difficulty of the text will be very close to the learner's actual developmental level. One can imagine that if a learner knows only about 50% of the words, it will be almost impossible for the learner to make sense of the text in any way. However, if the learner knows about 75% or 80% of the words and the text is on a topic the learner is familiar with, he can read it with the help of a dictionary and or teacher, so the task would be within the learner's ZPD.

Task A5.5

➤ Imagine the following text is written in a foreign language and the xxxx are words unknown to you. First every fifth word, then every fourth word, and every third word have been left off. At what point does the text become incomprehensible for you? Reflect on the strategies you use to understand the text as much as possible. At what point would you no longer be in your ZPD?

80%

Sano Halo, 90, her xxxxx of thick white hair xxxxx poking above the lectern, xxxxx the microphone down to xxxxx level and began reciting xxxxx Lord's Prayer in Greek.

xxxxx hush fell over the xxxxx in the Stathakion Center in xxxxx, Queens, on Friday evening. xxxxx 200 Greek-Americans there xxxxx and bowed their heads. xxxxx Mrs. Halo finished, they applauded.

'My xxxxx used to make us xxxxx by the fire and xxxxx it,' she said later, 'and xxxxx have repeated it to xxxxx over and over in all the xxxxx since.'

For 80 years, Mrs. Halo, xxxxx was born into one of the xxxxx of Pontic Greeks that were xxxxx along the Black Sea in xxxxx Turkey, had barely spoken her xxxxx tongue, having largely lost her first xxxxx to a hard life in one of xxxxx's ugly chapters of ethnic xxxxx.

75%

But the xxxx of her childhood xxxx is only one of xxxx satisfactions for Mrs. Halo xxxx. Spry and outspoken, she has xxxx something of a xxxx for many Greeks. xxxx daughter Thea, after xxxx Mrs. Halo to Turkey xxxx 1989 to try to xxxx the village of her xxxx's birth, decided to xxxx chronicle her mother's xxxx.

The resulting book, 'xxxxx Even My Name,' xxxxx the story of xxxxx and ethnic conflict xxxxx the Turks and Pontic xxxxx, of personal xxxxx and the great xxxxx of mere survival. xxxxx of the rare xxxxx in English, it has xxxxx one of the xxxxx books in Astoria, xxxxx to about 40,000 Pontic Greeks.

60%

On this xxx, Thea Halo xxx from her xxx, her mother xxx, the audience's xxx full of xxx and meaning. The xxx to Turkey xxx her mother xxx convinced her xxx her mother's xxx could allow xxx to tell of 'xxx land, my people and my xxx'.

Mrs. Halo's xxx story, set xxx years of xxx with the xxx, mirrors the xxx recent religious xxx ethnic conflicts xxx have torn xxx, Rwanda and East xxx. Not only xxx the Greeks xxx from their xxx, but their xxx, language and xxx monuments were xxx, along with xxx of their xxx.

Van Geert (1994b) offers a mathematical developmental model in which the ZPD and the change from actual to potential knowledge are built in. The equations he presents predict that development is typically discontinuous, and depending on the setting of parameters in the model, the growth curves can take different forms.

The settings of the parameters represent different settings of learning, difference in actual level of potential level and so on. A typical pattern is one in which development sets off slowly and then accelerates to slow down close to the potential level. Many processes of change appear to follow the patterns predicted on the basis of simulations, though the patterns may be different for different developmental aspects and stages. Another pattern is one in which the learner remains at a level close to the actual level, only to jump to a level close to the potential level at a late stage. The assumption is that knowledge stabilises at an equilibrium level, which is the optimal level that can be reached given the actual knowledge and the guidance provided. In some cases, such an equilibrium is never reached and the learner flips between the two levels. An example could be the use of articles in English for students whose L1 has a completely different article system (such as Chinese, Japanese and Vietnamese). A learner may use the articles correctly and incorrectly without apparent systematicity. For example, she may write 'I sat on chair' (where the zero article would indicate a non-count noun) and 'I bought a chair' (where the indefinite article indicates a singular count noun) in the same text.

Van Geert (1998) also points to an aspect that has not been dealt with much so far in discussions of Vygotsky's work: The actual and potential level are not fixed, but they interact. With learning, i.e. the carrying out of specific actions, the actual level of knowledge changes and with it the level of potential knowledge moves too. This shows one aspect of the dynamism of the system: the input interacts with the system, which leads to adaptations that not only bear on the present level of knowledge but also what the system can achieve under specific conditions. Note that for a language-teaching situation this means that the instruction should always stay ahead of the learners' present, but constantly changing level. 'Given the potential dynamics of a ZPD-driven developmental process . . . it is likely that the major function of, for example, instruction or help is not to offer a learning environment at the ZPD, but rather a learning environment at or around the ZPD that can also expand the ZPD' (Van Geert, 1998: 638). This idea is of course very similar to Krashen's notion of i +1 (see Unit A3).

A distinction needs to be made between learning in general, and optimal learning. Linking Piaget and Vygotsky, optimal learning takes place when the maximal accommodation takes place, that is when the system changes maximally or when the distance between the actual level and the potential level is optimal. For different learners and different aspects to be learnt, the optimal distance between actual a nd potential level will vary, and accordingly the ZPD is not based on what needs to be taught, but on the characteristics of the system at a given point in time. In other words, the system creates its own ZPD and it is up to a teacher to find out for an individual learner how to make optimal use of that gap.

THE IMPLICIT/EXPLICIT DISTINCTION

In discussing Piaget's 'accommodation' and Vygotsky's ZPD, we have not dealt with how an adult or peer can help the learner solve a problem. This may be done implicitly by giving the learner some extra cues so he can discover the 'rules' for himself, or explicitly by giving the learner some 'rules'.

In L2 teaching situations explicit teaching used to be common and students were asked to memorise lists of words and learn grammar rules, but as we illustrated in Unit A3, Krashen and Terrell (1983) argued that knowledge that was acquired explicitly was of little use in language acquisition, which has led to the extensive debate whether explicit input can lead to implicit knowledge. Clearly, this point is crucial for the type of instruction that needs to be provided to learners and the discussion in this unit is therefore very relevant to that of our next unit, on the role of instruction in SLA.

Krashen's theories are based on a non-interface position, i.e. that what is learned explicitly and consciously can be used only in a controlled manner and will never become part of implicit knowledge, which is used automatically. While this position has been attacked in various ways, more recent neurolinguistic evidence suggests that this distinction and the non-interface position are actually well grounded. As Paradis (1994; 2004) shows, there is evidence that implicit and explicit memory each have their own circuits in the brain and that the processes of implicit and explicit acquisition are fundamentally different and unrelated. However, Paradis does argue that there is some link between explicit and implicit knowledge. The explicit, controlled type of use may gradually be replaced by the implicit, automatic use.

> Skilled use of a second language indeed often begins as controlled processes and gradually appears to become automatic. In reality, controlled processing is gradually replaced by the use of automatic processing, which is

not just the speeding up of the controlled process, but the use of a different system which, through practice, develops in parallel.

(Paradis, 2004: 35)

Related to this is the role of metalinguistic knowledge. Metalinguistic knowledge is acquired consciously, while implicit knowledge is acquired unconsciously. Both types of knowledge can be used as a monitoring system in language use, but, according to Paradis, they never merge.

So how are implicit and explicit knowledge and learning and acquisition related, and if there is no transfer from explicit learning to implicit knowledge, what is the use of instruction? According to Paradis, implicit learning, which usually takes place without instruction and the learner being aware of learning something, may also result as a by-product of explicit learning. Instruction leads to explicit knowledge that is then used to produce and understand language. The perception and production of the (more and more correct) utterances serves as input for the implicit learning mechanisms that extract information from the input. This implies that what is implicitly acquired may be quite different from what the instruction was about. Explicit knowledge does not become implicit, but it generates relevant input and output. Also, explicit metalinguistic knowledge serves as a monitor to control the output, and it plays a role in generating more correct utterances, which again serve as input for implicit learning.

While there is still discussion on the strict separation between implicit and explicit learning and the existence of an interface between the two, we think that the claim Paradis makes is well founded. For a discussion of the role of input in SLA, this is an important starting point. There are two systems that can have input. The implicit learning system incorporates new information according to its own rules that are not open to inspection and probably not open to manipulation either. The other input is needed for the explicit learning system that cumulates declarative knowledge for conscious processing. The set of implicit knowledge develops parallel to the explicit system but how the latter influences the former is unclear. In other words, what is taught is not necessarily implicitly learned. Conscious processing and the application of explicit knowledge demand a lot of resources, mainly because it is not automatised. The implicit system is more efficient in that respect, and that is probably the reason why we have two such parallel systems. With learning a skill, we gradually rely more and more on the implicit knowledge and the explicit knowledge set can then be left to fade. It is a common finding among language learners that they have acquired a set of rules and applied them explicitly and consciously for a while, with the implicit knowledge system gradually taking over. In the end the explicit knowledge and the rules so laboriously learned are no longer needed, and learners may behave as if they are still applying the explicit rule knowledge, while in fact they use the implicit knowledge in which access to such rule systems probably play no role at all.

CONCLUDING REMARKS

In this unit we have argued that learning is basically connecting new information to old information (assimilation) and that strengthening of these connections is needed for a learner to remember the new information (accommodation). Optimal learning takes place when there is enough old information to connect the new information to, and there is enough new information offered to be assimilated. This works for single pieces of information as well as for pattern recognition. New information can be assimilated implicitly or explicitly, but in different and parallel systems. These systems are separate, but the information may move from one system to the other because information practised in the explicit system producing output may provide input for the implicit system and information obtained in the implicit system may provide input to be analysed, which in turn may result in an explicit rule.

Unit A6
Learners' characteristics

In the previous units, we have looked at the ways an individual may process information, and for the sake of the argument we have discussed these issues as if all language learners were similar. However, there are enormous differences between learners. Second-language learners may have learned additional languages, may have started learning their second language at different ages, may be more or less motivated, may be more or less intelligent, and may have more or less aptitude. In this unit, we will discuss the most important of these individual differences between learners to arrive at a better understanding of variation in second-language learning. Although a multitude of factors is mentioned in the literature, we will concentrate on age, on some social-psychological factors like motivation and attitude, and on cognitive factors like aptitude. Although we will discuss these factors separately, it is important to realise that each of them affects the other in a dynamic process of second-language acquisition, and it is impossible to come to exact conclusions about the effect of any of the factors in isolation.

AGE

A position that is strongly associated with the age issue is the *critical period hypothesis* (Lenneberg, 1967). This hypothesis claims that it is not possible to acquire a native-like level of proficiency when learning the second language starts after a critical period, normally associated with puberty. This position is most strongly associated with acquiring the phonological system of a second language. Scovel (1988), for instance, argues that late starters may be able to learn the syntax and the vocabulary of a second language, but that attaining a native-like pronunciation is impossible for them. Three relevant questions have to be answered in this respect. Is there a critical period for language acquisition and, if so, what causes does it have, and when does it start and end?

Task A6.1

➤ Imagine there are three groups of immigrants to the US. Group 1 is between the ages of 6 and 17, group 2 is between the ages of 17 and 30 and group 3 is over 31. They all come from the same country, have the same L1 and none of them speaks any English at the time of arrival. After five years they are tested on their English.

➤ What predictions would you make? Which age groups would have learned English best and why?

➤ Do you believe it is possible for the oldest group to become fluent in English – and why (not)?

➤ In what aspects of language (fluency, grammar, pronunciation) would you expect the biggest differences between the groups and why?

Whether there is a critical period or not has been a much-debated issue. Proponents of the CPH have demonstrated in several empirical studies that it is difficult, if not impossible, to acquire a native command of a second language when learning started after childhood. Johnson and Newport (1989) found a clear effect of age of arrival in the United States on a grammaticality judgement task, which they administered to 46 native speakers of Chinese and Korean who had lived in the United States for at least five years. Especially for the subjects who arrived between age 6 and age 17, a very strong negative correlation (–0.87) was found between their score and their age: the higher the age, the lower their score. For the adults in their experiment, no age effects were found. One point of criticism (Kellerman, 1995) was that the study concentrated on languages that are very different (Chinese and English) and that the outcomes might be different when related languages are used. However, age effects were also found for French learners of English (Coppetiers, 1987) and for English and French learners of Italian (Sorace, 1993). These studies convincingly show that young starters do better than late starters. The question is, however, whether this difference between young learners and adults *must* be due to a critical period. Three arguments against this idea are mentioned in the literature. First, the difference might simply be caused by the fact that young learners have more time and more exposure to attain L2 proficiency. Second, it is very difficult if not impossible to determine the boundaries of a critical period. This is illustrated by a study indicating data on 2.3 million US immigrants Hakuta *et al.* (2003: 31) conclude that early starters show higher second-language attainment, but that 'the pattern of decline in second-language acquisition failed to produce the discontinuity that is an essential hallmark of a critical period'. Third, in spite of the difficulty for most adults to achieve a native-like command of L2, some learners (Selinker's famous 5%)[1] do manage. This means that it is not impossible for late starters to reach full proficiency, which considerably weakens the position of the CPH: if some individual learners can do it, it will of course be very interesting to try and find out in what way these learners are different. The effect of what seems

---

1 Selinker (1972) argues that no more 5% of all adult L2 learners will reach native-like competence. Although this is the most widely quoted number, it is not based on empirical data and should be considered as a rough estimate.

to be a critical period will then be a matter of *individual differences* other than age. Several studies have therefore concentrated on learners who are late starters and who have nevertheless attained a native-like command of their L2. In a specific grammaticality judgement task, White and Genesee (1996) found that the 44 near-native late starters in their experiment could not be distinguished from the native speakers. A similar effect was reported by Birdsong (1992) in a test containing a wide range of morphosyntactic elements. Also in the domain of the acquisition of phonology a number of investigations have been carried out with learners who appear to be very good at L2 pronunciation. In a series of experiments, Bongaerts and his colleagues (Bongaerts *et al.*, 1997; Bongaerts, 1999; Bongaerts *et al.*, 2000) demonstrated that the pronunciation of the late starters in their experiments could *not* be distinguished from that of the native speakers in their test. One of these papers, Bongaerts (1999) has been included in Section B.

Concluding, we can say that the evidence for the CPH is mixed. There is ample evidence for the general observation that most learners who start late at acquiring their L2 never reach native-like proficiency. Whether this is due to a critical period or not is an unanswered question. On the other hand, we have seen that (a limited number of) very good learners do reach that level. This brings us to the question of what causes a critical period may have.

An influential explanation on the CPH has been the one initiated by Lenneberg (1967). Lenneberg's account was based on neurological development. He claimed that as the brain gradually matures, it loses its plasticity. The maturation process, called *cerebral lateralisation*, is a process of specialisation of the hemispheres. Once this process is completed, Lenneberg argued, the brain would no longer be able to take up a new language system. The completion of lateralisation was assumed to coincide with the start of puberty. However, later studies (such as Krashen, 1973) have argued that lateralisation is completed much earlier than that (around age 5). Moreover, it is unclear how this explanation can account for the fact that some learners do reach native competence. Apart from the neurological explanation, quite a number of other accounts of the critical period have been suggested in the literature, ranging from cognitive explanations (Johnson and Newport, 1989) to social-psychological explanations (Schumann, 1975). We will elaborate on two accounts that are most pertinent to current discussions in the field: a general linguistic explanation that claims to account for the critical period in the domain of grammar, and an explanation that is specific to the domain of phonology.

The first explanation, proposed by Bley-Vroman (1988) among others, asserts that L1 learning is based on innate mechanisms, which are no longer available to L2 learners (see Unit A5). In this view, second-language learning is seen as a process that is fundamentally different from first-language acquisition because children still have access to innate processes (UG), but that adult L2 learners will have to resort to a more explicit type of learning, which can never lead to the same kind of attainment as natural, implicit learning. A counter-argument for this position is that most L2 learning will also involve implicit learning. Also the claim that L1 learning is predominantly based on innate mechanisms is regularly challenged. To date, the question whether L1 and L2 acquisition are fundamentally different learning processes cannot be answered satisfactorily.

In the domain of phonology a similar assumption has been advanced. Flege (Flege *et al.*, 1999) attributes the general inadequacy of late starters' L2 pronunciation to their perceptual capabilities. When children learn the sounds of their first language, they perceive the sounds in what Wode (1994) labels the 'continuous mode': all sounds are perceived and qualified equally. However, once children have established a linguistic sound system, they start categorising the speech sounds they hear in terms of the sounds they already know ('categorical perception'). From that moment (around age 7), all L2 sounds that are similar to L1 sounds will be categorised as L1 sounds, so no new categories are created for 'similar' sounds. Only for sounds that cannot be classified in terms of L1 sounds, a new phonological category will be created. This would account for the observation that L2 sounds that are phonetically similar to L1 sounds are the most difficult ones to attain.

 Task A6.2

> In the perceptual account for the difficulty of learning L2 sounds, there is a crucial distinction between L2 sounds that are exactly the same as L1 sounds, L2 sounds that are similar to L1 sounds, and L2 sounds that are completely new to the learner. Comparing your own language to English, think of four sounds in each of these categories. Would you expect that the 'similar' sounds are indeed the most difficult ones to acquire, more difficult than the 'new' sounds?

However, if the fixation of perceptual categories were indeed the reason for the existence of a critical period, again the question can be raised how it is possible that some 'exceptionally good' learners are able to overcome this. Can the mode of perception be affected by other individual factors? It is conceivable that the perception of subtle L2 differences can be trained and thus be overcome. The fact is that all the 'good' L2 performers in the experiments carried out by Bongaerts received explicit pronunciation training, during which learners were made aware of the differences between L1 and L2 'similar' sounds. Other studies, especially focussed on the usefulness of explicit pronunciation instruction (Champagne-Muzar, 1996; Derwing, 1998) also point in that direction. Particularly when the instruction is focussed on individual needs and when global characteristics are emphasised (as opposed to concentration on individual phonemes), pronunciation instruction tends to be beneficial. Another observation made by Bongaerts *et al.* (2000) about their learners is that they were all very highly motivated. We will elaborate on the latter observation in the discussion on attitude and motivation below.

There is one more point in relation to the critical period that we need to address. The observation that younger starters have a greater chance of attaining full proficiency in their second language does not say anything about the speed with which they learn that language. In fact, several studies have shown that older learners learn a second language faster than younger learners do, given the same amount of time, which may be due to their more fully developed cognitive skills. This advantage for older learners has been taken as counter-evidence to the CPH. However, the rate of acquisition is not the same as the eventual level of attainment, and it may be assumed (as is done by the advocates of the critical period) that in the end the older starters are caught up by the younger starters. As these studies do not provide data about the eventual level of proficiency, it remains an empirical question whether or not the younger learners turn out to be better in the end.

The conclusions we can draw from our discussion about the critical period so far is that younger learners have a greater chance of attaining native-like proficiency in the L2, older learners may show faster progress at the beginning, but are probably surpassed by the young ones in the end. These observations have been made in all domains, but the phonology of a second language is beyond doubt the most difficult area to master for late starters. It has proven to be very difficult to point to the exact age at which the critical period ends and to explain what causes a possible critical period for language acquisition, so overall, the evidence for the existence of a critical period is not convincing.

APTITUDE AND INTELLIGENCE

Regardless of all other factors like age and motivation, some people happen to be better at learning a second language than others. In the literature about second-language learning, a person's inherent capability of second-language learning is labelled *language learning aptitude*. Aptitude can be seen as a characteristic that is similar to intelligence, which cannot be altered through training. As different skills are involved in language learning, aptitude needs to include several factors. In the literature, starting from Carroll (1958), aptitude is usually described as a combination of four factors:

- the ability to identify and remember sounds of the foreign language;
- the ability to recognise how words function grammatically in sentences;
- the ability to induce grammatical rules from language examples; and
- the ability to recognise and remember words and phrases.

Task A6.3

➤ Consider your own experience in second language acquisition. For each of the components of aptitude, can you say how good you think you are yourself on a 5-point scale? Would this be the same for all languages that you have learned?

➤ You have now assessed aptitude by using self-reflection. Would this be a good way of determining aptitude? And how else could this be tested?

➤ Do you think intelligence should be included in aptitude or should this be regarded as something totally different?

A number of tests have been developed to assess language aptitude. The most frequently quoted tests are the Modern Language Aptitude Test (MLAT) by Carroll and Sapon (1959) and The Pimsleur Language Aptitude Battery (PLAB), developed by Pimsleur (1966). These tests contain a wide range of tasks. For example, phonemic coding ability is tested by sound–symbol association tests in which the learner has to make a link between a sound and a symbol. Grammatical sensitivity was tested by recognising the function that a word fulfils in a sentence. The tests largely overlap, but Pimsleur includes intelligence as one aspect of aptitude, whereas Carroll claims that intelligence must be seen as distinct from aptitude. Both tests have shown high correlations with proficiency scores in schools. However, the tests are completely geared towards formal second-language learning and particularly towards the way in which languages were taught in the classroom of the 1960s. When teaching practice changed to include practice in actual communication, aptitude testing went out of fashion. Several studies have shown that MLAT and PLAB show high correlations with intelligence and controlled language production, but low correlations with free oral production and general communication skills. As the latter do play an important role in second-language acquisition as well, the conventional aptitude tests do not tell the whole story of a person's second-language learning ability. Consequently, as from the late seventies hardly any studies have been carried out on aptitude.

Not until the early 1990s did research on language aptitude come into vogue again. Recent approaches take into account that aptitude has shown to be a good predictor of achievement in classroom second-language learning, but also emphasise its information-processing side and consider the different components separately rather than as a fixed combination of factors. The article by Gardner *et al.* (1997) in Unit B6 shows how many of these factors may interact.

An aspect that is now generally considered as one of the components of aptitude is Working Memory (WM). WM must be seen as an active system in which information is stored and manipulated and which is required for complex tasks like language comprehension. Both the control centre that is at the heart of WM, the 'Central Executive' and the specific phonological component have been tested in a rapidly increasing number of studies. Both components generally show moderately strong correlations (around 0.50) with language proficiency scores like TOEFL. However, the studies investigating this are usually taken under strongly controlled laboratory conditions and it is unclear to what extent these findings can be generalised to real-life situations.

The question whether aptitude should include intelligence cannot be answered straightforwardly. After all, this depends on the definition of intelligence.

Conventional intelligence tests have recently been under attack. Sternberg (2002), for instance, claims that intelligence as measured by conventional American IQ tests does not account for more than half of people's intelligence. He proposes an alternative in which he distinguishes between analytical, creative and practical intelligence and argues that also language-learning aptitude needs to be redefined to include creative and practical language-acquisition abilities besides memory and analytical skills.

Task A6.4

➤ Gardner (1983; 1999) redefines intelligence in terms of 'multiple intelligences' of which seven are listed below:

- linguistic

- logical-mathematical

- spatial

- musical

- bodily-kinaesthetic

- interpersonal

- intrapersonal

Language use also consists of various components:

- articulation of sounds and intonation;

- use of gestures in speaking;

- construction of complex sentences;

- analysing the content of interactants' speech;

- monitoring one's own speech;

- assessing the specifics of a given speech situation.

➤ Which of Gardner's components of intelligence could be related to (which) aspects of language use?

Whatever the future of research into language aptitude may be, recent work has shown that the discussion on aptitude is very much alive after a relatively silent period of about thirty years! The focus of future developments will probably be on attempts to redefine aptitude in such a way that it includes communicative skills. Among other things, measures of working memory and processing may have to be incorporated. (See Unit C6, task C6.1, for a small-scale project involving working memory.)

ATTITUDE AND MOTIVATION

Teachers, learners and researchers will all agree that a high motivation and a positive attitude towards a second language and its community help second-language learning. However, when it comes to systematically investigating the effect of motivation on language learning, it appears that it is a rather difficult concept to operationalise. Everyone will agree that motivation is related to someone's 'drive' to achieve something, but what is the exact nature of motivation and how can we measure it? A very influential definition is given by Gardner and Lambert (1972), who distinguish *integrative motivation* and *instrumental motivation*.

Integrative motivation is based on an interest in the second language and its culture and refers to the intention to become part of that culture. Most research that has been done in this area investigates integrative motivation. Commonly, this is done by self-reporting in which learners answer a set of questions about their attitudes towards the second-language community, their interest in foreign languages and their desire to learn the second language. In a similar way to aptitude, several batteries were developed to measure motivation and attitude. The most influential test battery is the Attitude and Motivation Test Battery (AMTB) by Gardner (1985). It includes 130 items, measuring all kinds of factors that affect motivation and attitude, like language anxiety, parental encouragement and, of course, all the factors underlying Gardner's definition of motivation. As its name implies, in the AMTB the learner's attitude is incorporated into motivation, in the sense that a positive attitude is argued to increase motivation. The idea that attitude does not always reinforce motivation is exemplified by what has been called 'Machiavellian motivation' (Oller and Perkins, 1978): learners may strongly dislike the second-language community and want to learn the second language to manipulate and prevail over people in that community. In most cases, however, a positive attitude will strengthen motivation, whereas a negative attitude will negatively affect motivation.

Instrumental motivation is based on a more practical need to communicate in the second language. In its purest form, this type of motivation is sometimes referred to as the 'Carrot and Stick' type: the learner wants to learn the second language to gain something 'now' from it. To test if this type of motivation affects success in second-language learning, Gardner and Macintyre (1991) awarded $10 to students who succeeded in a vocabulary learning task. They found that learners did better when they were awarded, but that the extra effort ceased when the reward was taken away, indicating that 'eternal influences and incentives will affect the strength of the learner's motivation', as R. Ellis (1994: 509) points out.

Task A6.5

➤ The AMTB was first developed for English-speaking Canadians learning French. As you probably know, English has been the dominant language in Canada. To measure integrative and instrumental motivation, the AMTB includes the following categories:

A   attitudes toward French Canadians
B   interest in foreign languages
C   attitudes toward towards learning French.

Try to relate each of the following statements to one of the three categories of motivation in the AMTB.

1   French Canadians add a distinctive flavour to Canadian culture.
2   French Canadians are cheerful, agreeable and good-humoured.
3   Studying French can be important for me because it will allow me to meet and converse with more easily with fellow Canadians who speak French.
4   Studying French can be important for me only because I'll need it for my future career.
5   English Canadians should make a greater effort to learn the French language.
6   The more I learn about the Canadian French, the more I like them.
7   I think that learning French is dull.
8   French is an important part of the school programme.
9   It embarrasses me to volunteer answers in our French class.
10 I plan to learn as much French as possible.
11 My parents think I should devote more time to my French studies.
12 I always feel that the other students speak French better than I do.
13 I would like to know more French Canadians.
14 Studying French can be important for me because I will be able to participate more freely in the activities of other cultural groups.
15 Even though Canada is relatively far from countries speaking other languages, it is important for Canadians to learn foreign languages.

Although researchers claim to investigate different types of motivation, it is difficult if not impossible to strictly separate the types. Apart from very specific studies, like the one by Gardner and MacIntyre (1991) mentioned in the previous paragraph, it is hard to make separate claims about these types. Gardner's original definition was based on naturalistic language learning in Canada and cannot be simply generalised to other learning situations. For instance, a learner who learns a second language in a classroom situation may have an integrative motivation to learn the language, but at the same time an instrumental motivation to get high grades. Moreover, apart from these external types of motivation, a learner may also be intrinsically motivated. But whatever the exact nature of motivation may be, significant correlations (around 0.40) have been found between self-reported motivation (usually focussed on the integrative type) and success in L2 learning, which could suggest that motivation is one of the predictors of success in L2 learning.

A relevant question, however, is whether success should be seen as the result or as the cause of motivation. In Gardner and Lambert's definition, success is an integral part of motivation, but others argue that success arouses motivation: learners may like what they are good at. After all, a correlation does not say anything about cause and effect. Probably, motivation and success affect each other interactively, which points to a possible interaction between motivation and aptitude.

 Task A6.6

➤ In several countries in Western Europe the government wants older immigrants to integrate into society, for which they have to learn the national or local language. We know from research that with age both working memory capacity and perception generally decline. What specific problems are older learners likely to run into when they start learning the new language? Do you have friends or relatives who started learning a new language at an older age? What problems did they have?

In the literature on motivation, two methodological pitfalls of motivation research are regularly mentioned. The first is that, since motivation research is based on self-report, it cannot be determined what the learner's actual effort is. The actual effort is closely related to the second point: short-term motivation. The questionnaires usually enquire about the learner's goals, desires and attitudes in the long term, while the actual effort requires short-term motivation. The analogy with smoking may illustrate this: smokers may express the long-term desire to quit smoking, but will keep on lighting their cigarettes today. A learner may have a strong desire to learn a language, but does not feel like learning vocabulary items. As most motivation studies are based on self-report, no conclusions can be drawn about the actual (short-term) effort.

Recent developments in motivation are outlined by Dörnyei (2001), who mentions several new areas of motivation: social motivation, motivation from a process-oriented perspective, a neurobiological explanation of motivation and task motivation. From this, it becomes clear that there is a need to move away from the limited traditional division into instrumental and integrative motivation. The new conceptualisation of motivation from a dynamic point of view seems particularly promising, as in the course of the acquisition process, the level of motivation will constantly change due to a wide range of interrelated factors. Also the research methodology has lately seen major improvements. Besides improved methods of analysis used in quantitative studies, more qualitative approaches involving thinking out loud protocols may help unravel the true nature of motivation.

Task A6.7

➤ How does the definition of motivation below differ from the more traditional definitions of motivation?

> In a general sense, motivation can be defined as the dynamically changing cumulative arousal in a person that initiates, directs, co-ordinates, amplifies, terminates and evaluates the cognitive and motor processes whereby initial wishes and desires are selected, prioritised, operationalised, and (successfully or unsuccessfully) acted out.
>
> (Dörnyei and Ottó, 1998: 65)

CONCLUDING REMARKS

In this Unit, we have discussed three individual factors that are important in second-language acquisition: age, aptitude and motivation. With regard to age we can conclude that there is a general difference between early starters and late starters of second-language acquisition. It is unclear whether this points to the existence of a critical period for language acquisition. Also, the uncertainty about the causes of a critical period does not help the CPH. Only for the acquisition of phonology may a change in people's capacity to determine different sounds point to the existence of a critical period for speech perception. For aptitude research we have seen a clear development. After a period in which aptitude research was extremely popular, the interest declined. Aptitude, together with motivation, is probably the best predictor of success in a foreign language, and we have seen a clear upsurge in the interest in aptitude with new perspectives and new methods of investigation. Traditionally, the biggest challenge for motivation research has been to accurately define and investigate the concepts related to motivation. Here too, we have recently seen new insights, leading to new, dynamic definitions and new methods of investigation.

Besides the individual differences we have discussed here, there are many others that would merit further elaboration. Differences in learning style, the use of learning strategies, gender, personality factors and language anxiety may all affect the rate and attainment of second language acquisition. Some of these factors will be discussed in the articles included in unit B6; for others the reader is referred to the growing pile of specialist literature on this issue. What is most important to remember is that in a dynamic view of language acquisition, all individual factors strongly interact and that these interactions are constantly changing while the process of L2 acquisition proceeds.

Unit A7
The role of instruction

Throughout this book we have taken the view that SLA is a dynamic process, which means that it is impossible to extract and measure single factors that contribute to SLA because they all interact. For example, we showed in the previous unit on individual differences that many individual factors such as L1, age, aptitude, learning style, intelligence, personality, and so on may interact with the SLA process. Theories compatible with DST are 'emergentism' and 'connectionism' (see Unit A3), which assume that language can be acquired through input without a dedicated language learning device; the 'spreading activation model', which is also based on relative frequency of input and considers L1 and L2 as part of the same system; and views from neuro-linguistics. For example, we quoted Paradis (2004) in Unit A5, who said that explicit knowledge is qualitatively different from implicit knowledge, but what may happen is that an explicit system may gradually be replaced by an implicit system. This view, in turn, is compatible with the Vygotskyan view of the dialectic unity of learning and development, in which learning lays down the pathway for further development and in turn prepares the ground for further learning. Another interesting notion we incidentally dealt with in the reading span task (Unit A6) is 'selective attention' (Daneman and Carpenter, 1980). It is difficult to pay attention to more than only one level or one strand of events at a time (for example, to read sentences and at the same time remember the last words of each sentence read). Finally, the need for conscious attention to any input in order to notice it and learn from it has been made obvious by Schmidt (1990) (as pointed out in Unit A1).

What we can gather from almost all studies and theories (also those not compatible with DST) is that the amount of meaningful input is of crucial importance in the acquisition process. When taken together, these theories would predict that an L2 can be acquired in a natural setting, but because a learner in a naturalistic setting will most probably attend more to meaning and real communication rather than form (cf. Spada and Lightbown, 1989), it may not be difficult for the learner to acquire a high degree of fluency, but a high degree of accuracy in the L2 may be possible only if the learner also focuses her attention on forms.

If we take DST as our theoretical framework, we must accept that we will never be able to filter out the exact effect of explicit instruction, but we do know it has some effect. As Larsen-Freeman points out: 'Much learning may take place receptively only to be manifest productively when the requisite data have been taken in. Terrell

(1991), R. Ellis (1993), and VanPatten and Cadierno (1993) have all pointed out that explicit grammar instruction will not likely result in immediate mastery of specific grammatical items, but suggest nevertheless that explicit instruction does have value, namely, in facilitating intake' (Larsen-Freeman 1997: 155).

To show the issues involved in the debate on the goals of teaching and the role of explicit instruction in SLA, we will first present a brief overview of the way language teaching has developed over the last 50 years or so and then focus on the role that explicit instruction in SLA may have. We will show that explicit instruction indeed has a positive effect on SLA, even though – as we can presume from a DST perspective – we cannot explain exactly the cause of the effect.

DEVELOPMENTS IN TEACHING APPROACHES

Until the sixties, it was common practice to teach a foreign language by teaching the grammar in detail, providing students with bilingual word lists to memorise, and translating texts from L1 into L2 and vice versa. In other words, it was commonly assumed that formal, explicit instruction was the key to learning an L2. Of course, students did learn to read and understand the L2, but very often they did not learn to use the language actively in conversation with native speakers.

Task A7.1

➤ In several units, but especially in the Unit A3, we have discussed two major linguistic theories, structuralism (related to behaviourism) and Chomskyan Universal Grammar (related to mentalism). Try to recall their major claims and try to imagine with what kind of teaching approach they would be compatible.

➤ How do activities like memorising word lists, group discussions in the target language, translation from L2 into L1 and the learning of grammatical rules fit in these two theoretical perspectives?

During the Second World War, there was a great need for people who could actively speak a foreign language and the Army Specialised Training Program or 'Army Method' was developed in the US. It relied very heavily on intense exposure to the language. Amazingly, students learned to speak and understand the language in a relatively short time. This method had developed from practical needs. Of course, it was impossible to teach large L2 classes as intensively as the Army Method had taught small, highly motivated groups. To be able to teach bigger groups in a more systematic manner, the audio-lingual method was developed. It was based on the practical Army Method and two influential theories: structuralism in linguistics and behaviourism in psychology. Structural linguistics provided tools for analysing language into chunks and behavioural theory provided a model for teaching any behaviour by conditioning. One method that was based on behaviourist principles was the audio-lingual method (Lado, 1964). It was mainly oral, and consisted of drilling the L2 patterns as in the following example. No free use of language was allowed because it was believed that it would cause errors, which would interfere with the formation of correct habits in the foreign language.

Stimulus	Response
Peter went to school today. John	*John went to school today.*
Reinforcement and new element:	
John went to school today. Church	*John went to church today.*
John went to church today. Tomorrow.	*John will go to church tomorrow.*

Even though the audio-lingual method was similar to the 'Army Method' in that it provided input, it was quite different in the fact that the language structures were controlled by the teacher (or an audio tape) and because it was more concerned with providing the right structures and implicitly teaching grammar than with providing meaningful input, natural language in a natural setting. Students and teachers found the method rather restrictive and boring, and the results of the approach were not as good as had been expected. About the same time, changes in linguistic theory in the 1960s seriously challenged the premises on which the audio-lingual method was based. Chomsky (1966) argued that behaviour theory could not account for the fact that people do not use only those structures they have heard before but that they could create and generate new sentences and patterns all the time. These new insights and the dissatisfaction with the audio-lingual method in general set the stage for a complete shift in approaches to the teaching of second and foreign languages.

This shift was mainly caused by a move away from a focus on the language to a focus on the learner. There was a growing interest in sociolinguistic aspects of language as means of communication rather than as a system. This change of focus led to what became known as Communicative Language Teaching. According to Johnson (1996) the main characteristics of CLT are as follows:

1 It places much importance on the role of message focus in language practice.
2 It attempts to simulate processes of language use by employing techniques like 'Information gap' and 'Information transfer'.
3 It is part of learning, as opposed to an acquisition model. It does not avoid one of the characteristics which (. . .) Krashen associates with learning: rule isolation.

(Johnson, 1996: 173)

CLT starts with the message to be conveyed or the language function (request, complaint) to be carried out, and provides the learner with the structures needed to do that. So the focus shifted from the language as a system of rules to language functions and the structures needed to fulfil them. But the focus was still on the language rather than on the learner. This view of CLT is different, however, from the perspective on CLT taken by Breen and Candlin (1980), who argue that language learning is situated and socially constituted rather than consisting of the acquisition of a set of items to be applied in interaction.

Task A7.2

➤ Imagine a class of about 30 L1 speakers of English, approximately 7 years old, who are taught all normal subjects completely in French. The children receive input from the teacher and textbooks, but they are not taught French as a subject. How do you think their French will develop in fluency, in accuracy or in both?

A major impetus for CLT in the instructed language teaching sector in schools and colleges has come from a development that started in Canada. In the second half of the last century, immersion programmes became immensely popular. In immersion, part of the curriculum in schools is taught in the second language, in the Canadian case, mostly French. There is very little teaching of grammar or rules, and learning is supposed to result from exposure and use. It is to a large extent based on the general assumption that learning a second language should be like learning the first language as much as possible. Since infants do not generally receive grammar lessons, why should second-language learners need them? The immersion programmes were on the whole very successful: meta-analyses (Swain and Lapkin, 1982) show that learners in immersion programmes and schools with bilingual streams outperform learners in traditional classes in the second language, while their results in other school subjects do not seem to suffer from being taught in another language.

Out of the immersion experiences a new approach to language teaching emerged, content-based instruction (CBI), or what in the European context is now called Content and Language Integrated Learning (CLIL). In this approach the language to be learned is used to teach other subjects. Lessons are delivered in the second language and all reading and tasks have to be carried out in that language. CLIL has become one of the cornerstones of language-teaching policy in Europe (Marsh et al., 2001). It is obvious that CBI or CLIL satisfies the need to have meaningful interaction in the classroom: the focus is on the message rather than the language and learners have to listen and interact in order to learn the topic.

Also in non-immersion programmes, the role of meaningful communication in SLA has become recognised. According to Krashen (1982), who can be considered one of the main driving forces of a CLT, people acquire a second language much in the same way as they acquire a first language, not by talking *about* the language, but by talking *in* the language (see Unit A3). In other words, to acquire a language one needs a great deal of meaningful input. He also argued that explicit rules that were 'learned' did not lead to 'acquisition'. The implication is that languages were best acquired without any formal study of structure and form. However, this did not mean that no attention was paid to the role of grammar. To make the input 'comprehensible', teachers needed to be aware of a 'natural order' in the acquisition of grammatical structures, and the structures offered needed to be ordered in such a way that they were only slightly beyond the current level of the student.

In all communicatively oriented approaches in SLA today it is assumed that we cannot learn a language by just studying words and grammar rules, but we have to actually 'use' the language in a meaningful context; however, Vygotsky would argue that the meaningful context is not enough at early stages of development. One needs as well to be placed in a context where there is socially meaningful interaction for learners to progress. In SLA theories, Vygotskyan ideas find their place in what has been termed Sociocultural Theory (SCT). SCT can best be explained by first looking at some of the Vygotskyan concepts in more detail and then exploring how they apply to SCT. As pointed out in Unit A5, one of the key concepts in Vygotskyan thinking for SLA purposes is the notion of the zone of proximal development (ZPD). Here the crucial idea is that learning is of a social nature and that children grow intellectually only when they are in the action of interacting with people in their environment, and that it is only this interaction that allows a variety of internal developmental processes to operate. This interaction depends for a great deal on language.

When a child is still an infant, before she learns to speak, her intelligence is a purely natural, useful capacity. As a child begins to develop, so does her language. As a child begins to speak, her thought processes also begin to develop. In this final stage, the child, but also older children and adults, can think in language, called inner, soundless speech, which allows us to direct our thinking and behaviour. Once a person has reached this final stage, she can engage in all forms of higher mental functions such as reasoning about time and considering objects that are not present in the here and now. Therefore, in essence, it is language or signs which direct behaviour (Lefrancois, 1994).

As far as SLA is concerned, one of the basic principles underpinning SCT is that 'the human mind is always and everywhere mediated primarily by linguistically based communication' (Lantolf, 2002). In an earlier publication, he defined mediation as follows.

> Mediation, whether physical or symbolic, is understood to be the intro-
> duction of an auxiliary device into an activity that then links humans
> to the world of objects or to the world of mental behaviour. Just as physical
> tools (e.g. hammers, bulldozer, computers etc.) allow humans to organize
> and alter their physical world, Vygotsky reasoned that symbolic tools
> empower humans to organize and control such mental processes as volun-
> tary attention, logical problem-solving, planning and evaluation, voluntary

memory, and voluntary learning. . . . Symbolic tools are the means through which humans are able to organize and maintain control over the self and its mental, and even physical, activity.

(Lantolf, 1994: 418)

Language as a tool allows the learner to self-regulate the process of learning, and with increasing skill the learner will be more and more autonomous and less dependent on 'other-regulation'. Self-regulation takes the form of actions, e.g. by interacting with peers and by finding information that is needed to carry out a task. A special form of self-regulation is the use of self-directed speech. This serves to organise thinking and planning of action.

Task A7.3

➤ In your language learning experience, do you ever think in the L2 and if so, in what type of situations? Do you ever talk in the L2 with a fellow L2 learner? Do you feel it helps you in mastering the L2? Why (not)?

Observational studies have shown that young children in particular but also adult L2 learners talk to themselves when solving difficult tasks. According to SCT this self-directed speech develops into inner speech. SCT learning is by definition a dialogical activity, either with the self, as in private speech, or with peers, or with experts. Most of the research on SCT has been done on the role of peer interaction in SLA.

> Dialogue among learners can be as effective as instructional conversations between teachers and learners. Working collaboratively, people are able to co-construct distributed expertise as a feature of the group, and individual members are then able to exploit this expertise as an occasion for learning to happen. (. . .) Learners are capable of scaffolding each other through the use of strategies that parallel those relied upon by experts'.

(Lantolf, 2002: 106)

'Scaffolding' is another central Vygotskyan concept related to the ZPD in SCT. Scaffolding is understood as providing learners with relevant and increasingly more precise information in the environment at the right time to help to solve a particular problem. The information given allows for a stepwise solution of the problem through interaction. For SLA purposes, Lantolf describes the ZPD as 'the site where future development is negotiated by the expert and the novice and where assistance is offered, appropriated, refused and withheld' (Lantolf, 2002: 105) and Mitchell and Myles as 'the domain of knowledge and skill where the learner is not yet capable of independent functioning, but can achieve the desired outcome given relevant scaffolded help' (1998: 146).

The contrast between communicative language teaching and sociocultural theory can be made clear with two different metaphors concerning the role of the learner in the SLA process: the 'acquisition metaphor' and the 'participation metaphor'. In the acquisition metaphor (AM) the learner is seen as a 'container' who absorbs new information, and in the participation metaphor (PM) the learner is seen as a person who becomes part of an L2 community. Pavlenko and Lantolf (2000) define the two as follows:

> (We view) second language learning not as the acquisition of a new set of grammatical, lexical, and phonological forms but as a struggle of concrete socially constituted and always situated beings to participate in the symbolically mediated lifeworld (see Habermas, 1987) of another culture. These individuals have intentions, agency, affect, and above all histories, and are frequently, though not always, known as people. (. . .) Sfard (1998), in fact, observes that a new metaphor, *participation* (PM), has emerged in the education literature not as a replacement for, but as a complement to, the traditional learning as *acquisition* metaphor (AM), often associated with computer and the container metaphors. Leaving aside the informative details of her analysis of the two metaphors, we wish to highlight those aspects of her discussion that are relevant to our current project. AM, according to Sfard (1998: 5), compels us to think of knowledge as a commodity that is accumulated by the learner and to construe the mind as the repository where the learner hoards the commodity. In SLA such an approach allows us to see language as a set of rules and facts to be acquired and permits us to discuss learner language in all its complexity. PM, on the other hand, obliges us to think of learning 'as a process of becoming a member of a certain community' (Sfard, 1998: 6) which entails 'the ability to communicate in the language of this community and act according to its particular norms' (ibid.).
>
> Applying such an approach to SLA involves shifting the focus of investigation from language structure to language use in context, and to the issues of affiliation and belonging. Moreover, while AM is about states and the permanence implied by related terms such as 'having', and 'knowledge', PM is characterized by terms such as 'doing', 'knowing', and 'becoming part of a greater whole' (ibid.). AM implies somewhat discrete learning stages with a well-defined end point; PM 'leaves no room for halting signals' (ibid.). As Hanks (1996: 222) puts it, viewing language learning as participation, 'does not involve acquiring rules or codes, but ways of acting and different kinds of participation.' Thus, we can summarize by saying that AM focuses on the individual mind and the internalization of knowledge, which is crucial for the study of the *what* in SLA, while PM stresses contextualization and engagement with others in its attempt to investigate the *how*.
>
> (Pavlenko and Lantolf, 2000: 155–156)

The acquisition versus the participation metaphor can be related to two other well-known issues in SLA: *focus on the learner* vs. *focus on the language*. The participation metaphor focuses on the learner as the activist in the learning process, while the acquisition metaphor focuses on the acquisition of the language as a system rather than an instrument of use, and on the role of instruction. The two metaphors may also be helpful to guide our thinking about the role of instruction. It is obvious that the social setting will define to a great extent how far the educational practices that follow from the two perspectives can actually be implemented.

Task A7.4

➤ In what type of setting did your own L2 learning take place: in the country where the L2 is spoken, in a country where the L2 is available to a great degree, or in a country where the L2 is available only in the classroom? Which of the two metaphors of acquisition and participation applied to you most in your particular situation?

Even if we wanted to go by the participation metaphor, few language learners will have the opportunity to be engaged in the social interactions needed to learn through contextualization and engagement because much instructed language learning takes place in classrooms. Foreign language learning especially (where the L2 is spoken only in the classroom) does not provide much opportunity for such interactions. Of course, many teachers are aware of the need to have meaningful interaction in the classroom, but the artificiality of most classroom activities aiming at 'real' interaction is often painfully clear. Only through 'real' experiences such as international exchanges will students come into contact with native speakers in their community and only there will the kind of approach that follows from the participation metaphor be feasible.

The discussion on the different metaphors and their application needs to be related to the role of individual differences discussed in Unit A6, and in particular the role of level of proficiency, age and personality. While (very) young learners will probably learn best through comprehensible input and interaction (which for them is not yet artificial), older learners may be better served with a combination of input and rule learning. Likewise, the discussion on ultimate attainment has to be related to what participation means and whether the learner really wants to participate in the target language community.

THE ROLE OF FORM-FOCUSSED INSTRUCTION

In spite of its great successes, there has also been a degree of dissatisfaction with a communicative approach in its purest form. From general practice and research it has become clear that communicative practice alone is not sufficient to help learners become either completely proficient or accurate in the second language (cf. Lightbown, 2000). A considerable amount of research in SLA that has examined whether explicit focus on form has any effect on L2 acquisition has provided strong support for some focus on form in the Communicative Language Teaching classroom. For example, Norris and Ortega (2000) have conducted a meta-analysis of studies that looked at the effects of grammar instruction and they conclude that the research confirms that instruction that includes focus on form does make a positive difference for classroom SLA.

 Task A7.5

➤ If some sort of instruction is needed to achieve accuracy in the L2, which do you intuitively think is the most effective, and why?

1 a Providing students with examples and letting students discover 'rules' for themselves.
  b Providing students with examples and explaining the 'rule'.

2 a Grammar instruction according to a pre-determined syllabus.
  b Grammar instruction only when a learner produces an incorrect target form.

The question therefore no longer is whether some explicit teaching is helpful, but what type of explicit teaching is the most effective. Norris and Ortega distinguished between explicit (the textbook or teacher explaining the 'rule') and implicit instruction (the learner discovering the 'rule') and between Focus on Forms (treatment of the target L2 forms one by one in a sequence according to linguistic complexity) and Focus on Form instruction (brief, reactive interventions within the context of communication by drawing a learner's attention to a linguistic feature that appears to cause trouble on that occasion) (Long, 1991).

Norris and Ortega concluded that instruction definitely has a positive effect. Moreover, they found that instructional treatments involving an explicit focus on the rule-governed nature of L2 structures are more effective than treatments that do not include such a focus. The effects are also durable. In other words, what the students have learned explicitly is remembered over time. However, one problem is that the result may be partly due to the type of controlled tests that are used to measure the effect. Finally, even though they feel further research is needed, they tentatively suggest that an explicit focus is more effective for both a Focus on Form and a Focus on Forms, and that an explicit Focus on Form (brief reactive interventions) is more effective than an explicit Focus on Forms (a predetermined grammar syllabus).

The fact that brief reactive interventions seemed to have the most positive effect is in accordance with what one might expect in a Vygotskyan zone of ZPD. Brief interactive interventions are individualised and react to what an individual produces at a particular moment. By producing a certain construction, the individual shows that she has already partially mastered it and therefore she may be more 'ready' to receive additional information about it than when she has not yet started using it productively. The fact that explicit instruction seems more effective than implicit instruction could be attributed to the idea that in implicit learning one does not know for sure whether the learner has really inferred the rule as intended or inferred an 'incorrect rule'. Another possibility is that the learner has paid attention to and learned another aspect of the language (e.g. the meaning). And in some cases, the construction may be too opaque for the learner to distil the correct rule.

For example, depending on how closely related the L1 and L2 are, it may be difficult for the learner to discern the intricacies of the L2 grammatical system. Williams (2003) gives an example of how difficult it may be for adult learners to discern the 'rules' of a language that is very different from the L1. In his experiment, he taught native English speakers a 'new' version of English in which definite articles were replaced with four nonsense articles, two singular and two plural, that distinguished – as Japanese and many other Asian languages do – between whether the noun following was animate or inanimate. Subjects received extensive drills with short sentences, with plenty of examples of articles before animate and inanimate nouns. It was obvious to the students that the articles were the focus of attention. The question was whether they could 'infer' the rules on their own and produce the correct form before new nouns. It turned out that only two of the 18 subjects were able to do so. These two subjects happened to have other L2 learning experience and had developed language analytical skills. This simple experiment shows how difficult it may be for an adult L2 learner to discern conceptual distinctions that are not made in her own language and supports the view that at least in some cases explicit teaching could help the learner to see and understand the intricacies of the L2 system. Whether the learner then internalises the rules probably depends on how complex the rule is, how salient the construction is in the L2, and how much the learner practises it.

One of the only studies conducted that have really looked at the influence of input and the understanding of 'rules' is by Schmidt and Frota (1986). By keeping up a very detailed learner's diary, in which every newly noticed construction was noted, and by analysing regularly taped spontaneous conversations during the learning process, the authors concluded that improvement in SLL follows on the heel of understanding. Correct understanding led to correct production; incorrect understanding led to incorrect production. Schmidt (1990) concludes that attention is necessary for learning. Even though some 'rules' can be learned unconsciously through input (such as gender), many other 'rules' and vocabulary can be learned only consciously by paying attention. The role of explicit instruction is then to 'prime' for noticing and to make clear those rules that cannot be deducted easily without instruction.

In Unit B7, we will present another meta-study by Spada in detail, which looks more in depth into whether instruction is useful and which type seems the most effective. Spada concludes that explicit form-focussed instruction may be especially effective when combined with a communicatively or content-based approach (Spada, 1997: 82).

CONCLUDING REMARKS

This unit has shown some extremes in the view of what the role of teaching should be. Whereas the grammar-translation method consisted of mostly explicit focus on forms and the audio-lingual method on implicit focus on forms, the Communicative Language Teaching approach focussed especially on meaningful communication. But over the last decades it has become clear that providing a mixture of meaningful input and some explicit or implicit instruction on form may be the most effective in teaching an L2. This observation is in contrast with Krashen's claim that explicit rules that were 'learned' could not lead to 'acquisition' and a great deal of current SLA research is directed towards the question if and how declarative knowledge can become subconscious knowledge. In other words, it is obvious that the relationship between 'learning' and 'acquiring' must be a dynamic one.

SECTION B
Extension

Unit B1
Reading and finding SLA literature

In this section, we present excerpts of publications on the issues discussed in Section A. Most of the publications are journal articles. This form of publication is becoming the most important source of information, though books continue to play a role, along with electronic data. Of course, the selection is very small. There are literally thousands of books and articles that have been published in the field of applied linguistics (AL), and no doubt several hundreds of publications are relevant for our purpose. Nobody is able to read all of this, and therefore we need to be selective in what we read when we do our research. In this introduction to Section B, we want to give some information on how to read articles like the ones offered here and to assist you in finding the most pertinent literature on specific research topics.

READING CRITICALLY

Readers should be critical in what they read and how they read it. In our view, it is better to read a smaller number of articles carefully than to browse quickly through masses of publications. Obviously, this requires a strict selection of publications that are crucial for the specific topic that is studied. To help the reader focus their reading, we have provided some guidelines on how to do a proper literature search in the field of SLA.

Assessing information and argumentation

The most important motivation for reading is the need for information. Therefore, it is necessary to be able to assess how valid and reliable the information provided actually is. In other words, can it be verified that what an author says is well based? Is the author simply presenting a private opinion or is it based on solid research? It is not uncommon to find assertions like 'It is well known that most errors in L2 are caused by the L1', or 'There is consensus on the fact that children are better language learners than adults'. For the critical reader this raises the question of what these assertions are based on. Such broad statements are generally hard to substantiate, and it will not be easy to find publications directly supporting such statements. Even when well-known researchers make these statements, the reader can legitimately question them.

The opposite of such unsupported claims is what has been called 'black boxing'. This refers to the habit of listing an outrageous number of publications to support an assertion. The reader will be duly impressed by the extensive knowledge of the literature by the author and will probably be unwilling or unable to check all these references. Still it is worth doing this, because black boxing is typically used in cases where the evidence is at best circumstantial.

Task B1.1

➤ Suppose you find the following statement with citations in an article: 'For language learning, output is essential (Swain and Lapkin, 1995; Spada, 1997; Mackey, 1999, Hansen and Chen, 2002, Pallier *et al.*, 2003)'. Is this a case of black boxing? (The articles cited are all included in Part B. Just skim them to see what the articles are about.)

Another example of unsupported claims can be found in the line of argumentation. In English, in particular, the links between parts of the argumentation are often indicated with specific words and constructions such as 'thus', 'so', 'accordingly', 'therefore', 'we can conclude that . . .' and 'it shows that . . .'. These cohesive devices are used frequently, but not always with good reason. Authors may draw conclusions that are not really warranted, either by their own data or by the literature they cite. The critical reader should therefore be aware of the possible misuse of these types of cohesive transitions and assess their value.

Task B1.2

➤ Have the cohesive devices in the following text been used appropriately?

In our data we find a significant difference in proficiency scores between the 5 year olds and the 7 year olds. Therefore, young children are better language learners than older ones. It can be concluded that FL teaching should start in kindergarten rather than in secondary education.

Assessing research results

The articles included in this section represent a range of different research methods and techniques. This comprises both qualitative and quantitative methods. In the introduction to Section C, we will elaborate on the different methods of investigation that are relevant to conducting research. Some of this is equally relevant for critical reading of the research articles included in Section B. It is important to realise that both qualitative methods (aiming at detailed analyses of small groups of learners) and quantitative methods (investigating the behaviour of groups of learners) have advantages as well as disadvantages.

The most important merit of qualitative research is that it provides an in-depth and detailed analysis that can demonstrate the development of a particular learner beyond doubt. However, although a particular process or development may be demonstrated for one learner, this does not necessarily tell us anything about other learners of different ages, different language backgrounds or with different attitudes and motivations. In other words, the obvious weakness of qualitative research follows logically from its merit: it is not possible to generalise the findings of one or two learners to an entire population.

In quantitative research, especially when it takes the form of a statistical study, this drawback is overcome by calculating the chance of making the wrong decision when the results are generalised to a larger population. Such a degree of chance is expressed in the 'level of significance'. When an article reports a level of significance of '$p < 0.05$', this means that the chance of having obtained these results purely by chance is less than 5 per cent, so the results can be safely attributed to the variables under investigation. However, this approach also entails the danger that a significant result is interpreted as the proven 'truth'. This is by no means the case. Significant results indicate that within the conditions of the study the specific research hypothesis can be accepted (the 'internal validity'), but they may say nothing about the meaningfulness of the study (the 'external validity') in real life. Of course, if the conditions of the study are carefully considered and motivated, the study may be very valuable.

Task B1.3

➤ Suppose a researcher wants to investigate the influence of naturalistic input on the acquisition of L2. To this end, she sets up an experiment in which 40 Japanese learners of French are randomly attributed to two groups. One group (let's call this the 'experimental group') watches French television programmes for one hour a day in addition to their French foreign language classes. The other group (called the 'control group') does not watch French television at all, but just attends French classes. After two weeks, both groups are subjected to a proficiency test in which the number of French words is counted that the participants can mention in one minute. The results show that on average the learners in the experimental group produce more words in a minute than the ones in the control group. This difference is significant at $p < 0.05$. The researcher therefore claims it has been proven that naturalistic input helps L2 acquisition.

➤ As a critical reader, you will have several objections to this approach: draw up a list of points at which the study may be wrong.

From a DST perspective, both qualitative and quantitative research are necessary and useful. The case studies allow us to get a picture of the many possible interacting variables, but for the development of a formal model, which is ultimately the aim of DST research, we need quantitative data to test these models. The main difference with traditional approaches is that in DST the focus is on change over time, in particular changes in the interaction between a great many variables. For example, we know that language proficiency and attitude, motivation and confidence are interrelated, but how a learner's attitude, motivation and confidence might change as proficiency increases or decreases or the other way round has not been studied thus far in SLA. The mathematical models needed for this type of research are beyond the scope of this book.

So, when reading a research report, always take a critical stand. Do not accept one-on-one causal relationships because they do not exist and do not blindly accept all results reported. Whatever the method used, it is good to be aware of the fact that finding all relevant factors, generalisation and representativeness are very difficult to achieve.

Assessing variables

To be able to generalise findings from one study to another group, it is also important that researchers carefully define their groups, variables and conditions. One of the more frequently occurring problem areas in SLA research deals with defining the level of proficiency and the amount of exposure to the L2 a subject may have had.

In most SLA research, we are interested in the level of proficiency in L1/L2/L3. If the language background is not one of the main variables, it is likely to be one of the most important characteristics of individuals and groups studied. Unfortunately, there is no simple method or metric to describe level of proficiency uniformly. Various methods have been used to get an indication of level of proficiency. One is the use of standardised tests such as the Cambridge Exams or the TOEFL tests. Such tests are expensive and time consuming and are therefore rarely used for research purposes. Another method is the use of different types of self-assessments. The simplest one is to ask subjects to indicate on a 5- or 7-point scale how proficient they are in the language under investigation, which can be refined with different scales for skills like speaking, listening, reading and writing.

 Task B1.4

➤ The following example may help you become aware of some of the advantages and disadvantages of self-assessment scales. List the languages you are somewhat proficient in and indicate your level of proficiency on a 5-point scale (1= very bad, 5 = near native) in each skill separately.

	Speaking	Listening	Reading	Writing
L1				
L2				
L3				
L4				

Does your own evaluation present an accurate picture of the state of your languages at the moment? Would your own assessment be sufficient to characterise you as a subject in AL research? If not, what could be some reasons?

European researchers now often refer to proficiency levels as defined by the Common European Framework of Reference (CEFR), developed in the European Union to stimulate citizens of different countries to learn each other's languages. The DIALANG project (http://www.dialang.org) has developed an instrument that allows learners to assess their proficiency in the languages of the European Union through self-assessments. This test makes use of so-called 'Can-do-statements'. These statements refer to what someone can do in terms of language use in different situations. There are six levels of the four different skills (reading, writing, listening, and speaking). An example of a description of a level in speaking and the accompanying statement is:

Level B1

Description: The ability to express oneself in a limited way in familiar situations and to deal in a general way with non-routine information

Statement: I can ask to open an account at a bank, provided that the procedure is straightforward.

The CEFR instrument is now widely used to define targets of language proficiency for different types of education in many European countries. This framework could be very useful in applied linguistic research because it would offer a common standard and make comparing levels of proficiency possible. (For more information on levels and skills, see the CEFR website: http://www.coe.int/T/E/ Cultural_Co-operation/education/Languages/Language_Policy/Common_ Framework _of_Reference)

Another problem area in SLA research is defining and controlling the degree of contact a learner has had with an L2. For many forms of SLA research we need to know exactly how much and what type of contact individuals have had with the target language. For instance, in language attrition research, it is essential that 'non-use' indeed means that there has been no contact at all with that language. Similarly, in investigating the effects of a given teaching method, it is important to know whether the learners have had contact with the target language outside class.

 Task B1.5

➤ To help you become aware of how difficult it might be to define the degree and type of contact with a target language, it may be interesting to make a listing of the contact you have had with your L2 (or L3). Make a listing of the type and degree of contact you have had for your L2 in one of the skills (speaking, listening, reading or writing).

➤ What makes it difficult to make such a listing? Does the listing include all aspects that may be relevant to a potential researcher who wants to control for the exact amount of contact you have had with your L2?

There are many problems related to measuring contact. First, what should be considered contact? In the section on input, we discussed the distinction between input and intake. Someone could be listening to many hours of spoken Bulgarian without learning anything except the fact that Bulgarian has unusual sounds. Intake and accordingly relevant contact has to do with what can be understood and processed. What may be relevant contact for one person may be too difficult or too easy for someone else. Just saying 'Guten Morgen' to a Berlin neighbour will do little to improve or maintain one's German. Like input for learning, language contact needs to be of a specific type in order to be relevant in the study of development

Different types of contact will have different effects, but it is difficult to compare amounts of time devoted to specific types of contact. For instance, listening to a news broadcast in French on the radio and watching a French movie that has been subtitled in the L1 for an equal amount of time is likely to have different effects, but it is difficult to find out what the differences are. Not only may the subtitling be an advantage or disadvantage, but a learner may also be more interested in the movie and find it easier to follow it because words she does not know are likely to be used repeatedly, while in the news broadcast several topics and accordingly a wider range of words will be used. The amount of contact will tell us little about quality and relevance of that contact. Having a deep conversation with someone who is close to you is likely to be more relevant than some brief social talk in a shop. In short, simple listings of the amount of contact are not very effective in measuring contact. In recent years, there have been several attempts to replace language contact questionnaires with social network analyses. In language-related social network analyses, information is gathered about to whom an individual talks, writes or listens regularly, what topics are discussed, how important these are to the individual, who is the core of the network and most importantly, what language is used with each contact. Some examples of linguistic research using social network analysis can be found in a special issue of the *International Journal of the Sociology of Language* (issue 153, 2002).

Task B1.6

➤ Make a description of your social network in which another language than your first language is used. List the people you have contact with and indicate the type of contact you have with these people. Indicate on a 5-point scale how important these contacts are for you and how often you have contact with these persons.

➤ In your opinion, is the information from this network analysis more or less useful than the information you gathered with the listings of your language contact in task 5?

In the literature on SLA, the level of proficiency and contact with the language are important variables. In your reading of the literature, you may want to keep the observations given here in mind and critically evaluate the choices made by researchers. You may realise in some cases that the researcher had little choice in what he or she did, but in other cases improvements on these issues would have been possible.

FINDING RELEVANT LITERATURE IN SLA

In the first part of this unit, we discussed some aspects of reading the SLA literature critically. One of the issues was to evaluate the references to other literature used by authors to support their claims. We suggested checking the references an author uses carefully, but of course, that is not enough. To accurately evaluate the references used (or to be able to conduct SLA research yourself), a proper literature search is required. Only then can it be checked whether the references listed are the most relevant ones. What follows is not a manual on how to do the ultimate literature search on any topic, but merely an outline of how you might go about searching your literature. The focus is more on the strategy than on the finer and more technical details of searches.

Before going on, we need to consider why we use references and citations in the first place. Harwood (forthcoming) argues that there are two main perspectives on using citations. In the so-called 'normative' model, citation serves to 'record the debt the writer owes their colleagues for borrowing ideas and results'. In other words, citations are given to show on whose shoulders an author is standing. The other perspective is the social constructivist one in which citations serve primarily to make the publication more persuasive. In other words, citation is done to show that the author has read the relevant literature, knows what he is talking about, and therefore can be trusted. A possibly interesting facet in this perspective is the references that have not been cited. By not citing specific references, the author can take a stance with respect to a given issue. For instance, when an author talks about comprehensible input in SLA but does not cite Krashen's work (see Unit A7) then that author actually says: 'In my view Krashen's ideas on this are not worth mentioning.'

For a literature search, the following steps can be distinguished:

1   defining the topic
2   defining search terms
3   selection of relevant sources and resources
4   searching references in a database
5   evaluating references found
6   setting up a bibliography.

For this section, we assume that the researcher has access to the internet and preferably to some of the reference databases that are relevant for linguistic research, such as LLBA or Web of Science (http://isi4.isiknowledge.com/portal.cgi/wos). It is still possible to find literature non-electronically, but this requires a specialised library and reference books, and additional heuristic skills that are beyond the scope of this section.

Defining the topic

The most important step is to define and narrow down the topic. A researcher may be interested in 'something on adult SLA', but that is much too broad as a topic. There are literally thousands of publications on this topic, and it is not feasible to work with endless lists of references, as it will take too long to sort through them. The other extreme is a topic that has been defined too narrowly. One may be interested in a topic like 'The role of motivation in the acquisition of plural markers in Tunisian learners of Gujarati', but one is not likely to find any references on that specific topic. The aim is to find the right level of specificity to arrive at a sample of about 15 to 20 relevant publications on a topic. To define a topic it may be useful first to read some introductory chapters from one of the recent handbooks on applied linguistics, such as Kaplan (2002) and Davies and Elder (2004) or from the journal *Annual Review of Applied Linguistics*, which regularly contains overview articles on many aspects of SLA. From these overviews, some core publications on the topic can be gathered that may turn out to be useful at later stages of the search.

Defining search terms

When searching databases with a computer, it is important to use the right search terms for the topic. Computer programs are not as cleverly devised as we may suppose. For instance, when information is sought on the role of motivation in language attrition, and the terms 'motivation' and 'attrition' are used for a search, the result is probably a long lists of references on socio-psychological aspects of school dropout. The computer does not know that someone may be interested in language attrition. It often just looks for words in titles and summaries of articles and the way such words are used may be different from what is expected. When a topic has been defined as suggested above, the overview articles are likely to provide some ideas on terms to use. Another option is to use the list of search terms of the thesaurus of one of the reference databases. These lists contain all the valid search terms and going through those lists may be helpful in finding exactly the terms you need. In addition, the core articles that were found in the overviews can be used for this. Many journals now have a small number of key words attached to the title and summary. These keywords can also be used to refine a search.

Selection of relevant sources and resources

There are several databases for searching references. Probably the largest database that contains references relevant to SLA is the 'Web of Science' (http://isi4.isiknowledge.com), which is a network of networks covering many areas of science. Its size is both an advantage and a disadvantage. All major journals in the field of applied linguistics are included, so most of the relevant articles in SLA can be found in it. The disadvantage is that apart from journals in SLA, there are thousands of journals from other fields in the database. A complication is that search terms that are typical for applied linguistics may have their own senses in other fields. A term like 'intake' is likely to generate many articles on medicine, alcohol abuse and vegetation, but very few on SLA. Therefore, it is not always easy to curtail a search in the Web of Science in such a way that only the SLA references appear, and it may be a better strategy to go directly to more specialised databases such as LLBA (usually available through academic libraries) that are restricted to language-related topics. Searches will yield fewer, but probably more relevant references.

However, there is one very useful feature of the Web of Science that has to be mentioned here: the option to search for publications that cite a specific author or publication. Through this option, one key article on a given topic can be used to see what its impact is, who else is working on this topic, and how the topic has developed over time. Of course, it takes some time for a publication to be cited, so this option works only for publications that are at least two years old.

Another search option is to use one of the big internet search engines, such as Google or Yahoo. There is an incredible amount of information on language and language use on the internet, some of it extremely useful, and some of it completely useless. An alternative is to use a search engine that focuses especially on academic sites, like Scirus (http://www.scirus.com/).

Task B1.7

➤ The internet is probably the largest source of information we now have on almost anything, but the information available is also unstructured and uncontrolled. If you have access to one of the larger databases containing publications on applied linguistics, such as MLA, LLBA or Web of Science, do a search on a specific topic (e.g. 'Early bilingual education' or 'Interaction in the language class'). Then do a search with one of the internet search engines like Google or Yahoo. Compare the results and list the advantages and disadvantages of both.

The main problem with simple internet searches is that the information they yield is not filtered at all. There is no control over what is put on the internet, so for academic purposes, the more specialised databases are to be preferred. At the same time, the internet searches may provide interesting information about the role a given topic plays in the real world. Interest groups, organisations of parents and schools may be working on a particular topic and this may show to what extent a topic is relevant in society.

Searching references

Searches normally go in leaps and bounds. Some combinations of terms yield just the right references, while equally good-looking combinations may just miss what one is looking for. This can often be resolved by slightly adjusting the search terms, or by changing from a topic-based search (e.g. searching for references on the role of output) to a more author-based search (e.g. searching for publications by Merrill Swain or publications citing her work). There is no single strategy that will give all and only those references needed. Play with terms and strategies is required to become proficient in this.

Once the relevant sources have been found, it is very useful to store them and include the abstracts when provided. In most reference databases, it is possible to select references from the large lists that a search has produced and save them. Such a selection can be saved as a text file or it can be imported in a special computer program such as Endnote, Procite or Reference Manager, which helps in organising references and setting up bibliographies.

Evaluating references

Some titles found may look very promising. With a little luck, there is also an abstract that can make clear if the title of the publication matches the content. If there is no abstract in the database, the only way to assess the usefulness of a publication is to read it. It is very tempting to use references on the basis of the abstract only, but abstracts will typically conceal the weaker parts of the research reported on, so for a real evaluation reading the publication itself is the only solution. Many universities now have subscriptions to on-line versions of journals, which makes it easier to obtain a printed version of an article without going through the trouble of going to the library and making copies of the article. Still, going to libraries and browsing through journals and books on the shelves may lead to interesting and unexpected findings. Also, the databases referred to cover refereed journals only, and hardly any in languages other than English. Monographs and edited books as well as more teaching-oriented journals will not be found in them, while for many topics on SLA they may contain very useful information.

Setting up a bibliography

Above we mentioned special database programs for organising references and setting up bibliographies. Endnote, Procite and Reference Manager are probably the best known of them. These are commercial products, but many universities have licences that allow staff and students to use them on university computer networks. These programs allow the researcher to put references in a database in such a way that they can be used in different ways later on. Different journals and publishers use different styles of references. Some well-known formats are MLA, APA and Chicago. Those formats stipulate in detail how a publication should be referred to both in the text and in the list of references. Here are some examples of formats. Note the minor (but relevant!) differences between them:

APA format

Mackey, A. (1999). Input, interaction and second language development: an empirical study of question formation in ESL. *Studies in Second Language Acquisition, 21*, 557–587.

MLA format

Mackey, A. 'Input, interaction and second language development: an empirical study of question formation in ESL.' *Studies in Second Language Acquisition 21.4 (1999)*, 557–87.

Chicago format

Mackey, A. 1999. Input, interaction and second language development: an empirical study of question formation in ESL. *Studies in Second Language Acquisition 21*, no. 4, 557–587.

Doing this formatting by hand is very time consuming and error-prone, so if access to one of the programs mentioned above is available, we highly recommend using them. They will do the formatting on command in any style. Once a reference has been inserted in the database, it can be retrieved in many different formats depending on the publication for which it is used.

CONCLUDING REMARKS

In this introductory unit to Part B, we have provided some help in reading the literature in the field of SLA critically. Such critical reading should be applied to the articles in the units in this part as well. In the second part, we provided some information on how to do a literature search. This information cannot only be used to get the most out of the publications selected for this part of the book, but also to enable finding sources for research.

Unit B2
Dynamic systems of SLA extended

In Section A in the unit on Dynamic Systems of SLA, we discussed the main characteristics of Dynamic Systems Theory. In this unit, we present three articles that are related to DST and SLA. The authors of the three articles were probably not aware of the relevance of their work for a dynamic view on SLA. The first article is by Vivian Cook (1995), who coined the term 'multicompetence' to describe multi-lingual speakers whose language system consists of a number of language specific subsystems that interact. The second article, by Hansen and Chen (2002), takes two specific aspects of language as a dynamic system together: language acquisition and language attrition. The third article, by Pallier and his colleagues (2003), comes from a very different field: Neurolinguistics and Neuro-Imaging. Like the Hansen and Chen article, it deals with language attrition, but here the focus is to what extent the learning of a second language can replace the learning of the first one.

Text B2.1 by Vivian Cook on multicompetence has been included because it is the first to use this label to refer to the fact that bilinguals and multilinguals have an integrated system of elements from different languages. This contrasts with earlier models of multilingual processing in which the bilingual was seen as two monolinguals in one. (This is also argued in Unit A5 on the developing system.) From a DST perspective, Cook's ideas make a lot of sense: languages are interacting subsystems of a larger language system.

Task B2.1

➤ How would you define a 'successful' second language learner: a person who speaks the L2 so fluently that s/he is held for an L1 speaker, a person who communicates well in the L2 although s/he has an accent, or a person whose competence in the L2 is only as much as s/he needs for his/her individual purposes?

After suggesting that people are often defined by what they can *not* do, rather than by what they *can* do, he goes on to make the same point about L2 learners.

'Multi-competence and the learning of many languages' by Vivian Cook (1995) in *Language, Culture and Curriculum*, 8, 93–98

But something rather similar is happening in much of our talking and thinking about second languages. Second Language Acquisition (SLA) researchers spend a lot of time lamenting the lack of success of L2 learners, as we see from the quotes above. It is not difficult to find others. 'In L2 acquisition, on the other hand, it is common for the learner to fail to acquire the target language fully; there are often clear differences between the output of the L2 learner and that of native speakers and learners differ as to how successful they are' (White, 1989: 41). Or 'Those adults who seem to achieve native speaker "competence", i.e. those who learn a second language so that their "performance" is indistinguishable from that of native speakers (perhaps a mere 5% of all learners)' (Selinker, 1972). Or again, 'Unfortunately, language mastery is not often the outcome of SLA' (Larsen-Freeman and Long, 1991: 153).

But are the L2 learners unsuccessful in some absolute sense or are they unsuccessful only when measured against native speakers, a group to which, by definition, they can never belong? The image of successful language learning in our minds is the first language acquisition of a native speaker. We measure the strivings of a second language learner against this. Obviously, very few of them succeed in this sense: hence, the gloom in quotations like the ones above; hence, the depression in the educational system when children leave school apparently ill-equipped in the second language.

But why should monolingualism be the norm? L2 learners could only become native speakers by time-travel back to their date of birth. The proper comparison is not with native speakers at all, but with people who successfully use second languages in their lives to meet their own needs; the norm is the competence of L2 users, not of monolinguals. Their L2 grammatical structure, their vocabulary, their pronunciation should be evaluated against this target.

Multi-competence

For this kind of reason, I felt a few years back that it was necessary to invent a new term that would recognise that knowledge of more than one language is different from the knowledge of one. For knowledge of one language, we have the term 'linguistic competence'; for knowledge of a second language, the term 'interlanguage'; for knowledge of both a first language and other languages, that is to say L1 linguistic competence plus L2 interlanguage, I coined the term 'multi-competence'. The fact that there is an apparent gap in our vocabulary for the total knowledge of languages in one mind is in itself interesting and shows the inherent theoretical assumption that no such term is necessary, that is to say, all we need is native competence and whatever approximation to it can be achieved by L2 learners. L1 competence and L2 competence are never treated together, as a single system.

The idea is that multi-competence is a different state of mind from monolingual linguistic competence. The knowledge of the second language is not an imitation knowledge of a first language; it's something that has to be treated on its own terms, alongside the knowledge of a first language. A single mind with more than one language has a totality that is very different from a mind with a single language. This idea seems almost a commonplace in bilingualism studies. It is only in the fields of SLA research and language teaching that it is considered controversial.

[. . .]

But the idea of a different multi-competent mind can also be put to the test: do people with several languages have different minds from those with only one? There is a variety of evidence that says 'yes' to this question. Let us summarise some of it quickly (see Cook, 1992 for a fuller presentation).

Knowledge of L1 is different in L2 users

Some people find it slightly uncomfortable to be told that their competence in a second language has an effect on their first language. However, the effects are mostly subtle. Take Hebrew/English bilinguals. One of the areas of pronunciation that has received much attention in recent years is Voice Onset Time (VOT). This is a technical term for the moment at which voicing starts in certain speech sounds, a /p/ has late VOT, a /b/ early VOT. Loraine Obler (1982) found Hebrew–English bilinguals exaggerate VOT differences for each language in production but occupy an intermediate position between the two languages for perception. So people who speak two languages have marginally different L1 systems to monolinguals. Not that this would be detectable to the human ear; it's a matter of 23 milliseconds in Hebrew /p/ that only comes to light under instrumental analysis.

Advanced L2 users differ from monolinguals in knowledge of the L2

If you already have an L1 in the mind, can the knowledge of the L2 be the same as that in the mind of a person with only one language? Some research has indeed shown that Americans who can pass for balanced bilinguals in French still differ from native speakers in their grammaticality judgments of sentences. Also, for example, one's vocabulary is influenced by the various languages one knows. Take the word COIN. An English person who knows French cannot entirely free themselves from the meaning of 'corner' even when they are using the word in English meaning 'piece of money'.

People who know an L2 have a different metalinguistic awareness from people who know only an L1

One of the benefits of learning a second language is that it sharpens one's awareness of language in general, as witness writers such as Conrad, Beckett, or Nabokov. Research with children shows that the child with an L2 outscores the monolingual child on tests of sheer grammaticality and on tests where form has to be separated from meaning.

L2 users have different cognitive processes from monolinguals

It is not sheer pretentiousness that has made educators claim that L2 learning helps one to think in more flexible ways – what Latin teachers used to call 'brain-training'. Children who learn second languages indeed score better on tests of creativity and cognitive flexibility. To quote Peal and Lambert (1962), 'the bilinguals appear to have a more diversified set of mental abilities than the monolinguals'.

Multi-competence is, then, a different state of mind; people who know more than one language are different from those who speak only one. On many counts, if we were to compare the two groups, multilinguals function better than monolinguals. It is only in comparison to native language use that they are clearly deficient.

Task B2.2

➤ This article by Vivian Cook can best be characterised as an 'opinion' article and contains a few general statements that are not supported. This author can get away with it easily, because he is considered an authority in his field who knows what he is talking about. However, suppose you were to read the four sections above critically, where would you have expected more specific evidence or references?

Text B2.1
V. Cook

Universal Grammar

[. . .]

But suppose we start from the multi-competence position. To accommodate L2 learning, a parameter has to be able to have two or more settings simultaneously in the same mind, a flexibility denied in the monolingualist approach. They know at the same time one language that has subjects, one that doesn't have them. The multi-competent person may have two settings for the parameter simultaneously available to them. Evidence such as code-switching and lexical access show that the second language is never totally switched off but it is still latent whenever the speaker uses the L2. For example, speakers of postpositional languages like Japanese are quicker to spot that English phrases like 'the table on' are ungrammatical than speakers of prepositional languages like French. Why? Because they have the other parameter-setting already active in their minds.

[. . .]

Task B2.3

➤ In the following section, Cook advises L2 teachers not to use a real 'native-like' language as the ultimate target and to make use of the L1 when appropriate in the classroom. Before reading the next section, decide whether you would agree with him on both points. Why (not)?

Text B2.1
V. Cook

Language teaching

What does all of this have to say for language teaching? For a start, syllabuses and examinations need to specify a target other than the native speaker; again something that is in a sense obvious and which has been advocated on various grounds already. I feel more and more guilty that in the teaching materials I used to write, I assumed that non-native speakers had to behave like native speakers. But they can't. For example, the presence of a non-native speaker in a conversation immediately changes it. As natives, we expect particular behaviour from non-natives and are upset when it is not provided. An experiment of mine showed that non-native learners of English tended to be more formal in expressing their thanks than natives: 'Thank you very much' rather than 'Thanks'. My first reaction to this was that we should teach our students to speak less formally. My second, however, was that the learners were right and I was wrong: non-native speakers are expected to be more formal than natives. A syllabus that does not take the particular nature of L2 users into account will be inadequate. . . .

Secondly, the form of examination. What we need to test is how effective students are at using second languages as multi-competent speakers, not as imitation natives. Obviously, in many cases the standards will be similar. But sometimes it may have to be better than native models. I went to a conference on languages for business in Belgium a couple of years ago at which a constant refrain was the failure of British businessmen to adapt their speech to non-native speakers. Business people in continental Europe are amazed at the linguistic insensitivity of the British, which we certainly would not want people to imitate.

Finally the concept of multi-competence seems to me to make us think again about what is going on in the classroom. There has been a continuing TEFL tradition, from the 1920s, through the structural method, up to the communicative approach to ignore the first language in the students' minds. We have behaved as if the students knew no language rather than no English.

The impression is given that L2 teachers should be actually teaching speech functions such as arguing or describing rather than teaching students, who already have these functions, how to perform them in a second language. (It is hard, though not impossible, to find speech functions that do not exist in some form in the Ll.) The same with vocabulary. Teachers sometimes spend a lot of time carefully explaining some word, miming it, defining it, illustrating it. The students suddenly nod their heads, and the teachers think what good teachers they were, when all they have in fact done was enable the student to find a translation equivalent in their first language. When the students are sitting in the classroom their minds are not empty waiting to be filled by the second language: they already have their own language. Our teaching techniques must recognise this constant feature of the L2 mind, and avoid forcing the student to treat L1 and L2 as separate systems. We don't wish to return to simple translation, it is true. But certainly we should not be working with monolingual concepts of linguistic competence, and thus prevent the student from developing an efficient, multi-competent mind.

Task B2.4

➤ Suppose you were asked if it is a good idea to bring up a child bilingually rather than monolingually. Based on the information given by Cook about the differences between monolinguals and multilinguals, what would you say?

This article has presented three main ideas: no matter how fluent in an L2, a multilingual should be recognised for the competences in the L2 in their own right, a multilingual mind is per definition different from a monolingual mind, and one of the implications for teaching an L2 is that the L1 should be regarded as an asset rather than a disadvantage. As we mentioned before, these ideas are quite compatible with DST because the multilingual mind is regarded as one system that is continually changing, depending on both internal and eternal factors. The next article will show quite convincingly that the knowledge of L2 may fluctuate to a great extent, depending on the amount of recent exposure.

Text B2.2
L. Hansen and
Y.-L. Chen

'What counts in the acquisition and attrition of numeral classifiers?' by Lynne Hansen and Yung-Lin Chen (2002) in *JALT Journal*, *23*, 90–110

As indicated in Unit A2, attrition is as much a part of language as a dynamic system as acquisition. Both processes have in common that they are influenced by many interacting factors, but one obvious difference is that for attrition one particular factor stands out as an explanation: the fact that a language is not used anymore. However, this does not necessarily mean that attrition is a simple or a linear process. As in acquisition, many variables interact in attrition: the amount of use, the level of mastery before attrition sets in, cognateness of the language that is forgotten and other languages in the system, motivation to use (or maybe even forget) a language, and so on.

This article by Hansen and Chen is an excellent example of language attrition research, especially because it aims at testing one of the most frequently mentioned, but hardly ever systematically studied hypotheses, Jakobson's Regression Hypothesis. This hypothesis states that language attrition is the mirror image of language acquisition: whatever is learned first is forgotten last, and whatever is learned last is forgotten first. While many researchers have referred to it and have given it an almost magical explanatory power, there has been little empirical evidence. The problem with this hypothesis is that proving it requires the presence of a set of phenomena in a language that constitute an implicational scale, i.e. a sequence of developments in which one phenomenon clearly precedes another development. So if someone has acquired the last element on this scale, he or she will have acquired all the other elements before it. For example, let's consider children who learn to count and assume they first learn the single digit numbers (1–9), then the two-digit numbers (11–99), and then the three-digit numbers (100–999). This would mean that if they know how to count from 100–999, they also know how to count from 1–9.

There are few phenomena that show such a clear order of acquisition in language, but Hansen and Chen have made use of numeral classifiers in Chinese and Japanese. A numeral classifier is somewhat similar to English partitive constructions such as 'a piece of' 'a loaf of' in constructions such as 'a piece of pie' or 'two loaves of bread'. Numeral classifiers form complex systems that show a regular pattern in acquisition that form an implicational scale, and are therefore ideally suited to test the regression hypothesis. For example, such classifiers occur most often before animate nouns, which are therefore the most frequent type of numeral classifier. They occur less often before nouns referring to tools, which are therefore less frequent. (The authors also use the terms 'unmarked', which means, not unusual or exceptional and 'marked', which means rather unusual or exceptional for the language.) The hypothesis is that the subjects learn the most frequent and unmarked forms first and forget those last.

The study reported on here is a very 'clean' study in the sense that the subjects, who were native-English-speaking missionaries who were living or had lived in Japan and China for varying lengths of time, met specific requirements. Half of the group were still living abroad and were actively using and learning Japanese or Chinese for varying amounts of time. For this half, it could be established in what order the different classifiers were acquired by testing different cohorts of subjects, who had lived abroad for different lengths of time. The other half of the subjects had previously lived in China and Japan and had been back for varying amounts of time. Consequently, the pattern of forgetting the classifiers could be measured, because they were no longer using the language that they were very fluent in at some point.

On the one hand, this group of missionaries is ideal to test attrition in real time, but on the other hand, this group has some unique features, which may make comparisons to other groups and generalisations problematic.

Task B2.5

➤ A language such as English has an article system that marks whether an entity is definite or not (for example, in '*The street is wet*', the definite article indicates that the speaker refers to a street the hearer can identify) and to whether an entity is countable or not (for example, in '*Humans need water*' the zero article before *water* indicates that *water* is a non-countable entity). In classifier languages such as Chinese, Japanese, and Vietnamese different semantic distinctions are made. Briefly scan through the article to find out what semantic distinctions classifiers make other than the ones discussed above.

This paper examines interlanguage classifier systems, an aspect of second language (L2) semantics and lexicon that has scarcely been touched upon in previous research. The focus is on the accessibility [= ability to recall] of numeral classifiers in the learning and subsequent forgetting of two East Asian languages by English-speaking adults. The aims of the investigation are (a) to determine the stages of classifier syntax in learning and loss, (b) to examine semantic accessibility in classifier systems in learning and loss, and (c) to explain the findings in light of considerations of markedness, frequency, and the regression hypothesis. A comparison of data from two groups within the same population who learned unrelated languages, Japanese or Chinese, increases the transparency of the window that is provided into universals in second language progression and regression.

Text B2.2
L. Hansen and
Y.-L. Chen

Numeral classifier systems

The languages of the world can be divided into two groups with regard to numeral classifiers: those that have classifiers, such as the majority of languages in East and Southeast Asia, and those that do not, such as most European languages, including English (Allan, 1977). In Japanese and Chinese the numeral classifiers, or 'counters' as they are also called, are morphemes which occur adjacent to numerals and categorize the noun referent based on semantic features such as animacy, shape, size, arrangement, and function. A counter is obligatory in a noun phrase containing a numeral, and, as shown in the following examples, occurs between the number and the noun referent:

(1) English   three   books
(2) Japanese   *san*   *satu*   *no*   hon
                (three   classifier   poss.part   book)
(3) Mandarin   *san*   *ben*   *shu*
                (three   classifier   book)

The authors explain that there are many of these types of counters in both Japanese and Chinese. A specific counter will occur only with nouns that have something in common semantically. For example, in English the partitive 'piece' will occur only before nouns that refer to entities that can be divided into different pieces, such as 'cloth', 'pie'. It will not normally occur before a noun such as 'sand'.

In the schematic organizations of the Japanese and Mandarin classifier systems, we include the particular classifiers that are examined in the present study. While these two systems have many similarities, they do differ in the details of the semantic classifications as well as in the amount of variability allowed in reference. Chinese noun classes are more variable than those in Japanese, with a greater tendency for fuzzy sets that are often mutually overlapping.

The research on the semantics, frequency, and historical development of classifiers in many languages has established an implicational scale of the semantic features of classification (Craig, 1986). This scale is derived from cross-linguistic investigations such as Adams and Conklin's (1973) study of the classifier inventories of 37 Asian languages. This study reports that animacy, in the form of a human/nonhuman distinction or an animate/inanimate distinction, is always encoded. The three basic shape categories of long, round, and flat usually appear also. Secondary parameters, such as rigidity and size, are often found but usually in combination with the primary parameters instead of serving as the sole basis for classification. Functional parameters such as tools, footwear, and written materials also appear frequently, but, unlike the parameters of shape and animacy, are quite language-specific, reflecting the interests of members of the particular culture in which the language is spoken. The points on the implicational scale of semantic features, the Numeral Classifier Accessibility Hierarchy (NCAH), are ordered as follows:

Animate human > Animate non human > Shape > Function

In applying this hierarchy of markedness to the issues raised in the present study, we hypothesize that the accessibility of classifiers in acquisition and attrition follows the order of this implicational scale. That is, we expect the least marked distinction, animate: human, to be the earliest to appear and the longest to be retained, and the distinction at the end of the scale, function, to be the last to appear and the earliest to be lost after the onset of attrition.

Task B2.6

➤ The term 'implicational scale of semantic features' refers to the items that are encoded before any other items. For example, the scale above implies that if a language codes for 'animate non human', it will also encode 'animate human', but not necessarily 'shape' or 'function'. The authors hypothesise that those items that are encoded most will be learned before the others. Can you think of any common-sense reasons for this to be the case?

In the following section, the authors first explain what the regression hypothesis is and what their research questions are. Then to be able to test the regression hypothesis, the authors will first have to show what order these classifiers are acquired in L2.

The regression hypothesis

Text B2.2
L. Hansen and
Y.-L. Chen

Since the study of language attrition is relatively recent (for overviews of this sub-field of applied linguistics, see De Bot and Weltens, 1995; Hansen and Reetz-Kurashige, 1999; Hansen, 2000a; Hansen, 2000b), much more is known about the sequences of language learning than of language loss. In the second-language acquisition field, interlanguage, the language of L2 learners, is seen as a series of stages that all learners pass through in acquiring a language. In language attrition, the regression hypothesis is the idea that, in losing a language, attriters will follow an order opposite to the stages of acquisition. Dating back to Jakobson (1968), the hypothesis describes the path of language loss as the mirror opposite of acquisition, with the last learned being the first forgotten, the first learned being the longest retained (for a review of regression theory, see De Bot and Weltens, 1991).

In the language-attrition literature the regression hypothesis has been supported in a general sense at the inter-linguistic skills level: receptive skills precede productive skills in acquisition and the reverse holds true for attrition. At the intra-linguistic level (within morphology, syntax, semantics, and the lexicon), however, documenting that the stages of development are reversed in attrition is more difficult. Tracking both acquisition and attrition is time consuming and a universal or predictable developmental ladder has been established for only a limited number of linguistic structures. However, a number of studies have demonstrated through testing that the regression hypothesis holds. (. . .)

Research focus

In examining the acquisition and attrition accessibility of numeral classifier systems, the present study looks for evidence of regression in semantics and the lexicon as well as syntax. The research questions are:

1 What are the stages in the learning and loss of numeral classifier syntax in Japanese and Chinese by English-speaking adults?
2 What are the sequences of semantic accessibility?
3 To what extent are the accessibility sequences of the numeral classifiers explained by considerations of language universals and frequency in input?
4 Does classifier accessibility in attrition follow a reverse order to that of acquisition?

Task B2.7

➤ Of course, the main question in this study is number 4, but to be able to answer that question, the three other questions have to be asked. In order to understand the next sections it might be useful to consider the following questions:

1   No single subject was studied while s/he was learning and forgetting the L2, but the different subjects studied were living abroad or had been back for varying amounts of time. How, in your opinion, could the researchers have determined the different stages of learning and loss by studying these subjects?

2   'The sequence of semantic accessibility' is the sequence in which the learners acquire the L2 feature. For this question, the authors used pictures to elicit nouns with classifiers. Looking back at the semantic features (animacy, non-animacy, shape and form) of the implicational scale mentioned earlier, what types of items do you expect the authors to have used on the pictures?

3   Why would the researchers not only look at the universal implicational hierarchy but also at the frequency of occurrence of classifiers?

Text B2.2
L. Hansen and
Y.-L. Chen

Method

Subjects and data collection

The subjects included two groups of learners and attriters from the same population. They were native speakers of English in the western United States who, as young adults, had worked (or, in the case of the learners, were working) as full-time missionaries in Japan or Taiwan. Immersed in the culture of their target language, Japanese or Mandarin Chinese, they had acquired (or were acquiring) fluent competence in the spoken language through daily interaction with native speakers. The length of time spent in the target culture by the subjects varied from as little as 18 months (for females over the past two decades) to as long as three years (for males before 1959). Upon completion of their missions, the attriters (those who were or would be losing their L2) returned to an English environment in the western United States where L2 exposure was discontinued or greatly reduced.

The L2 Japanese learner/attriter group consisted of 204 learners (153 male, 51 female), 189 attriters (138 male and 54 female), and a control group of 14 native speakers of Japanese. The learners in Japan were selected randomly at missionary conferences attended by all missionaries serving in a particular area. The data were collected individually from each subject in a classroom. The attriters back in the western United States were found through lists of returned missionary organizations which included virtually all who had served during particular times in particular areas of Japan, and also by word of mouth from other missionaries. (. . .)

The L2 Mandarin learner/attriter group consisted of 167 learners (140 male, 27 female), 143 attriters (109 male, 34 female), and a control group of 35 native speakers of Mandarin. The learners in Taiwan were selected randomly at missionary conferences attended by all missionaries serving in a particular area. (. . .) The 35 native Mandarin

Text B2.2
L. Hansen and
Y.-L. Chen

speakers were Taiwanese students at Brigham Young University, Hawaii and were met in their homes or in a classroom on the university campus.

Elicitation instruments

The instrument administered to the L2 Japanese learners/attriters consisted of a set of 24 line drawings, each displaying between one and five exemplars of the pictured object on a 4″ x 6″ card. Presented in two alternating randomized orders, there were two items for each of the following twelve classifiers: humans (*nin*), small animals (*haki*), pieces of paper/leaves (*mai*), pens/tulips (*hon*), small round pieces of candy (*ko*), books (*satu*), vehicles (*dai*), buildings (*ken*), birds (*wa*), pairs of footwear (*soku*), large animals (*too*), and letters (*tuu*). Each subject was given the cards and asked to tell the number of items pictured. The responses were recorded on an answer sheet by the investigator.

In the Chinese data collection sessions, one of three tasks completed was a modified version of the Japanese instrument described above. In replicating the Japanese elicitation task for the Chinese study, we found that for three of the 12 Japanese counters (*mai, hon, hiki*) the exemplar pairs elicited two different classifiers from native speakers of Mandarin. For example leaves and pieces of paper, which had been used to elicit the single classifier, *mai*, in Japanese, fell into two separate semantic categories in Mandarin, *pin* being used for the classification of leaves; *zhang* for paper. In these three cases of semantic split of the Japanese categories, the new classifications were added to the Chinese version of the task, with a pair of exemplars included for each (the additional items are shown in Appendix II, Items 25 to 30). The Mandarin instrument therefore consisted of 30 line drawings (rather than 24 as for the Japanese), two items for each of the following fifteen classifiers: humans (*ge, wei, dui*) books (*ben*), pieces of paper (*zhang*), small animals (*zhi*), large animals (*tao, zhi*), birds (*zhi*), pencils/pens (*he, zhi*), fish (*taio*), letters (*feng*), pairs of footwear (*shuan*), vehicles (*liang, tai, bu*), buildings (*jian, don, zou*), small round pieces of candy (*ke, li*), flowers (*duo*), and leaves (*pin*). The drawings were presented on a picture sheet mailed or faxed to the subjects. In the telephone interview the learners/attriters were required to orally specify the number of items shown in each drawing. Again, the responses were recorded on an answer sheet by the investigator.

Calculating suppliance

Correct classifier suppliance in both the Japanese and Chinese data was determined by the responses of the native speaking control groups. The patterns of correct suppliance between the two languages vary because of basic differences in their systems of classification. The semantic criteria for determining Mandarin classifier classes appear to be more complex than in Japanese and the relations among different classifier categories in Mandarin are more complicated and overlapping. (. . .)

Results and Discussion

(. . .)

Sequences of semantic accessibility in acquisition and attrition

The percentages of target language responses for the elicited classifiers are provided in Table B2.1 for the Japanese data, and Table B2.2 for the Chinese data. Notice that

Text B2.2
L. Hansen and
Y.-L. Chen

under Time on each table, the first four columns, representing the Learning Period, indicate the percentage of correct suppliance for 6-month time cohorts over the two-year exposure period in Japan or Taiwan. On the right side of the table, representing the Attrition Period, are the percentages of correct suppliance for the attriters in time-cohorts based on the number of years since their departure from the target culture. In both the Japanese and Mandarin data sets there are wide disparities between classifiers in their levels of accessibility.

 Task B2.8

➤ In the following two sub-sections, the acquisition and attrition data are compared to the implicational scale (language universals and markedness) and frequency of input data. As was expected, correlations are found with both. However, the frequency of input data is more detailed and seems to explain the acquisition and attrition stages best. Keeping DST in mind, can you think of a common sense argument for this observation?

Text B2.2
L. Hansen and
Y.-L. Chen

Language universals and markedness

The accessibility patterns in the L2 data displayed on Tables B2.1 and B2.2 show conformity to the constraints of the Numeral Classifier Accessibility Hierarchy: Animate human > Animate non human > Shape > Function. The most accessible non-general classifier category in both acquisition and attrition is the least marked position on the hierarchy, animate: human; in Japanese *nin* (with its suppletive variants, *hitori* [one person], and *futari* [two persons]), and in Chinese *ge, wei*, or *dui*. The classifier for small animals also makes an early appearance in Interlanguage, *hiki* in Japanese, and *zhi* in Chinese. As pointed out above, a strong tendency for overgeneralization of these counters to other non human animates is most pronounced in early acquisition and late attrition. As for the next position on the markedness scale, shape, the three Japanese classifiers, *hon, mai,* and *ko* come in relatively early, while in Chinese the status of this larger, fuzzier set of classifiers is less clear. The counters of function included in our elicitation tasks tend to be least accessible of all, and, particularly in Japanese, in some cases do not occur in the data from the majority of learners and attriters. An exceptional case of earlier than predicted acquisition in both Japanese and Chinese, the functional counter for books, may be so because of its high frequency in missionary language.

Frequency in input

In as much as numeral classifier frequency data have not been reported for Mandarin, we focus in this section on the evidence from the Japanese data. Notice in Table B2.2 that the classifiers are arranged according to their frequency in oral conversational input, shown as a percentage in the leftmost column. The oral sample upon which the frequency count is based was collected by Downing (1984) from a number of transcribed Japanese conversations and conversational segments which involved a variety of interlocutors. We see in these frequency data that a small number of forms constitute a disproportionately large percentage of actual classifier usage. As pointed out by Downing (1984), although average Japanese native speakers may have a large

Table B2.1 Percent suppliance of Japanese numeral class fiers

Classifier		Frequency[1]	Time[2]								
			Learning period				Attrition period				
Counter*	Item	Oral %	0–6m	6–12m	12–18m	18–25m	0–2y	3–4y	5–15y	16–30y	>30y
			n = 59	n = 51	n = 49	n = 45	n = 59	n = 39	n = 30	n = 32	n = 29
nin	Human	36	63	90	96	99	96	87	73	67	49
tu[3]	General	26	33	27	23	19	19	23	31	35	18
hiki	small animal	8	15	52	82	87	77	72	46	22	20
mai	paper, leaf	7	30	70	73	80	78	71	48	46	41
hon	pen, tulip	5	23	42	64	70	73	70	44	39	26
ko	piece of candy	3	7	49	70	77	73	66	37	13	4
satu	Book	1	10	49	82	87	69	59	42	41	11
ken	Building	1	1	5	39	37	31	35	21	8	11
wa	Bird	1	4	7	17	14	24	18	10	12	7
dai	Vehicle	>1	4	27	61	82	78	63	19	22	11
soku	pair of footwear	>1	9	8	9	17	19	15	0	0	0
too	large animal	>1	2	5	9	17	19	12	4	0	0
tuu	Letter	>1	3	3	12	19	18	11	5	0	0

* The counters are listed in the order of frequency in conversational input.

1. From Downing (1984).
2. Time for learners indicates the number of months in Japan at the time of data collection; for the attriters the number of years since leaving Japan.
3. Percentages for tu indicate the substitution rate of this general classifier in place of the twelve more specific ones which the 24 items of the instrument were designed to elicit.

Table B2.2 Percent suppliance of Chinese numeral classifiers

Classifier		Time*							
		Learning period				Attrition period			
Counter*	Item	0–6m	7–12m	13–18m	19–25m	0–2y	3–5y	6–10y	20–30y
		n = 46	n = 57	n = 25	n = 39	n = 28	n = 25	n = 46	n = 46
ge, wei, dui	Human	99	96	98	87	100	100	100	98
Zhi	small animal	59	77	88	92	84	72	60	26
tiao, zhi	Fish	33	61	73	85	66	56	44	33
Zhang	Paper	61	88	96	97	79	58	55	33
Pin	Leaf	0	5	12	28	7	6	5	10
zhi, he	Pen	22	61	60	77	59	54	55	26
Dao	Tulip	0	16	20	15	16	14	15	6
ke, li	piece of candy	5	18	26	28	11	6	7	8
Ben	Book	85	98	98	100	93	92	91	72
jian, don, zou	building	6	21	38	61	23	24	18	6
Zhi	Bird	38	61	78	86	61	50	43	18
tai, liang, bu	vehicle	6	37	72	90	50	36	22	10
Shaun	Pair of footwear	9	46	80	86	72	64	62	37
tao, zhi	large animal	51	63	74	86	68	50	44	13
Feng	letter	13	48	74	81	79	68	37	29

* Time for learners indicates the number of months in Taiwan when data were collected; for the attriters the number of years since leaving Taiwan

Text B2.2
L. Hansen and
Y.-L. Chen

inventory of forms at their command, only a small number of these commonly play a part in their everyday language use.

As seen in an overview of the acquisition and attrition data in Table B2.2, classifier accessibility is quite consistent with a frequency explanation. The most frequent counters, *nin* and *tu*, are acquired earliest and tend to be retained longest. The next most frequent classifiers, *hiki*, *mai*, *hon* and *ko*, pattern in a second acquisition group. Notice also that the counters which are most resistant to loss over decades of non-use, *nin*, *tu*, *hiki*, *mai*, and *hon*, are the very five that, according to the frequency count, are most numerous in input during the learning period.

With regard to the two Japanese classifiers that were learned more quickly than Downing's (1984) frequency count or markedness considerations would have predicted, *satu* (the counter for books), and *dai* (the counter for large mechanical objects), we observe that these classifiers were highly frequent in the learning environment of the subjects. Their daily preoccupation with reading and persuading others to accept and read copies of a book of scripture undoubtedly increased their use of the classifier for books. Similarly, with bicycles as a daily means of transportation and a high level of interest of many in this 19 to 24 age group in mechanical objects such as automobiles, we suspect that the proportion of dai used in their conversations may have also exceeded that reported by Downing.

Regression hypothesis

The overall percentages of accuracy for the individual classifiers are compared between the acquisition data and the attrition data for the L2 Japanese in Figure B2.1, and the L2 Chinese in Figure B2.2. Notice the similarities in the relative accessibility of the counters in the acquisition and in the attrition data. These views of our two data sets make even more clear what is also evident in Tables B2.1 and B2.2, that, in the case of numeral classifiers, those which are most accessible in learning are retained longest, and those which are less accessible are more susceptible to loss.

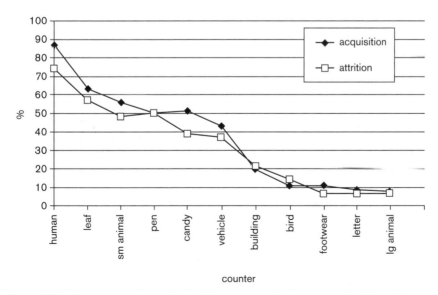

Figure B2.1 Mean percentages of classifier accuracy for learners and attriters: Japanese

Text B2.2
L. Hansen and
Y.-L. Chen

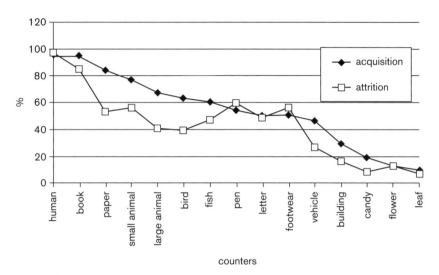

Figure B2.2 Mean percentages of classifier accuracy for learners and attriters: Chinese

 Task B2.9

➤ In their conclusion, the authors suggest that there are some individual differences, especially motivation, that may have caused the variation in 'correct' usage among the different learners, a view quite compatible with DST. In Unit 6, some other individual differences such as age, aptitude, intelligence, and attitude were discussed. In your opinion, which other ones could have played a role in explaining the differences among learners?

This article has shown, as DST would predict, that learning and forgetting takes place over time of use and non-use of an L2 and that frequently occurring items are acquired first and forgotten last. Therefore, it has also given strong evidence for the regression hypothesis. In the following article, we will look at language loss again, but this time at whether or not a language can be lost completely.

Text B2.3
C. Pallier,
S. Dehaene,
J. B. Poline,
D. LeBihan,
A. M. Argenti,
E. Dupoux and
J. Mehler

'Brain imaging of language plasticity in adopted adults: can a second language replace the first?' by C. Pallier, S. Dehaene, J. B. Poline, D. LeBihan, A. M. Argenti, E. Dupoux and J. Mehler (2003) in *Cerebral Cortex*, *13*, 155–161

In this part of Unit B2, we want to draw on an article by Christoph Pallier and his colleagues to do two things. One is to convey some information on the attrition of a first language learnt early in life. The second is to show how more recent research techniques using brain imaging techniques can be used to gather data in the field of SLA and multilingualism. The main aim of the article is to find out whether neural circuits that are involved in language acquisition lose plasticity after they have become tuned to the first language to which one has been exposed. In other words, does learning a specific language right after birth have an impact on our brain that at the same time leaves a life-long mark on the system and prevents us from acquiring a second language at a native level? This phenomenon is referred to as 'the crystallisation hypothesis'.

The crystallization hypothesis predicts that the later a second language is learned, the more the cortical representations of the second and the first languages will differ. This prediction, however, has received only mixed support.

Another prediction of the crystallization hypothesis is that exposure to the first language should leave long-lasting traces in the neural circuits subserving language processing. In the present study, we explore this issue by using fMRI to study the cerebral bases of speech comprehension in a special group of subjects: children adopted from foreign countries who have ceased to use their first language and speak only the language of their new parents. When tested as adults, they are apparently fluent in their second language and report having completely forgotten their first language (Maury, 1995). Has L2 completely replaced L1? According to the crystallization hypothesis, exposure to L1 during the first 3–8 years of life should have left traces.

Text B2.3
C. Pallier,
S. Dehaene,
J. B. Poline,
D. LeBihan,
A. M. Argenti,
E. Dupoux and
J. Mehler

In this study, Koreans adopted in France at an early age are studied in order to find out what happened with the Korean they must have acquired in childhood. Two types of data have been used, one based on behavioural measures and one based on neuro-imaging. Functional Magnetic Resonance Imaging (fMRI) is a technique that is used to measure brain activity in different tasks. Using this technique, the locus of activity, the parts of the brain that are active in language processing can be visualised. (For an explanation of fMRI and other neuro-imaging techniques see the introductory chapters in Brown and Haagoord, 1999).

Task B2.10

➤ A group of children learned Korean as their first language. Some were already 8 years old when they first learned French. After that, they had no exposure to Korean anymore. Do you think these subjects, who are tested again in their twenties, will recognise Korean sentences better than subjects who did not learn Korean as their first language when they hear them?

Exposing adopted subjects to sentences in their original language should elicit some remnant activity in language areas. If, on the other hand, the brain circuits for language remain plastic then learning a new language may have completely overridden the traces laid down by the first. To our knowledge, this is the first behavioral and neuro-imaging study that uses evidence from adopted children to examine the plasticity of language acquisition when the child's main language suddenly ceases to be used.

Text B2.3
C. Pallier,
S. Dehaene,
J. B. Poline,
D. LeBihan,
A. M. Argenti,
E. Dupoux and
J. Mehler

(. . .)

After excluding those who had had contacts with Korean since their arrival, and those who could not participate in the fMRI experiment for various reasons, we ended up with eight individuals for whom we had good evidence of sudden and definitive

Text B2.3
C. Pallier,
S. Dehaene,
J. B. Poline,
D. LeBihan,
A. M. Argenti,
E. Dupoux and
J. Mehler

isolation from the initial maternal language (two females, six males ranging in age from 20 to 32, mean = 26.8; the ages of adoption were 3, 3, 5.5, 5.5, 5.5, 7, 7.5 and 8 years). All claimed to have completely forgotten their native language, as is generally the case for children adopted from foreign immigration (Maury, 1995). When interviewed about their skills in French, only one (who arrived at 5.5) reported significant problems in learning to speak French. The others reported having learned French rather quickly, and had no perceptible foreign accent in French.

Task B2.11

➤ Below the authors explain their concerns about the subjects' L1 exposure. To what extent could an adopted child's L1 exposure be different from a child who has not been adopted?

Text B2.3
C. Pallier,
S. Dehaene,
J. B. Poline,
D. LeBihan,
A. M. Argenti,
E. Dupoux and
J. Mehler

Given their history of adoption, a concern is the extent to which those subjects' initial language acquisition was normal and, in particular, whether they had received sufficient inputs in the Korean language. Though we have little information on their individual history, the adopting organisms informed us that, in the orphanages they came from, they had interaction not only with other children but also with Korean-speaking adults. Older children went to Korean schools. Thus, it is likely that they received a normal exposure to Korean. The control group comprised eight native monolingual French speakers (two females, six males ranging in age from 22 to 28, mean = 23.5), who had had no exposure to any Asian language. All subjects were right-handed according to the Edinburgh questionnaire.

All subjects participated in two behavioral tests out of the scanner, and one test inside the scanner.

Task B2.12

➤ There are two types of data used. The first is a set of behavioural tests in which students had to identify orally whether the language they heard was Korean or not or whether a Korean word was the correct translation for a French word. The second set of data was obtained by fMRI techniques, which may detect very subtle differences in brain activity such as the places where or the intensity and speed with which processing takes place. In this case, would you expect such techniques to yield results different from the behavioural tests?

Text B2.3
C. Pallier,
S. Dehaene,
J. B. Poline,
D. LeBihan,
A. M. Argenti,
E. Dupoux and
J. Mehler

Behavioral test 1: language identification

The subjects listened to a total of 60 sentences, 12 in each of five languages unfamiliar to French subjects (Korean, Japanese, Polish, Swedish and Wolof). Sentences were read by three different female native speakers. After each sentence, the subject had to provide, on a scale from 1 to 7, a degree of confidence that the sentence was in Korean or not: '7' meant that he/she was sure the sentence was in Korean; '1' meant that he/she was sure that the sentence was not in Korean; 4 indicated a complete lack of confidence.

Behavioral test 2: word recognition

Text B2.3
C. Pallier,
S. Dehaene,
J. B. Poline,
D. LeBihan,
A. M. Argenti,
E. Dupoux and
J. Mehler

The experiment consisted of a series of 24 trials that started with the display of a word (written in French) followed by the auditory presentation of two Korean words. The task was to decide which of the two Korean words was the correct translation of the word displayed. Subjects could replay the Korean words as often as they wanted before responding.

fMRI design and acquisition

Brain imaging was performed using event-related fMRI while the participants listened to a total of 128 sentences in four different languages: French, Korean, Japanese and Polish. Japanese and Polish were both unknown to our subjects, and thus served as a control for French and Korean sentences. In addition, Japanese was more similar to Korean than Polish, as attested by our pre-test. We were interested in assessing whether this difference in similarity would show up on the cortical activations. (. . .) To ensure that the subjects paid attention to the sentences, they were required to perform a fragment detection task. Following each sentence, after a 500 ms delay, a 400 ms fragment was played. The subject had to indicate, by pressing one of two response buttons, whether this fragment had appeared in the sentence or not. Before scanning, subjects performed a practice run of 12 trials on this task. (. . .)

We studied language perception and comprehension using behavioral methods and fMRI in a group of Korean adults adopted in their youth by French families, as well as in a control group of native French subjects. Three main results were observed. First, behaviorally, the adopted subjects could not distinguish sentences in their native language from sentences coming from various languages. Nor could they identify Korean words in a forced-choice task, or detect fragments from Korean sentences better than native French controls. Second, the fMRI data revealed no differences in brain activation when the adopted subjects listened to Korean relative to an unknown language such as Polish or Japanese. Third, the cortical regions that responded more to the known language, French, than to other foreign languages were similar in the adopted subjects and in the native French control group. However, the observed activations in this comparison had a broader extent in the native French subjects than in the adopted subjects. (. . .)

These data do not support a strong version of the crystallization hypothesis. Indeed, this hypothesis led us to expect activations specific to Korean in the adopted Koreans, and a differential pattern of activated areas between the French and Korean groups, while listening to French. Actually, the activation patterns in the Koreans were remarkably similar to those of the native French group, at least in terms of the regions that were activated. Slight differences were detected in the extent and amount of activation; these are further discussed below. In both groups, there was a large activation of left-lateralized temporal and interior frontal regions when listening to French sentences, but essentially no detectable activation of this network when listening to Korean sentences relative to two other, unknown, languages. This provides evidence in favor of the reversibility of plastic changes associated with language acquisition in the first few years of life. The subjects in our study had been adopted between 3 and 8 years of age. If the brain circuits that subserve language acquisition had started to crystallize during this time period, we would have expected to see larger differences between the two groups. Our data rather suggest that when a second language is learned early on, this acquisition does not necessarily involve different brain systems

Text B2.3
C. Pallier,
S. Dehaene,
J. B. Poline,
D. LeBihan,
A. M. Argenti,
E. Dupoux and
J. Mehler

than those involved in learning the native language. On the contrary, the second language may become represented in the very areas that normally represent the first language. This conclusion fits with a previous PET [Positron Emission Tomography] study of spoken language comprehension in which late but highly fluent learners of a second language were found to have patterns of activation indistinguishable from those of native speakers (Perani, Paulesu, Galles, Dupoux, Dehaene, Bettinardi, Cappa, Fazio, & Mehler, 1998). Compared with this previous study, the present study has the advantage that the adopted subjects were not selected because they were exceptionally gifted for foreign languages. Our study suggests that any child, if placed in the unusual situation of having to learn a new language between 3 and 8 years of life, can succeed to a high degree, and that they do so using the same brain areas as are recruited for first-language acquisition.

The behavioral observations that we collected also support the adopted subjects' claim that they have forgotten their native language. On a Korean sentence identification test, they did not perform any better than native French subjects. This was true also in the lexical test that involved selecting the appropriate meaning for common words, and in the speech segment detection test. One limitation of these tests (except possibly for the third) is that they were not designed to test for subtle, implicit, remnants of Korean in the adopted subjects. Early experience with Korean may have left implicit unconscious traces at the level of the microcircuitry of the language processing areas that our behavioral and fMRI methods did not detect. If they exist at all, however, such traces must be small and perhaps take the form of 'dormant' synaptic changes that cannot be revealed with classical fMRI subtraction methods. Such traces might be revealed by using a learning paradigm. For example, more extensive retraining experiments (which could not be performed in the half-day visit on the present study) might reveal faster learning of Korean in subjects who had early exposure to Korean relative to control subjects, as has been observed in both animals and humans (Tees & Werker, 1984; Knudsen, 1998; Au, Knightly, Jun, & Oh, 2002). We are in the process of devising such a training test, to assess whether the adopted Koreans can perceive phonetic contrasts that exist in Korean but not in French better than native French listeners. (. . .)

 Task B2.13

> Although no differences were found between the adopted Korean and French subjects in the detection of Korean, some small differences were found between the two groups when being exposed to French. What, in your opinion, would that suggest about the ability to learn a new language at a later age?

Text B2.3
C. Pallier,
S. Dehaene,
J. B. Poline,
D. LeBihan,
A. M. Argenti,
E. Dupoux and
J. Mehler

Although the bulk of our results suggests a high degree of similarity between adopted subjects and native French subjects, we found two differences between the groups worth discussing. First, when listening to French relative to foreign stimuli, although the same anatomical regions were activated, the extent of activation was larger in the native French participants relative to the Korean adopted subjects. This result speaks to the main question that our experiment was designed to address: can the second language replace the first? The results discussed above imply that it can, but this latter finding suggests that such replacement may not be complete. (. . .) The native French subjects' greater experience with French may have resulted in a widening of the cortical

Text B2.3
C. Pallier,
S. Dehaene,
J. B. Poline,
D. LeBihan,
A. M. Argenti,
E. Dupoux and
J. Mehler

maps for language processing, and/or an increase in their responsivity, in comparison to the Korean subjects. Though we have informally observed that the adopted Koreans have a very good command of French, subsequent research will be needed to assess whether they might differ from native speakers in subtle ways. Alternatively, the relative difference in the extent of activation between groups, could be due to larger activation in the adopted subjects by the foreign stimuli. Contrary to the control group, which was composed of native students from the Paris area, the adopted subjects had agreed to participate in the study because of their adopted status, and were coming to Orsay from other parts of France specifically for this study. Given their natural curiosity for their special status, we cannot exclude the possibility that they deployed greater attention to the foreign language stimuli than the control subjects. It is also possible that their unusual history of language acquisition has caused a greater responsivity of left-hemispheric language areas to any form of linguistic input. At present, we cannot discriminate between the above explanations.

A second difference between the groups was observed in the Korean–Polish subtraction, which revealed an activation in the right STS that was stronger in the native French group than in the adopted subjects. This unpredicted result may be due to a relative inhibition in the Koreans relative to the French group, when listening to Korean. This interpretation raises the issue of the possible role of inhibition in the forgetting of the first language. However, the fact that the two groups did not differ in the Korean–Japanese and French–Korean substractions, mitigates this interpretation. (. . .) It is often not realized that this sort of empirical finding can be submitted to two radically different theoretical interpretations. It is useful to distinguish between interference and 'crystallization' accounts of the critical period hypothesis. Both accounts agree that language acquisition starts very early on, probably guided by genetically driven mechanisms partly dedicated to processing speech inputs. However, they differ in their interpretation of subjects' difficulties in acquiring a second language. According to the crystallization account, a window of brain plasticity is open at birth and progressively closes as the brain networks for language become stabilized, under the possible influence of maturational and/or experiential factors. In this view, plasticity is temporally limited and progressively lost. According to the interference account, on the other hand, the presence of processes and representations attuned to the first language acts as a filter that distorts the way a second language can be acquired. In this view, the loss of plasticity in language areas, if it exists at all, plays only a minor role compared to the interference imposed on the maintenance of a first language by the processing of the second.

Task B2.14

➤ In Unit B1 we noted that reading critically means to be aware of inappropriate cohesive devices such as 'therefore' or phrases such as 'it shows that' that may reflect conclusions and that are not really warranted by the data of the literature cited. In the next section of the article in which the authors draw their conclusions, can you detect any such unwarranted conclusions?

Text B2.3
C. Pallier,
S. Dehaene,
J. B. Poline,
D. LeBihan,
A. M. Argenti,
E. Dupoux and
J. Mehler

The study of adopted children provides a unique opportunity to address this theoretical distinction. Contrary to immigrants, who usually stay in contact with their home family and local language community, adopted children do not need to maintain any representation of the first language, from which they are suddenly deprived. In this situation, our data tentatively suggest that the native language is, in large part, lost and replaced by the language of the new environment. Even by 7 or 8 years of age, plasticity in language areas is still sufficiently high to promote an essentially complete recovery of normal language. This conclusion fits with lesion studies that found good, if incomplete, recovery from large left hemisphere lesions, or even from left hemispherectomy when performed before the age of 9 (Vargha-Khadem, Carr, Isaacs, Brett, Adams, & Mishkin, 1997). Our results complement these studies by showing that this form of plasticity is not limited to exceptional situations of brain insult or intractable epilepsy, but that it also occurs in the normal brain. This view is not incompatible with the notion that puberty is associated with a biologically determined reduction in language learning ability.

 Task B2.15

➤ In Unit A6, we discussed the evidence for and against the 'critical age' hypothesis. In your opinion, are the results presented in this article relevant to the critical age hypothesis or not? And if so, would they support the critical age hypothesis?

The results from this study support the idea that languages can be completely lost when there is no longer exposure to the language. On the other hand, we have to keep in mind that the techniques mentioned can only measure what they measure, and they can certainly not detect every possible brain activity going on. Therefore, for the moment, such results are valid, but more refined techniques may tell us more. In addition, there is always the need to compare this type of neuro-imaging with other types of data, in particular behavioural data. In that sense the article presented here is a good example of both the possibilities and limitations of neuro-imaging.

CONCLUDING REMARKS

In this unit we have discussed three different articles that each support the DST view that the language knowledge in the mind is not static but in a continuous flux. Cook argued that the multilingual mind is not the same as the monolingual mind. Hansen and Chen showed that aspects of languages that were once learned may be forgotten after a time of non-use and that the stages of forgetting mirror those of learning. The final article by Pallier *et al.* shows that even an L1 learned and used for several years may be forgotten after an extended period of non-use.

Unit B3
Historical perspectives extended

In Unit A3, we gave a brief overview of the influences of theories on the development of SLA research and then focussed on how the presumed role of L1 on L2 in SLA research has shifted over the years. Therefore, in this unit we have selected two articles that also focus on the influence of the L1 on L2. At the end of Unit A3, we pointed out the enormous popularity and influence of Krashen's hypotheses, and we will end this unit with an article that addresses these hypotheses.

Corder's, 'The significance of learner's errors' (1967) gives a good flavour of the time when Contrastive Analysis had fallen out of favour and the newly accepted claim was that L2 acquisition is very similar to L1 acquisition. The second reading provides an example of cross-linguistic influence, but an unusual one: Kellerman (2000) shows that L2 users are cautious in transferring their L1 knowledge. The third reading is by Gregg (1984), who, as we shall see, reacted quite strongly against Krashen's idea that 'learning' could not lead to 'acquisition'.

'The significance of learners' errors' by S. P. Corder (1967) in *International Review of Applied Linguistics in Language Teaching*, 5, 161–170

Text B3.1
S. P. Corder

This article was written after the Contrastive Analysis Hypothesis (CAH) had fallen into disfavour. Corder first summarises the demise of the CAH and explains in what way error analysis (EA) may still be useful for several reasons. He seems to accept the idea of an innate grammar without much hesitation, but maintains that L2 learning is different from L1 learning. Corder argues that even though not all L2 errors are caused by the L1, error analysis could be useful because L2 errors could give us insight into the processes of second-language acquisition.

Task B3.1

➤ In this article, Corder focuses on the differences between L1 and L2 learning. He wrote this article at the time that behaviourism and contrastive analysis had fallen into disfavour and the emphasis was on innateness. Corder, who was a proponent of error analysis, argues that L2 errors (like L1 errors) can give insight into the learning process. Can you think of an example of an L2 error that you (or someone else) used to make that would evidently reveal an aspect of the L2 learning process.

Both linguistics and psychology are in a state at the present time of what Chomsky has called 'flux and agitation' (Chomsky, 1966). What seemed to be well established doctrine a few years ago is now the subject of extensive debate. The consequence of this for language teaching is likely to be far reaching and we are perhaps only now beginning to feel its effects. One effect has been perhaps to shift the emphasis away from a preoccupation with teaching towards a study of learning. In the first instance this has shown itself as a renewed attack upon the problem of the acquisition of the mother-tongue. This has inevitably led to a consideration of the question whether there are any parallels between the processes of acquiring the mother-tongue and the learning of a second language. The usefulness of the distinction between acquisition and learning has been emphasised by Lambert (1966) and the possibility that the latter may benefit from a study of the former has been suggested by Carroll (1966).

The differences between the two are obvious but not for that reason easy to explain: that the learning of the mother-tongue is inevitable, whereas, alas, we all know that there is no such inevitability about the learning of a second language; that the learning of the mother-tongue is part of the whole maturational process of the child, whilst learning a second language normally begins only after the maturational process is largely complete; that the infant starts with no overt language behaviour, while in the case of the second language learner such behaviour, of course, exists; that the motivation (if we can properly use the term in the context) for learning a first language is quite different from that for learning a second language.

On examination it becomes clear that these obvious differences imply nothing about the processes that take place in the learning of first and second language. Indeed the most widespread hypothesis about how languages are learned, which I have called behaviourist, is assumed to apply in both circumstances. These hypotheses are well enough known not to require detailing here, and so are the objections to them. If then these hypotheses about language learning are being questioned and new hypotheses being set up to account for the process of child language acquisition, it would seem reasonable to see how far they might also apply to the learning of a second language.

Within this new context the study of errors takes on a new importance and will I believe contribute to a verification or rejection of the new hypothesis.

This hypothesis states that a human infant is born with an innate predisposition to acquire language; that he must be exposed to language for the acquisition process to start; that he possesses an internal mechanism of unknown nature which enables him from the limited data available to him to construct a grammar of a particular language. How he does this is largely unknown and is the field of intensive study at the present time by linguists and psychologists. Miller (1964) has pointed out that if we wished to create an automaton to replicate a child's performance, the order in which it tested various aspects of the grammar could only be decided after careful analysis of the successive stages of language acquisition by human children. The first steps therefore in such a study are seen to be a longitudinal description of a child's language throughout the course of its development. From such a description it is eventually hoped to develop a picture of the procedures adopted by the child to acquire language (McNeill, 1966).

Task B3.2

➤ In Unit B1, we suggested that sometimes authors leave off references on purpose, for different reasons. Although we cannot be certain anymore, it seems as if one reference has been left out on purpose in the paragraph above. Which reference seems to be implicit and what could possibly have been a reason for leaving off this citation?

The application of this hypothesis to second language learning is not new and is essentially that proposed fifty years ago by H. E. Palmer (1917). Palmer maintained that we were all endowed by nature with the capacity for assimilating language and that this capacity remained available to us in a latent state after the acquisition of a primary language. The adult was seen as capable as the child of acquiring of foreign language. Recent work (Lenneberg, 1966) suggests that the child who fails for any reason i. e. deafness, to acquire a primary language before the age of 12 thereafter rapidly loses the capacity to acquire language behaviour at all. This finding does not of course carry with it the implication that the language learning capacity of those who have successfully learned a primary language also atrophies in the same way. It still remains to be shown that the process of learning a second language is of a fundamentally different nature from the process [of] primary acquisition.

Text B3.1
S. P. Corder

If we postulate the same mechanism, then we may also postulate that the procedures or strategies adopted by the learner of the second language are fundamentally the same. The principal feature that then differentiates the two operations is the presence or absence of motivation. If the acquisition of the first language is a fulfilment of the predisposition to develop language behaviour, then the learning of the second language involves the replacement of the predisposition of the infant by some other force. What this consists of is in the context of this paper irrelevant.

Let us say therefore that, *given motivation*, it is inevitable that a human being will learn a second language if he is exposed to the language data. Study of language aptitude does in some measure support such a view since motivation and intelligence appear to be the two principal factors which correlate significantly with achievement in a second language.

I propose therefore as a working hypothesis that some at least of the *strategies* adopted by the learner of a second language are substantially the same as those by which a first language is acquired. Such a proposal does not imply that the course or *sequence* of learning is the same in both cases.

Task B3.3

➤ In the paragraph above Corder postulates the working assumption that whereas the *strategies* may be the same in the acquisition of L1 and L2, the course or *sequence* of acquisition may not. He does not expound on this further. What could he mean by strategies and sequence of learning? Based on your reading of Section A, do you find this a reasonable working hypothesis?

Text B3.1
S. P. Corder

We can now return to the consideration of errors made by learners. When a two year old child produces an utterance such as 'This mummy chair' we do not normally call this deviant, ill-formed, faulty, incorrect or whatever. We do not regard it as an error in any sense at all, but rather as a normal childlike communication which provides evidence of the state of his linguistic development at that moment. Our response to that behaviour has certain of the characteristics of what would be called 'correction' in a classroom situation. Adults have a very strong tendency to repeat and expand the child's utterance in an adult version; something like 'Yes, dear, that's Mummy's chair'.

No one expects a child learning his mother-tongue to produce from the earliest stages only forms which in adult terms are correct or non-deviant. We interpret his 'incorrect' utterances as being evidence that he is in the process of acquiring language and indeed, for those who attempt to describe his knowledge of the language at any point in its development, it is the 'errors' which provide the important evidence. As Brown and Fraser (1964) point out the best evidence that a child possesses construction rules is the occurrence of systematic errors, since, when the child speaks correctly, it is quite possible that he is only repeating something that he has heard. Since we do not know what the total input has been we cannot rule out this possibility. It is by reducing the language to a simpler system than it is that the child reveals his tendency to induce rules.

In the case of the second language learner it might be supposed that we do have some knowledge of what the input has been, since this is largely within the control of the teacher. Nevertheless it would be wise to introduce a qualification here about the control of input (which is of course what we call the syllabus). The simple fact of presenting a certain linguistic form to a learner in the classroom does not necessarily qualify it for the status of input, for the reason that input is 'what goes in' not what is *available* for going in, and we may reasonably suppose that it is the learner who controls this input, or more properly his intake. This may well be determined by the characteristics of his language acquisition mechanism and not by those of the syllabus. After all, in the mother tongue learning situation the data available as input is relatively vast, but it is the child who selects what shall be the input.

(. . .)

It is in such an investigation that the study of learner's errors would assume the role it already plays in the study of child language acquisition, since, as has been pointed out, the key concept in both cases is that the learner is using a definite system of language at every point in his development, although it is not the adult system in the one case, nor that of the second language in the other. The learner's errors are evidence of this system and are themselves systematic.

 Task B3.4

> In the following few paragraphs, Corder explains a distinction between 'mistake' and 'error', a distinction he was the first one to make. If you are not familiar with this distinction, try to predict for yourself what the distinction could be, and if you are already familiar with these terms, you might try to remember what they entail and see if they match Corder's original definition. In your opinion, is it always possible to differentiate between an error and a mistake?

The use of the term systematic in this context implies, of course, that there may be errors which are random, or, more properly, the systematic nature of which cannot be readily discerned. The opposition between systematic and non-systematic errors is important. We are all aware that in normal adult speech in our native language we are continually committing errors of one sort or another. These, as we have been so often reminded recently, are due to memory lapses, physical states, such as tiredness and psychological conditions such as strong emotion. These are adventitious artefacts of linguistic performance and do not reflect a defect in our knowledge of our own language. We are normally immediately aware of them when they occur and can correct them with more or less complete assurance. It would be quite unreasonable to expect the learner of a second language not to exhibit such slips of the tongue (or pen), since he is subject to similar external and internal conditions when performing in his first or second language. We must therefore make a distinction between those errors which are the product of such chance circumstances and those which reveal his underlying knowledge of the language to date, or, as we may call it his transitional competence. The errors of performance will characteristically be unsystematic and the errors of competence, systematic. As Miller (1966) puts it, 'It would be meaningless to state rules for making mistakes'. It will be useful therefore hereafter to refer to errors of performance as mistakes, reserving the term error to refer to the systematic errors of the learner from which we are able to reconstruct his knowledge of the language to date, i. e. his transitional competence.

Mistakes are of no significance to the process of language learning. However the problem of determining what is a learner's mistake and what a learner's error is one of some difficulty and involves a much more sophisticated study and analysis of errors than is usually accorded them.

A learner's errors, then, provide evidence of the system of the language that he is using (i. e. has learned) at a particular point in the course (and it must be repeated that he is using some system, although it is not yet the right system). They are significant in three different ways. First to the teacher, in that they tell him, if he undertakes a systematic analysis, how far towards the goal the learner has progressed and, consequently, what remains for him to learn. Second, they provide to the researcher evidence of how language is learned or acquired, what strategies or procedures the learner is employing in his discovery of the language. Thirdly (and in a sense this is their most important aspect) they are indispensable to the learner himself, because we can regard the making of errors as a device the learner uses in order to learn. It is a way the learner has of testing his hypotheses about the nature of the language he is learning. The making of errors then is a strategy employed both by children acquiring their mother tongue and by those learning a second language.

Although the following dialogue was recorded during the study of child language acquisition (Van Buren, 1966) it bears unmistakable similarities to dialogues which are a daily experience in the second language teaching classroom:

Mother: Did Billy have his egg cut up for him at breakfast?
Child: Yes, I showeds him.
Mother: You what?
Child: I showed him.
Mother: You showed him?
Child: I seed him.
Mother: Ah, you saw him.
Child: Yes I saw him.

Text B3.1
S. P. Corder

Here the child, within a short exchange appears to have tested three hypotheses one relating to the concord of subject and verb in a past tense, another about the meaning of *show* and *see* and a third about the form of the irregular past tense of see. It only remains to be pointed out that if the child had answered I *saw him* immediately, we would have no means of knowing whether he had merely repeated a model sentence or had already learned the three rules just mentioned. Only a longitudinal study of the child's development could answer such a question. It is also interesting to observe the techniques used by the mother to 'correct' the child. Only in the case of one error did she provide the correct form herself: *You saw him*. In both the other cases, it was sufficient for her to query the child's utterance in such a form as: *you what?* or *You showed him*? Simple provision of the correct form may not always be the only, or indeed the most effective, form of correction since it bars the way to the learner testing alternative hypotheses. Making a learner try to discover the right form could often be more instructive to both learner and teacher. This is the import of Carroll's proposal already referred to.

We may note here that the utterance of a correct form cannot be taken as proof that the learner has learned the systems which would generate that form in a native speaker, since he may be merely repeating a heard utterance, in which case we should class such behaviour, not as language, but in Spolsky's term (Spolsky, 1966) 'language-like behaviour'. Nor must we overlook the fact that an utterance which is superficially non-deviant is not evidence of a mastery of the language systems which would generate it in a native speaker since such an utterance must be semantically related to the situational context. The learner who produced 'I want to know the English' might have been uttering an unexceptionable sentiment, but it is more likely that he was expressing the wish to know the English language. Only the situational context could show whether his utterance was an error or not.

 Task B3.5

> In Unit A4 on the Multilingual Mind, we argued that the different languages a person knows are all part of one dynamic system, which would imply that L1 rules or habits may play an important role in the learning of an L2. Keeping in mind what Corder has argued so far, what kind of view do you expect him to have concerning the role of L1 in the learning of an L2?

Text B3.1
S. P. Corder

Although it has been suggested that the strategies of learning a first and second language may be the same, it is nevertheless necessary at this point to posit a distinction between the two. Whilst one may suppose that the first language learner has an unlimited number of hypotheses about the nature of the language he is learning which must be tested (although strong reasons have been put forward for doubting this) we may certainly take it that the task of the second language learner is a simpler one: that the only hypotheses he needs to test are: 'Are the systems of the new language the same or different from those of the language I know?' 'And if different, what is their nature?' Evidence for this is that a large number, but by no means all, of his errors, are related to the systems of his mother-tongue. These are ascribed to interference from the habits of the mother-tongue, as it is sometimes expressed. In the light of the new hypotheses they are best not regarded as the persistence of old habits, but rather as signs that the learner is investigating the systems of the new language. Saporta (1966) makes this point clear, 'The internal structure of the (language acquisition) device, i. e. the learner, has gone relatively unexplored except to point out that one of its components is the grammar of the learners native language. It has generally been assumed that the effect of this component has been inhibitory rather than facilitative'. It will be evident that the position taken here is that the learner's possession of his native language is facilitative and that errors are not to be regarded as signs of inhibition, but simply as evidence of his strategies of learning.

Text B3.1
S. P. Corder

Task B3.6

➤ Many applied linguists would agree that Corder's article is a 'classic' that contains many ideas that are still pertinent today. Read through the article again and try to distil a list of five or six main observations and/or distinctions that Corder makes concerning learners' errors. Do you feel that some of these observations are compatible with ideas you have read about earlier in the book, such as DST, Vygotskian notions or Krashen's hypotheses? In what ways do you think they are compatible or not?

Even though Corder argues for many notions and distinctions that are important in SLA and that were later put forward and popularised by Krashen, error analysis as a separate discipline became outmoded for many linguists who focussed more on language universals. However, many second-language teachers and applied linguists, especially those teaching or studying homogeneous groups of L1 speakers, have remained appreciative of the approach because it has been self-evident that learners with the same L1 have similar problems in learning a particular L2.

In the next reading, we will address another way in which the L1 may influence the L2, but this time on how the knowledge of L1 may inhibit choices in the L2.

'What fruit can tell us about lexicosemantic transfer: A non-structural dimension to learners' perceptions of linguistic relations' by Eric Kellerman, 2000

Text B3.2
E. Kellerman

(Translated as 'Lo que la fruta puede decirnos acerca de la transferencia léxicosémantica: una dimensión no estructural de las percepciones que tiene el aprendiz sobre las relaciones lingüísticas' in C. Muñoz (Ed.), *Segundas lenguas. Adquisición en la aula.* Barcelona: Ariel, pp. 21–37)

The second reading is from Kellerman, who gives an overview of his research over the years on the role of the mother tongue in SLA. He focuses on what he calls 'homoiophobia'. He shows that L2 learners are often very cautious in transferring L1 structures to the L2 because they seem to work on the hypothesis that there are constraints on how similar the L1 can be to the L2. In this paper he expands on findings reported on in 1978 by arguing that these constraints are related to 'prototypicality' effects, a notion borrowed from the field of cognitive linguistics. A prototypical use of the English verb *break* is in a sentence such as 'I broke the cup', but a non-prototypical use would be 'His voice broke when he was 14.'

 Task B3.7

➤ Sometimes expressions or proverbs can be translated literally from one language to another and sometimes they cannot. Think of such a proverbial expression in your language that is similar to an expression in another language. Does this surprise you? Try to think of the nature of your surprise and think of other similar pairs of constructions that might add further to your explanation.

Text B3.2
E. Kellerman

Homoiophobia describes the feelings learners of second languages sometimes have that for particular language structures (syntactic, lexical, whatever), L1 and L2 *should* differ from each other. While expectations of difference are unlikely to be confounded when L1 and L2 are typologically very remote (let us say Spanish and Japanese), such feelings have been shown to occur even when L1 and L2 are actually closely related and the structures in question are in reality congruent.

Homoiophobia can be clearly seen in the reactions of Dutch learners to English idiomatic expressions with direct equivalents in Dutch. Unless these appear in authentic English texts (where they are gratefully received), they are viewed with suspicion or amusement. Potentially bilingual idioms will be rejected in acceptability tasks, for instance Kellerman (1977). A useful example of such an idiom (which also shows how close Dutch and English are) is *to drink someone under the table/iemand onder de tafel drinken* ('to win a bout of competitive drinking'). No doubt partially as a response to the unusual combination of manner and motion in the verb, Dutch speakers of English treat the English version as a jokey literal translation. It seems as if confrontation with one's native language structures through the mirror of another language heightens metalinguistic awareness, and the sudden appreciation of the unusual in one's own tongue serves to constrain expectations about what is possible in the language one is learning.

(. . .)

 Task B3.8

➤ In this article, Kellerman refers back to a much-cited article he wrote in 1978. Based on that article, Second Language Acquisition specialists often use the term 'Kellerman effect', but Kellerman himself calls it homoiophobia (from Greek *homoio* meaning 'similar or same' and *phobia* meaning 'fear'). How would you define this term in your own words?

Text B3.2
E. Kellerman

As mentioned above, English and Dutch are closely related languages. Take the highly polysemous verb *break*. This verb has literal usages, such as in *he broke his leg* or *she broke the vase*, and metaphorical usages like *she broke his heart, he broke his promise*. Another way to look at the different usages of break is in terms of concreteness: *legs, vases, a voice breaking with emotion*, and *the waves breaking on the shore* are all concrete, while *broken promises*, *hearts* and *world records* are clearly abstract. All these usages and several more can be translated into Dutch using the cognate verb *breken*. Nevertheless, despite the considerable overlap between English and Dutch in this respect, Dutch learners of English have remarkably consistent expectations of equivalence of *breken* and *break*, but these expectations also happen to *under*estimate the degree of usage similarity between the two verbs.

In the 1978 study, I asked a large number of Dutch learners of English with widely varying proficiencies to decide whether *break* would be the appropriate translation for *breken* in a number of exemplary sentences similar to those in the previous paragraph. Bar one exception (light rays *refract*, rather than break, in water, though the Latin origin of that verb is revealing), all the Dutch cases could be directly translated using *break*. Thus if learners rejected L1–L2 equivalence, they would not be doing so because of their knowledge of English – the intuition had to come from within, so to speak. The percentage of acceptances of translation equivalence for each usage is given below in Table B3.1, which, for purposes of clearer exposition, has been reduced from the original 17 stimuli to 12:

Table B3.1 Does 'breken' = 'break'?

%	Does breken = break?
100	1. he broke his *leg*
97.5	2. she broke his *heart*
79	3. the *cup* broke
75	4. a broken *man*
74	5. he broke his *word*
63	6. they broke the world *record*
43	7. the *waves* broke against the rocks
35	8. Who broke the *ceasefire*?
27	9. The enemy *resistance* was broken
21	10. His *fall* was broken by a tree
21	11. His *voice* broke when he was 13
11	12. Some workers broke the *strike*

In Table B3.1, no account has been taken of different proficiency levels of the subjects, as these do not materially affect the overall rank ordering of predictions of equivalence. It will be noted that there is considerable variation in acceptability of equivalence, ranging from 100% acceptance for *breaking a leg* to 89% rejection for *breaking a strike*.

The nice spread of acceptance scores begs explanation: why should some usages be deemed more likely to be English than others, given the obvious cognateness of the two verbs? Let us just consider the implications of Table B3.1. The variable acceptability of usages of *break* in English does not support a transfer position of the type proposed by Andersen's 'transfer to somewhere' principle (Andersen, 1983), which, among other things, predicts that learners will only transfer an entity from the L1 when the L2 seems to provide evidence of equivalence. As *breken* and *break* are obviously cognate, there is 'transfer to somewhere', but it is not wholesale. At least as far as this study is concerned, there are constraints on the assumption of equivalence. This is what is meant by *homoiophobia*.

(. . .)

Text B3.2
E. Kellerman

If one takes those *breken* usages which have a high rejection rate in English and asks other Dutch learners to translate them, we gain insight into the strategies employed to avoid equivalence in performance. Consider the following examples:

Original text	**Dutch learner's translation**
Zijn val werd door een boom gebroken	As he hit a tree in his fall, his fall was not that serious
His fall was by a tree broken	His fall was softened by a tree
'His *fall was broken by a tree*'	

Original text	**Dutch learner's translation**
Het kopje brak	The cup was broken
The cup broke	The cup burst
'The *cup broke*'	

Original text	**Dutch learner's translation**
Zijn stem brak toen hij 13 jaar oud was	His voice changed when he was 13
His voice broke when he 13 year old was	His voice deepened when he was 13
'His *voice broke when he was 13 years old*'	

Cases like these are examples of what might be called 'avoidance' (Schachter, 1974), though avoidance in Schachter's sense is usually understood to occur as a response to prior experience of problematic differences between L1 and L2 – one avoids what is known to be difficult. Here, however, we are dealing with anticipated differences, *homoiphobia* again.

Let us now return to the various usages of *breken* in Dutch and seek an explanation for the variable constraints on translatability we detected in Table B3.1. To do this, I will invoke the notions of prototypicality and category membership by considering fruit. 'Fruit' is a natural category, a superordinate term, with very many members. Suppose one were asked to list as many different types of fruit as one can in 30 seconds. My list (and other northern Europeans' lists) might differ from a Spaniard's list, but I would certainly include apples, pears, bananas, oranges, and a good sprinkling of strawberries, raspberries, peaches, and cherries as well. No doubt fruits like figs, kiwis, mangos, and various other berries would also be named. Some European show-offs might even list durians, mangosteens, rambutans or tomatoes. However, not only are fruit like durians and tomatoes unlikely to appear frequently, but even when they are listed, they will probably appear towards the end (as 30 seconds flies by!). *They are not what we think of as prototypical fruits.*[1] Those which we think of first are seen as the best examples of the category fruit; they are representative of the category. Even though a botanist will classify a tomato as a fruit, in the popular conception it is only a marginal one, if one at all. It is more likely to find itself among the vegetables.

---

1   This is not to deny that for people living in SE Asia, durians, mangosteens and rambutans may indeed be prototypical fruits.

Task B3.9

➤ As mentioned above, a prototype is basically a 'best example' of a category. If you were to write three sentences in your L1 with the equivalent of the verb 'break' to show clearly what it means, which sentences would you write? We will return to this question later.

Now take the category 'types of *breken* or *break*'. My hypothesis was essentially this: the more prototypical a usage of *breken* is perceived to be, the more likely a learner is to assume equivalence in English. If we were to ask Dutch speakers to list example sentences illustrating how this verb may be used, one might guess that some usages would appear more frequently than others. Perhaps usages involving concrete brittle household goods or bones would figure prominently. However, such a task might never elicit the more marginal usages. A different approach is needed to determine whether the variation in perceived translatability of *breken* by *break* is determined by intuitions about prototypicality of the usages in Dutch.

Text B3.2
E. Kellerman

At this point in the article, Kellerman describes how he went about obtaining a prototypicality index for all his sentences. He asks native speakers to sort the sentences according to 'similarity'. For example, he would ask subjects to judge whether 'to break someone's heart' was more similar to 'to break a cup' than 'to break a record'. (In Unit C3 we suggest another way of obtaining a prototypicality index.)

Here is the similarity matrix deriving from the Dutch speakers' judgements for the 12 *brekens* reported in this chapter. Figures represent the percentage of subjects who placed a given pair in the same pile.

Text B3.2
E. Kellerman

Table B3.2 Similarity matrix for Dutch usages of *breken*

waves	leg	Cup	Man	heart	word	ceasefire	strike	record	voice	fall	resistance
28	leg										
28	90	Cup									
06	02	02	Man								
06	02	02	82	heart							
06	0	0	16	30	word						
08	0	0	08	14	40	ceasefire					
06	0	0	08	14	36	90	strike				
08	06	06	12	18	26	30	26	record			
14	04	04	12	14	08	06	12	18	voice		
36	14	14	02	08	10	08	02	04	22	fall	
08	0	0	04	12	30	68	34	22	08	12	resistance

The matrix is to be read rather like a distance chart in a road atlas, though in reverse, as the higher the figure the closer the two meanings are assumed to be. Note below how, for instance, 12% placed the Dutch equivalent of *a broken man* and *they broke the world record* in the same pile, indicating that these two *breaks* were not considered particularly alike, while 82% placed *a broken man* and *she broke his heart* together. He *broke his leg* and *the cup broke* are placed together by 90% of the subjects, while the same number placed *who broke the ceasefire?* and *some workers broke the strike* together. There are, however, 8 potential pairings which never occur, and a further 26 (out of a grand total of 66) which fewer than 10% of subjects sort together:

Then Kellerman describes a specific visualisation method to show that the judgements can be organised along two dimensions a N–S [North–South] dimension and an E–W [East–West] dimension:

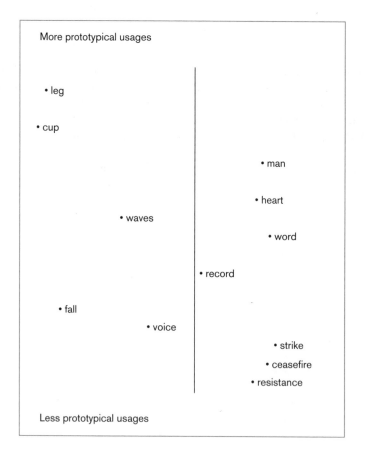

Task B3.10

➤ Below, in accounting for the differences in translatability judgments, Kellerman makes a distinction between 'prototypicality' (going from top to bottom), which also involves frequency of use, and 'concreteness' (going from left to right), which has to do with the more literal sense of a word referring to things or events that can be seen. Which do you predict will account better for the choices made by Dutch students? Why?

Text B3.2
E. Kellerman

Now what does the arrangement of the usages along these dimensions mean, if anything? My suggestion is that the N–S dimension is actually a scale of prototypicality; the most northerly usages are the ones that best exemplify the prototypical meaning of *breken*. As we move down south, so we encounter usages which are increasingly removed from this prototypical sense. What is interesting about this ordering is that metaphorical usages like *man* and *heart* are positioned relatively high up, yet I would maintain that the sense of breaking in these usages is still prototypical.

(. . .)

Now to the W–E dimension. This seems much easier to interpret. As we move in an easterly direction, it seems as if the first five usages, *cup*, *leg*, *fall*, *waves* and *voice* are all concrete or literal or imaginable or however we want to label usages that refer to directly perceivable events: we hear or see cups breaking, feel or see (on an X–ray) or hear legs being broken; see or experience a fall being broken, see or hear waves breaking on the rocks, and hear a breaking voice. It is debatable whether the remaining senses along the W–E axis are perceivable at all, though their effects may well be. For this reason, let us call this dimension the concreteness dimension.

(. . .)

The next step is a simple one – we are looking for evidence that prototypicality plays a role in determining Dutch learners' judgements about the translatability of the various meanings of *break*, so all we need to do is statistically compare the rank order of the usage translatability judgements in Table B3.1 with the ordering of the usages along the prototypicality dimension (. . .), and for good measure we can also compare those judgements to the rank ordering of the usages along the concreteness dimension (. . .), as in Table B3.3 below:

Table B3.3 Comparison of translatability data with ordering of usages along prototypicality and concreteness dimensions

Prototypicality dimension	Translatability judgements	Literal–metaphor dimension
1. leg	1. leg	3. cup
3. cup	2. heart	1. leg
4. man	3. cup	10. fall
2. heart	4. man	7. waves
7. waves	5. word	11. voice
5. word	6. record	6. record
6. record	7. waves	9. resistance
10. fall	8. ceasefire	2. heart
11. voice	9. resistance	4. man
12. strike	10. fall	8. ceasefire
8. ceasefire	11. voice	5. word
9. resistance	12. strike	12. strike

Task B3.11

➤ Look back at the three examples you wrote down with your L1 equivalent of 'break' (see Task B3.9). Are they similar to the first five or six in the two left-hand columns? Can you think of an explanation for the differences or similarities that are in line with Kellerman's reasoning?

Text B3.2
E. Kellerman

It does not require a statistician to see that there is a clear resemblance between the rank orders of the left (prototypicality) and the middle (translatability) columns, and that there is little resemblance between the rank orders of the right (concreteness) and translatability columns. Indeed statistical tests would bear this out. A reasonable inference is, then, that the dimension of prototypicality, rather than concreteness, largely underlies the translatability of *breken* by *break*.

How then to explain the fact that 'the cup broke' was only deemed acceptable English by 79% of subjects, if it represents a prototypical *breken* usage? Here we must acknowledge an additional factor, the pragmatic force of an utterance. Although *het kopje brak* (literally 'the cup broke') is correct Dutch, a number of learners (21%) in fact rejected 'the cup broke'. The majority of these were amongst the most proficient learners (3rd year university level). Some were asked why they had rejected this stimulus, and the response was that 'things do not break spontaneously – there must be an agent'. Hence their translation of *het kopje brak* would be 'the cup was broken', or 'someone broke the cup'. A further solution was 'the cup cracked'. This latter is interesting as 'to crack' in Dutch (*barsten*) can only be used intransitively, unlike *breken*. Less proficient learners were less troubled by this transitive/intransitive problem, and furthermore, if one provides a warrant for the act of breaking (e.g. 'he squeezed the cup until it —'), no learner of English hesitated to fill in the single word 'broke'.

These results show that the influence of the first language, at least where word meaning is concerned, can be rather subtle. One might expect that Dutch learners would happily capitalise on cross-language similarity, but the ones I typically come into contact with do not, not even the least experienced. They proceed with caution; they assume a subset of potential equivalence, and that subset can be predicted probabilistically from their intuitions as native speakers of Dutch. No amount of structural linguistic comparison in the spirit of Lado's Contrastive Analysis Hypothesis would predict or account for the phenomena I have described above, nor would Schachter's Avoidance Hypothesis. The above data stress the need for a psycholinguistic dimension to predicting and explaining transfer from L1 to L2.

(. . .)

Conclusion

In this chapter, I have suggested that even in cases of languages which are typologically close, learners may not fully exploit obvious similarities between L1 and L2 (homoiophobia). Instead they adopt a conservative approach to parallelism between languages. Decisions as to what usages may be translated into the L2 seem to depend on intuitions of prototypicality in the native language. The notion of prototypicality, it is claimed here, derives from actual physical experience of activities like breaking (and standing), and it is the degree of prototypicality of a particular usage that will determine whether it is considered transferable or not. As far as polysemy is concerned, it is clear that structural comparison of L1 and L2 will not necessarily serve as a source of predictions about transfer, necessitating a search for psycholinguistic constraints that determine homoiophobia.

Task B3.12

➤ Kellerman argues that neither the Contrastive Analysis Hypothesis nor Avoidance strategy (Schachter, 1974) can account for his findings. Therefore, he suggests a 'psycholinguistic dimension' to the explanation. What does he mean by 'psycholinguistic' in particular? Do you find this an appropriate term for the phenomenon?

Among other things, Kellerman's article nicely points out that even such a phenomenon as 'transfer' is not a straightforward matter. Corder, in the first reading in this unit, argued that the L1 may facilitate the acquisition of L2, but as we have now seen, in non-prototypical instances, the learner may be careful in transferring the L1 knowledge to the L2. We can assume that in Kellerman's translatability judgments the learner is conscious of the choices s/he makes. The next article focusses on the notion of 'consciousness'.

'Krashen's Monitor and Occam's Razor' by Kevin R. Gregg in *Applied Linguistics* (1984) 5, 79–100

The final article in this chapter is an excerpt from Gregg (1984) who wrote a very critical review of Krashen's five hypotheses, as discussed in Unit A3. In this excerpt, we have kept only comments on the 'acquisition versus learning' hypotheses because it is most pertinent to the focus of this book. The review was not very well received because of its abrasive tone, but it has been included here because he was one of the first ones to point out that although he agrees that Krashen's observations make common sense, Krashen had failed to give any substantial evidence to support his claims. However, Gregg himself also appeals very much to anecdotal and subjective information to substantiate his own claims.

Task B3.13

➤ The expression 'Occam's razor' in Gregg's title refers to a logical principle attributed to the mediaeval philosopher William of Occam. The principle states that one should not make more assumptions than the minimum needed. In other words, those concepts, variables or constructs that are not really needed to explain the phenomenon should not be mentioned. By doing so, a theoretical model will become much easier, and there is less chance of introducing inconsistencies, ambiguities and redundancies.

Keeping the title in mind, what do you predict Gregg will say about the 'acquisition' versus 'learning' distinction that Krashen makes (see information in Unit A3)?

**Text B3.3
K. R. Gregg**

Among the effects on second language acquisition research of the Chomskyan revolution in linguistics has been the creation of something of a vacuum as far as theory is concerned. The older behaviorist model of acquisition has been discarded, for the very good reason that it was hopelessly inadequate, but no new model of comparable scope has been put forward, although a great deal of interesting work has been done in specific areas of acquisition research. There are several possible explanations for this state of affairs. One is that second language acquisition may simply be too difficult and too complex to be dealt with in a single theory. This seems like a reasonable idea, especially as Chomsky (1980: 90) has suggested the same sort of thing for first language acquisition, where there are arguably fewer variables to worry about:

> (. . .) we should not expect a unitary answer to the question 'What is knowledge of human language and how does it arise?' Rather, we will find that the question was wrongly put; it does not identify a natural kind.

Another possible reason for this absence of an overall theory of second language acquisition, I believe, is the growing rift between second language acquisition research and generative linguistic theory, which itself is a consequence of the increasing difficulty of linguistics, and of what is perceived as the increasing irrelevance of theoretical linguistics to acquisition research. This, if true, is to be regretted, since a theory of language acquisition without a linguistic theory is doomed to inconsequentiality. Both of these reasons should be kept in mind when we examine, as I propose to examine, what is probably the most ambitious and most influential attempt in recent years to construct an overall theory of second language acquisition; namely, Stephen Krashen's 'Monitor Theory'.

Krashen presents five main hypotheses that 'make up a coherent theory of second language acquisition' (1982: 2). I propose to examine these hypotheses one by one, to look at the evidence and argumentation that Krashen offers in support of them, and (to let the cat out of the bag) to show that he has not in fact presented us a coherent theory of second language acquisition. The hypotheses are:

1. the Acquisition/Learning Hypothesis
2. the Monitor Hypothesis
3. the Natural Order Hypothesis
4. the Input Hypothesis, and
5. the Affective Filter Hypothesis.

1. The acquisition/learning hypothesis

The Acquisition/Learning Hypothesis 'states that adults have two distinct and independent ways of developing competence in a second language' (1982: 10): acquisition, which is 'subconscious', and learning, which is conscious. Evidently, 'acquisition' is to be identified with Chomsky's language acquisition device (LAD), although Krashen is not very clear on this: 'acquisition' is 'a process similar, if not identical, to the way children develop ability in their first language' (1982:10). 'Learning', on the other hand, refers to 'conscious knowledge of a second language, knowing the rules, being aware of them, and being able to talk about them' (1982: 10).

The distinction between conscious and unconscious knowledge, or between conscious and unconscious mental processes, is certainly by now uncontroversial. But

Krashen of course recognizes this, and his hypothesis goes much further. Specifically, he claims that (1) 'adults can access the same natural "language acquisition device" that children use' (1982: 10), and (2) that 'learning does not "turn into" acquisition' (1982: 83).

One effect of these two claims is to reduce drastically the difference in language learning ability between children and adults, since on the one hand both have the same LAD, and on the other the adult's superior cognitive abilities, memory, pragmatic knowledge, etc., are apparently next to useless. Thus the Acquisition/Learning Hypothesis places a heavy burden on Krashen to explain just why it is that so few adults successfully acquire a second language. This is where the Affective Filter Hypothesis comes in, which we will consider later.

First of all, it is important to see just what is involved in the claim that acquisition in adults is the same as acquisition of a first language by children. Although Krashen does not make himself clear on this, he seems to be giving the LAD a scope of operation much wider than is normally the case in linguistic theory. Indeed, he seems to equate the LAD with unconscious acquisition of any sort. This is certainly not in the spirit of the inventor of the term: as Chomsky and others have argued (see, e.g. Chomsky, 1980: 40–4, 54–5, 92 ff.; Lightfoot, 1982: 42–9), the mind is modular, that is, LAD is but one of various 'mental organs' that interact with each other and with input data to produce linguistic competence. Conceptual knowledge, real-world knowledge, common sense, pragmatic competence, etc., are all necessary for understanding and using language, but they are not part of LAD.

In any case, the LAD as a construct is intended to describe the child's initial state, before being presented with primary linguistic data (PLD). The LAD is constrained by innate linguistic universals (Universal Grammar, or UG) to project grammars to account for the PLD. Indeed, the terms LAD and UG are in effect interchangeable (see, e.g. Chomsky, 1981: 34–5). It is not immediately clear how this concept of LAD can be applied to an adult. Not only is an adult not in an initial state with respect to language, but he also is endowed with a much richer set of cognitive structures, which theoretically at least could enable him to violate the constraints of UG (and thus put him at a disadvantage vis-à-vis the child in terms of language acquisition). For instance, to take an example frequently used by Chomsky (e.g. 1975: 30–3):

1   The man is tall.
2   Is the man tall?
3   The man who is tall is in the room.
4   Is the man who is tall-in the room?
5   *Is the man who-tall is in the room?

As Chomsky points out, given (1)–(3) as PLD, it would be perfectly logical to form a hypothesis about yes/no question formation in English that would lead to the production of (5) rather than (4). In fact such a hypothesis is simpler than the correct hypothesis. None the less, children do not form such hypotheses, presumably because they cannot, their hypothesis-forming powers are restricted by UG; here, by the principle of structure-dependency. But what is to the point here – an adult can form such a hypothesis; Chomsky did it, and so can you. Whether in fact adult second language learners do violate UG is another question; a very interesting question in fact, and one that is worth investigating. Krashen provides no evidence one way or the other. In any case, it is not enough merely to say that adults have a language acquisition device, without specifying what that device does.

Task B3.14

➤ In the following sections Gregg (and Krashen) use the term 'conscious' and 'unconscious' in rather non-technical terms. Drawing on the information presented in Unit A1, what do you think that they mean by these terms?

Text B3.3
K. R. Gregg

Of course, some adults do attain native-speaker competence in a second language, and of course such competence is largely unconscious; no one has ever denied this. In this sense, the Acquisition/Learning Hypothesis is not a hypothesis, but simply an observation. But Krashen also claims that 'learning' cannot become 'acquisition', and this is what makes the hypothesis interesting. Unfortunately, it also makes the hypothesis a bit inconsistent, since if 'learning' cannot become 'acquisition', and if as Krashen goes to unnecessary lengths to remind us (1982: 92–4) most of our knowledge of a second language is necessarily unconscious, then it makes little sense to call 'learning' one of 'two distinct and independent ways of developing competence in a second language'. But that is by the way. The question is, is the claim a valid one?

On the face of it – and this is what makes it the interesting part of the hypothesis – it is nonsense, and Krashen himself seems to be aware of this: 'The idea that we first learn a new rule, and eventually, through practice, acquire it, is widespread and may seem to some people to be intuitively obvious. It was, I thought, exactly the way I learned languages myself (1982: 83). Well, it certainly does seem intuitively obvious that at least some rules can be acquired through 'learning'. I learned the rules for forming the past tense and gerundive forms of Japanese verbs by memorizing the conjugation chart in my textbook and – like most of my classmates – was pretty much error-free after a couple of days, with no input other than a bit of drill. I learned the super-polite forms of Japanese adjectives by asking a friend for a few examples and a short explanation. I know these rules, I am aware of them, I can talk about them. These seem to me to be cases of 'learning' becoming 'acquisition', and fairly typical cases at that.

It is worth emphasizing not only that I 'learned' these rules, but that I 'acquired' them – if error-free, rapid production is a criterion for 'acquisition'. And I acquired them instantaneously, to all intents and purposes, and in the absence of virtually any input. I stress this point since Krashen insists on several occasions that 'acquisition' 'always takes time and requires a substantial quantity of input data' (1982: 114). This seems plausible on the face of it, but it is not enough simply to make such an assertion dogmatically, in the absence of evidence. After all, first language acquisition proceeds on the basis of a rather small quantity of PLD, and at such a rapid pace that linguists in the Chomskyan tradition feel justified in idealizing to instantaneous acquisition. And, as Roeper (1981:5) points out, 'later stages in acquisition are often marked by a sudden ability in children to move from no response to a correct response (in an experiment) with no evidence of intermediate trial hypotheses'. (See, e.g. Carey, 1978 on lexical acquisition in three- and four-year-olds.)

 Task B3.15

➤ Paradis, quoted in Unit A5, argues that controlled processing is quite different from automated processing, but that automated processes can replace controlled processes. In the previous section, Gregg argued that learning can lead to acquisition. In your opinion, is his explanation compatible with Paradis's observations?

The burden is thus on Krashen to disprove the intuitively obvious proposition that 'learning' can become 'acquisition'. Unfortunately, he does not do this. He does show (1982: 84–7) that 'learning' need not precede 'acquisition', but he does not show that it cannot. He gives three arguments: (1) sometimes there is 'acquisition' without 'learning'; (2) sometimes 'learning' never becomes 'acquisition' – e.g., someone who knows the rule but still keeps breaking it; (3) no one knows anywhere near all the rules. These are all true, but are not evidence that 'learning' cannot become 'acquisition'. More specifically, Krashen has not shown that presentation of rules, explanation, etc., cannot facilitate the acquisition of a second language, which is the very strong claim that he is making.

> Text B3.3
> K. R. Gregg

One of the problems with the Acquisition/Learning Hypothesis is that Krashen plays fast and loose with his definitions. 'Acquisition' is a process leading to competence; 'learning' is evidently a state ('knowing the rules, being aware of them, and being able to talk about them'). If Krashen means that a given state cannot become a process, he'll get no argument from me, or from anyone else. But the position that he is attacking is the position that learning (not 'learning') can lead to acquisition (not 'acquisition') of what one has learned. Krashen is simply wrong when he says, 'Some second language theorists have assumed that children acquire, while adults can only learn' (1982: 10). He is confusing learning with 'learning'; I know of no one who has maintained that adults can only 'learn', and to argue against such a position is to attack a straw man.

Task B3.16

> In the previous section, Gregg distinguished learning (without quotation marks) from 'learning' with quotation marks, without really defining the difference between them. In your opinion, what difference is he trying to point out and do you agree with him that there may be a difference between the two kinds of learning?

Similarly, Krashen fails to make clear what he means by 'conscious' and 'subconscious', as McLaughlin (1978) has pointed out. Specifically, does 'subconscious' mean 'not accessible to the conscious', or simply 'not conscious at a given moment'? Does 'conscious' entail 'incapable of becoming unconscious'? If by definition the 'subconscious' is inaccessible, and conscious 'learning' is always accessible, then Krashen's claim that 'learning' does not become 'acquisition' is of course trivially true, but uninteresting. On the other hand, if (some) unconscious knowledge is capable of being brought to consciousness, and if conscious knowledge is capable of becoming unconscious – and this seems to be a reasonable assumption – then there is no reason whatever to accept Krashen's claim, in the absence of evidence. And there is an absence of evidence.

> Text B3.3
> K. R. Gregg

As it stands, then, the Acquisition/Learning Hypothesis, far from being 'potentially the most fruitful concept for language teachers that has come out of the linguistic sciences' in recent years (Stevick, 1980: 270), is either clearly false or trivially true.

Task B3.17

➤ Krashen's hypotheses, especially the distinction between acquisition and learning, have had an enormous influence on the way teachers (especially in the US) thought a second language should be taught in schools: much less focus on grammar and form and much more emphasis on 'comprehensible input'. If Gregg were right in his conclusion that the distinction is false or only trivially true, what would the consequences for teaching a second language be?

Gregg's article pointed out that Krashen's model needed empirical evidence and as we have shown in Units A1 and A5, a great deal of research has been done to test Krashen's hypotheses, but there is still no hard evidence whether learning can lead to acquisition. On the other hand, as we will show in Unit B7, there is a great deal of evidence that explicit focus on the grammar of a second language does in many cases lead to better mastery of the L2. From a DST perspective this is not surprising: all kinds of different factors will affect the system continuously, including explicit instruction.

CONCLUDING REMARKS

Both the Corder and the Gregg article in this unit on the historical perspectives in SLA have shown some of the debate that has gone on since behaviourism was challenged and universalist theory, including Krashen's SLA model, became in vogue. In universalist theory the role of the L1 in SLA was downplayed, but as all three articles have argued and Kellerman's article has shown with empirical evidence, the L1 does indeed play a role. This is no surprise if we accept the premise that all the languages a person knows are part of one system.

Unit B4
The multilingual mind extended

The main focus in Unit A4 was on processing in relation to the multilingual lexicon. Two of the most pertinent questions raised there were: do bilingual (or multilingual) speakers have separate lexicons for the different languages they know, and can languages be switched off. The articles we have included here address these questions.

In the first article, Kroll and Stewart (1994) provide evidence for the 'Revised Hierarchical Model' (RHM). This model deals with the relation between the concepts (abstract 'ideas' that can, but need not be verbalised), the L1 lexicon and the L2 lexicon. The main point of this model is that words in the L1 have direct links to their conceptual representations (these words are 'conceptually mediated'), whereas words in the L2 do not have direct links to the related concepts and have to be accessed via the L1. Their paper is a report of an empirical study involving reaction time measurements. Since this is a method of investigation that is frequently applied in this field of research, we have included the methodological details of their paper to illustrate the type of argumentation and the methodological issues for this type of studies.

The second article, by Kroll and Dijkstra (2002), approaches the multilingual lexicon from the point of view of activation theory, which we discussed in Section A. This article provides an overview of the most relevant questions in relation to the multilingual lexicon. These questions are answered with reference to the Bilingual Interactive Activation (BIA) model, of which the authors first give an outline. The most important point raised in this article is whether selective access must be assumed; i.e. when we read or listen to language utterances, do we concentrate on one particular language only, or are all the languages we know always active in processing? These and other issues are discussed in separate sections for comprehension and production.

The two articles in this unit are logically linked because the Revised Hierarchical Model proposed in the article by Kroll and Stewart (1994) is criticised in the article by Kroll and Dijkstra (2002). According to Kroll and Dijkstra, Kroll and Stewart's major assumption that the lexicons of different languages are stored separately must be questioned.

Text B4.1
J. F. Kroll and
E. Stewart

'Category interference in translation and picture naming – evidence for asymmetric connections between bilingual memory representations' by Judith F. Kroll and Erika Stewart (1994) in *Journal of Memory and Language, 33*, 149–174

A frequently quoted article about the differences between translating from L1 to L2 and L2 to L1 (referred to as *translation asymmetry*) is Kroll and Stewart (1994). In this rapidly developing field, this article is now rather dated because it still worked with the assumption that the L1 and L2 lexicons are separated, from a spatial point of view. However, it is a good example of the focus of the research in the early 1990s. The article describes three experiments involving picture naming and bilingual translation to investigate the role of the conceptual representations in translation tasks. The researchers want to find out if lexical items in the second language have direct links with the relevant concepts or if that link is mediated by the related items in the first language. These two possibilities are graphically represented in Figure B4.1. Referring to the terminology introduced in Unit A4, the article is about the question whether the organisation of the multilingual mind is co-ordinate or subordinate (see Figure A4.3 in section A4). An additional question that is addressed is how the organisation develops with increasing levels of L2 fluency.

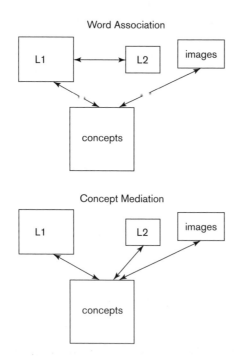

Figure B4.1 Two models of language interconnection in which second language (L2) words are associated to first language (L1) words (Word Association) or directly linked to concepts (Concept Mediation).

Task B4.1

➤ Suppose you are quite fluent in an L2 and you have to translate L1 words into L2 words for a series of items, under which of the following two conditions do you think you will be able to do so faster? Why?

(1) All the pictures are related to the same semantic domain (e.g. words all pertain to clothing items).
(2) The pictures are not related to the same semantic domain (e.g. words pertain to different fields such as clothing, body parts, musical instruments, kitchen items, transportation, tools, buildings, household objects, fruits, toys, animals, and food).

The article starts with a review of earlier studies in this area. The authors then describe the current study, which is a follow-up study of Kroll and Curley (1988), summarised as follows:

Kroll & Curley (1988) argued that if fluent bilinguals were conceptually mediating L2 words, then it should be possible to obtain direct evidence of having accessed conceptual or semantic information during translation by manipulating a variable that should influence the speed of conceptual access. Subjects named words, translated words, and named pictures in Ll and L2 under two different list conditions. In one, the lists of words or pictures were semantically categorized; in the other, the lists contained a mixed set of exemplars from a number of different semantic categories. Kroll and Curley (1988) predicted that only bilingual subjects who were relatively fluent in L2, and hence concept mediators, should benefit from the semantic organization of the list.

Text B4.1
J. F. Kroll and
E. Stewart

The results were counterintuitive. The translation performance of the more fluent subjects was indeed influenced by the semantic organization of the list, but the effect was one of interference rather than facilitation. Fluent subjects took longer to translate into L2 when the list was semantically categorized than when it was randomly mixed. Similarly, it took all subjects longer to name pictures in L1 when the list was categorized than when it was randomly mixed. This pattern of results supported the claim that there was a developmental shift from word association to concept mediation because only the more fluent subjects, whose overall data provided support for concept mediation, also showed category inference in translation. Still, it was puzzling that there was category interference rather than category facilitation.

Task B4.2

➤ Are the results found by Kroll and Curley in agreement with your expectations expressed in Task B4.1? Could you account for this result from the point of view of a spreading activation model as discussed in Unit A4?

In the present article, we have left out the discussion of the first experiment, the purpose of which was to replicate the Kroll and Curley study with a larger subject group and a more sophisticated design, in which all participants are tested in all conditions (a 'within subject design'). The results of this experiment (a translation task) showed the same effect as the one that was found in the earlier study: fluent subjects took longer to translate into L2 when the list was semantically categorised than when it was randomly mixed. The authors label this finding in the rest of the article as the 'category interference effect'. They argue that this interference is caused by the linking ('mapping') between the concepts and the words. Apparently, it takes more time to find the right word when one has to respond to pictures that represent related concepts. These findings lead the authors to investigate these matters further in two additional experiments, using different research techniques. In the first of these (the second experiment), the links between concepts and lexical items is investigated for native speakers of English using a picture naming task. In a picture naming task, the participants sit behind a screen on which a picture appears. As soon as the picture appears, they have to say what the picture represents. The time elapsed between the moment the picture appears on the screen and the participant's reaction is measured. Clearly, picture naming can be done in L1 and in L2. In their final experiment, the authors investigate the direction of the links between concepts and lexical items in L1 and L2 using a bilingual translation task. We have included the report on the latter experiment without further abridgement to demonstrate all the conventional steps in this type of research, followed by an abbreviated version of the final experiment.

In the following section, the authors argue that conceptual activation may actually account for the interference effects found in advanced subjects. When a concept such as clothing is activated, subjects may need more time to 'inhibit' the competing lexical entries. (For an analogy see the 'ping pong balls' analogy in Unit A4). The authors also argue that such conceptual activation may be deactivated by an intervening task, namely reading a word aloud, even if this word is semantically related to the same semantic domain.

Experiment 2: naming pictures and words in alternation

Text B4.1
J. F. Kroll and
E. Stewart

The results of Experiment 1 replicated the category interference effect in picture naming reported by Kroll and Curley (1988). The results also showed that the category interference effect can be obtained using a within-subject design. We suggested earlier that the source of semantic interference in picture naming is in the mapping between semantic representations and lexical entries. If this interpretation is correct, then repeated access to concepts within the same semantic category should increase activation at the conceptual level and produce corresponding activation at the lexical level. If the task is to choose a single lexical entry that is the best name for the pictured object, then the additional activation should produce competition among close alternatives, and hence interference, rather than facilitation.

In the second experiment we tested this hypothesis by spacing picture naming trials and thereby reducing the requirement for repeated conceptual access. Subjects named the pictures and words used in Experiment 1 in lists that were again seman-tically categorized or randomly mixed. However, each list alternated between words and pictures from trial to trial. For example, in a categorized list a subject might name a picture of a mitten, read the word 'hat' aloud, name a picture of a jacket, read the word 'belt' aloud, and so forth. A great deal of evidence suggests that word naming can be accomplished without conceptual access (e.g. Lupker, 1984; Potter, Kroll, Yachzel, Carpenter, and Sherman, 1986). Therefore, the strict alternation of words and pictures in Experiment 2 should maintain the same level of lexical activation within lists but diminish the degree of conceptual activation relative to Experiment 1. If category interference in picture naming is a result of selecting a lexical candidate amidst greater lexical activation, then we would expect to find the same interference effect in Experiment 2 as observed in Experiment 1. If, however, the category inter-ference effect results from increased conceptual activation and its lexical consequences, then we would expect the effect to be substantially diminished in Experiment 2 as compared to that in Experiment 1.

Task B4.3

➤ One of the most difficult things in running an experiment is to show cause and effect between the factors under investigation in different conditions. To be certain that only the relevant factors affect the results, the possible other factors need to be kept as constant as possible. In the following sections, what are the factors under investigation and which factors have been controlled for?

Method

Stimulus materials

The stimulus materials were identical to those described for Experiment 1 with a single change. Each of the lists contained alternating trials of words and pictures. The order of alternation was counterbalanced across stimulus lists.

mitten

hat

jacket

belt

shirt

The *Stimulus materials* section for Experiment 1 was as follows: The pictures were 120 line drawings of objects from 12 semantic categories (clothing, body parts, musical instruments, kitchen items, transportation, tools, buildings, household objects, fruits, toys, animals, and food). The words were the names of the objects in English. The word frequency of the object names ranged from 0 to 413 times per million with a mean of 31.7 (Francis and Kucera, 1982). Categorized lists of words and pictures were constructed such that each list included between 2 and 4 categories. All of the members of a given category appeared in sequence within the list. Four lists of 30 items each were generated for pictures and a corresponding set of four lists was generated for words. A set of randomized lists was constructed such that each random list of

Figure B4.2 Examples of categorized picture and word lists used in Experiment 1

pictures or words contained exemplars from each of the semantic categories in a random order. The modality of each list was blocked so that pictures and words never appeared in the same list. Examples of the categorized stimulus lists are shown in Figure B4.2.

Apparatus and procedure

The apparatus and procedure were similar to those described for Experiment 1. There were some changes, however. Subjects were instructed to name aloud whatever stimulus appeared and were told to anticipate that the stimulus modality would alternate from trial to trial. They again named words and pictures in four lists, of which two were categorized and two were randomized. In addition, the incidental recall task was not given at the end of the session.

The *Apparatus and procedure* section for Experiment 1 was as follows: Stimulus words and pictures were presented one at a time in one field of a three and one-half field tachistoscope (Scientific Prototype Model N-1000). [A tachistoscope is a device that shows pictures very briefly for a fixed amount of time. Now computers are used for this kind of experiment.] A second field contained a fixation point. Prior to the presentation of the word or picture there was a 100-ms warning tone followed by a 400-ms delay. During this initial 500-ms period the fixation field remained in view. Immediately following the delay period the word or picture target was presented for 500-ms. A voice-activated relay (Scientific Prototype audio threshold detection relay, 761 G) stopped a counter (Scientific Prototype Model N-1002) that was activated at the onset of the target display [The relay and counter, also outdated devices now, served to measure the exact amount of time before the subject started to speak.] Each subject viewed four lists: categorized words, categorized pictures, randomized words, and randomized pictures. Different versions of the stimulus materials were constructed to ensure that subjects would receive different words and pictures in the categorized and randomized conditions and that no word or picture would be repeated for a given subject. The order of lists was counterbalanced across subjects. Subjects were instructed to name the word or picture as rapidly and as accurately as possible. Naming latencies [latencies are the amounts of time needed to respond to the stimulus] were measured to the nearest millisecond.

Subjects

Sixteen undergraduate college students participated in the experiment for course credit. All subjects had normal or corrected-to-normal visual acuity and were native English speakers.

 Task B4.4

➤ In the following section, the results of the experiment are given. If you are familiar with statistical analyses, you will probably have no trouble understanding them. If not, you may just have to assume that the authors have done the analyses correctly and read for those findings that are significant ($p < .05$) or not. To keep track of the findings, you may want to write down in two separate columns the factors that are significant and those that are not.

Results and discussion

Text B4.1
J. F. Kroll and
E. Stewart

Analyses of variance were performed on mean naming latencies and percentage errors. The means are shown in Table B4.1.

Table B4.1 Mean response latencies (in milliseconds) and percentage errors (as shown in parentheses) to name words and pictures in Experiments 1 and 2 in categorized and randomized lists contexts and mean percentage incidental recall in Experiment 1

	Target modality			
List conditions	Words		Pictures	
Experiment 1: Blocked modalities				
Categorized lists	514	(0%)	819	(7.3%)
Mean % recall	18.5%		43.2%	
Randomized lists	516	(0.0%)	783	(6.4%)
Mean % recall	13.3%		27.4%	
Magnitude of category interference	−2ms		36ms	
Experiment 2: Alternating modalities				
Categorized lists	549	(2.1%)	792	(14.7%)
Randomized lists	542	(2.3%)	798	(11.4%)
Magnitude of category interference	7ms		−6ms	

Reaction times

Word naming was again reliably faster than picture naming (by approximately 250-ms), $F(1,15) = 150.87$, $p < .001$ in the analysis by subjects, and $F(1,238) = 932.95$, $p < .001$ in the analysis by items. However, the category interference effect in picture naming was completely absent under the alternation conditions. The interaction between stimulus modality (word or picture) and type of list (categorized or randomized) was not significant, $F(1,15) = 1.02$, $p < .10$ for subjects, and $F(1,238) < 1$, for items. The type of list had no overall effect on naming either words or pictures, $F(1,15) < 1$ for subjects, and $F(1,238) < 1$ for items.

Percentage errors

The overall error rate was higher in Experiment 2 (7.6%) than in Experiment 1 (3.4%), but as in Experiment 1, there were more errors in picture naming (13.1%) than in word naming (2.2%), $F(1,15) = 34.22)$, $p < .001$. Although there were slightly more errors in picture naming under the categorized conditions, the interaction between type of list and stimulus modality was not significant, $F(1,15) = 3.01$, $p > .10$.

The main result of Experiment 2 was that the category inference effect in picture naming was eliminated when picture naming alternated with word naming. A second aspect of the results was that a comparison of Experiments 1 and 2 showed that the alternation of word and picture naming produced a cost in the speed of word naming. Word naming was approximately 35 ms longer in the mixed modality lists of Experiment 2 than in the blocked conditions of Experiment 1. However, picture naming took approximately the same time in the two experiments. The cost to word

SECTION
B

Extension

Text B4.1
J. F. Kroll and
E. Stewart

naming is consistent with the interpretation that word and picture naming require different processing. The results of Experiment 2 suggest that it is not simply increased lexical activation that produces category interference in picture naming. Rather, continuous access to related concepts produces increased activation at the conceptual level which makes it more difficult to then select the single lexical entry that best names the picture.

Task B4.5

➤ In the section above it has become clear that native speakers, like advanced non-native speakers, show an effect of 'category interference' and that the previously 'counterintuitive interference effects' for advanced L2 speakers are actually due to the fact that the lexical items in the two lexicons are conceptually mediated. Now, let us return to the two models represented in Figure B4.1. Does either of these models say anything about the direction of the links between L1 and L2 lexical items? In other words, does it say in which direction – from L1 to L2 or from L2 to L1, the translation would go fastest? If you are bilingual yourself, what is your experience? Can you translate a word from L1 to L2 as fast as the other way round?

In their third experiment, the authors want to find out why bilinguals translate faster from their L2 into their L1 than the other way round. This effect is called translation asymmetry or directional asymmetry. We have included a report of Experiment 3 without experimental detail, followed by the general discussion and conclusion of the article.

Unpublished data from Kroll and Curley (1986) and from Kroll and Stewart (1989) are shown in Table B4.2 as a function of the direction of translation and the fluency of the subjects. The specific details of these two experiments differ, but the main point is that in each experiment subjects performed the translation task in both directions and the results were always the same: Subjects were consistently faster to translate into the first language than into the second language. This translation asymmetry requires modification of both the concept mediation and word association models shown in Figure B4.3. Each of those models makes differential predictions about translation into L2 and picture naming in L2, but neither model specifies any directional asymmetry. In past studies we considered the possibility that it was harder to access the pronunciation of an L2 word than of an L1 word. However, when we compared translation performance with naming performance on the same words, we found that subjects were somewhat slower to name L2 words, but the magnitude of the difference between L1 and L2 naming was small relative to the difference between the two forms of translation. We hypothesized (Kroll and Sholl, 1991; Kroll and Sholl, 1992; Kroll and Stewart, 1990) that the two forms of translation reflect two distinct routes to translation: Translation from L2 into L1 is accomplished on a lexical basis, whereas translation from L1 to L2 requires concept mediation. The process of concept mediation should require additional time for the same reason that pictures take longer to name than words, and thus the time to translate from L1 to L2 should be longer than the time to translate from L2 to L1.

Table B4.2 Data from Kroll and Curley (1986) and Kroll and Stewart (1989) on
the time to perform bilingual translation (in milliseconds) as a function of the
direction of the translation task

| | Direction of translation | |
Study	L1 to L2	L2 to L1
Kroll and Curley (1986)*		
More fluent subjects	1729	1318
Less fluent subjects	2079	1596
Kroll and Stewart (1989)		
More fluent subjects	1267	1175
Less fluent subjects	1612	1230

*In each of these studies L1 was English and L2 was German. Data are shown for more
and less fluent subjects in each study.

To accommodate the translation asymmetry, Kroll and Stewart (1990) proposed a
revised version of the hierarchical model (see Figure B4.3). According to the model,
both lexical and conceptual links are active in bilingual memory, but the strengths of
the links differ as a function of fluency in L2 and relative dominance of L1 to L2. As
shown in Figure B4.3, L1 is represented as larger than L2 because for most bilinguals,
even those who are relatively fluent, more words are known in the native than in the
second language. Lexical associations from L2 and L1 are assumed to be stronger than
those from L1 to L2 because L2 to L1 is the direction in which second language
learners first acquire the translations of new L2 words. The links between words and
concepts, however, are assumed to be stronger for L1 than for L2.

According to this asymmetric strength model, when a person acquires a second
language beyond a stage of very early childhood, there is already a strong link between
the first language lexicon and conceptual memory. During early stages of second
language learning, second language words are attached to this system by lexical
links with the first language. As the individual becomes more proficient in the second
language, direct conceptual links are also acquired. However, the lexical connections
do not disappear when the conceptual links are established. The model also assumes
that both lexical and conceptual links
are bidirectional, but that they differ in
strength. The lexical link from L2 to L1 is
assumed to be stronger than the lexical
link from L1 to L2 because L2 words were
initially associated to L1. Likewise, the link
from L1 to conceptual memory is assumed
to be stronger than the link from L2 to
conceptual memory.

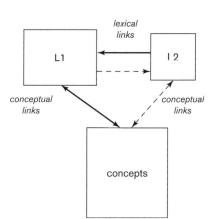

Figure B4.3 Revised hierarchical model of
lexical and conceptual representation in
bilingual memory

Text B4.1
J. F. Kroll and
E. Stewart

A clear implication of the claim that there are two routes to translation is that the two directions of translation should differ in the degree to which they are influenced by conceptual factors. Translation from L1 to L2 should be sensitive to the manipulation of semantic or conceptual information, whereas translation from L2 to L1 should be relatively independent of this type of manipulation. In Experiment 3 we asked whether there would be category interference in translation. The model makes the clear prediction that category interference should occur for fluent bilingual subjects only when they translate from L1 to L2.

The results of this experiment replicate 'the translation asymmetry found in previous studies (Kroll and Curley, 1986; Kroll and Stewart, 1989) in that translation from L1 to L2 took reliably longer than translation from L2 to L1'. Below, the authors argue that if translation from L1 to L2 requires concept mediation, then there should also be some semantic context effects (same domain versus different domains) as were found in Experiment 2, supporting their predictions on the revised hierarchical model.

Text B4.1
J. F. Kroll and
E. Stewart

The question of interest, given that we were able to replicate the translation asymmetry, was whether the two directions of translation were differentially sensitive to the effects of semantic context. If L1 to L2 was longer than L2 to L1 because the L1 to L2 translation route required concept mediation, then translation from L1 to L2 should also have been influenced by the semantic context of the lists in which translation was performed. However, if translation from L2 to L1 was performed lexically, it should not have been influenced by semantic context, and, naming latencies should also have been independent of the semantic form of the list. The data (. . .) support each of these predictions

A further analysis shows that:

Text B4.1
J. F. Kroll and
E. Stewart

. . . as predicted, there was no effect of the type of list for naming in either language. For translation, there was a category interference effect when translation was performed in the direction that was hypothesized to require concept mediation. Translation from L2 to L1 was immune to the effects of list context, consistent with the hypothesis that translation in this direction can be accomplished at a level of lexically mediated connections between the two languages.

The authors summarise the overall results of the third experiment as follows:

Text B4.1
J. F. Kroll and
E. Stewart

Overall, then, the results of Experiment 3 support the predictions of the revised asymmetric hierarchical model. Translation from L1 to L2 required concept mediation and therefore took longer to perform than translation from L2 to L1 and was also influenced by the presence of semantic context. Translation from L2 to L1 appeared to be lexically mediated, and, like naming, was uninfluenced by the semantic context in which the task was performed.

Then, the authors separately discuss the subjects' behaviour with regard to cognates, words that are very similar in both form and meaning in L1 and L2 (e.g. French *rivière* and English *river*) and non-cognates. Their data showed that category interference occurred for non-cognates. This was to be expected, as finding an L2 word for a given L1 word that is dissimilar may well involve concept mediation. However, their data show that the same effects were found for cognates. This is surprising, since concept mediation is not strictly necessary when translating an L1 word that is very similar to a word in the L2. This demonstrates that even for words that are very similar in form (and in meaning) in L1 and L2, concept mediation is used for both cognates and non-cognates, in this experiment. In their general discussion, the authors summarise their findings and draw conclusions about the underlying model.

General discussion

Text B4.1
J. F. Kroll and
E. Stewart

The three experiments described here show that there is category interference when pictures are named in semantically categorized lists (Experiment 1), that this category interference is eliminated when picture naming alternates with word naming (Experiment 2), and that a bilingual translation task which requires processing that is formally analogous to picture naming also produces category interference (Experiment 3). The findings go beyond past research in demonstrating that the analogy between picture naming and translation is limited to translation from the bilingual's first language into the second. We have hypothesized that only this translation process requires concept mediation. Translation from the second language to the first is both faster than translation from the first language to the second and is not susceptible to the effects of category interference, consistent with the claim that translation in this direction can be accomplished at a lexical level. Furthermore, words that are cognates in Dutch and English, although translated more rapidly than noncognates, also produce category interference when translation is performed from L1 to L2. This result demonstrates that the availability of shared lexical features does not necessarily imply that concept mediation can be overridden.

Task B4.6

Ask a few fluent bilinguals if they intuitively agree with what Kroll and Stewart argue. You can do so by asking them if they agree with the following two statements:

(1) When I translate a word from my L1 (e.g. *imagination*) to my L2, I first think of the general concept and then 'find' the appropriate L2 word.
(2) When I translate a word from my L2 (e.g. *attention*) to my L1, I will almost automatically 'find' the appropriate L1 word without having to think of the concept first.

Evaluating the Revised Hierarchical Model

Text B4.1
J. F. Kroll and
E. Stewart

The results of Experiment 3 supported the predictions of the revised model of bilingual memory representation shown in Figure B4.3. Translation from L2 to L1 was faster than translation from L1 to L2, as it should be if the former task could be accomplished

Extension

by accessing lexical-level language connections whereas the latter task required concept mediation. In addition, there was category interference only for the conceptually-based translation from L1 to L2. Translation from L2 to L1 was performed similarly in categorized and randomized list conditions. The conditions that produced category interference in translation also selectively produced category facilitation in recall, demonstrating the expected advantage of having translated by conceptual rather than lexical mediation. The analysis of naming latencies in Dutch and in English also supports the assumption of the model that the L2 lexicon is smaller and requires additional access time. The analysis of the cognate data in particular suggests an asymmetry in lexical processing consistent with the claim that the lexical connections are stronger from L2 to L1 than from L1 to L2. Naming latencies in L1 were unaffected by whether L2 cognates shared phonological features. In contrast, naming latencies in L2 were long when an L1 cognate had a different pronunciation, and they were fast when an L1 cognate had the same pronunciation. If the lexical connections from L1 to L2 are weaker than those from L2 to L1, and if translation from L1 to L2 requires conceptual access, as we have suggested, then the finding that cognates, like non-cognates, produced category interference in translation from L1 to L2 can be explained by the fact that cognate words in L1 do not automatically activate their L2 lexical representations.

In other work we have considered a number of additional predictions based on the asymmetry model. One hypothesis concerns the course of second language development. If second language learners acquire lexical links between L2 and L1 before they are able to conceptually mediate L2, as previous research has suggested (Chen and Leung, 1989; Kroll and Curley, 1988), then they should be able to quickly and accurately translate from L2 to L1 before they can do the same from L1 to L2. In other words, the difference between the translation performance of less and more fluent bilinguals should be greater for translation from L1 to L2 than for translation from L2 to L1 This is precisely the result we have obtained in other studies in which we have compared the translation performance of more and less fluent bilinguals (e.g., Kroll *et al.*, 1991; Kroll *et al.*, 1989). The result supports the notion that it is the ease of accessing connections between L2 words and concepts that changes most dramatically as proficiency in L2 increases.

(. . .)

Conclusions

The experiments we have reported show that there are category interference effects when picture naming and bilingual translation are performed in the context of semantically organized lists. We have argued that category interference occurs when conceptual activation in a specific semantic field creates difficulty in selecting a single lexical entry for production. We have also obtained evidence that suggests that, at least for relatively fluent but unbalanced bilinguals, there is an asymmetry between the two directions of translation that reflects differential reliance, on lexical and conceptual activation during the translation process. The data we have presented support the claim that translation from the first language to the second is conceptually mediated, whereas translation from the second language to the first is lexically mediated. Taken together, the data support the predictions of a revised model of bilingual memory representation in which crosslanguage connections between lexical representations, and between lexical representations and concepts, are asymmetric. We believe that this proposal has important implications, not only for revealing aspects of translation performance, but also for illuminating the role of language dominance in determining the form of bilingual memory representations and for suggesting new directions for exploring the general course of second language acquisition.

The basic assumption in this article by Kroll and Stewart has been that the lexicons for different languages are essentially separated. After all, if there is one big lexicon for all languages it would not make sense to argue differential access to the lexicons of different languages. In Unit A4 we have argued that the question whether or not we must assume separate lexicons for different languages is based on a spatial metaphor. When this question is approached using the activation metaphor as a starting point, the question has in fact become irrelevant. Any item from any language can be activated given the relevant combination of activators, especially frequency.

Task B4.7

➤ In the introductory section about the multilingual mind (Unit A4), it was concluded that interactive activation approach to the multilingual mental lexicon probably provides the strongest possible explanation of empirical data. How can the two statements below be explained in terms of activation?

1 Cognates are faster to translate than non-cognates.
2 Translation from L2 words to L1 words is faster than the other way around.

The next article, which was written eight years later, is an overview article for a handbook on applied linguistics by Kroll and Dijkstra (2002). Based on more recent research, it argues for the bilingual activation model and no longer accepts Kroll and Stewart's Revised Hierarchical Model as it has just been presented.

'The bilingual lexicon' by Judith F. Kroll and Ton Dijkstra in R. Kaplan (Ed.) *The Oxford handbook of applied linguistics.* Oxford: Oxford University Press, 2002, pp. 301–321

Like Unit A4, this article argues that the bilingual mental lexicon should not be seen as consisting of two separate systems in which a language must be selected before a word can be found in that language (called 'selective access'), nor should it be seen as one whole system in which one cannot select for a language (called 'nonselective access'). This article presents the Bilingual Activation Model (BIA) as the most likely model to account for the facts known so far. The information not yet covered in Unit A4 concerns the different conditions that may affect the selection of one language rather than the other one.

Even though this article was written to give non-specialists in this field an overview of the most recent findings, it is very technical and uses quite a few specialists' terms, only some of which were introduced in Unit A4. To help you through the article, we have added clarifications in square brackets and included quite a few tasks to make specific points clear.

Text B4.2
J. F. Kroll and
T. Dijkstra

How do bilinguals recognize and speak words in each of their two languages? Past research on the bilingual lexicon focused on the questions of whether bilinguals represent words in each language in a single lexicon or in separate lexicons and whether access to the lexicon is selective or not.

These questions endured because they constitute a set of correlated assumptions that have only recently been teased apart. One concerns the relation between representation and process. [Representation has to do with the architecture of the lexicon and process has to do with accessing specific items.] As Van Heuven, Dijkstra, and Grainger (1998) note, it is not logically necessary to identify selective access with segregated lexical representations and nonselective access with an integrated lexicon; the form of representation and the manner of access can be treated as independent dimensions. Another issue concerns the way in which the lexicon itself has been operationalized. Different assumptions about the information required to recognize and speak a word in the first (L1) or second (L2) language have led to models of the bilingual lexicon that differ in the types and levels of codes [codes are the phonological, morphological and semantic aspects of lexical items] that are represented.

In this chapter, we review the way in which models of the bilingual lexicon reflect different assumptions about the architecture and processing of words in two languages and then consider three central questions about lexical access:

1   What codes are activated?
2   When are these codes activated?
3   What are the critical factors that affect lexical selection?

We examine the answers to these questions first for comprehension and then for production. Because we assume that comprehension and production rely on a common representational system but differ in the problems that they pose for the system, we finally consider the implications of the comparison for reaching general conclusions about the nature of the bilingual lexicon.

Models of the bilingual lexicon

The Revised Hierarchical Model

Initial attempts to model the bilingual lexicon proposed a hierarchical arrangement to represent word forms and word meaning (e.g. Potter, So, Von Eckhart, and Feldman, 1984). These models solved the problem of whether there were integrated or separate lexicons by assuming that both alternatives were accurate but that they described different levels of representation; at the level of word form, they proposed independent lexical representations for each language, but at the level of meaning they assumed a single conceptual system. The empirical basis for these assumptions has been reviewed extensively in the recent literature, so we will not describe it here.

With these assumptions in place, the focus shifted to consider whether words in the bilingual's two languages are connected via the lexical representations or by direct access to the conceptual representations. Initial evidence suggested that the connections between lexical forms in L1 and L2 might be active early in L2 acquisition but that, by the time the bilingual achieved proficiency in L2, words in each language could access concepts directly (e.g. Chen *et al.*, 1989; Kroll *et al.*, 1988).

Kroll and Stewart (1994) proposed the revised hierarchical model (RHM) to capture the developmental consequences of a shift from lexical to conceptual processing with increasing L2 proficiency. They argued that, early in acquisition, the reliance on lexical-level connections between words in the two languages provided a means for transfer; L1 could provide the meaning for an L2 word if L2 activated its respective translation equivalent. However, unlike other models, the RHM assumed that the lexical level links remained even after conceptual processing was established for L2. The implication of the sequential acquisition of these links was a set of hypothesized asymmetries. Lexical links were assumed to be stronger from L2 to L1 than the reverse, as this was the initial direction of transfer during acquisition, and L1 was assumed to have stronger connections to concepts than L2.

(. . .)

The RHM assumed independent lexical representations for words in each language. As we will see in the sections that follow, more recent studies on comprehension and production of words in two languages suggest that the assumption of independence at the lexical level was incorrect. (See also Brysbaert, 1998; Van Heuven, Dijkstra, and Grainger, 1998.) However, even models of the bilingual lexicon that assume an integrated lexicon and parallel access must address asymmetries in the way in which words in the two languages are processed by virtue of the relative dominance of one language over the other and the context in which they occur. In comprehension, these asymmetries may be revealed in greater or faster activation of orthography and/or phonology associated with L1. In production, there may be a bias to activate and select lexical candidates in L1 even when the task requires that words are spoken in L2.

Task B4.8

➤ According to the last two sentences, where comprehension and production are compared, there is a bias to activate an L1 word rather than an L2 word. In your experience, is that always true or do you sometimes think of an L2 word before an L1 word? If so, when is this most likely to occur? Can the phenomenon be accounted for with the Bilingual Interactive Activation Model (see below and Unit A4).

The Bilingual Interactive Activation Model (BIA)

Which mechanisms should be incorporated in a processing model to implement the assumptions of an integrated lexicon and parallel access and at the same time allow simulation of asymmetric L1/L2 processing and context effects? In the domain of language comprehension, Van Heuven, Dijkstra, and Grainger (see, for instance, Van Heuven *et al.*, 1998) developed a computer model for bilingual visual word recognition that incorporates one possible proposal. The bilingual interactive activation (BIA) model (Figure B4.4) is a bilingual extension of the well-known interactive activation (IA) model for monolingual visual word recognition (McClelland and Rumelhart, 1981).

Extension

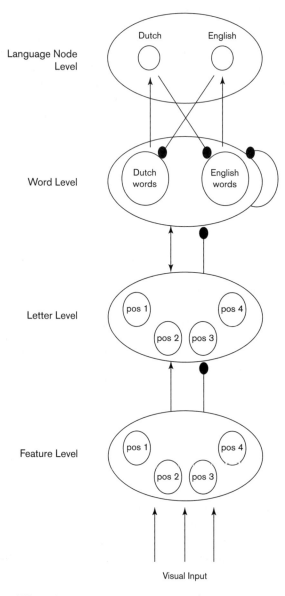

Figure B4.4 Bilingual interaction activation model (adapted from Dijkstra, Van Heuven, and Grainger 1998)

It consists of a network of hierarchically organized representational units of different kinds: features, letters, words, and language nodes. The model differs from the original IA model in two main respects: First, it *incorporates* an integrated lexicon with words from two different languages rather than one, and, second, it includes an extra layer of two language nodes that can be considered as language labels (tags) that indicate the language membership of each word.

According to the model, presentation of an input letter string leads to parallel activation of several possible words (the 'neighbourhood') irrespective of language.

Next, activated lexical candidates compete and suppress each other's activation until one item surpasses its activation threshold and is recognized. Competition takes place between items from the same and different languages through the mechanism of lateral inhibition. By means of this mechanism, the model simulates the results of several studies that showed both within- and between-language effects of the number of lexical competitors (Dijkstra, Van Heuven, and Grainger, 1998; van Heuven, Dijkstra, and Grainger, 1998).

Text B4.2
J. F. Kroll and
T. Dijkstra

Task B4.9

> Imagine a bilingual English–French speaker wants to say 'pride' and the following words (English: praise, pray, prey, pride, prove, prude. French: prier, prise, . . .) in the 'neighbourhood' become activated, how will she select the appropriate word according to the authors of this article?

The BIA model accounts for asymmetries observed in unbalanced bilinguals (stronger effects from L1 on L2 than vice versa) by assuming that, relative to L1 words, the subjective frequency of L2 words is lower for participants with lower L2 proficiency. This is implemented in terms of the model's resting level activations, which are generally lower for words in L2 than L1. As a consequence, L2 words on the whole become activated more slowly and to a lesser extent than L1 words.

Text B4.2
J. F. Kroll and
T. Dijkstra

The language nodes in the BIA model account for context effects that are dependent on specific characteristics of experiment and task. (Such context effects are discussed in detail in the next section.) These nodes modulate the relative activity in the L1 and L2 lexicons during lexical processing by exerting top-down inhibitory effects on all words of the other language (e.g., the English language node suppresses all active Dutch words). This mechanism induces stronger or weaker interactions between words from L1 and L2, thus allowing the simulation of the relative degree of language selectivity observed under various experimental circumstances.

We now review empirical studies in comprehension that support the language non-selective access hypothesis. Next, we specify under which experimental circumstances more or less selective results have been observed.

Comprehension

What codes are activated?

One of the most frequently used tasks in monolingual and bilingual word recognition research is lexical decision. In this task, participants decide as quickly and accurately as possible whether presented letter strings are words in a pre-specified target language. In monolingual lexical decision, response times are usually in the order of 500–550 ms. The same experiments performed in L2 with relatively proficient Dutch–English bilinguals led to response times of about 600 ms in L2, but for less proficient participants considerably longer latencies may be obtained (e.g. Dijkstra, Grainger, and Van Heuven, 1999).

It has been shown that presentation of a word to monolinguals induces activation not only of orthographic codes but of phonological and semantic codes, as well (e.g. Frost, 1998; James, 1975). Furthermore, monolingual studies involving ambiguous

Text B4.2
J. F. Kroll and
T. Dijkstra

words (e.g., 'bug,' referring to an insect, a spy, or a programming error) suggest that different meanings of these words are initially activated during recognition (Kawamoto and Zemblidge, 1992; Simpson, 1984). In a study on word naming, Gottlob, Goldinger, Stone, and Van Orden (1999) found that English homographs (words with separate pronunciations and meanings, such as 'lead') were read slower than homonyms (with a single pronunciation but separate meanings, such as 'spring') and control words (e.g., 'clock'). Thus, during monolingual word recognition there is *intra*lingual co-activation of lexical candidates with overlap in meaning or form.

According to a nonselective access view, it should not matter very much whether the coactivated lexical candidates belong to the same language or to another. In other words, this view predicts that there will be *inter*lingual activation of similar words during bilingual word recognition as well. In contrast, according to a language-selective access view, a presented word will activate the form and meaning representations only from the language that is currently selected.

A study by Dijkstra *et al.* (1999) indicates that cross-linguistic competition between form-similar and meaning-similar words does indeed occur. In a series of experiments, Dutch-English bilinguals were tested with English words varying in their degree of orthographic (O), phonological (P), and semantic (S) overlap with Dutch words. Thus, an English word target could be spelled the same as a Dutch word and/or could be a near-homophone of a Dutch word. Whether such form similarity was accompanied with semantic identity (translation equivalence) was also varied. This led to six different test conditions, exemplified by the following words: 'hotel' (overlap in S, O, and P codes), 'type' (S, O), 'news' (S, P), 'step' (O, P), 'stage' (O), and 'note' (P). The first three conditions are what are usually called 'cognates,' while the last three conditions contain 'interlingual homographs' or 'interlingual homophones.' Lexical decisions were facilitated by cross-linguistic orthographic and semantic similarity relative to control words that belonged only to English. However, phonological overlap produced inhibitory effects. This study indicates that (at least for L2) a presented word form leads to the activation of all representations that it is associated with, irrespective of the target language.

 Task B4.10

> ➤ The authors argue that experimental results clearly contradict the idea that first the language is selected and then the word. In what way do the intralanguage (within one language) results relate to the interlanguage (between language) results?

Text B4.2
J. F. Kroll and
T. Dijkstra

When are these codes activated?

The empirical evidence just discussed indicates that, under particular experimental circumstances, form and meaning representations of lexical candidates that belong to different languages become activated and may affect the pattern of results. A further question concerns the time course of such effects. At which moment in time is the necessary lexical candidate selected? Given that all three types of representations (Semantic, Orthographic, and Phonological) may affect the response, earlier views that assume that lexical selection always occurs at the orthographical level clearly cannot be correct.

Task B4.11

➤ In the next section the authors explain how until the very last moment items from the different languages may compete for activation. To understand the reasoning, you may want to outline the experimental set up while you are reading. Some of the words used were:

1 high frequent English–low frequent Dutch
2 low frequent English–high frequent Dutch
3 low frequent English–low frequent Dutch

You may also want to consider the following question: If you are just beginning to learn an L2, has a highly frequent L2 word been activated much in your mental lexicon?

A recent study by Dijkstra, Timmermans and Schriefers (2000) suggests that co-activation of lexical candidates from different languages occurs until relatively late in the word recognition process. In three experiments, bilingual participants processed the same set of interlingual homographs embedded in identical mixed-language lists, but each experiment had different instructions. Homographs of three types were used: high-frequent in English and low-frequent in Dutch (HFE–LFD); low-frequent in English and high-frequent in Dutch (LFE–HFD); and low-frequent in both languages (LFE–LFD). In the first experiment (involving language decision), one button was pressed when an English word was presented and another button for a Dutch word. In the second and third experiments, participants reacted only when they identified either an English word (English go/no-go) or a Dutch word (Dutch go/no-go). It turned out that participants were able to exclude effects from the non-target language on homograph identification only to a limited degree. Target-language homographs were often 'overlooked,' especially if the frequency of their other-language competitor was high. The results suggest that the two readings of a presented homograph are involved in a 'race to recognition' that is won by the fastest candidate. Even more interesting, it appeared that a slowing down of the response occurred if two candidates were relatively close to the 'finish,' that is, their recognition activation threshold. For instance, in the Dutch go/no-go task, responses to homographs were much slower in the HFE–LFD condition than in the LFE–LFD condition, although the proportion of responses did not differ between the two conditions. This suggests that selection takes place relatively late, implying coactivation of lexical candidates from different languages over a considerable period of time.

The observed effects were dependent on the relative word frequency of the two readings of the interlingual homograph. This factor, of course, is an approximation of the participants' subjective frequency, that is, the number of times they have encountered or used the word in question. For bilinguals, this subjective frequency is lower for items that belong to their L2 than to their L1, it being correlated to their L2-proficiency. If the subjective frequency of the L2-reading is negligible relative to its L1 frequency, the L2 reading will not be able to affect the lexical processing to any considerable extent. In other words, low proficiency bilinguals might show relatively weak effects from their L2 on their L1, lexicon (but strong effects from their L1 on their L2 lexicon). This point brings us to a consideration of critical factors that may affect the selection of lexical candidates during the bilingual word recognition process.

Text B4.2
J. F. Kroll and
T. Dijkstra

Critical factors that affect lexical selection

We have seen that different codes are activated and competition may occur even during response selection. However, we have already suggested, as well, that observed result patterns may not be a direct reflection of an underlying architecture. They may have been 'changed' by processing or decision strategies from the participant that relate to task demands and stimulus presentation conditions. In other words, even though the bilingual word recognition system may be basically nonselective in nature, seemingly selective results may be obtained under particular experimental circumstances. A number of influential factors have been identified in earlier studies (e.g. Grosjean, 1998), including L2-proficiency, language intermixing, task demands, and instruction. Apart from proficiency, which we referred to earlier, we now discuss these factors and their relative effect on the (non) selectivity of bilingual word recognition in more detail by summarizing a few recent studies that examined them.

Language intermixing and task demands

Language intermixing refers to whether an experiment contains exclusively items that belong to one language (blocked presentation) or items from two languages (mixed presentation). The term thus refers to one aspect of 'stimulus list composition.' In a series of three lexical decision experiments, Dijkstra, Van Jaarsveld, and Ten Brinke (1998) showed that interlingual homographs may be recognized faster than, slower than, or as fast as single language control words, depending on language intermixing and task demands. In Experiment 1, Dutch bilingual participants performed an English lexical decision task on a list that included English/Dutch homographs, cognates, and purely English control words. Response times to interlingual homographs were unaffected by the frequency of the Dutch reading and did not differ from monolingual controls. In contrast, cognates were recognized faster than controls. The first result seems to be in support of selective access models, while the second result favors non-selective access. In Experiment 2, Dutch participants again performed an English lexical decision task on homographs, but, apart from nonwords, Dutch words were included that required a 'no' response. Strong inhibition effects were obtained that depended on the relative frequency difference of the two readings of the homograph, as in the study by Dijkstra, Timmermans, and Schriefers (2000), discussed earlier.

In retrospect, the different pattern of results in Experiments 1 and 2 may be due to differences in language intermixing in the two experiments. The selective access view of bilingual word recognition is evidently rejected by the results of Experiment 2; therefore it must be that Experiment 1 created experimental circumstances in which null results for interlingual homographs arose in a language nonselective access system. Other studies have confirmed the importance of language intermixing for performance and have proposed accounts to explain the null effects (De Groot, Delmaar, and Lupker, 2000; Dijkstra et al., 1999).

In Experiment 3, Dijkstra, Van Jaarsveld, and Ten Brinke (1998) used the same stimulus materials but changed the task demands. Participants now performed a general lexical decision task, responding 'yes' if a word of either language was presented (rather than saying 'no' to Dutch words). In this experiment, frequency-dependent facilitation effects were found for the interlingual homographs. Dijkstra et al. explain these results by pointing out that the task in Experiment 2 required the participants to make a distinction between the two readings of interlingual homographs, while they were able to use either reading in Experiment 3. Thus, the same underlying architecture (involving representations for homographs in different languages) could lead to both inhibition and facilitation effects.

Text B4.2
J. F. Kroll and
T. Dijkstra

Task B4.12

➤ In the section above, there are two variables mentioned: language intermixing and task. What differences were found with respect to whether subjects were asked to say 'yes' only to English words or to both English and Dutch words?

Effect of Instruction

Text B4.2
J. F. Kroll and
T. Dijkstra

We have seen that several factors (proficiency, language intermixing, task demands) may affect the (non) selectivity of the result patterns in bilingual word recognition experiments. In this context, the question arises to which extent top-down factors, such as participant expectancies based on the instructions of the experimenter, may affect the observed result patterns.

While adequate evaluation of this issue will require additional empirical evidence, it appears that bottom-up factors, such as language intermixing and stimulus characteristics (e.g., frequency, code similarity), are the more important ones. Dijkstra, De Bruijn, Schriefers, and Ten Brinke (2000) contrasted the effect of instruction-induced expectancies and language intermixing in an English lexical decision task performed by Dutch–English bilinguals. At the start of the experiment, participants were explicitly instructed to respond 'yes' to interlingual homographs and exclusively English words and 'no' to English nonwords and to exclusively Dutch words. In the first part of the experiment the stimulus list did not contain any Dutch words. In the second part of the experiment, Dutch items were introduced. No significant differences were found between interlingual homographs and controls in the first part of the experiment, while strong inhibition was obtained for interlingual homographs in the second part. This effect is demonstrated for words with a low-frequency reading in Dutch and a high-frequency reading in English.

The reader will note that these results converge with those of Experiments 1 and 2 by Dijkstra, Van Jaarsveld, and Ten Brinke (1998), discussed earlier. They suggest that language intermixing, rather than instruction-based expectancies, drives the bilingual participants' performance. However, the issue is still not decided, because a study by Von Studnitz and Green (submitted) suggests that the result patterns may yet be modulated by participant strategies.

To summarize this section on bilingual comprehension studies, it appears that:

1 Lexical codes from different languages are activated in parallel on the basis of an input string.
2 Selection of the lexical candidate that is identified appears to take place rather late in the recognition process.
3 Several factors affect the ultimately arising result patterns, the most important of which are a participant's L2-proficiency level, the requirements of the task, and the blocked or mixed presentation of items from different languages.

Task B4.13

➤ The sections above have been dealing with comprehension (recognising words) in the L1 or L2. In what respect would you expect the three statements above to apply to production?

Subsequently, the authors go through the same steps for language production. We will limit our current focus to comprehension, and refer to the author's summary of the differences between comprehension and production.

Text B4.2
J. F. Kroll and
T. Dijkstra

Discussion: similarities and differences between comprehension and production

In this chapter, we have contrasted comprehension and production to reveal those aspects of bilingual lexical representation and processing that are common to both modes of language use. We now evaluate the outcome of this comparison. It is important to note that some of our conclusions will necessarily be influenced by the fact that most of the research on bilingual word recognition and comprehension has been in the visual domain. The small number of studies on the recognition of spoken words in bilinguals (e.g. Grosjean, 1988; Li, 1996; Spivey and Marian, 1999) makes it difficult to compare the comprehension and production of spoken language alone.

Perhaps the most striking similarity between comprehension and production in bilinguals is the overwhelming evidence for nonselective access to words in both languages, regardless of whether the task logically permits the language of processing to be selected in advance. Comprehension and production also share the consequences of the lower L2 than L1 proficiency in unbalanced bilinguals. In both modes of language use, there appears to be more evidence for effects of L1 on L2 than the reverse, and a suggestion that the relative asymmetry in the magnitude of these cross-language influences may be larger for less fluent bilinguals.

Though the two domains share the aspect of language nonselective access, this does not imply that orthographic, phonological, and semantic codes are used in the same way or at the same moment in processing. For example, the bottom-up nature of comprehension requires that orthographic codes play a larger and earlier role in word recognition than they do in word production, although little is known about the activation of orthography during production. Likewise, the role of phonology is likely to be more critical in production than in comprehension, although, as we have seen, there is overwhelming evidence to suggest that phonology is involved in bilingual word recognition and that it determines, at least in part, the magnitude of cross-language influences. In both domains, there is evidence for semantic processing, but again the contribution of meaning is generally more reliable in production than in comprehension. In comprehension, semantics appear to play a role when there is a consistent correspondence between lexical form and meaning, as in the case of cognates, suggesting that semantic codes are activated even when they are not required by the task.

The time course over which these lexical codes are activated must also be different for comprehension and production. Because the longer time course associated with production provides additional opportunities for feedback and interaction between codes, there is the possibility that the cohort of activated lexical competitors will differ from those available in comprehension. The different nature of orthographic and

Text B4.2
J. F. Kroll and
T. Dijkstra

conceptual representations makes such a difference all the more likely. For instance, it may be that more lexical alternatives are initially activated in comprehension than in production because there are simply more orthographic neighbors of the input word than semantic alternatives for the output concept.

The inherent different nature of comprehension and production also has its effects for factors that may potentially affect lexical selection. There are a large number of variables (e.g., stimulus list composition, language mixing, instructions, language cues, and aspects of attentional control) that may influence lexical selection in each domain. Because comprehension and production differ in the cognitive resources that they require, and because we know that the ability to understand precedes the ability to speak, it seems likely that the role that external factors play in moderating the relative activation of alternatives in each language and in potentially inhibiting the unintended language, will be different.

Furthermore, in production, the language of speaking can and must be determined by the language user; in comprehension the requirement to determine the language in which the task is performed depends in a more complex way on the nature of the task itself. For example, to perform a generalized lexical decision task, it is logically not necessary to specify the language of the activated lexical form. But, to speak a word in order to name a pictured object, it is mandatory that language be specified. Even in the case of highly similar cognate translations, words in two languages rarely have an identical pronunciation, so language must be known if performance is to be error-free.

Conclusion

The answers to the questions that we have posed about the bilingual lexicon are, of course, preliminary. As noted earlier, we have said nothing about the comprehension of spoken language in the bilingual, nor have we considered how these questions might be answered for bilinguals for whom the two languages do not share the same alphabet. Rather, our discussion reflects the fact that we are just beginning to develop a theoretical framework for how words in the bilingual's two languages are represented and processed. The current issue driving experimental research is no longer simply whether or not there are two lexical representations, or whether or not processing is language selective. Research has gone beyond that point and now focuses on investigating how the output of activity from the representational system interacts with the processing goals and context in which the languages are used.

Task B4.14

➤ The authors first discussed the Revised Hierarchical Model (RHM) and then the Bilingual Interactive Activation Model (BIA). How does the RHM deal with the fact that an L1 word is usually selected faster than an L2 word in translation tasks and how does the BIA model deal with this phenomenon? Accepting the Bilingual Interactive Activation model, what would you predict for the following situations:

A proficient bilingual has spoken her L2 only for about a year while she was abroad and now she returns to her country. Will she have more difficulty finding cognates? Will she have more difficulty finding the right pronunciation than before she went abroad? Can you explain this?

CONCLUDING REMARKS

In this unit, you have seen two of the original articles on which the information in Unit A4 was based. The focus has been on a pair of closely related languages, English and Dutch, which lends itself well to separate out the subtle differences between semantic, orthographic and phonological factors. This type of research is highly specialised and one may wonder what it contributes to the bigger picture of second language acquisition. However, we feel that with the findings as presented and the Bilingual Interactive Activation model, we can account for quite a few phenomena that have puzzled SLA researchers for many years such as instances of language interference and code switching.

Unit B5
The developing system extended

In Unit A5, we discussed the Vygotskyan idea that optimal learning may take place when the information to be learned is within the learner's zone of proximal development. We also reasoned that new information could be assimilated when it is linked to old information. Information can be assimilated implicitly or explicitly. Even though the implicit and the explicit system, are separated, we argued that information practised in the explicit system produces output that may provide input for the implicit system. In this unit, we want to present two articles that address this point. The first article is by Swain and Lapkin (1995), who examined the thought processes involved while a learner produces output in writing. As mentioned in Unit A3, in the Krashen tradition, comprehensible input was initially strongly emphasised, but later the interest shifted to output. In this article, the background of that shift and the methodology used to study the role of output are laid out. The second article by Gass *et al.* (1998), which was written as an introduction to a special issue on the role of input and interaction in SLA, is a survey article and provides a summary of research on input and interaction over the past decades.

'Problems in output and the cognitive processes they generate: A step towards second language learning' by Merrill Swain and Sharon Lapkin (1995) In *Applied Linguistics 16*, 371–391

Text B5.1
M. Swain and
S. Lapkin

In this article, Swain and Lapkin present the output hypothesis for the first time. Since that time, there has been quite some discussion and research on the output hypothesis (see the Mackey article in Unit B7 for an update). We have included this article, because it is a good example of a qualitative approach to SLA. It shows both the advantages and disadvantages of such an approach. The method used is introspective think-aloud protocols, a commonly used methodology to learn more about thought processes. Through the protocols, the researchers try to get insight into what goes on in the mind of the learner and the kind of decisions he or she makes and on what grounds.

Introspective methodologies have met with quite some criticism, mainly because it is not clear to what extent the think-aloud information really reflects what goes on in the mind: it may be restricted to that part that can be verbalised, and that may not be the most significant part or the part we are really interested in. Nevertheless, we have gained considerable insight into language processing through these methods, and even if they cannot really prove anything with certainty, they are useful as ways to generate hypotheses that can subsequently be tested in quantitative studies. At the same time, the question has to be raised whether quantitative methods can prove anything definitively at all, and this, too, has been and continues to be a matter of considerable debate. In research on SLA, fortunately, the fierce debates on the strengths of qualitative versus quantitative research and vice versa have settled and their respective contributions are now being stressed more than their weaknesses.

This article argues that in addition to the study of input, more study of output is needed. The background of the study is one taken from a Canadian context, where French immersion teaching has been one of the battlefields of SLA. A consistent finding in evaluations of immersion teaching is that students reach a fairly high level of fluency, but show a lack of accuracy and correct use of grammar. In addition, analyses of school practices showed that students are hardly ever pushed to use the language actively, and this lack of output may be the reason for the low accuracy scores.

Text B5.1
M. Swain and
S. Lapkin

Functions of output

The relative lack of sustained talk in French in these immersion classes was an unexpected finding and led to a consideration of how output might be important in L2 learning beyond that of simply enhancing fluency. The proposal developed (Swain, 1985; 1993) and briefly explicated below, goes as follows: in producing the L2, a learner will on occasion become aware of (i.e. notice) a linguistic problem (brought to his/her attention either by external feedback – e.g. clarification requests – or internal feedback). Noticing a problem 'pushes' the learner to modify his/her output. In doing so, the learner may sometimes be forced into a more syntactic processing mode than might occur in comprehension. Thus, output may set 'noticing' in train, triggering mental processes that lead to modified output. It is the purpose of this paper to determine if learners' own output does, on occasion, serve as an attention-getting device, and if it does, does it sometimes serve to stimulate the learners to engage in linguistic analysis?

Task B5.1

➤ In Unit A1 we discussed Schmidt's 'noticing' hypothesis: to learn a form one has to notice it and pay attention to it. Why do you think output may be helpful to notice a form?

Text B5.1
M. Swain and
S. Lapkin

But let us first examine the proposal in a little more detail. Schmidt and Frota (1986: 311) offer a 'notice the gap principle' which states, 'a second language learner will begin to acquire the target like form if and only if it is present in comprehended input and 'noticed' in the normal sense of the word, that is consciously'. Our hypothesis is that output is one of the triggers for noticing. That is to say, in producing the target language, learners may encounter a problem leading them to recognize what they do not know, or know only partially. In other words, the activity of producing the target language may prompt second language learners to consciously recognize some of their linguistic problems; it may bring to their attention something they need to discover about their L2.

The 'output hypothesis' (stripped to its bare bones) is that even without implicit or explicit feedback provided from an interlocutor about the learners' output, learners may still, on occasion, notice a gap in their own knowledge when they encounter a problem in trying to produce the L2. (. . .)

Research is beginning to accumulate evidence supporting the theoretical claim that 'pushing' learners beyond their current performance level can lead to enhanced performance, a step which may represent the internalization of new linguistic knowledge, or the consolidation of existing knowledge. In this paper, we wish to examine what mental processes learners engage in as they move from the original output to their modified output, as they move from encountering a linguistic problem in L2 production to developing a solution.

It has been demonstrated that the processes involved in producing language can be quite different than those involved in comprehending language. Van Dijk and Kintsch (1983) have shown with native speakers that comprehension will sometimes rely on comprehension strategies rather than on a closed, logical system of rules required to produce a grammatical utterance. For example, in comprehending an utterance, a native speaker may make guesses about the probable structure of what they are hearing (or reading) based on syntactic or semantic clues. One strategy, for example, is 'try and make sense of a sentence using content words alone'.

Krashen (1982: 66) has pointed out that 'In many cases, we do not utilize syntax in understanding – we often get the message with a combination of vocabulary, or lexical information plus extra-linguistic information. Similarly, Gary and Gary (1981: 3) state, in speaking of the comprehension-based approach to language teaching, that:

> Speech requires linguistically more complex tasks than comprehension. Comprehension – at least all but the most advanced levels – allows many linguistic signals to be ignored: redundant grammatical and semantic functions such as concord, definite/ indefinite distinctions, singular/plural distinctions, etc., can very often be ignored without seriously distorting the message being comprehended.

(. . .)

On the basis of theoretically and empirically based arguments, Swain (1985; 1993) suggested that perhaps one function of output in second language learning might be to force the learner to move from the semantic processing prevalent in comprehension to the syntactic processing needed for production. It might be that producing language forces learners to recognize what they do not know or know only partially. This may trigger an analysis of incoming data, that is, a syntactic analysis of input, or it may trigger an analysis of existing internal linguistic resources, in order to fill the knowledge gap.

The study

This study (. . .) began with a specific interest in whether our young learners would identify problems as a result of trying to produce the target language and what they might report doing to overcome them. Could what they reported be related to processes of second language learning? Would we see evidence of grammatical analysis as they struggled to produce the target language?

Text B5.1
M. Swain and
S. Lapkin

Thus, our research questions in this study were as follows:

1   As young adolescent learners produce their L2, do they ever become aware of the gaps in their linguistic knowledge? In other words, can producing the L2 lead to a conscious awareness by a learner of what he/she does not know or knows only partially?
2   If young adolescent learners do become aware of linguistic gaps in their knowledge as a result of attempting to produce the L2, what do they do? Specifically, are cognitive processes ever triggered which theoretical and empirical accounts suggest are involved in second language acquisition?
3   Do these learners ever engage, in trying to solve their linguistic problems, in grammatical/syntactic analyses?

 Task B5.2

➤   To test the above questions, how would you go about it? Would you use a speaking or writing task? The authors used a writing task. Can you imagine why? When would you know that there is a 'linguistic gap'? How would you determine whether the learner is consciously aware of not knowing something?

Text B5.1
M. Swain and
S. Lapkin

Methodology

1 *Subjects*

The subjects in this study were 18 students from a grade 8 early French immersion class of 21 students. The 18 students were those whose parents had signed permission forms allowing their children to participate in the study. Students in this class were from a lower-middle to middle class socio-economic background (the school is located in the inner city of a large metropolitan area in Ontario, Canada). The students, whose average age was 13, had a wide range of academic abilities.

The students also had had generally similar educational backgrounds in that they had all participated in an early French immersion program since kindergarten. Immersion teachers are encouraged to use approaches that are similar to those being used by their English language counterparts. (. . .)

In spite of the overall experiential nature of L2 learning in the immersion classroom, formal grammar instruction is often an important feature of the French immersion classroom. It is thus highly likely that as these students entered their grade 8 year, they would have been exposed to an eclectic second language teaching approach consisting of learner-centered activities fortified with a regular dose of traditional grammar activities (Kowal and Swain, 1994).

Of the 18 students from whom we collected data, 9 were selected for data analysis. The procedures for selecting these 9 students were as follows. At the end of the year, their French language arts teacher ranked her students according to their overall proficiency in French. The top two students and the bottom two students were chosen for inclusion in our sample. These students are referred to as the 'most proficient' and 'least proficient' students respectively. Then 5 additional students were randomly

Text B5.1
M. Swain and
S. Lapkin

selected from among the middle group. The final sample consisted of 6 girls and 3 boys.

2 *Procedure*

The writing task was developed in consultation with the students' homeroom teacher. It was decided that students should be given a theme that they had covered in class. Their familiarity with the topic, it was hoped, would allow the students to focus attention on their writing and the need to think aloud. An environmental theme was therefore chosen.

Each student met individually with the researcher in a small, quiet room. Procedures suggested by Ericsson and Simon (1993) for eliciting think-alouds were followed. Students first received a brief introduction in English outlining the task which they would be expected to do. They were told that the researcher was interested in knowing what they were thinking as they were writing. In order to accomplish this, they would be asked to write a short article in French of one or two paragraphs, on an assigned topic. As they performed the writing task, they were to think aloud. To illustrate, the researcher thought aloud while solving a multiplication problem. The students were then given a similar problem to solve.

The students were then given the specific writing task: 'You are a reporter for your local newspaper. You have been asked to write an article about an environmental problem facing your community. In your article, describe the problem and offer one or two possible solutions to the problem.'

The students were told that they must write in French, but that it would be fine for them to use either French or English as they thought aloud. They were asked not to erase any mistakes that they might make, but simply to cross them out and continue. They were told that if they stopped talking for very long, the researcher would remind them to think aloud.

Whenever students made a change without commenting on it, they were prompted to verbalize what they were thinking. The probe used was 'what are you thinking?' Finally, students were advised that they could not have access to a dictionary or any other aid, and that the researcher would not be able to help either.

Upon completion of a draft, students were asked to edit their work using a red pen to record any of their changes, and to think aloud while they were editing. A tape-recorder was placed on the table where the student was working. The researcher remained in the room, sitting close to the student so she could see when the student crossed out something. Each session lasted approximately one hour.

Language-related episodes

1 *Definition*

Language-related episodes were identified in the think-aloud protocols of our sample of students. We defined a language-related episode as any segment of the protocol in which a learner either spoke about a language problem he/she encountered while writing and solved it either correctly (see example 1) or incorrectly (see example 2); or simply solved it (again, either correctly or incorrectly) without having explicitly identified it as a problem (see example 3).

Example 1 (translations in italics)

S17: [S17 has written an article about how phosphates released into lakes and oceans cause plants in them to grow quickly to such an enormous size that they *will* kill all the fish. She struggles in the following think-aloud episode with how to say 'kill all the fish'.] 'et mort (*and dies*). I don't know. I don't know because mour . . . mourir les poissons (*to die the fish*), it's like mourir is something that you do. It's not something that someone does to you. So it's more like they're being murdered and not dying. So, uhm, et tue toutes les poissons (*and kills all the fish*), or something like that.'

In example 1, the student has produced 'mort' (*die*), and is not pleased with this lexical choice. Her explanation for the change she makes is in fact a rather sophisticated one, relating to the need to use a transitive verb 'tuer' (*to kill*) rather than an intransitive one 'mourir' (*to die*). Recognizing her difficulty, she searches her own linguistic knowledge for information which might help to solve her problem. Of course, we cannot tell whether the analysis she conducts reflects some generalized knowledge she has of transitivity/intransitivity that she is possibly applying for the first time to the difference in meaning between 'mourir' and 'tuer', or whether she is struggling consciously for the first time with the concept as she senses the difference in meaning between the two verbs. (. . .)

Example 2

S3: [S3 has just written: 'Il y a trop d'utilisation des chemicaux toxiques qui détruissent l'ozone'. (*There's too much use of toxic chemicals which destroy the ozone layer.*) In his think-aloud, we hear him trying to produce a noun form of the verb he has just used.] 'La dé...truc...tion. Et la détruction. No, that's not a word. Démolition, démolisson, démolition, démolition, détruction, détruision, détruision, la détruision des arbres au forêt de pluie (*the destruction of trees in the rain forest*).'

It is difficult to know in example 2 the extent to which the student's attempts to produce 'la déstruction' are English- or French-based. Both languages are probably influencing his choice of words (e.g. demolish/démolir). It is clear from his pronunciation, however, that the endings he tries out are French, being either the noun suffix 'on' or 'tion' (Grevisse, 1980). His final solution, 'la détruision' is wrong, but he has made use of his knowledge of French by using the stem of the verb he has just produced and adding a French-sounding suffix. This example is revealing, because the incorrect solution allows us to conclude that new knowledge has been created through a search of his own existing knowledge. His search began with his own output which he heard as incorrect.

 Task B5.3

➤ In example 2, the authors mention that it is difficult to know whether the attempt to find a word was French or English based. Using your knowledge of the Bilingual Interactive Activation model, can you explain why it might be quite natural for these students to access both languages?

Text B5.1
M. Swain and
S. Lapkin

Example 3

S3: [S3 is writing about how products such as aerosols destroy the environment. He then says aloud the following, while writing.] 'C'est pour ça qu'on doit arrêter . . . qu'on doit les arrêter. (*That's why one must stop . . . one must stop them.*)'

In example 3, the sentence would have been better rendered as 'On doit arrêter de les utiliser'. However, the student appears to have recognized the need for 'arrêter' to have a complement, and inserts one to refer to 'the products'. The initial omission, or incorrect placement, of the direct object pronoun is a relatively common error made by immersion students (Selinker, Swain, and Dumas, 1975), and this student's self-correction to include it could be considered as a step in his linguistic development, if only as a consolidation of procedural knowledge.

Returning now to our definition of language-related episodes, as we have said, each one is related to a problem the student had with the production of the target language. In almost all of our examples, the resolution of the problem involved drawing simultaneously on both gist (meaning) and language use (Scardamalia and Paris, 1985) (. . .) However, in a few instances in our data, only language use was focused on, and these tended to be in reference to the written form of the target language (see example 4). We have included these as language-related episodes because we consider them to be examples of the consolidation of linguistic knowledge as the learner applies existing knowledge to old contexts, or as would seem likely in example 4:

Example 4

S16: [S16 writes 'Pour solve] 'OK, I shouldn't have an accent there. I should have an 'r' because it's l'infinitif.'

(. . .)

Each language-related episode dealt only with one linguistic item. Sometimes episodes overlapped, and sometimes one was embedded in another. In example 6, there are three episodes. One episode continues throughout: what tense should be used for 'envoyer', and how is it formed. Embedded in that larger episode are two others: one where the student changes 'de chemiques' to 'des chemiques'; and one in which 'qui' is inserted as subject of 'envoyer':

Example 6

S12: [S12 has just written: 'Cette problème est causé par de chemiques envoyé' (*This problem is caused by chemicals sent*)]. 'Uhm, is it passé composé or what? Cette problème est causé par des . . . just had de, so you change it 'cause it's des chemiques. Envoyé . . . sent . . . well it might be passé composé because xxx. It's in the past. So, I . . . 'cause it says that are sent. So I could change this. Cross out envoyé and write uhm des chemiques qui sont envoyé. If I did it that way [the way she originally had it] then I would have to put it in either uhm imparfait or, or in infinitive or a verb tense, but I think it would be better in passé composé, and I have to put uhm who are. I can't just put . . . I have to put which are, or whatever, so I have to add the qui, and then because it's passé composé I add the uhm sont before the verb. Wait, would it be sont? Uhm, Ya.'

2 Reliability

Four researchers independently identified the language-related episodes in one think-aloud protocol and subsequently discussed their decisions. Where there was disagreement initially, it was possible to reach a consensus among the researchers as to what precisely a language-related episode was and how to identify it as detailed in the preceding section. Subsequently, another protocol was examined by the same four researchers, and, although there were minor discrepancies about when an episode actually began or ended, there was full agreement on what constituted an episode.

The next step was to categorize the language related episodes.

3 Classification

We proceeded to classify the data – the language-related episodes – in the following way. The same four researchers who identified the language-related episodes in the two protocols mentioned above, independently categorized each episode from one protocol. No categories were pre-established; rather they were entirely data-dependent.

Our intent was to categorize each language-related episode according to how the learners solved, in the way that they did, the linguistic difficulties that they identified as they produced the target language. In other words, *we wanted to try to arrive at the mental processes we thought were reflected in the changes the students made to their output.* In our first pass through the data, we tried to stay as close to the data as possible. A second-level analysis presented later relates these categories to cognitive processes that have been identified in the SLA literature as potentially involved in second language learning.

The descriptive categories were discussed at a meeting in which consensus emerged among the four researchers as to the categories and labels for them. These seven descriptive categories are listed below along with examples.

Due to space limitation, we present only the categories, without the examples.

1   Sounds right/doesn't sound right

   a   lexical
   b   grammatical

2   Makes more sense/doesn't make sense
3   Applied a grammatical rule
4   Lexical search

   a   via English
   b   via French
   c   via both

5   Translation (phrase or greater)
6   Stylistic
7   Spelling

4 Reliability

Text B5.1
M. Swain and
S. Lapkin

The four researchers independently classified the language-related episodes in the second protocol and attained a consensus on how to classify each episode. Following that, one researcher classified the remaining data (7 protocols). The episodes of one of those protocols, selected at random, were independently classified by a second researcher. Agreement was 82 per cent.

(. . .)

Findings

The first result is the finding that young adolescent second language learners do indeed become aware of gaps in their linguistic knowledge as they produce their L2. Furthermore, when they encounter difficulties in producing the target language, they do engage in thought processes of a sort which may play a role in second language learning. They do so even when external feedback is unavailable to them. It will take further research to trace the effect of these cognitive processes on learning. However, the thought processes identified represent processes similar to those other theorists and researchers (Cohen and Robbins, 1976; Corder, 1981; Kellerman and Sharwood Smith, 1986; Larsen-Freeman and Long, 1991; McLaughlin, 1987; e.g. Selinker, 1972) have hypothesized to be involved in second language learning: extending first language knowledge (particularly meanings) to second language contexts; extending second language knowledge to new target-language contexts; and formulating and testing hypotheses about linguistic forms and functions. In doing so, these learners some-times engage in grammatical analysis which, though not essential to comprehension, is essential to accurate production.

   It needs to be pointed out that, for these learners at least, the substance of their thoughts was sometimes faulty, leading to incorrect hypotheses and inappropriate generalizations, suggesting that relevant feedback could play a crucial role in advancing their second language learning.

Task B5.4

➤ Why, in your opinion, do the authors suggest that relevant feedback could play a crucial role in advancing second language learning? From a Vygotskian perspective, what would be the role of relevant feedback at the moment that a learner is struggling with a particular point?

After this, the authors present quantitative data on the occurrence of different categories for different types of learners. This highlights some of the problems with this kind of qualitative research that is by definition unsolvable: how can you on the one hand look at individual behaviour and patterns, and at the same time generalise findings to a larger population. In DST the interest is in both: the larger pattern and the individual variation in patterns, as well as the recognition that different methodologies are required for each.

Text B5.1
M. Swain and
S. Lapkin

In summary, this study has suggested that the communicative need engendered by the task did force the learners into thinking about the form of their linguistic output. In other words, it moved learners from semantic to grammatical processing. The data have allowed us to derive a set of descriptive categories for the language-related think-aloud episodes. Reflection on the categories led to our identification of two different dimensions: cognitive processes involved in second language learning, and aspects of language focused on.

 ### Task B5.5

➤ The purpose of this study was to discover the mental processes the subjects are engaged in while producing output. The general findings were that (a) subjects extend first-language knowledge to new target-language contexts and (b) they formulate and test hypotheses about linguistic forms and functions. Can these findings be related to the learning theories presented in Unit A5? For example, are Piaget's notions of 'assimilation' and 'accommodation' involved? Are new connections made that remain? Or, in terms of Anderson's theory of semantic networks, are certain items elaborated, creating more retrieval paths. Or, in terms of Vygotsky, how does producing output relate to the students' zone of proximal development? And finally, if the students are learning by doing and thinking about linguistic forms and functions, are they dealing with these forms in an explicit or implicit manner?

This article has made clear that by producing output the learners interact with the L2 differently than when they just listen to the L2. What seems to be involved is that by producing the language, in this case in writing, learners are interacting with a virtual reader and want their text to be understood by that reader. Therefore, attention is paid to the correct forms. In this study, the subjects received no feedback at all, but the authors themselves suggested that relevant feedback could play a crucial role in advancing their second language learning. In the next article, we will look at what exactly the role of feedback may be, this time in spoken interaction.

Text B5.2
S. Gass,
A. Mackey and
T. Pica

'The role of input and interaction in second language acquisition' by Susan M. Gass, Alison Mackey and Teresa Pica (1998) in *Modern Language Journal*, 82, 299–307

The main argument put forward in this article is that input is most effective in learning when it is part of interaction, and not when the learner is simply exposed to spoken or written text. What matters is the involvement of the learner in the interaction, the intention to understand what is said, and the contribution to the interaction in a meaningful way. Measuring the role of input or interaction in learning is extremely complicated, and many studies show little effect or appear not to be replicable. In the light of what we have said before on the complexity of systems and learning, this is not very surprising. Input and interaction are part of the larger picture of the learner as a situated learning system with all the individual differences and contextual variations that are implied. The instability of findings can be interpreted as a confirmation of our claim that isolating a single aspect of the learning process may tell us little: it is part of the larger complex system. This does not imply that it would be pointless to study the role of input and interaction: we do need that information to enhance our understanding of the process of SLA. Although the unique contribution of such factors to learning success is limited, it is certainly a crucial part of the picture.

Task B5.6

➤ If you are a fluent L2 speaker who has learned the L2 primarily through formalised L2 instruction, try to remember your earliest real, meaningful conversations with native (or fluent non-native) speakers of your L2. Can you remember what you did? In your attempt to produce understandable language, did you focus on form or content? Were you consciously applying 'rules' you had learned in class? Did your interlocutor correct your speech when there were grammatical mistakes, or did he or she signal only that he or she did not understand something? Did you find the interaction useful in your quest to master the L2? And did you find it more, less, or equally useful compared to an instructional setting? Why?

If you do not have experience learning an L2 through instruction and interaction, you might want to interview someone who does.

THE THEORETICAL BASIS FOR THE ROLE OF CONVERSATION IN SLA

Text B5.2
S. Gass,
A. Mackey and
T. Pica

The study of conversational interaction involving second language (L2) learners and their interlocutors has been central to second language acquisition (SLA) research since the early 1980s. A good deal of this work has focused on the ways in which interaction can be influenced by factors of gender, ethnicity, and the role in the social relationship of learners and their interlocutors, and by the nature of the topics, tasks, and activities in which they engage. Considerable attention has also been directed towards the role of interaction with respect to the conditions considered theoretically important for SLA, such as the learner's comprehension of input, access to feedback, and production of modified output (Gass, 1997).

The role of interaction has long been central to the study of language acquisition theory. For example, Vygotsky and his colleagues working in Russia in the 1920s conceptualized many constructs that continue to have relevance in interactionist research to date (see Swain and Lapkin, 1998). With the advent of interactionist perspectives in SLA, emphasis was placed on the empirical study of language learner discourse and social interaction, as SLA researchers gathered data on learners and interlocutors as evidence of language development. Extensive empirical studies of input and interaction explored the ways in which learners manipulated their interlanguage (IL) resources when asked to make their messages more comprehensible. These manipulations, in turn, led learners to restructure their IL toward greater accuracy and complexity. (. . .)

Text B5.2
S. Gass,
A. Mackey and
T. Pica

Despite the large number of studies dealing with input and interaction in SLA, and, indeed, the wealth of information that such studies have provided, the precise role of interaction in actual development and internalization of L2 knowledge has continued to challenge researchers. As early as 1986, for example, Sato, drawing from her longitudinal research initiated in 1981, proposed that the relationship between learners' participation in conversational interaction and their L2 development was one of selectivity and indirectness. This theme has now become central to work on conversational interaction and SLA (. . .)

Until the 1970s, conversational interaction was believed to serve a reinforcing function in SLA, whereby learners could take grammatical features, structures, and rules that had been presented in classroom lessons and other assignments and apply them to spoken discourse itself – often carefully organized and orchestrated by their teachers and textbooks – to showcase particular grammatical items. This common orthodoxy changed in 1975 when Wagner-Gough and Hatch (also see Hatch, 1978; Hatch and Wagner-Gough, 1976)(see also Hatch, 1978; Hatch & Wagner-Gough, 1976) illustrated how learners' participation in conversational interaction provided them with opportunities to hear and produce the L2 in ways that went beyond its role as simply a forum for practice. Their analysis of conversations between learners and interlocutors suggested that L2 syntax might develop out of conversation, rather than simply feed into it.

From this basic insight stemmed a number of studies that described L2 interaction and attempted to relate it to the linguistic needs of L2 learners, particularly the need for comprehensible input, which, at the time, was considered to be the driving force behind the acquisition process (see Krashen, 1985; Long, 1983a; 1983b). With these studies in the 1980s, Long launched a series of studies that shed light on this relationship. One of Long's foremost contributions was to distinguish between the talk directed toward L2 learners by native speakers (NSs) and the interactions in which they engaged. He showed that such interactions differed from native speaker–non-native speaker (NS–NNS) conversation in terms of the conversational structure. Such differences include clarification requests, confirmation of message meaning, and comprehension checks. Long's research revealed that these conversational modifications were not unique to non-native discourse, and, indeed, were found in NS conversations as well. However, as they were significantly more abundant in conversations that involved L2 learners and even more so in learner-to-learner conversations (cf. Varonis and Gass, 1985), Long suggested that they could serve a role in providing the comprehensible input needed for successful L2 learning and proposed a two-step argument concerning the relationship between conversational interaction and acquisition.

 Task B5.7

➤ Based on the information given above, can you illustrate (with fictitious examples) possible differences in the interaction between a NS–NS, a NS–NNS, and a NNS–NNS conversation? How would you characterise these differences?

Text B5.2
S. Gass,
A. Mackey and
T. Pica

Long's (1980) proposal went as follows: First, we need to show that comprehension promotes acquisition, and second, we need to show that conversational modifications lead to better comprehension. From this, we would be able to deduce that

Text B5.2
S. Gass,
A. Mackey and
T. Pica

conversational modifications promote acquisition. Long argued that the first part of his proposal was already supported, albeit indirectly given the lack of evidence that there had ever been a successful language learner in the absence of comprehensible input.

Despite the promising results of this early research, however, the effect of interaction on acquisition has remained a complex issue. As Long himself pointed out (1985), comprehensible input, in itself, was necessary but not sufficient to promote the acquisition process. Interactional modifications, therefore, cannot be the only mechanism behind the learner's L2 development. As noted above, Sato (1986) began to question the claim concerning a direct relationship between interaction and acquisition. She based her argument on findings from her earlier research on two Vietnamese boys learning English as a second language (ESL), whom she had studied intensively for 10 months and whose primary source of L2 input came from conversational interaction with their teachers and schoolmates, their foster parents, and Sato herself.

Sato found that the boys made little progress toward L2 proficiency, particularly with respect to their application and control of past tense inflections, despite the opportunity to hear and produce these linguistic features in their social discourse on a daily basis. Sato's analysis of her own conversational interactions with the boys revealed that they were able to establish time reference in ways that were comprehensible but often obviated the need for the application of temporal and aspectual morphosyntax. Relying on the knowledge that they shared with their interlocutor, conversational features (such as their interlocutor's use of past tense markings), and their own insertions of adverbial phrases and calendric expressions to indicate time, the boys were able to achieve mutual comprehensibility with Sato and other interlocutors without the need for complex grammar.

Task B5.8

➤ Apparently the two Vietnamese boys had 'fossilised' their incorrect use of the past tense, or as we claim in Unit A2, reached an 'attractor' state. Even though from a DST perspective we cannot be sure, can you think of a reason why the boys had fossilised this particular structure?

Text B5.2
S. Gass,
A. Mackey and
T. Pica

On the basis of her research, Sato did not rule out the importance of conversational interaction in learners' access to input for past time marking but suggested that it served more as a source for linguistically salient features such as adverbial phrases and calendric expressions than for verb inflections and other structures that were less perceptible in conversational discourse. She also argued that the role of interaction in acquisition was far more complex than had been heretofore conceived. It was becoming increasingly apparent that researchers would need to look for additional interactional processes that could assist the learners' access to L2 forms not readily apparent in the comprehensible input generated by conversational interaction. One such interactional process was advanced by Swain (1985) and led to a line of research that Swain has continued to date. (See the Swain and Lapkin article in this unit.)

Swain (1985) has argued for the utility of what she has called 'comprehensible output.' Her work has expanded and diversified the role of conversation in SLA, as she has suggested that conversation (and production, in general) pushes learners to impose syntactic structure on their utterances. This is in contrast to comprehension, in which it is not always essential for learners to draw on knowledge of L2 syntax. Thus, with respect to the more complex dimensions of L2 syntax, it is the necessity for learners to strive toward comprehensibility in responding to interlocutor feedback, rather than to reach comprehension of interlocutor input, that may play a pivotal and yet somewhat selective role in the acquisition process.

The importance of feedback, particularly as a source of negative evidence, as a way of elucidating the inadequacy of learners' own rule systems, has also been pointed out by White (1987), who suggested that what is necessary for L2 development is not comprehensible input, but incomprehensible input. By this she means that modifications to language (triggered by something incomprehensible) become the impetus for learners to recognize the inadequacy of their own rule system. As Gass (1997) argues, it is incomprehensible input that may trigger learners' recognition of mismatches between their IL grammar and that of their L2 target. In essence, this is the crux of the current argument as to the possible role that interaction plays in the learning process. As illustrated in a series of articles by Gass and Varonis (see, e.g. Varonis *et al.*, 1985), comprehension difficulties or 'instances of non-understanding' are what allow a learner to realize that linguistic modification is necessary. In essence, then, interactional modifications or 'negotiations' (as they have long been referred to by Gass and Varonis and, increasingly, by researchers throughout the field of SLA), can serve to focus learners' attention on potentially troublesome parts of their discourse, providing them with information that can then open the door to IL modification. These modifications may, in turn, lead to subsequent stabilization or language change. Through clarification and elaboration of the message, non-native speakers (NNSs) can receive more usable input in their quest to understand the L2 and, further, this new or elaborated input can draw attention to IL features that diverge from the L2. It is the realization of divergence between L2 forms and target language (TL) forms that becomes the catalyst for learning. Therefore, negotiation, along with certain classroom activities such as teacher explanation, can bring particular forms to a learner's attention – forms that might otherwise be unnoticed – thus enhancing the input (Sharwood Smith, 1986) and making it more salient. This perspective on the relationship between interaction and, more specifically, negotiation and L2 development has, in turn, stimulated research of considerable scope and theoretical import. Long (1996) presents a similar view of the role of interaction/negotiation, noting how it 'connects input, internal learner capacities, *particularly selective attention*, and output in productive ways' (1996: 452) (emphasis ours).

Task B5.9

➤ The discussion above does not mention individual differences. For example, a learner who is mostly interested in communicating messages may not pay that much attention to form, whereas another type of learner, for example someone who is learning the language to become a teacher later on, may pay selective attention to form, too. With which of the learners' characteristics mentioned in Unit A6 would this difference most clearly be associated?

Any sort of reformulation of an incorrect utterance (assuming that a learner recognizes it as a reformulation), such as an expansion, recast, or rephrasing, can serve to draw a learner's attention to the fact of the 'incorrectness' and can thereby trigger learner-internal mechanisms (e.g., hypothesis testing), which may, in turn, result in immediate output change on the part of the learner. Immediate output change can lead to a quick response to the revised hypothesis and hence a tentative confirmation or rejection of that revised hypothesis.

Text B5.2
S. Gass,
A. Mackey and
T. Pica

Recent empirical studies of conversation and SLA

The considerable expansion in the body of work on the role of interaction in SLA in the past several years has, in part, been made possible through the use of more innovative and varied methods of data collection – including interactive tasks and computer controlled interaction – and through a focus on cognitive processes such as attention and recall. These have long been considered important in L2 development and are now beginning to be operationalized carefully for empirical investigation. From this recent research has emerged a more focused view of the relationship between interaction and L2 development and a reinforcement of the notion that the development outcomes of interaction are indeed complex.

A number of studies have shown that interactional modifications that are brought about through negotiation for meaning can have a positive effect on the quality of learners' immediate production. Studies by Holliday (1995) and Linnell (1995), which have been able to track changes in learner production through their participation on interactive computer tasks, have suggested that the modifications in output that occur as a result of negotiation for meaning are often target-like in direction. Review papers by Pica (1994; 1996) have extended the claims for negotiation, outlining the ways in which interaction modified through negotiation brings about reformulations, segmentations, and movement of constituents that can provide learners with both lexical and grammatical information about the L2 as well as their own IL system. Such adjustments might also serve as a source of linguistic data for the learner both immediately and possibly also in the longer term.

Recent research has also addressed the question of whether the increasingly target-like output that learners can obtain through their negotiation for meaning can benefit their L2 development over time. With respect to retention in the short run, Nobuyoshi and Ellis (1993) explored this issue with a small-scale study examining the developmental outcomes of 'pushed output' (i.e., the construct that Swain [1985] had originally labelled 'comprehensible output'). Two of their three experimental learners maintained an improvement in accuracy after 1 week of treatment. This finding indicated that output that is 'pushed' may increase learners' control over structures they have already acquired. However, questions remained as to whether it could help learners internalize and retain these and other linguistic features over the long term. Further studies in this area by LaPierre (1994) and Donato (1994) have suggested that pushed output may result in more permanent IL restructuring (see references in Swain, 1995). Mackey (1995; 1997) also suggested that changes can be maintained, at least for a short period of time. Taken together, these studies of adult and adolescent L2 learners have found that interactional modifications that occur through pushed output can be maintained at least in the short run. Longitudinal data or delayed post-tests are obviously a necessary step in order to test this hypothesis with respect to long-term retention.

This is one of the more complicated aspects of research on the impact of teaching practices on learning: a given approach or method may be effective in the short run, but may fail to show an effect in the long run. This is unfortunate for the researcher who wants to claim to have found an important contribution to language learning, but it is not surprising. The new approach has become integrated in the repertoire of strategies of a learner, but it will also interact with other strategies present, thus blurring the specific effect of what was aimed at. In accordance with DST, the fact that no specific effect can be detected in the end does not mean that there is no effect at all, but its unique effect can simply not be singled out.

**Text B5.2
S. Gass,
A. Mackey and
T. Pica**

Other recent studies of the effects of interaction that bring up the topic of long-term change have been reported in the research literature. Gass and Varonis (1994) compared the impact of prescripted modified and unmodified input, with and without the opportunity for interaction, on both comprehension and production, as measured by their NS partner's success in following the directions. They found that both the negotiated and modified input positively affected comprehension. In addition, they found that prior negotiation, but not prior modified input, significantly affected subsequent production, leading them to suggest that interaction, with the opportunity for modifications, may impact positively on later language use.

Other research has also explored the short-term effects of interactional modifications on comprehension and acquisition of vocabulary as well as the development of targeted grammatical structures. Loschky's (1994) study focused on these processes with respect to vocabulary items and locative constructions in Japanese as a L2. His results showed a positive effect on comprehension of the vocabulary but no effect on retention or acquisition of the vocabulary and the locatives. With respect to vocabulary, however, a study by Ellis, Tanaka, and Yamazaki (1994) found a greater role for interactional modifications than that of Loschky. This research revealed that, when compared with premodified input, interactionally modified input resulted in both better comprehension and greater vocabulary acquisition. As explained by Ellis *et al.*, these differences in results on acquisition may have been due to the items under study. Loschky investigated locative constructions, whereas Ellis *et al.* used vocabulary items. The research of Ellis *et al.*, together with that of Gass (1988) and Gass and Varonis (1994), further emphasize the relationship among interaction, comprehension, and SLA as one in which interaction allows learners to comprehend TL input and in which comprehended input is important for SLA.

 Task B5.10

➤ Ellis *et al.* found different learning effects for vocabulary items than Loschky did for locative constructions: affixes or particles that express place. Often they are not very transparent in meaning. For example, the 'ke' particle at the end of the following two Mingo words expresses 'place', a near equivalent of the English 'on'.

o'nehsa' – sand; o'nehsa'ke – on, in the sand

atekhwaahkwa' – table; atekhwaahkwa'ke – on the table

Ellis *et al.* argue that these different effects may be related to the items under study. In your opinion, why are vocabulary items different from locative constructions? What would make learning vocabulary items more amenable to acquisition in a conversational setting than locative constructions?

Additional research has also suggested ways in which both the measure of development and the differences in the interactional conditions might account for their different findings. Mackey (1995; 1997) found that certain types of interaction can have a positive effect on L2 development. [See article in Unit B7.] She examined the effects of different types of input and interaction on the short-term development of question formation in ESL. Using a pretest, delayed post-test design, Mackey (1995; 1997) found a positive effect for negotiated interaction where there was active participation in the interaction, but no effect for observing interaction without opportunities for production or for receiving modified input with no opportunity for interaction. The interaction in Mackey's study involved NS–NNS dyads [pairs of speakers] carrying out communicative tasks that provided contexts for learners to produce specific morphosyntactic forms.

> Text B5.2
> S. Gass,
> A. Mackey and
> T. Pica

In addition to the research mentioned above, expansions of this line of enquiry continue through a variety of empirical studies in the area of conversational interaction and L2 development. The focus of these studies is increasingly on such issues as the role of negative feedback received through conversational interaction and the role of conversational interaction in promoting noticing and attention to form (e.g. Schmidt, 1994; Tomlin and Vilia, 1994).

Then this introductory article presents a short overview of the articles in this special issue that is definitely worth reading for those interested in more detailed accounts of research on input and interaction. After this, the authors conclude:

Despite the emphasis in this special issue on the role of interaction studies in L2 development, it is still advisable to be cautious about the nature of the claims for the role of the environment in SLA. Although interaction may provide a structure that allows input to become salient and hence noticed, interaction should not be seen as a cause of acquisition; it can only set the scene for potential learning. As Long (1996) has pointed out, there are many factors involved in L2 learning: the role of interaction is claimed only to be facilitative. The sources of learning are complex and can be seen as stemming from learner-internal factors, some of which have received extensive treatment in the SLA literature (see Gass, 1997, for a review).

> Text B5.2
> S. Gass,
> A. Mackey and
> T. Pica

However, current research on the role of interaction in L2 development continues to contribute to our understanding of the relationship between input, interaction, and SLA. (. . .) It seems that interaction can have positive effects on L2 development and that the complex matter of individual differences needs to be considered carefully.

Task B5.11

Suppose a group of secondary school L2 teachers asked you, as an expert, to advise on whether they should incorporate exercises to encourage output and communicative interaction in their classes. What would you advise these teachers? Should they include time for conversational interaction? Should they give feedback on form and meaning or limit their feedback to meaning only?

Base your answer on the two articles in this unit (but you could also include Mackey's article in Unit B7).

CONCLUDING REMARKS

In this unit, we have presented two articles, both dealing with output. The first one dealt with writing and the mental processes that the student experiences while producing a text. The second one dealt with the effect of output in spoken interaction. It is clear that acquisition may take place during interaction, but keeping a DST perspective and the learning theories presented in Unit A4 in mind, we very much agree with Gass *et al.*'s conclusion that, no matter how useful, interaction should not be seen as a cause of acquisition, but as a scene in which potential learning can take place.

Unit B6
Learners' characteristics extended

In Unit A6, we have discussed a range of individual learner's characteristics, like age, motivation, attitude and aptitude. The main point of this chapter was that all of these factors interact in a complex and dynamic way. The current section contains three extracts from original articles that demonstrate the variety of research done in this area. Bongaert's article (1999) is an example of the discussion that is in progress on the issue of age. Bongaert's study concentrates on late starters who did manage to achieve native-like L2 pronunciation. The second excerpt is from an article by Sparks and Ganschow (1991), in which the authors discuss individual differences with a special focus on Foreign Language Aptitude. The authors give a comprehensive overview of the field that can be seen as complementary to our discussion in Unit A6. Among other things, the authors elaborate on the role of *anxiety* in second language. A further complementation is found in the final extract from an article by Gardner, Tremblay and Masgoret (1997). In this article, the authors attempt to provide an integrated picture of 34 of the most important individual differences, leading to an obviously complex overall picture. The focus of their article is on the role of motivational factors.

'Ultimate attainment in L2 pronunciation: The case of very advanced late L2 learners' by T. Bongaerts in D. Birdsong (Ed.) *Second language acquisition and the critical period hypothesis*. Mahwah, NJ: Erlbaum, 1999, pp. 133–159

Text B6.1
T. Bongaerts

The first excerpt included in this extension is from one of the articles by Theo Bongaerts (1999). In this article, Bongaerts begins by summarising some of the earlier studies involving the group of learners who turned out to have acquired a native-like accent in their second language, even though they started learning this language as adults. From this article we have selected the author's summary of the first two experiments. The third study, which was also reported on in this paper, refers to the same review questions and uses the same methodology as the first two. The difference was that in the third study the participants' L1 was not typologically closely related to the L2. Also for this group of learners, the same results were found.

(. . .) I will report on three studies, two with Dutch learners of English and one with Dutch learners of French. The aim of the studies, which were all conducted at the University of Nijmegen, was to find out whether or not some learners could be

Text B6.1
T. Bongaerts

Text B6.1
T. Bongaerts

identified who, in spite of a late start, had attained such a good pronunciation of an L2 that native listeners would judge them to be native speakers of the language. The studies were inspired, as were similar studies on ultimate attainment in the domain of grammatical competence by Birdsong (1992), Van Wuijtswinkel (1994), and White and Genesee (1996), by Long's suggestion that future ultimate attainment studies should focus on very advanced learners. The studies I review in this chapter, therefore, all included a group of carefully screened, highly successful learners in their designs. For reasons of space I cannot give full accounts of any of the three studies. Rather, I briefly summarize the design and main findings of the first study and give more detailed information on what I consider the central aspects of the second and third studies.

Task B6.1

➤ Imagine you were going to conduct a study to see whether advanced learners can attain a native-like pronunciation. Where would you find your learner subjects? Who would be your control subjects? How would you go about finding judges? What types of tasks would you ask your subjects to perform?

Text B6.1
T. Bongaerts

The first study[1]

There were three groups of participants in this study: a control group with 5 native speakers of British English and two groups of learners. One group consisted of 10 Dutch learners of English who had been brought to our attention by English as a Foreign Language (EFL) experts, who described them as highly successful learners with an excellent command of British English. The English learners in this group were the key participants in our study. The other experimental group was composed of 12 learners of English at various levels of proficiency. None of the learners had received instruction in English before the age of 12. All participants provided four English speech samples: They talked briefly about recent holiday experiences and they read aloud a brief *text*, 10 sentences and a list of 25 words. Four linguistically inexperienced native speakers of British English rated the four speech samples for accent, using a 5-point scale, which ranged from 1 (*very strong accent: definitely non-native*) to 5 (*no foreign accent at all: definitely native*). The most important result of the study was that the judges appeared to be unable to make a distinction between the group of highly successful learners and the native speaker control group. In addition, there were some results that we had clearly not expected: (a) the average score assigned to the group of native speakers was rather low (3.94) and (b) half of the participants in the group of highly successful learners received higher ratings than any of the native speakers. We hypothesized that an explanation for these unexpected results might perhaps be found in the composition of the group of native speakers and the group of judges. The participants in the former group were from the south of England or from the Midlands, and their pronunciation contained some regional features. The participants from the group of very successful learners had all been intensively trained to speak the supraregional variety of British English known as Received Pronunciation (RP).

---

1   For a full report on this study, see Bongaerts, Planken, and Schils (1995).

The judges all lived in York, in the north of England. We speculated that there may have been an inclination on the part of the judges to assign higher scores to participants who spoke the supraregional variety than to those who spoke English with a regional accent with which they may not have been very familiar. As these are mere speculations, however, we decided to conduct a follow up experiment in which we took care to match native speaker controls and judges more closely in terms of the variety of English that they spoke.

Text B6.1
T. Bongaerts

Task B6.2

➤ In the first study discussed above, there were some unexpected results: the non-native speakers were judged more native-like than the native ones. Would you agree with the explanation the author gives? In the second study, the authors try to avoid such problems by asking different controls and judges. What criteria the native speaker controls and judges, in your opinion?

The second study[2]

Text B6.1
T. Bongaerts

Participants

As in the first experiment, there were three groups of participants:

Group 1 was composed of 10 native speakers of standard English (mean age 27). They all spoke British English with a 'neutral,' supraregional accent, which is the target of instruction in most Dutch schools. They were selected from a larger pool of candidates who were originally recruited for the experiment. Only those candidates were invited to participate who had indicated on a questionnaire that they did not speak English with a regional accent and whom we had judged to have no regional accent after listening to four different speech samples they had provided.

Group 2 consisted of 11 native speakers of Dutch (mean age 42), 9 of whom had also participated in the first study. They were selected for the experiment because university-based EFL experts had designated them as highly successful, very advanced learners with an exceptionally good command of British English. The participants reported to have been not more than incidentally exposed to English input, through the Dutch media, before entering high school at or around the age of 12. While at high school, they received 2 hours of instruction in English per week from native speakers of Dutch, who most of the time did not use English as the medium of instruction. After graduating from high school, they all studied English at a university, where they were for the first time exposed to a large amount of English input. During their first year at the university, they also received intensive instruction in the pronunciation of the supraregional variety of British English known as RP. During the last stage of their study, most participants spent a year abroad at a British university. At the time of the experiment, all but 2 of the 11 participants taught English at a Dutch university or a Dutch teacher-training institute. All participants reported in a questionnaire that it was very important for them to have very good pronunciation in English.

---

2 For more details, in particular on the preparation of speech samples and on procedures, as well as for extended discussion, see Bongaerts, Van Summeren, Planken, and Schils (1997).

Group 3 consisted of 20 native speakers of Dutch (mean age 30) at widely different levels of proficiency in English. This group was composed of students of English, Dutch, and history, and of professors from various departments.

Speech samples

All participants read aloud the following six sentences a total of three times:

1 Arthur will finish his thesis within three weeks.
2 My sister Paula prefers coffee to tea.
3 The lad was mad about his dad's new fad.
4 Mat's flat is absolutely fantastic.
5 It's a pity we didn't go to the city.
6 You'd better look it up in a cookbook.

The sentences were picked such that they contained phones ranging from very similar to very different from Dutch phones. Only the participants' last two renderings were used for the experiment (henceforth called first and second versions, respectively), except when they contained irregularities such as slips of the tongue.

Judges and procedure

The speech samples were judged by 13 native speakers of British English (mean age 44), who were selected from a larger pool of candidates using the following criteria: Their level of education should be comparable to that of the Dutch participants in the study, they had to be residents of Great Britain, and most important, they had to speak standard British English without a regional accent. Spontaneous speech samples the prospective judges had provided enabled us to ascertain whether the latter criterion had been met. Thirteen judges met all criteria; 6 of them were or had been EFL teachers or phoneticians (the experienced judges), and 7 had not received any formal training in languages or linguistics after high school (the inexperienced judges).

For each judge, a unique tape was prepared that contained 12 sets of speech samples, each set consisting of one sentence pronounced by all 41 participants. Within each set, the order of the participants was randomized. The 12 sets were administered to the judges in the following order: The first six sets, which contained the first versions of the sentences, were presented in the order 1, 2, 3, 4, 5, 6; and the second six sets, with the second versions, in the order 5, 3, 1, 6, 4, 2. The judges rated all ($2 \times 6 \times 41$ = 492) speech samples for accent on the same 5-point scale that was used in the first study. They were told that they would hear sentences pronounced by an unspecified proportion of native and non-native speakers of British English.

 ### Task B6.3

➤ The procedure described above is one of 'random sampling', very common in research. Why, in your opinion, is it so important to conduct sampling randomly?

Results

First, we calculated the scores assigned to each participant and averaged them across 12 samples (two renderings of six sentences) and 13 judges. These scores are displayed in Table B6.1.

Table B6.1 Mean participant scores averaged across samples and judges

Group 1[a]		Group 2[b]		Group 3[c]			
Participant	M	Participant	M	Participant	M	Participant	M
1	4.75	11	4.75	22	2.88	32	1.46
2	4.93	12	4.32	23	3.04	33	3.10
3	4.94	13	4.47	24	1.88	34	3.76
4	4.67	14	4.65	25	1.53	35	3.26
5	4.86	15	4.18	26	1.79	36	2.43
6	4.93	16	4.93	27	1.92	37	4.14
7	4.93	17	4.71	28	3.92	38	1.74
8	4.90	18	4.32	29	3.18	39	3.57
9	4.72	19	4.83	30	1.60	40	2.47
10	4.74	20	4.72	31	1.90	41	2.29
		21	4.83				

[a]$M = 4.84$ [b]$M = 4.61$ [c]$M = 2.59$

Inspection of Table B6.1 reveals that the native speakers of English received very high scores: Individual means range from 4.67 to 4.94, with a group mean of 4.84, which is much higher than the average score of 3.94 assigned to the native speakers in the first study. The table also shows that the highly successful learners, too, were given high scores: Their means ranged from 4.18 to 4.93, with a group mean of 4.61.

In the section that follows, Bongaerts shows that there were significant differences between the groups. Group 2 and especially Group 3 clearly deviate from the native speaker scores.

(. . .) However, the main aim of the study was to find out whether or not at least some learners could be identified whose scores were comparable to those assigned to the native speakers. Our next analyses, therefore, focused on individual learners. In these analyses, we adopted the criterion of nativelikeness that Flege *et al.* (1995) used in their study of the strength of perceived foreign accent in the English spoken by Italian immigrants in Canada. They considered participants who received a mean rating for the sentences they had been asked to pronounce that fell within 2 standard deviations of the mean rating assigned to the native speakers of English in their study to have spoken the sentences with an authentic, nativelike accent. The results of the analyses of the ratings assigned to individual participants, adopting Flege *et al.*'s '$z < 2$' criterion, are displayed in Table B6.2.

As Table B6.2 shows, there are 5 participants in group 2 marked with an asterisk in the table (11: $z = 0.98$; 16: $z = 0.28$; 19: $z = 0.14$; 20: $z = 1.12$; 21: $z = 0.66$), who meet this criterion. In other words, this analysis, which was based on scores averaged across sentences, led to the conclusion that the pronunciation of five highly successful learners could be characterized as authentic.

Text B6.1
T. Bongaerts

Table B6.2 Standard scores for 'native(-like)ness' for all participants

Group 1[a]		Group 2[b]		Group 3[c]			
Participant	z	Participant	z	Participant	z	Participant	z
1	1.70*	11	0.98*	22	25.06	32	40.41
2	−1.10*	12	5.73	23	22.92	33	22.17
3	−1.16*	13	3.53	24	37.26	34	13.77
4	0.34*	14	2.41	25	40.86	35	20.07
5	−0.10*	15	6.69	26	37.26	36	29.77
6	−1.26*	16	0.28*	27	35.67	37	5.59
7	0.33*	17	2.64	28	8.57	38	37.62
8	−0.44*	18	4.80	29	19.75	39	13.88
9	0.64*	19	0.14*	30	40.17	40	27.99
10	1.06*	20	1.12*	31	35.62	41	30.77
		21	0.66*				

[a]$M = 0.00$ [b]$M = 2.63$ [c]$M = 27.26$

Note. * = native(-like).

(. . .)

A further investigation of the data shows that 5 highly successful learners meet the criterion of nativelikeness on Sentences 1, 2, 3, 4, and 6 and that 3 of these participants reach the criterion on Sentence 5 as well. In comparison, the native speakers, whose scores are not displayed in Table B6.3, meet the criterion on all six sentences. The conclusion we can draw, then, is that, using very strict criteria, we have been able to identify a number of learners who, in the present study, have consistently managed to convince native English judges that they are native speakers of British English.

It could be objected that the results of the experiments might not be generalizable to L1–L2 pairings other than the one in the present study or to other learning contexts, in view of the prominent position that English has in the Dutch media in comparison with other foreign languages. Such considerations led us to set up a third experiment.

The aim of the third study was to find out if the results of the second study could also be obtained in an experiment with languages that are typologically less related than Dutch and English. Therefore, the learners in this study were Dutch learners of French. The results of this experiment show that as a group the highly successful learners were outperformed by the native speakers. However, this conclusion does not apply to all learners individually. The individual scores show that three highly successful learners could be identified who managed to attain an 'authentic, nativelike French accent'.

Text B6.1
T. Bongaerts

Conclusions and discussion

According to those who support the notion of a critical period for accent, it would be impossible to achieve a native-like pronunciation in an L2 after a specified, biological period of time. The three studies summarized in this chapter were, unlike most previous studies on age-related differences in ultimate attainment, specifically designed to test this claim. Each of the studies included a carefully selected group of very advanced, highly successful late learners in its design. These learners of English or French with a Dutch L1 background had, at least initially, primarily learned the

Text B6.1
T. Bongaerts

L2 in an instructional context, in high school. They had not been massively exposed to input from native speakers of the target language until they were about 18 years of age, when they went to the university to study English or French. The main conclusion to be drawn from the combined results of the three studies is that the pronunciation of some of these learners was consistently judged to be native-like, or authentic, by listeners who were native speakers of the language. We argue that such results may be interpreted as evidence suggesting that claims concerning an absolute biological barrier to the attainment of a nativelike accent in a foreign language are too strong.

Having said this, it should also be pointed out that nativelike attainment in the domain of pronunciation seems to be a fairly exceptional phenomenon. The question that needs to be addressed is what is it that makes the exceptional learners identified in our experiments so different from the general population of less successful learners? We are far from being able to give a conclusive answer to this question, as we did not make a detailed study of the specific characteristics of these learners. We do not know, therefore, to what extent these learners differ from less successful learners in terms of cognitive variables such as language aptitude, cognitive style, or the use of learning strategies, or affective variables such as anxiety, empathy, or what Guiora (e.g. 1990; 1991) termed *ego permeability*. [i.e. the willingness of learners to give up part of their own (L1) identity].

Yet, on the basis of what we know about the learning histories of the highly successful learners in our studies, we would like to suggest that a combination of the following learner and context factors may have contributed importantly to their success. In the introduction, we referred to Klein's (1995) suggestion that a nativelike accent may be attainable for late L2 learners, provided that it is of vital importance to them to sound like native speakers and provided they have continued access to massive, authentic L2 input. As the description of the participants in our studies showed, both factors were clearly operative in the case of the very successful learners. They were all highly motivated individuals who reported that it was very important to them to be able to speak English or French without a Dutch accent, and they all received a large amount of input from native speakers from the time they entered the university around the age of 18. Another important learning-context factor may have been what we have elsewhere (Bongaerts, Van Summeren, Planken, & Schils, 1997) called *input enhancement through instruction*, using a term adapted from Ioup (1995). In the introduction, we cited evidence that the original perceptual and motoric abilities that enable children to master the pronunciation of their L1 are not lost over time and can still be accessed by adults. We also cited evidence that late L2 learners tend to (over)rely on the categorical mode of perception and thus to perceive L2 sounds in terms of firmly established L1 phonetic categories. In this connection, we remind the reader that, in the course of their studies at the university, the highly successful learners in our experiments had received intensive perceptual training that focused their attention on subtle phonetic contrasts between the speech sounds of the target language and those of their L1. We suggest that this may have helped them to rely less on the categorical mode and more on the continuous mode of perception, as they did when they acquired their L1, and thus to gradually work out what the relevant sound cues in the L2 are (see also Hammond, 1995; Martohardjono and Flynn, 1995) and to establish correct perceptual targets (Flege, 1995) for the L2 speech sounds. In addition, the very advanced learners had all received intensive training in the production of L2 speech sounds aimed at developing the finely tuned motor control required for accurate pronunciation. In sum, what we suggest is that the success of the exceptional adult learners we identified may have been at least partly due to the combination of three factors: high motivation, continued access to massive L2 input, and intensive training in the perception and production of L2 speech sounds. Clearly, much more work in this area is called for, and subsequent studies of ultimate attainment should put more effort into identifying the psychological and contextual correlates of exceptionally successful L2 learning.

⭐ **Task B6.4**

➤ In their conclusion, the authors try to account for the fact that some non-native speakers who were not exposed extensively to the language before the age of 12 are nonetheless able to attain native-like pronunciation. Most of them were students of English language and literature and were teaching at Dutch higher education level. Are the possible reasons given for the fact that these L2 learners performed like natives in pronunciation in line with the observations made concerning learners' characteristics in Unit A6?

So far, our studies have focused on the pronunciation of British English and French by adult learners with a Dutch L1 background. It is an empirical question whether the findings we reported in this chapter can be generalized to pairings of L1s and L2s that are typologically more distant than the L1–L2 pairings in our experiments. We intend to explore this issue in future studies with very advanced learners of Dutch who have Turkish, Moroccan Arabic, or Berber L1 backgrounds.

To conclude, although the speech of adult L2 learners is typically accented, it seems that we have identified at least some individuals who have beaten the predictions of the critical period hypothesis for accent by attaining a native-like pronunciation of an L2. A major challenge for the future would be to identify which (combinations of) learner, context, and language variables (L1–L2 pairings) are instrumental in making native-like attainment possible.

⭐ **Task B6.5**

➤ To what extent does the author's explanation correspond with Schmidt's views on the need for attention to learn something and the idea that instruction may help to raise awareness (see Unit A1), and Paradis's view on how controlled processes may be replaced with automatic processes (see Unit A5)?

This study by Bongaerts was meant to provide evidence for or against the critical period hypothesis, but one of the side benefits of this study has been to show that certain learners are capable of attaining native-like pronunciation, one of the most difficult things to acquire in an L2. Probably, only certain learners may be able to achieve this. These learners had the following in common: they are native speakers of Dutch, a language very closely related to English. Moreover, they were English majors at university, who are obviously intelligent and motivated, and have a great language aptitude. The following article will also concern learners' characteristics, but concentrates on learners that may have problems in acquiring an L2.

'Foreign language learning differences: Affective or native language aptitude differences?' by Richard L. Sparks and Leonore Ganschow (1991) in *Modern Language Journal* 75, 3–16

Text B6.2
R. L. Sparks
and
L. Ganschow

This extract comes from a frequently quoted article on language learning aptitude: Sparks and Ganschow (1991). In their article these authors suggest that learners who have problems learning a second language may also have problems in their first language. After an introduction and a discussion on how learning styles and affective factors may influence FL learning, they concentrate on one of these affective factors, *anxiety*. They refer to a study by Horwitz *et al.* (1986), who claim that poor FL performance may be due to anxiety.

Anxiety and FL learning

Text B6.2
R. L. Sparks
and
L. Ganschow

In proposing an alternative hypothesis that considers native language ability as a variable in L2 learning, the possibility of a confounding interaction between an affective variable, such as anxiety, and receptive/expressive language skills (such as listening, speaking, and auditory memory) in the FL might be hypothesized. Positive correlations, for example, have been found between anxiety and speech and between anxiety and listening comprehension and ability to imitate. These correlations suggest that difficulties in speaking and listening skills and poor memory for language may contribute to the anxiety that students experience in FL classes.

(. . .)

In our view, the speculation of Horwitz (1986) and her colleagues that anxiety is the likely cause of FL failure must be approached with caution. First, they fail to use a comparison group and therefore provide only anecdotal information about the possible contribution of anxiety to poor FL performance. Second, neither the students' native nor FL aptitude was assessed to ascertain if highly anxious students have learning problems in their native language or poor aptitude for L2 learning. It is, therefore, conceivable that other factors, such as difficulties with one or more aspects of one's native language, may contribute to poor performance in FL classes and that undue anxiety may *result from* native language learning problems. The affective qualities then, may only be symptoms – behavioral manifestations – of a deeper problem. In the next sections, we examine research on FL aptitude and explore the hypothesis that students with FL learning difficulties may have underlying native language problems that impact on their learning of another.

After this point, the authors elaborate on the components that constitute language-learning aptitude, which we have discussed in Unit A6. Then the authors concentrate on the relationship between native and foreign language learning difficulties and introduce their Linguistic Coding Deficit Hypothesis. The abbreviation LD in this fragment stands for 'learning disabilities'.

Task B6.6

➤ Below you will find some definitions of learning disabilities (Lokerson, 1992). In your opinion, which of the learning disabilities mentioned might be especially troublesome in learning an L2?

Attention Deficit Disorder (ADD) – A severe difficulty in focussing and maintaining attention. Often leads to learning and behaviour problems at home, school and work. Also called Attention Deficit Hyperactivity Disorder (ADHD).

Brain injury – The physical damage to brain tissue or structure that occurs before, during or after birth that is verified by EEG, MRI, CAT, or a similar examination, rather than by observation of performance. When caused by an accident, the damage may be called Traumatic Brain Injury (TBI).

Developmental aphasia – A severe language disorder that is presumed to be due to brain injury rather than because of a developmental delay in the normal acquisition of language.

Dyslexia – A severe difficulty in understanding or using one or more areas of language, including listening, speaking, reading, writing and spelling.

Dysnomia – A marked difficulty in remembering names or recalling words needed for oral or written language.

Learned helplessness – A tendency to be a passive learner who depends on others for decisions and guidance. In individuals with LD, continued struggle and failure can heighten this lack of self-confidence.

Locus of control – The tendency to attribute success and difficulties either to internal factors such as effort or to external factors such as chance. Individuals with learning disabilities tend to blame failure on themselves and achievement on luck, leading to frustration and passivity.

Minimal Brain Dysfunction (MBD) – A medical and psychological term originally used to refer to the learning difficulties that seemed to result from identified or presumed damage to the brain. Reflects a medical, rather than educational or vocational orientation.

Perceptual handicap – Difficulty in accurately processing, organising and discriminating among visual, auditory or tactile information. A person with a perceptual handicap may say that 'cap/cup' sound the same or that 'b' and 'd' look the same. However, glasses or hearing aids do not necessarily indicate a perceptual handicap.

Specific Language Disability (SLD) – A severe difficulty in some aspect of listening, speaking, reading, writing or spelling, while skills in the other areas are age-appropriate. Also called Specific Language Learning Disability (SLLD).

Specific Learning Disability (SLD) – The official term used in federal legislation to refer to difficulty in certain areas of learning, rather than in all areas of learning. Synonymous with learning disabilities.

Relationship of native and FL learning difficulties

The suggestion that FL learning problems may occur in association with, or perhaps as a result of, L1 learning problems was first made in studies associated with students with learning disabilities. Strong support is evident in LD research results that learning disabilities have their genesis in oral and/or written language problems. As increasing numbers of LD students entered college in the 1980s and were required to take a foreign language, references to the FL learning problems of students with LD began to appear in professional publications. Informal reports at several universities showed that substantial numbers of students were being referred for suspected LD after college entry. The referrals were made because of the students' inability to meet the FL requirement at the university, giving rise to speculation that subtle *native* language problems became evident primarily because of the demands that the study of a new and unfamiliar symbol system placed on these students. Prior to 1980, only one reference, a chapter in a book by Harvard counselor Kenneth Dinklage about Harvard's students, addressed the possibility of *language* disabilities among students who had difficulties in FL classes. Dinklage stated that these bright students who could not seem to learn a FL exhibit three types of problems: 1) difficulty with the written (reading and writing) aspects of their native language; 2) inability to distinguish the sounds of the FL and, thus, difficulties with an oral communication approach to FL learning; and 3) memory problems for sounds and words. While memory problems may occur in conjunction with auditory discrimination difficulties, the former is characterized by difficulty in discriminating between sounds and words whereas the latter refers to the inability to hold auditory material in memory long enough to complete the task. According to Dinklage, many of these students had an early history of reading, writing, and spelling problems similar to what was described in the literature at that time as 'dyslexia,' a type of learning disability. While affective symptoms frequently accompanied the students' failure, Dinklage and his staff ruled out lack of motivation or anxiety and, instead, supported the idea of an underlying language processing disability as the cause of FL failure.

Text B6.2
R. L. Sparks
and
L. Ganschow

Task B6.7

➤ In the following section, it is argued that phonological awareness is a key predictor to reading ability in a language such as English. Phonological awareness is the ability to 'conceive of spoken words as a sequence of phonemic segments and the capacity to identify these segments in spoken words and syllables'. How, in your opinion, does a child learn to read a word like 'dog'? Reading such a word at the beginning stages is probably a controlled process. How, in your opinion, does the reading of a word like 'dog' develop into an automatic process?

Text B6.2
R. L. Sparks
and
L. Ganschow

Research shows that an underlying language processing difficulty appears when children first learn to speak their native language. While it is true that most children acquire oral language, all children do not necessarily acquire these skills at the same rate. Often, overt or subtle speech articulation difficulties, language delay, otitis media [middle ear infection], or other language-related problems are the precursors of later differences in a student's language profile. Even though children with a history of language difficulties eventually learn to speak and understand their native language, their FL aptitude profile could be related to and/or affected by these earlier problems. The LD literature, in fact, strongly supports the position that early problems in acquiring oral language lead to later written language difficulties and that language difficulties, both written and oral, may continue into adulthood. Studies also show that *reading* disabled children display large deficits in *listening* comprehension. Researchers have recently begun to focus upon a small set of skills which play a significant part in later reading/writing performance, i.e., the ability to access the phonological code in both oral and written language. Accumulating evidence has indicated that learning to read and spell depends upon the ability to conceive of spoken words as a sequence of phonemic segments and the capacity to identify these segments in spoken words and syllables. This particular skill has been shown to be a significant predictor of success in learning to read even when the effects of IQ and family status have been accounted for, and evidence is mounting that 'phonological awareness' is causally related to later reading disability.

Phonological awareness and phoneme segmentation not only play a part in the acquisition of written language but also in the development of oral language. Recent research indicates that reading disabled children have limited awareness and sensitivity to the speech sound structure of the language. They also have word-finding and naming problems and poor verbal short-term memory. Studies also have shown that these children have difficulty comprehending lengthy oral sentences or carrying on conversations and articulating the language. Implications from this research are that poor readers need a higher quality of signal than do good readers for error-free performance in speech (which is not the case for non-speech sounds in the environment) and that poor readers have deficits which are *specific* to difficulties with the phonological structure of words.

While the belief is common that high school or college level FL learners have acquired or discovered at least some basic principles of phonology, the 'phonological awareness' research suggests that such may *not* be the case. Moreover, older learners, even adults, may not necessarily acquire phonological or syntactic rules faster with age, as has been suggested.

Whether the problem is called 'phonological awareness,' 'phonetic coding,' or 'auditory ability,' it seems clear that specific difficulty at the phoneme level can cause difficulties with the acquisition of oral and written language in both the native and the FL. Carroll (1962) makes the point that 'phonetic coding' ability is a '. . . cognitive process which cannot be directly observed' (1962: 128) and that '. . . a person low in this ability will have trouble not only remembering phonetic material, word forms, etc., but also in mimicking speech sounds' (1962: 129). Pimsleur (1968), too, notes that poor 'auditory ability' often accounted for intelligent or motivated students who could not learn a FL. These intuitions about language factors, especially the phonological component, affecting FL learning are consistent with recent literature on L1 learning difficulties.

We propose now to relate our understanding of L1 problems of students with LD to FL learning by proposing that students with FL difficulties may have underlying linguistic coding deficits which interfere with their ability to learn a FL.

Task B6.8

➤ Using a common-sense approach, decide which of the following statements you would expect to be true. For each try to think of reasons why you thought they were true (or not).

1 Good readers use context clues more than poor readers to understand difficult words.
2 Good reading involves, among other things, relatively complete processing of the individual letters of print.
3 Students who have trouble learning a foreign language (in an instructed setting) may also have some language problems in their first language.
4 The problems that learners who have difficulties processing the structural and formal properties of spoken and printed words (i.e. learners with a 'Linguistic Coding Deficit') have in learning their L1 are usually very noticeable.

Linguistic coding deficit hypothesis

Text B6.2
R. L. Sparks
and
L. Ganschow

We cited studies above which show that some individuals have difficulty learning their native language in oral and/or written form and that this difficulty is likely to affect ability to learn a FL. We also provided growing evidence indicating a lack of phonological awareness as a primary source of difficulty in learning to read and write one's native language. In our view, the hypothesis of language-based difficulties provides a viable alternative to affective explanations for FL learning problems. Our hypothesis, which we will call the Linguistic Coding Deficit Hypothesis (LCDH) is derived from the work of Vellutino and Scanlon (1986), who found that poor readers/writers had difficulties processing the structural and formal properties of spoken and printed words. Vellutino and Scanlon coined the term 'linguistic coding' to refer to the use of phonological, syntactic, and semantic aspects of the language to code information. Their findings suggested that good readers were attuned to *both* the meaning (semantic) and structural (syntactic and phonological) components of language but that poor readers were attuned primarily to the meaning. Poor readers were found to be especially deficient in phonological coding or the ability to access the phonological code rapidly and automatically to read individual words.

Until recently, many educators assumed that skilled readers generate hypotheses about text as they read; using contextual knowledge and focusing on the decoding of individual words only when a hypothesis fails to be confirmed. In this view, skilled readers' attention is driven by higher-level comprehension processes and is directed to and by the meaning of the text. Recent research indicates that poor readers also use context to facilitate word recognition and that they actually rely on context to enhance decoding *more than* good readers do. 'Top down' models of reading have been criticized in scholarship because good readers seem to acquire greater knowledge of context but use this knowledge minimally, if at all, to speed word recognition. In an exhaustive review of the reading literature Adams (1990: 105) states clearly that '. . . the single immutable and non-optional fact about skilful reading is that it involves relatively complete processing of the individual letters of print'.

To investigate the LCDH in relation to learning a FL, Sparks, Ganschow and Pohlman (1989) tested a group of twenty-two college enrolled students who had petitioned and been granted a waiver from the FL graduation requirement because of their inability to pass a FL course. Diagnostic inferences from their test results indicated a common thread among the students, an overt or subtle oral and/or written native language problem, which matched the three components described by Vellutino and Scanlon in their linguistic coding hypothesis. Sparks and colleagues speculate that phonological problems have the most severe as well as immediate impact upon the learning of a FL because, of the thirteen students with phonological deficits, seven failed the FL in the first semester and six failed in the next semester. Of the eight students with intact phonological skills but with syntactic or semantic deficits, seven reached the third semester of the language, one made it to the second semester, and none failed the first semester.

In another recent study (Ganschow *et al.*, 1991) we compared the performance of successful and unsuccessful FL learners on several variables including FL aptitude, intelligence, and L1 oral and written language skills. Students were college level juniors and seniors, fifteen of whom had received an 'A' or 'B' in at least two semesters of a FL course and fifteen students whose petitions for an alternative to the FL requirement had been approved by their institutions. Students were matched for GPA [grade point average], sex, and year in college. The results showed no differences in intelligence between the two groups. Yet, the petition students scored significantly poorer on the total MLAT [Modern Language Aptitude Test] and specific MLAT subtests (which supports Gajar's study described earlier in this paper). In addition, oral and written language test scores showed significant differences between successful FL learners and petition students on measures of phonology, word identification, spelling, and grammar but *not* in reading comprehension. Results suggest that petition students had particular difficulties at the phonological and syntactic levels of language but not at the semantic level, in terms of comprehension.

With its emphasis on the specific components of language, i.e., phonological, syntactic, and semantic, the LCDH provides an explanation for why secondary or postsecondary students who appear to have learned their native language adequately, in fact, have problems that have gone unnoticed but have been compensated for over the years. Generally, the problem areas are subtle, e.g., relatively weak spelling or a slow rate of reading. For the most part, the compensatory strategies used by these students mask their linguistic coding deficits in the native language, and they often succeed well in academic settings. Most of the college students reported in studies by Dinklage (1971), Pompian and Thum (1988), Lefebvre (1984), and Sparks, Ganschow, and Pohlman (1989) were identified as LD after college entry because of FL learning difficulties.

In our view, what happens to these students is that their compensatory strategies become unworkable when they are placed in situations where they must learn a totally unfamiliar and new linguistic coding system. The student is virtually 'thrown back' into the situations s/he experienced in learning to talk and/or learning to read and write. Our studies on petition students, Gajar's MLAT research with students with LD, and Dinklage's case studies on Harvard's FL failures all support the idea that FL proficiency involves factors that extend beyond motivation, attitude, anxiety, or intelligence.

In a review of aptitude research done in the 1990s, Sparks *et al.* (2001) summarise the work done on their LDHC. Their main conclusion is that there is a clear and significant relationship between a learner's native language skills and her FL skills, especially at the level of phonology and orthography.

In the same article, these authors list what they think are important directions for the future of aptitude research. They emphasise the importance of new norms for the MLAT and the development of appropriate phonological measures for aptitude, as these measures most strongly affect linguistic coding deficiency. Furthermore, they argue that future research into affective variables should include native language skills. In view of the findings discussed in the articles included in this unit, the latter point certainly merits follow-up.

Sparks and his colleagues stress the importance of including several factors at the same time in studies investigating individual differences between learners. Obviously, all individual learner characteristics continuously affect each other and this seems to be a valuable recommendation. The interaction of a wide range of learner characteristics in one complex design is precisely the topic of the next article we have included.

'Towards a full model of second language learning: An empirical investigation' by R. C. Gardner, Paul F. Tremblay and Anne-Marie Masgoret (1997) in *Modern Language Journal* 81, 344–362

Text B6.3
R. C. Gardner,
P. F. Tremblay
and
A.-M. Masgoret

Even though the authors never intended to do so, we believe the next article supports DST to a great degree. In the previous article it was claimed that it is not really possible to separate 'affective' factors from others such as L1 ability.

In this article, the authors (Gardner, Tremblay and Masgoret, 1997) have investigated several individual differences in one study, emphasising the interaction of factors like anxiety, aptitude, motivation, field dependence, language learning strategies and self-confidence. The 'causal model' proposed by the authors in the result section showing the connections between these affective variables and achievement resembles a DST model. Not one single factor stands out, they are all interconnected, and it is impossible to establish or separate causal relations among them.

After an introduction, the authors provide an overview of previous studies for all of the factors. Only those factors that were not discussed in Unit A6 will be included here.

Language anxiety

Text B6.3
R. C. Gardner,
P. F. Tremblay
and
A.-M. Masgoret

Early research suggested that the relation of anxiety to SLA was equivocal. Scovel (1978) reviewed a number of studies investigating the relation between anxiety and L2 achievement and found evidence for positive, negative, and no relationships. Based on these findings, he proposed that there might be two types of anxiety, which he referred to as *facilitating* and *debilitating* anxiety. Other research being conducted at the time, however, found evidence to suggest that anxiety specific to the language learning context (i.e., language anxiety) tended to be negatively related to L2 achievement (see, e.g. Gardner, 1985: 33–6).

In recent years, there has been much more interest in the role of language anxiety. Horwitz, Horwitz, and Cope (1986) developed the Foreign Language Classroom Anxiety Scale (FLCAS), assessing three components of anxiety (communication apprehension,

Text B6.3
R. C. Gardner,
P. F. Tremblay
and
A.-M. Masgoret

test anxiety, and fear of negative evaluation) that they believed were responsible for its detrimental effect on language learning. Other researchers have also developed measures of language anxiety. Examples of such measures are the French Class Anxiety Scale (Gardner and Smythe, 1975), the English Use Anxiety Scale (Clément, Gardner, and Smythe, 1977), the Anxometer (Macintyre and Gardner, 1991), and other measures that are conceptually related to language anxiety (e.g. Ely, 1986).

Research using these various scales indicates that language anxiety is negatively related to achievement in the L2 (see, e.g. Clément *et al.*, 1977; Gardner *et al.*, 1975; Horwitz, Horwitz, and Cope, 1986; Macintyre *et al.*, 1991). These studies have found that language anxiety is associated with deficits in listening comprehension, impaired vocabulary learning, reduced word production, low scores on standardized tests, low grades in language courses or a combination of these factors. This anxiety is hypothesized to develop out of negative experiences in L2 contexts, where students may begin to associate the L2 with feelings of apprehension (Macintyre and Gardner, 1989). These anxiety-provoking experiences may create difficulties in the cognitive processing of L2 material (see, e.g. Macintyre, 1995).

Field dependence/independence

A number of studies have demonstrated a relationship between field dependence/ independence and achievement in the L2, with high levels of achievement being associated with field independence. Field-dependent individuals are characterized as sensitive and interested in others, while field-independent individuals are described as able to distinguish between figure and ground, and tending to be self-sufficient and analytical (Witkin, Goodenough, and Oltman, 1979). Often, in the studies concerned with SLA, field dependence/independence is measured using the Embedded Figures Test (Oltman, Raskin, and Witkin, 1971).

Several studies have reported relationships between field independence and L2 achievement (Genesee and Hamayan, 1980; Hansen and Stansfield, 1981; Naiman, Frölich, Stern, and Todesco, 1978). Krashen (1981) argues that because field independent individuals have an analytic orientation, they are potentially better language learners. Naiman *et al.* (1978) proposed that field-independent individuals would be successful language learners because they would distinguish between important elements to be learned and other less salient background factors. Hansen and Stansfield (1981) found, however, that most of the relationship between field independence and L2 achievement disappeared when the effects of scholastic ability were partialled out. In their review of a number of studies showing relationships between field independence and L2 proficiency, Chapelle and Green (1992) view field independence as a fluid ability closely related to language aptitude.

Language learning strategies

Language learning strategies are techniques that individuals use to help them learn L2 material and improve their skills. Oxford (1986) developed the Strategy Inventory for Language Learning (SILL), a self-report assessment designed to determine the extent to which individuals use various strategies to promote learning. In a factor analytic investigation of language learning strategies, Oxford, Nyikos, and Crookall (1987) identified five factors underlying the SILL: (a) General Study Habits, (b) Functional Practice, (c) Speaking and Communicating Meaning, (d) Studying and Practising Independently, and (e) Mnemonic Devices.

Other researchers have also proposed classifications of strategies. Thus, for example, Chamot (1990) proposed three major classes of strategies: (a) Metacognitive, (b) Cognitive, and (c) Socio-Affective. Regardless of how they are classified, research indicates that language learning may involve the use of several independent learning strategies that may have different effects on proficiency. Investigations confirm that there are relationships between the frequent use of learning strategies and achievement in the language (Green and Oxford, 1995; Oxford and Burry-Stock, 1995; Oxford, Park-Oh, Ito, and Sumrall, 1993).

Text B6.3
R. C. Gardner,
P. F. Tremblay
and
A.-M. Masgoret

Task B6.9

➤ In this section, strategies are mentioned without taking into account the fact that different types of learners may use different ones, or that different types of strategies might be more effective with different types of learners. In your opinion, would all types of learners use the same type of strategies?

Do you think some strategies might be more effective for some learners, depending on their level of proficiency, their motivation, and their aptitude?

Self-confidence

The concept of self-confidence is conceptually related to that of language anxiety, except that it emphasizes a positive as opposed to a negative component. Clément (1980) proposed that self-confidence was an important determinant of the motivation to learn a L2, and that this self-confidence developed in multicultural contexts as a function of the frequency and quality of contact with members of the L2 community. He proposed that self-confidence consisted of perceptions of confidence in the L2 as well as an absence of anxiety about learning or using the language. As stated by Clément, Dörnyei, and Noels (1994: 443) 'self-confidence includes two components . . . : anxiety as the affective aspect and self-evaluation of proficiency as the cognitive component'. Clément and his associates have found that indices of self-confidence correlate significantly and appreciably with measures of proficiency in the L2 (Clément, Dörnyei, and Noels, 1994; Clément et al., 1977; Clément, Gardner, and Smythe, 1980; Clément and Kruidenier, 1985).

Text B6.3
R. C. Gardner,
P. F. Tremblay
and
A.-M. Masgoret

Relationships among the individual difference variables

As demonstrated, there is evidence to indicate that all of these variables are related to indices of achievement in the L2, and that there are also relationships among many of these measures themselves. In addition to the obvious relationships between indices of attitudes and motivation (Gardner, 1985), relationships have been reported between self-confidence and both motivation and anxiety (Clément et al., 1985), and between self-efficacy (conceptually similar to self-confidence) and the frequency of use of language learning strategies (Chamot, 1994). Gardner (1985) presents evidence indicating that motivation and language aptitude are relatively independent, although other studies indicate that language aptitude tends to be related to field independence (see Genesee et al., 1980). Other research suggests that attitudinal/motivational variables could influence the extent to which individuals make use of various language

Text B6.3
R. C. Gardner,
P. F. Tremblay
and
A.-M. Masgoret

learning strategies (see, e.g. Oxford, Nyikos, and Crookall, 1987; Politzer, 1983; Politzer and McGroarty, 1985).

Some researchers have proposed models of SLA that have discussed the possible role of these types of variables in learning. Gardner (1985) reviews a number of such models; among the oldest appears to be the socio-educational model of SLA, which dates back to 1974, but has been revised and expanded since then (see e.g. Gardner and Macintyre, 1993; Tremblay and Gardner, 1995). Another is Clément's (1980) social context model. Both of these models have been subjected to empirical evaluation using causal modelling procedures, and both have received considerable support. Other, more complex, models have been proposed but, although they are based on interpretations of the literature, they have not themselves been put to direct empirical evaluation. One such model was proposed by Stern (1983: 498ff), while another was presented by Spolsky (1989). Both of these models are excellent overviews of the complex processes involved in language learning with many implications for language teaching and learning. They are, however, less concerned with functional relationships among the major variables that could be put to empirical test than are other models like the socio-educational and social-context models.

Existing research and theory make it clear that a number of variables relate to achievement in the L2, and it seems obvious that the variables do not operate independently of one another. The present investigation focuses on measures from all the classes of variables discussed above, and directs attention to the factorial composition underlying the relationships among them. A second objective is to investigate the relation of each of these variables to measures of achievement in a L2, so that their relative relationship to achievement can be considered with the same sample of students. A third objective is to assess the adequacy of fit of a causal model based on the socio-educational model of SLA, as described by Gardner (1985) and Gardner and MacIntyre (1993), but modified to incorporate the variables discussed above.

Method

Participants

The sample consisted of 82 female and 20 male university students enrolled in introductory French. Participants were recruited from their French classes and were paid $15 for their cooperation. Demographic information obtained from participants indicated that they had studied French for an average of 11.37 years (SD = 3.01), and that 86% of them had spent 9 or more years studying French. Other information revealed that 38% of them had between 1 and 14 years of French immersion experience (M = 2.96, SD = 4.43), and that 55% of them had spent at least a month in a French country or region.

 Task B6.10

➤ From the remaining discussion, it is not clear whether individual learning background (e.g. immersion versus non-immersion) has been taken into account in the analysis. As you read further consider whether individual learning background should have been taken into account, or not.

Procedure

Text B6.3
R. C. Gardner,
P. F. Tremblay
and
A.-M. Masgoret

Participants were tested in two stages. In the first session, they completed a question-naire containing measures of attitudes, motivation, achievement, and self-rating scales of French proficiency. Administration of this questionnaire took approximately 90 minutes and was conducted in small groups. Following this, participants made appointments for the second testing session that also lasted approximately 90 minutes. In this session, they completed a questionnaire containing measures of anxiety, learning strategies, aptitude, and field dependence/independence. Next, the participants completed a short language history questionnaire and were asked to sign a release form providing access to their final French grades. Following the second session, they were thanked for their participation and were paid $15.

Measures

Measures were obtained on 34 variables. The authors then provide a description of all 34 variables. They used nine variables from the AMTB, adjusted to make them suitable for university-level testing. In addition, they included six other self-report variables, taken from different sources and relating to factors like self-confidence and anxiety. French achievement was measured using eight variables like a cloze test, a spelling test, a theme test, a paired associates test and grades in French. Finally, several measures were included to express learning strategies, emotion management and self-perception of L2 performance. The correlations are expressed in a rotated factor matrix in which five factors emerge. Factor I is best expressed as 'self con-fidence in French'; Factor II as 'language learning strategies', Factor III as 'motivation to learn French', Factor IV as 'language aptitude' and Factor V as 'orientation to learn French'. The loadings are summarised in Table B6.3.

Next, the authors calculate aggregated scores for the most important underlying factors and investigated the correlation of these aggregated scores with achievement in French. The results of this step are represented in Table B6.4.

Table B6.4 shows that there is a moderately strong correlation (0.36) between moti-vation and the French grades. Correlations always vary between −1 and 1; the highest the number – positive or negative – the higher the correlation. The table also shows a moderately strong negative correlation between language anxiety and French grades. So the higher the motivation, the higher the French grades and the higher the anxiety, the lower the French grades (−0.33). However, correlations in themselves say nothing about cause and effect. The correlation between motivation and French grades, for instance, may imply that motivation helps the acquisition of French, but it may also imply that motivation increases when the grades go up!

Therefore, the final step the authors take is what is called 'causal modeling'. Causal modelling can be illustrated as follows. Let us accept that there is a correlation between a person's height and weight: the taller someone is, the heavier he or she is likely to be. In this case, there is a causal relation between height and weight: if the

Table B6.3 Rotated factor matrix: I = self-confidence in French; II = language-learning strategies; III = motivation to learn French; IV = language aptitude; V = orientation to learn French

Factors

Variables	I	II	III	IV	V
Spelling clues	.01	−.07	.23	.65	−.08
Words in sentences	.04	.03	.10	.73	.08
Paired associates	−.11	.05	.03	.51	−.10
Instrumental orientation	.21	.06	.05	−.27	.55
French use anxiety	−.82	−.08	−.27	.03	−.21
French class anxiety	−.86	.16	−.28	−.15	−.09
French language anxiety	−.81	.05	−.34	−.13	−.05
Attitudes toward French Canadians	.06	.12	.07	−.06	.77
Interest in foreign languages	.01	.26	.42	.28	.25
Integrative orientation	.12	.14	.15	.02	.85
Motivational intensity	.20	.52	.59	−.16	.01
Attitudes toward learning French	.27	.33	.73	.05	.20
Desire to learn French	.33	.36	.73	−.03	.15
Self-confidence (SCC)	.87	.00	.23	−.02	.03
Self-confidence (SCAC)	.87	.07	.17	−.11	.27
Self-confidence (SCGA)	.87	−.03	.26	−.04	.14
French class evaluation	.27	.03	.82	−.05	.03
French teacher evaluation	.11	−.24	.63	.19	.00
Memory strategies	−.07	.68	.11	−.06	−.05
Processing information strategies	.16	.86	.03	.10	.06
Missing information strategies	.10	.20	−.30	.36	.14
Meta-cognitive strategies	.03	.83	.17	−.09	.09
Emotion management strategies	.01	.75	.04	.00	.08
Learning with others strategies	.10	.72	−.11	.10	.27
Group embedded figures test	.01	−.11	−.17	.60	−.09
Can do–writing	.80	.18	−.03	.00	−.05
Can do–reading	.83	.05	−.01	−.12	.02
Can do–understanding	.86	.05	−.04	−.05	.07
Can do–speaking	.91	.13	−.02	.05	.01

Table B6.4 Correlations of the aggregate scores with achievement

Variables	Objective measures	French grades
Motivation	.27**	.36***
Language attitudes	.23*	.09
Language anxiety	−.66***	−.33**
Self-confidence	.64***	.29**
Can do	.64***	.33**
Learning strategies	−.10	.04
Language aptitude	.37***	.35**
Field independence	.14	.17

person becomes taller then he or she is likely to become heavier. However, there is no causal relation the other way round between weight and height. In other words, if the person becomes heavier, he or she is not necessarily likely to become taller. In causal modelling, a statistical procedure first estimates scenarios or hypotheses and then tests these hypotheses or scenarios. The results of this operation are graphically represented in Figure B6.1.

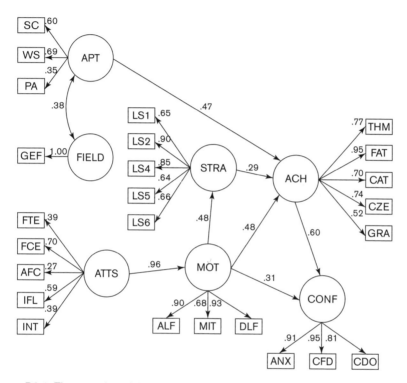

Figure B6.1 The causal model

APT: Language Aptitude; SC: Spelling Clues; WS: Words in Sentences; PA: Paired Associates; FIELD: Field Independence; GEF: Group Embedded Figures Test; ATTS: Language Attitudes; FTE: French Teacher Evaluation; FCE: French Course Evaluation; AFC: Attitudes toward French Canadians; IFL: Interest in Foreign Languages; INT: Integrative Orientation; STRA: Language Strategies; LS1: Remembering More Effectively: LS2: Using Mental Processes; LS4: Organizing and Evaluating Learning; LS5: Managing Emotion: LS6: Learning with Others; MOT: Motivation; ALF: Attitudes toward Learning French; MIT: Motivational Intensity; DLF: Desire to Learn French; ACH: Language Achievement; THM: Theme Test; FAT: French Achievement Test; CAT: Thing Category Test; CZE: Cloze Test; GRA: Grades in French; CONF: Self-Confidence, ANX: Language Anxiety; CFD: Self-Confidence; CDO: Self-Rated Proficiency (Can Do).

Even though this picture may seem overwhelming at first sight, it is not too difficult to interpret if it is clear what to look at. The circles represent the main factors such as attitude (ATTS) and motivation (MOT). Each circle points to a set of small squares, which represent causally related sub-fields on which the score for the main factors are based. For example, the motivation score is based on the attitude to learn French (ALF), the motivational intensity (MIT), and the desire to learn French (DLF). For instance, 'Motivation' shows a moderately strong correlation with language achievement of (.48); Self-confidence shows an even stronger correlation with language achievement (.60). Motivation, which is comprised of 'attitude toward learning French' (ALF), 'Motivational intensity' (MIT) and the 'Desire to learn French' (DLF), shows the strongest relation with ALF. This picture provides an interesting summary of the interaction of a wide variety of individual variables. In their conclusion, the authors explain how complex the relations are.

Text B6.3
R. C. Gardner,
P. F. Tremblay
and
A.-M. Masgoret

Integration and conclusions

This study examined a number of variables that have been shown to correlate significantly with indices of L2 achievement. The results are instructive. The exploratory factor analysis was performed to determine how the variables related to one another without any preconceived structure imposed on them. It is clear that despite the different theoretical models represented in the various measures, they group together into five relatively independent clusters. These clusters (factors) were identified as: (a) Self-Confidence with French, (b) Language Learning Strategies, (e) Motivation to Learn French, (d) Language Aptitude, and (e) Orientation to Learn French. That is, the various measures can be seen to fall into one of these five categories (factors), although examination of the factors themselves indicates that some measures contribute to more than one factor. This, in turn, suggests that there are some functional relationships among the measures and that even these categories are not mutually exclusive.

When attention is directed to the correlations between achievement in the L2 and the major variables researchers have identified by the measures, it is clear that different types of processes are implicated depending upon how one assesses achievement. Thus, when achievement is assessed by relatively objective measures taken at the same time as the other measures, indices of Language Anxiety, Self-Confidence, and Can Do evidence much higher correlations with this achievement than do indices of Language Aptitude, Motivation, or Language Attitudes. However, when achievement is measured in terms of more global and less time-specific indices, such as final grades in French, the correlations of all of the above measures with achievement are similar. One interpretation that might be put on these results is that the indices of Language Anxiety, Self-Confidence, and Can Do are simply better correlates of objective measures of proficiency than are the other measures studied here, but this begs the question as to why. Another interpretation might be that these three indices all involve some self-examination of French proficiency as well as of feelings of anxiety or self-confidence, and consequently that these indices were partially confounded with proficiency at the time they were taken. This would, in turn, increase the magnitude of the correlations between these indices and measures of achievement taken at the same time. Further research might well profit by investigating such possible confounds.

Task B6.11

➤ The information above is quite difficult to understand, and it may help you to make sense of it by answering the following questions:

1   Is the model presented in Figure B6.1 (a) a reflection of a pre-existing theoretical model, (b) a representation of the researchers' hypotheses, (c) the result of the statistical analysis?

2   Is there a one-on-one relationship among the factors? (In other words, is motivation related only to achievement and no other factor?)

3   How can achievement be assessed? In other words, what is the difference between 'relatively objective measures taken at the same time as the other measures' and 'more global and less time-specific indices' of achievement?

4   In their speculations, which of the following two explanations do the authors find more likely? (a) Language Anxiety, Self-Confidence, and Can Do correlate more with objective tests of proficiency than are the other measures studied here. (Note that all these different tests – the confidence and objective proficiency tests – are taken on the same day.) (b) The fact that a student did not do so well on an objective proficiency test on a particular day may have affected the scores on the language anxiety, self-confidence and can-do surveys.

Whenever individual difference measures are involved, there is always the question as to how one might account for the relationships among them. Many different models are possible; often it is not possible to compare them directly. Causal modelling is, however, a procedure that permits one to evaluate how well a model accounts for the relationships obtained. In this investigation, we have attempted to show how the variables investigated can be incorporated into an extended version of the socio-educational model of SLA (Gardner, 1985; Gardner *et al.*, 1993). The results provide strong support for the model, suggesting that the model permits one way of under-standing how the variables interrelate and complement one another. However, this support should not be taken as proof that this is the correct or only model. It is a useful model, but various other models might have been proposed that may have fit the data equally well. The intent of demonstrating this model at this time is not to argue for its superiority, but simply to demonstrate that it is meaningful for interpreting the relationships among the variables and for postulating how they relate to L2 achievement. This seems to be a fruitful purpose at the present time. It is hoped that future research may continue to attempt to determine the processes by which individual difference variables influence how well people acquire a L2.

Text B6.3
R. C. Gardner,
P. F. Tremblay
and
A.-M. Masgoret

Task B6.12

➤   This model, even though it represents language achievement as a static organ-isation, is in several aspects compatible with the hypothesis that second language development is a dynamic process and DST is an appropriate theory to model this process. In your opinion, which of the following statements pertaining to DST (taken from the concluding remarks of Unit A2), does this model explicitly support?

1   All parts of the system are interconnected.
2   The system is continually changing, either through external input or through internal reorganisation.

3 Growth and decline are normal characteristics of a system.
4 Variation, discontinuity and attractor states are characteristics of a dynamic system.

CONCLUDING REMARKS

In this unit we have included three articles that have to do with learners' characteristics. In the first article, Bongaerts presented counter evidence to the Critical Period Hypothesis. He demonstrated that, given sufficient motivation and language aptitude (and an L1 similar to the L2), at least some learners can acquire a native-like pronunciation. The second article by Sparks and Ganschow has argued that second-language learning may very well be related to L1 ability in general and learning disabilities in particular. Finally, the model by Gardner *et al.* has shown how complex the interrelationships are between Aptitude, Field Independence, Attitude, Learning Strategies, Motivation, Confidence and Achievement. We can conclude from all this that L2 achievement depends on a variety of factors and that the research has given insight into general tendencies. However, we can also conclude that these factors are interrelated, so it is impossible, but also unnecessary, to predict exactly either how each factor contributes to the language learning process in general or how any one particular learner will behave under any given circumstances.

Unit B7
The role of instruction extended

In the introductory unit on the role of instruction, we pointed out that the notion of what constitutes good language teaching has moved from a strong focus on form in the early 1900s to a strong focus on meaning and meaningful interaction in more recent years. However, the fact that children who learned an L2 in an immersion programme were not able to acquire the L2 completely accurately, among other things, has given researchers the impetus to study not only exactly what the role of instruction is but also what exactly the role of meaningful interaction is and how it can be best achieved. We have maintained that the entire SLA process is too complex to be able to filter out the exact effect of instruction, but that it was clear that instruction does have an effect in many cases. In this unit we present two articles: the first one, Spada (1997) reviews the classroom and laboratory research into the role of instruction and the second one, by Mackey (1999), is a classic laboratory research experiment into the effect of interaction, a source of input that is often overlooked in traditional classroom settings.

'Form-focussed instruction and second language acquisition: A review of classroom and laboratory research' by N. Spada (1997) in *Language Teaching*, 30, 73–87

> Text B7.1
> N. Spada

This article provides a useful overview of research on the role of form-focussed instruction (FFI) in SLA. Spada argues that several definitions of FFI have been used, which has led to considerable confusion. There is now a rich literature on this topic, but, as the overview will show, many questions remain. Spada provides strong arguments for a combination of classroom observation studies and experimental laboratory studies, because they both have their advantages and disadvantages, which can only be overcome by combining them.

In the research reviewed, the implicit/explicit distinction comes back again and again, and following Nick Ellis's suggestions, Spada does not opt for an either/or position but again argues for a combination of the two.

Introduction

> Text B7.1
> N. Spada

This paper presents a review of research which has investigated the effects of form-focussed instruction on second language acquisition (SLA). This includes

Text B7.1
N. Spada

descriptive/interpretive and quasi-experimental classroom-based studies as well as experimental laboratory-based research. The studies have been contextualised within the 'process/product' paradigm of classroom research (Rosenshine and Furst, 1973). This tradition, with its roots in first language education, has also had a considerable influence on classroom SLA research. Within this paradigm, the research process is viewed as cyclical with the elements of observation, correlation and experimentation contributing equally to the direction of the research and to the specification of research questions. (. . .) The research is examined from an evolutionary perspective to demonstrate how research questions about the role of instruction in SLA have become increasingly precise and finely-tuned over the past two decades.

★ Task B7.1

➤ To be able to understand the relevance of the article, it is important to have a clear notion of what Spada considers FFI. After reading the following section, try to formulate her definition in your own words. Pay specific attention to the *focus on form* vs. *focus on forms* difference.

Text B7.1
N. Spada

What is form-focussed instruction?

In reviewing the relevant research on the role of form-focussed instruction in SLA, one is immediately faced with the problem of defining it. Indeed, one of the problems with undertaking a cross-study comparison such as this is the lack of clarity and consistency in the definition of terms such as form-focussed instruction and related ones (e.g. focus on form, focus on forms, explicit/implicit instruction, corrective feedback, analytic/experiential teaching) which are regularly referred to in the literature on instructed SLA. The difficulty is that in some instances different terms have been used to express the same meaning and in others, the same term has been used to express different meanings. The problems which arise from the discrepancies in the definition and operationalisation of terms will become evident in the review of research which follows.

For the purposes of this paper, form-focussed instruction (hereafter referred to as FFI) will mean any pedagogical effort which is used to draw the learners' attention to language form either implicitly or explicitly. This can include the direct teaching of language (e.g. through grammatical rules) and/or reactions to learners' errors (e.g. corrective feedback). These pedagogical techniques have been associated with traditional approaches to L2 instruction which provide discrete-point grammatical presentation and practice – i.e. what Long (1991) has referred to as a *focus on forms*. However, they can be (and have been) incorporated within an instructional approach which is primarily meaning-based – i.e. what Long (1991) has referred to as a *focus on form* or what I will refer to as FFI. Long's *focus on form* and my use of FFI are not identical. The essential difference between the two is that Long's definition of *focus on form* is restricted to meaning-based pedagogical events in which attention is drawn to language as a perceived need arises rather than in predetermined ways. The term FFI is used here to refer to pedagogical events which occur within meaning-based approaches to L2 instruction but in which a focus on language is provided in either spontaneous or predetermined ways.

Research questions

Text B7.1
N. Spada

The paper is organised around the seven research questions listed below. The majority of the studies reviewed in the sections that follow are most directly relevant to questions 3–7. The first two questions have been included to provide a brief historical context to research on the role of FFI in classroom SLA. The questions are:

1   Does second language instruction make a difference?
2   Does type of instruction make a difference?
3   Is form-focussed instruction beneficial to SLA?
4   Are particular types of form-focussed instruction more beneficial than others?
5   Is there an optimal time to provide form-focussed instruction?
6   Are particular linguistic features more affected by form-focussed instruction?
7   Do particular students benefit more from form-focussed instruction?

Task B7.2

➤   Before reading the remainder of the article, try to think – rather quickly and immediately – what kind of answer would you give to the questions above? What type of evidence do you think you would need to gather to substantiate your answer for each question?

Text B7.1
N. Spada

Although these are separate questions which can be (and have been) investigated individually, they are inextricably linked. For example, question #3: 'Is *form focussed instruction beneficial to* SLA?' cannot be fully answered without investigating whether particular types of FFI are more beneficial than others, or whether particular linguistic features or types of learners benefit more from FFI. As classroom research on SLA continues to develop, it is becoming increasingly important to take into account the inter-dependency of these questions.

While classroom research on the role of instruction in SLA is a productive area of applied linguistics study, we do not yet have clear answers to any of these questions. Furthermore, even though considerable research has investigated some of the questions listed above, there are others for which the research is just beginning. Thus, while this paper is intended to serve as a review of the major findings related to research on the role of FFI in SLA, it is also intended to provide a framework and direction for future research.

The review begins with a brief description of some of the research and theory relevant to the first two questions: *Does second language instruction make a difference?* and *Does type of instruction make a difference?*

Task B7.3

➤   The following section deals with a bit of history in the 1980s. As you may recall from Unit A7 , the notion of what constitutes effective second-language teaching had swung from a rather pure focus on form (such as a grammar–translation approach) to a rather pure focus on meaning (such as Krashen's version of the communicative approach). To put the next section in perspective, you may want to recall what is meant by the 'strong version of the communicative approach'.

Does second language instruction make a difference?

In a 1983 article published in the TESOL *Quarterly*, Long posed this provocative question. He asked the question partly in response to increasing support for a theoretical position which had gained prominence in SLA research in North America in the early 80's, and which also had an enormous impact on L2 pedagogy. This position maintained that all L2 learners needed in order to successfully acquire a second language was exposure to comprehensible input and motivation to acquire the L2 (Krashen, 1985). It was further argued that instruction which provided learners with metalinguistic information or pedagogical rules and corrective feedback was not an effective way to acquire a second language and could actually interfere with the natural developmental process. (. . .). Following from this came the argument that SLA was best 'nurtured' in ways which were consistent with and similar to the environmental characteristics of natural L1 acquisition.

The impact of this research on L2 pedagogy was considerable and led to the adoption of the 'strong version' of a communicative approach to language teaching – one which is defined exclusively in terms of the provision of meaningful comprehensible input with no attention to language form or error correction (Howatt, 1984). Although there have been other interpretations of communicative language teaching (CLT), both theoretical and pedagogical, some of which argue for more of a balance between form and meaning (see for example, Brumfit, 1984; Littlewood, 1981; Widdowson, 1978), the strongest voices in the early 80's were those which encouraged an emphasis on meaning over form and fluency over accuracy – a version which has been referred to by Johnson (1982) as the 'separationist' view of CLT.

If one accepts the view that instruction can potentially interfere with SLA, then assumptions about the benefits of instruction are naturally called into question. It was within such a context that Long chose to investigate the question: *Does second language instruction make a difference?* In a cross-study comparison of 11 studies, he compared the achievement 'of learners after comparable periods of classroom' instruction, natural exposure or combinations of the two. He concluded that there were clear advantages for L2 instruction over exposure in 6 of the studies reviewed as well as some benefits for instruction in two others. Acknowledging the difficulty of cross-study comparisons in which differences between subjects, teaching methodologies and proficiency measures vary considerably, Long argued for more systematic research to focus on a set of specific questions on instructed SLA. One of them was whether type of instruction makes a difference.

Does type of instruction make a difference?

In the studies Long reviewed, there was no information about the kind of instructional practices and procedures which took place in the classrooms. While one might assume that the instruction was traditional discrete-point grammatical teaching given the era in which these studies were done, there were no classroom data to confirm this. Thus, Long could not (and did not) address the question as to whether differences in the type of instruction may have played a role in the results obtained. In fact, virtually no studies had been done at that time which examined L2 learning in relation to systematic descriptions of teacher and learner behaviours. This was partly due to the fact that instruction was viewed globally and somewhat monolithically. This problem had been acknowledged in the earlier product-oriented global method comparison studies which failed to find substantial differences in learning outcomes between L2 learners who received inductive (e.g. audiolingual) versus deductive (e.g. grammar translation) instruction (Chastain, 1969; Scherer and Wertheimer, 1964; Smith, 1969). The lack of sufficient classroom observation data in these studies made it difficult to interpret these findings.

Text B7.1
N. Spada

Task B7.4

➤ To help you focus on the following section, you may want to consider the following question: Which type of method do you think showed to be most effective for adult second or foreign language learners: (a) pure focus on form, (b) pure communicative method, or (c) a combination of both? Why?

Efforts to systematically observe and describe classroom practices and procedures came later. This period of classroom observation (or process-oriented) research provided much needed information about what goes on inside the L2 classroom or what Long (1980) referred to as the 'black box'. (. . .) Notwithstanding the benefits of this productive period of process-oriented research, like the exclusively product-oriented research which preceded it, it was one-sided, and it took several more years before researchers began to examine both process and product in studies designed to examine relationships between instructional input and learning outcomes. (. . .)

Text B7.1
N. Spada

During the period of extensive classroom observation research, there were also a few studies which explored the question that the earlier global method comparison studies had tried but failed to adequately respond to: *Does type of instruction make a difference*? These studies examined L2 learning outcomes in programs where either a communicative component was added to structure-based teaching, or a form-focussed component was added to primarily meaning-based instruction. The studies varied in their methodology and in terms of whether classroom observation data were included.

While the enthusiasm for CLT continued to mount in the 80's, the empirical evidence to support (or refute) it was slim. One of the earliest efforts to investigate the effects of CLT on L2 learning was Savignon's (1972) experimental study of the acquisition of French by American college students. In this research, learners who received a steady diet of audiolingual instruction were given an additional communicative component and their performance was compared with that of learners who had received an additional component of either culture-based instruction (in English) or additional audiolingual practice. Savignon's findings revealed that the communicative group significantly outperformed the other two groups on communicative measures and did as well on linguistic measures. Curiously, while her findings have often been interpreted as support for the strong version of CLT, the learners who benefitted most in her study were in fact those who had received attention to form in addition to opportunities for communicative practice. (. . .)

Other researchers who examined the inclusion of FFI within communicative programs also reported that a combination of form and meaning was more beneficial than the exclusive use of either one (Harley, Allen, Cummins, and Swain, 1990;

Lightbown, 1991; Lightbown and Spada, 1990; Spada, 1987). Despite these early findings, the strong version of CLT prevailed. This was primarily due to the fact that: 1) little classroom research had been done, thus, the available findings were limited and 2) the few studies which had been done were descriptive (apart from Savignon's), and any claims about the observed relationship between instructional input and learning outcomes were based on post-hoc analyses.

 Task B7.5

> If we work on the Vygotskian premise that each learner at any given point in time has a ZPD, a time when he or she has not quite accomplished mastering something but is ready to do so (see Unit A7), what do you think would happen if someone was offered a task or problem to be solved beyond his or her ZPD?

Is form-focussed instruction beneficial to SLA?

Observations of the francophone children's L2 development in intensive ESL classes revealed that, while five months of communicative exposure to English contributes greatly to their fluency and confidence in using English, their language is characterized by many morphological and syntactic errors (Spada and Lightbown, 1989). These errors are not only highly frequent, but also similar across learners due to the fact that they share a common first language. Similar observations were made in French immersion programs. Students attain high levels of functional competence in their L2, yet continue to experience considerable and persistent morphological and syntactic difficulties even after several years of exposure to French (Harley and Swain, 1984; Lyrter 1987).

 Task B7.6

> In DST it is assumed that a period of strong development of learning of a certain construction is accompanied by a high degree of variation in learner performance of that construction (for example, learning to use the simple present tense versus the progressive tense in English correctly). What effects of instruction would you expect in a post-test immediately after instruction and on a post-test about two weeks later? Will a greater degree of variation in the second post-test necessarily mean nothing was learned?

Early process-product research in intensive ESL classes led to the hypothesis that there would be benefits for the inclusion of some FFI in these highly communicative programs (Lightbown *et al.*, 1990; Lightbown, 1991). Subsequent quasi-experimental research to test this hypothesis was carried out with two linguistic features known to present problems for francophone learners of English: adverb placement and question formation (see White, 1991 for a discussion of L1/L2 differences in adverb placement; and White, Spada, Lightbown, and Ranta, 1991 for a discussion of L1/L2 differences in question forms). In two studies, the regular classroom teachers provided 9 hours of FFI over a two-week period. This included explicit information about how the target

Text B7.1
N. Spada

forms work in English in addition to feedback on students' errors. The results were mixed. In the adverb study, the instructed learners performed significantly better than the comparison group on immediate post-tests but these gains were lost in the delayed post-tests (White, 1991). In the question formation study, the instructed groups were also significantly better in their accuracy and development of questions and these gains were maintained on the delayed post-tests (Spada and Lightbown, 1993; White *et al.*, 1991). The type of instruction was the same in both studies, yet the effects of instruction were not. (. . .)

The results [of a series of studies in French immersion classes] were mixed. Harley's (1989) study showed only short-term benefits for instruction, Day and Shapson's (1991) study showed immediate and delayed benefits for written but not oral performance and Lyster's (1994) study showed immediate and delayed effects on productive and receptive tasks. Given these conflicting results, the answer to the question: Is *form-focussed instruction beneficial to* SLA, is 'yes' and 'no'. To help disambiguate these findings, it is important to break down the question further and consider the results in relation to the next question.

Are particular types of form-focussed instruction more beneficial than others?

(. . .) [The general finding is that] learners who benefited most in these studies were those who received FFI which was operationalised as a combination of metalinguistic teaching and corrective feedback provided within an overall context of communicative practice. (. . .)

The overall results of the classroom research with young school-age learners suggest that FFI in communicative programs may require explicit information and/ or corrective feedback when the L2 is learned via content-based instruction. This does not mean that explicit FFI is necessary (or beneficial) for all features of language. There is considerable evidence that a great deal of L2 learning takes place through exposure to language in the input. Furthermore, research with adult L2 learners offers a challenge to such a conclusion by reporting findings which, on the surface, appear to support less explicit methods of FFI.

Task B7.7

> In what ways could you make a certain type of 'word-order rule' clear to (your) learners? For example, how could you 'explain' the fact that in English the subject and verb change place after a negative adverb such as *not only*.

   a   *He* not only *is* a teacher but also a student.
   b   Not only *is he* a teacher but also a student.

   Do you think that an L2 learner will find it much easier to comprehend the (a) sentence than the (b) one?

Text B7.1
N. Spada

In an innovative computer-based comprehension study with adult L2 learners, Doughty (1991) investigated whether learners who received visual enhancement in their exposure to relative clauses without any metalinguistic rule statements improved as much as learners who, in addition to the visual cues, received explicit metalinguistic rules. She found that both groups improved significantly more than a control group on post-tests administered immediately after the instruction. Doughty interpreted her findings as evidence for Schmidt's (1990) 'noticing hypothesis' and his claim that getting learners to attend to forms in the input is the basic prerequisite for learning. Her findings also support the argument that there are different ways to get learners to 'notice' which may be equally successful. (. . .)

Corrective feedback

In most of the FFI studies discussed above, the effects of instruction with or without corrective feedback were not investigated separately. This makes it difficult to know whether the instruction or the corrective feedback (or both) led to the results obtained. In fact, little research has been done to isolate error treatment and examine its effect on SLA either in the classroom or laboratory setting. (. . .) The conflicting results between the classroom and laboratory studies on the potential contributions of recasts (and other more implicit types of feedback) may be related to differences in the purpose, focus and context of the different research settings. For example, in the laboratory studies, the focus has been on one or two specific linguistic features, whereas in the classroom research, corrective feedback has been examined in relation to a large number of learner errors. Thus, even though recasts do not include explicit markers to draw learners' attention, the fact that the same feature is consistently recast may increase the salience of the feature.

(. . .)

Processing instruction

Another question relevant to the role of FFI is whether it is more effective when provided via one modality versus another (i.e. comprehension versus production). Operating from the premise that FFI instruction helps the learner build a cognitive representation of the L2, VanPatten (1993) argues that instruction which enables learners to 'process' information via comprehension practice may be more effective than that which requires learners to produce language prematurely. 'Processing' instruction is thought to be more effective because it provides a more direct route for the learner to convert input into intake. In a series of classroom studies with adult L2 learners of Spanish, VanPatten and his colleagues have compared the effects of traditional instruction (i.e. production practice) and processing instruction on the acquisition of object pronouns and preterite verbs. In all studies, learners receiving processing instruction outperformed learners receiving traditional instruction (VanPatten and Cadierno, 1993a; VanPatten and Cadierno, 1993b; VanPatten and Sanz, 1995).

 Task B7.8

> Because the number of studies are limited and too varied, the author can draw only tentative conclusions in the two sections above. Why, in your opinion, is it so difficult to design studies that look at the effects of corrective feedback and processing instructions?

Is there an optimal time to provide form-focussed instruction?

Text B7.1
N. Spada

As indicated above, previous research in SLA has shown that learners go through a series of predictable and ordered stages in their L2 development. Meisel, Clahsen and Pienemann (1981) have argued that learners' progress through these stages is dependent on their psycholinguistic processing abilities. Pienemann (1984; 1985; 1989) formulated a 'teachability hypothesis' based on the psycholinguistic research in L2 acquisition. His hypothesis is that instruction which targets a learner's next developmental level will be more effective than that which targets features too far beyond the learner's current level. Pienemann refers to those features which are amenable to instruction at specific times as 'developmental' and those which are considered to respond to instruction at just about any time as 'variational'.

The research discussed in this section does not give us a clear answer to the question of an optimal time. There seems to be agreement on the need to make the gap between what is known and what is taught not too big, but the definitions of stages depend very much on the type of language phenomena studied. In addition, most of the research not only looked at stages of development of learners but also included frequency of input or amount of feedback in the design, which makes it difficult to keep the effects of timing separate.

Are some linguistic features more affected by form-focussed instruction than others?

Text B7.1
N. Spada

This question is one which has received increasing attention by SLA researchers. It is an important question because, as VanPatten (1994) and others have pointed out, those who have investigated the effects of different types of instruction on SLA 'have not paid much attention to the *what* of their investigations' and must recognize that 'perhaps different aspects of language are processed and stored differently' (VanPatten, 1994: 31). As indicated above, this may explain why L2 learners appear to benefit from input which contains linguistic features at stages which are much more advanced than their level of development in some instances (e.g. with relative clauses and possessive pronouns), but may require input which is targeted to the next stage of development in others (e.g. question formation).

Task B7.9

➤ Can you think of examples from your own L2 learning experience of 'rules' in the L2 that you acquired totally on your own and probably would not have benefited much from explicit instruction, and some others that you feel you acquired, probably because you received some explicit instruction on the topic? In what ways do you think such differently acquired 'rules' might be different?

There is also evidence from some of the classroom studies reviewed here that certain linguistic features may not only benefit from FFI but require it for continued development (e.g. adverb placement for francophone learners of ESL). White's (1985; 1987) explanation for this is that input data or 'positive evidence' alone is not always sufficiently informative for learners to work out the complex properties of the target

Text B7.1
N. Spada

language. That is, while positive evidence contains information about what is possible in the target language, it does not contain information about what is not possible. Thus, 'negative evidence' (i.e. grammar teaching and corrective feedback) may be required in such instances especially when similarity between the L1 and L2 leads learners to assume that they have acquired accurate knowledge of the L2. As indicated above, it has also been observed by Swain (1988) and Harley (1993) that the input in L2 classrooms is 'functionally restricted' and often fails to provide learners with information about the full range of semantic and syntactic uses of particular forms (e.g. distinctions between *tu/vous* and *passé composé/l'imparfait* in French immersion classrooms. (. . .)

Some recent laboratory research has sought to explore the effects of explicit and implicit instruction on the acquisition of grammar rules. DeKeyser (1994; 1995) predicted that explicit instruction would be better for easily-stated categorical grammar rules and that implicit instruction would be as good as or better than explicit instruction for prototypes. This hypothesis was confirmed. In a related study, Robinson (1996) investigated L2 learners' performance on 'complex' and 'simple' rules under implicit and explicit learning conditions. The results indicated that while the explicit condition led to greater short-term learning than the implicit for simple rules, there were no advantages for the implicit condition with complex rules.

In another laboratory study N. Ellis (1993) examined the acquisition of complex rules for the soft mutation of initial consonants in Welsh. One of the experimental groups received exposure to the different kinds of consonant alternations in random order; a second group (i.e. 'grammar' group) received explicit rule instruction followed by examples in the same random order; and a third group (i.e. 'structure' group) received rules which were accompanied by two examples of each rule and then followed by the same random presentation of examples as the two others. The 'structure' group outperformed all groups by showing the most solid explicit knowledge of the rule as well as greater ability to transfer this knowledge to new analogous structures. Ellis interprets this as support for explicit instruction with complex rules. Because the study did not include a group which received only the rule, however, it is difficult to know whether it was the rule itself or the presentation of examples which led to the more positive results for the 'structure' group.

Direct comparisons of these studies are problematic for several reasons including differences in the linguistic features investigated and the criteria used to distinguish between 'easy' and 'hard' and 'simple' and 'complex' rules. In Robinson's study, the procedure used to select 'hard' and 'easy' rules was to ask experienced ESL teachers to decide from a list of grammatical rules which ones they considered to be more difficult for their students. Although teachers are very good at identifying students' problem areas, these difficulties may or may not be related to whether the forms themselves are more or less structurally complex. Theory-driven approaches to distinguish rule complexity are needed, and Hulstijn and De Graaff (1994) have made some proposals in this regard. Research in the cognitive sciences literature has also provided some useful insights. For example, in Pinker and Prince's (1988) 'dual mechanism model', it is hypothesised that while the acquisition of regular inflectional morphology in English is learned through a rule-governed process, irregular inflectional morphology is learned through an associative learning process which requires each irregular item to be learned individually. (. . .)

Task B7.10

➤ Apparently, there are no set criteria yet that can predict which rules are 'easy' or 'difficult' to acquire. What examples of L2 rules can you think of that were easier or more difficult to acquire? Can you think of some criteria that could explain the difference between these rules?

➤ Do you intuitively agree with the basic idea of Pinker and Prince that there are different ways to learn rules? For example, is the formation of regular plurals in English (house–houses, dog–dogs) learned differently from the formation of irregular plurals (mouse–mice, child–children)?

Do particular students benefit more from form-focussed instruction than others?

Text B7.1
N. Spada

The question of how individual learner differences interact with instructional (and other) variables, and how we might best investigate these complex relationships is an important area of research that Skehan (1989; 1991) has been instrumental in drawing our attention to in recent years. The work on individual learning styles by Oxford (1990) and others has also been important in addressing issues such as whether learners with a more analytic orientation benefit more from FFI than those who are less analytic. Yet little systematic research has been done to investigate interactions between different instructional and learner variables (see Wesche, 1981 for one exception). This is another area where much more work is needed.

One difference which has been raised in relation to some of the research reviewed here is the age of the learner. For example, in the French immersion research, the grade 6 learners in Harley's (1989) study may not have benefitted as much from the analytic instruction as the grade 8 learners in Lyster's (1994) study because they were younger and less cognitively mature. Unfortunately, because age differences were not examined separately from type of instruction in these studies, it is impossible to know how they might have interacted.

In the intensive ESL research, the effects of different types of instruction on L2 learners at the same grade level were investigated. That is, learners who received high frequency exposure to adverbs were the same age as learners who received explicit FFI on adverbs. Yet the latter group outperformed the former. This suggests that young learners can benefit from explicit FFI when it is contextualised in meaningful, communicative practice. A study under way with intensive ESL learners (Ranta, 2004) further indicates that those who possess high levels of grammatical sensitivity are very successful in combining their individual analytic learning orientations in these communicative programs.

Task B7.11

➤ Drawing on your reading of the extracts from the Spada article, what conclusions would you draw concerning the following statements? In particular, are they in your view true or false?

1   FFI is beneficial to SLA.
2   Explicit FFI may be particularly effective in L2 classrooms which are communicatively-based and/or where the L2 is learned via subject-matter instruction.
3   The research has clearly shown that there is an optimal moment to provide FFI dealing with a certain construction.
4   The research has shown that all constructions lend themselves equally well to being learned implicitly as well as explicitly.

The Spada article is a typical overview article that looks at different studies at a meta-level. As she indicated in this overview of research on the role of role of instruction in SLA, there has been a good deal of empirical research which has tried to show the effects different variables in the classroom, such as instruction, input and interaction, have on SLA. Some of the work in this area is more of the laboratory type in the sense that the treatments and their effects are controlled as much as possible, while other studies are based on observations of what goes on in real-life language classes. As Spada argues, both types of studies are useful and combinations of both are needed to learn more about the complexity of the process of SLA. In the next article, we will examine the laboratory type of study.

Text B7.2
A. Mackey

'Input, interaction, and second language development: an empirical study of question formation in ESL' by Alison Mackey (1999) in *Studies in Second Language Acquisition*, 21, 557–587

This article by Mackey is included here as an example of a carefully set up and carried out laboratory type of study. The article tests the 'interactionist hypothesis', which claims that an L2 learner benefits from meaningful interaction because his or her conversation partner may not understand everything that is said and therefore give 'implicit negative feedback'. This hypothesis is very difficult to test 'objectively' because it is very difficult to control for all the different variables. We will focus on the quantitative part of the study. In the summary, the research question and results are made clear.

Text B7.2
A. Mackey

This study examines the relationship between different types of conversational interaction and SLA. Long's (1996) updated version of the interactionist hypothesis claims that implicit negative feedback, which can be obtained through negotiated interaction, facilitates SLA. Similar claims for the benefits of negotiation have been made by Pica (1994) and Gass (1997). Some support for the interaction hypothesis has been provided by studies that have explored the effects of interaction on production (Gass & Varonis, 1994), on lexical acquisition (Ellis, Tanaka, and Yamazaki, 1994), on the short-term outcomes of pushed output (see Swain, 1995), and for specific interactional features such as recasts (Long, Inagaki, and Ortega, 1998; Mackey and Philp, 1998). However, other studies have not found effects for interaction on grammatical development (Loschky, 1994). The central question addressed by the current study was: Can conversational interaction facilitate second language development? The study employed a pretest–post-test design. Adult ESL learners (N = 34) of varying L1 backgrounds were divided into four experimental groups and one control group.

They took part in task-based interaction. Research questions focused on the developmental outcomes of taking part in various types of interaction. Active participation in interaction and the developmental level of the learner were considered. Results of this study support claims concerning a link between interaction and grammatical development and highlight the importance of active participation in the interaction.

> Text B7.2
> A. Mackey

The first part of the article contains an extensive overview of the literature on input and interaction. It overlaps to a large extent with Spada's overview in this Unit and is therefore not reproduced here.

The studies reviewed above [not included in this excerpt] demonstrate that, although some aspects of the interaction hypothesis have been explored, to date the central claim made by the hypothesis – that taking part in interaction can facilitate second language development – has not been fully tested empirically. The current study aims to test that claim. The following research questions were addressed: (a) Does conversational interaction facilitate second language development. And (b) Are the developmental outcomes related to the nature of the conversational interaction and the level of learner involvement. These questions led to the central prediction that interaction would lead to development, and an associated prediction that the extent of the development would be related to the nature of the interaction and the role of the learner, such that learners who actively participated in interaction would receive the most benefit and learners who did not actively participate, namely those who observed interaction without taking part in it, or who took part in scripted interaction, would receive less benefit.

> Text B7.2
> A. Mackey

Method

(. . .)

Operationalizations

Interaction. The study was designed to investigate the connection between interaction and SL development. Interaction was operationalized following Long (1996), who claimed, as discussed above, that it is beneficial because It can provide implicit reactive negative feedback that may contain data for language learning. Such feedback can be obtained through interactional adjustments that occur in negotiated interaction. In Table B7.1, from data used for this study, both examples are of negotiated interaction containing question forms. Example (a) shows implicit negative feedback in the form of negotiation (which is also a recast), and example (b) shows implicit negative feedback in the form of negotiation (without a recast). Both types of feedback follow the NNS's nontargetlike utterance. In example (a) the NNS's modified response takes the form of a question. In example (b) the response is not a modified question form.

Table B7.1 Examples of interactional modifications/negotiation sequences

Description	Example (a) Negotiation/Recast	Example (b) Negotiation
The initial utterance that is not understood	A-NNS: *So your dogs are in space . . . vee er vee er ship*?	A-NNS: *I have a kind dog man*
Implicit reactive negative feedback: The utterance that lets the first speaker know that her message was not understood	B-NS: *Are my dogs in a spaceship or space vehicle you mean*?	B-NS: *You have a what*?
The first speaker's reaction to the feedback: responses can be modified, as in (a), or unmodified, as in (b)	A-NNS: *Yes are your dog in space ship*?	A-NNS: *A kind dog man.*

Task B7.12

➤ Mackey decided to use English question formation as the construction to be examined in interaction. In your opinion, why are questions good candidates?

If you want to test development, you have to know in what order L2 learners usually acquire the different types of structures. Below, some English question constructions (three correct, one incorrect) have been put in random order. In what order do you think correct constructions are usually acquired? Why?

1   Can you tell me where the cat is?
2   Have you drawn the cat?
3   Where does your cat sit?
4   Where the cats are?
5   Your cat is black?

Second language development

Question forms were chosen as the measure of development, the dependent variable in the current study, because previous research had shown that they were readily elicited (Mackey, 1994a; Mackey, 1995; Spada *et al.*, 1993) and that different question forms were present at all stages of learning, and because question forms fall into the category of complex structures that some researchers have suggested may be affected by interaction.

(. . .)

All question forms targeted in treatment and tests were part of the developmental sequence for question formation in ESL identified by Pienemann and Johnston (1987) and illustrated in Table B7.2. This sequence was adapted by Spada and Lightbown for their 1993 study of the effects of instruction on question formation and used by Mackey (1995) and Mackey and Philp (1998).

Text B7.2
A. Mackey

Table B7.2 Examples of question forms and developmental stages

Stage	Description of stage	Examples
2	SVO Canonical word order with question intonation	*It's a monster?* *Your cat is black?* *You have a cat?* *I draw a house here?*
3	Fronting: *Wh*/Do/Q-word Direct questions with main verbs and some form of fronting	*Where the cats are?* *What the cat doing in your picture?* *Do you have an animal?* *Does in this picture there is a cat?*
4	Pseudo Inversion: Y/N, Copula In yes/no questions an auxiliary or modal is in sentence-initial position. In *wh*-questions the copula and the subject change positions.	(Y/N) *Have you got a dog?* (Y/N) *Have you drawn the cat?* (Cop) *Where is the cat in your picture?*
5	Do/Aux-second Q-word? Aux/modal? subj (main verb, etc.) Auxiliary verbs and modals are placed in second position to *wh*-questions (and Q-words) and before subject (applies only in main clauses/direct questions).	*Why* (Q) *have* (Aux) *you* (subj) *left home?* *What do you have?* *Where does your cat sit?* *What have you got in your picture?*
6	Cancel Inv, Neg Q, Tag Q Cancel Inv: *Wh*-question inversions are not present in relative clauses. Neg Q: A negated form of *do*/Aux is placed before the subject. Tag Q: An Aux verb and pronoun are attached to end of main clause.	(Canc Inv) *Can you tell me where the cat is?* (Canc Inv) *Can you see what the time is?* (Neg Q) *Doesn't your cat look black?* (Neg Q) *Haven't you seen a dog?* (Tag Q) *It's on the wall, isn't it?*

Development was operationalized as movement through this sequence. Only development in terms of question forms was investigated. Pienemann and his colleagues suggested that two different usages of two different structures is sufficient evidence that a stage has been acquired. The current study imposes the more stringent criterion of requiring the presence of at least two examples of structures in two different post-tests, to strengthen the likelihood that sustained development had occurred.

Task B7.13

➤ If you wanted to elicit as many questions as you could possibly obtain in a conversation between two people in a classroom setting, what type of task would you assign?

Materials

The tasks used in this study were developed to (a) provide contexts for the targeted structures to occur and (b) provide opportunities for the interactional adjustments described above to take place. The tasks were used for both tests and treatment. They were produced and tested in a number of research projects with both adults and children (Mackey, 1994a; Mackey, 1994b; Pienemann & Mackey, 1993).

Conversational tasks with face validity as familiar classroom materials, for example 'spot the difference' were used to promote production of the targeted forms. Examples of the task types, classification features, and structures that they targeted can be found in Table B7.3.

Table B7.3 Task materials used for tests and treatment

Task	Description	Structures targeted
Story completion	Working out a story by asking questions	*Wh*-questions, Do/Aux questions, SVO questions, *Neg/Do*-second questions
Picture sequencing	Discovering the order of a picture story	SVO questions, Negatives (Neg & SVO and Neg & verb)
Picture differences	Identifying the differences between similar pictures	*Wh*-questions, Copula inversion questions, Yes/no inversion questions, *Wh/Do*-fronting questions, Negatives (Neg & SVO and Neg & verb), *Neg/Do*-second questions
Picture drawing	Describing or drawing a picture	*Wh*-questions, Copula inversion questions, Yes/no inversion. questions, *Wh/Do*-fronting questions, Negatives (Neg & SVO and Neg & verb)

 Task B7.14

Independent variables are variables that affect the score. In an experiment, it is important either to control independent variables (the variables that are the same across all groups) as much as possible, or to vary them systematically, as you do not want factors other than the ones under investigation to affect the results. Reading the section below, you will see that there were quite some differences between the subjects (L1, age, amount of instruction). What is the independent variable by which the researcher has categorised the participants?

Participants

Text B7.2
A. Mackey

ESL *learners*

Participants in this study were 34 adult ESL learners from a private English language school in Sydney, Australia. Participants were selected at random on the basis of enrollment in lower proficiency level programs in the school. Total enrollment in these programs was 147 students, who all had the option of volunteering for the study or writing an essay for extra credit. They all volunteered for the study. All participants were from beginner and lower-intermediate intensive English language classes. Participants were from various L1 backgrounds (including Korean, Japanese, Spanish, French, Arabic, Cantonese, Mandarin, Indonesian, Thai, and Swiss German). There were equal numbers of male and female participants. Their ages ranged from 16 to 32 years. Length of residence was 6.1 months on average. Length of residence corresponded with amount of instruction in Australia, although not in the country of origin. In terms of level, 27 participants were classified by the school as lower-intermediate and 7 participants were classified as beginners. A before and after proficiency test was administered to confirm the school's rating. All participants scored within a similar range for their level. The lower-intermediate participants were randomly assigned to four groups: three treatment and one control group. The beginner participants were assigned to a group that received identical treatment to one of the experimental groups but was at a lower developmental level. The average length of residence for this low-level group was 1.7 months. The study took place during the summer vacation when students were not receiving formal instruction.

Native speakers

The native speakers included six native speakers of English. There were four females and two males. The native speakers were between the ages of 24 and 36. Test and treatment sessions were counterbalanced so that all learners were randomly assigned to interact with all NSs. The NSs were trained in the use of the pre- and post-test task materials. This training consisted of the following: (a) reading a written overview of the tasks and a description of the targeted structures, (b) viewing videos of the tasks being carried out by NSs and Spanish L1 children, (c) reading transcripts of the tasks being carried out by adult NSs and NNSs, and (d) carrying out examples of each of the different task types in NS pairs. This training was carried out 2 days prior to the beginning of the study. Step (a) was repeated the evening before each session.

Task B7.15

➤ Judging from the information given above and below, would you consider some of the conversation sessions more 'instructed' or 'non-instructed' or both? Which of the five groups (italicised) mentioned below had the most 'natural' interaction? Which of the groups would you expect to develop most? Which of the groups do you expect to develop least?

Design

Interactors: Interactionally Modified Input through Tasks (n = 7). This group carried out the tasks in NS-learner pairs. The learners asked whatever questions were necessary in order to carry out the tasks and the NSs answered, asking their own questions when necessary. This treatment was termed 'interactionally modified input.' Any interactional adjustments that took place in response to communication breakdowns arose naturally through the interaction.

Interactor Unreadies: Interactionally Modified Input through Tasks (n = 7). This group received the same input as the interactors. In terms of their developmental level (Pienemann and Johnston, 1987), these participants were lower than the other groups and were not developmentally ready to acquire structures at the highest level. The group was termed 'Interactor Unreadies' because they were different from the interactors group only in that respect of readiness.

Observers: Watch Interactionally Modified Input (n = 7). This group observed the same input that was given to the interactors. They had a copy of the same pictures for the task that was being carried out and could hear and see both the learner and the NS. However, they were not permitted to interact in any way. It was considered important to monitor the involvement and attention that this group paid to the task. A pilot study had shown that some observers were observing other things, for example, the scene outside the classroom window, rather than the task, so a post hoc Ll comprehension check was administered. Participants were told that they would need to (a) supply the missing information for the task completion (usually one simple sentence, e.g., *The cat ate the lost dinner*) in their L1 and (b) draw the picture that had been described.

Scripteds: Premodified (Scripted) Input through Tasks (n = 6). This group carried out the same tasks in NS learner pairs. However, the input that the learners received from the NSs was premodified using the system outlined in such studies as Pica, Young, and Doughty (1987), Pica (1992), and Gass and Varonis (1994). This system produces a script that was followed by the NSs. The NNSs interacted naturally. In effect, the instructions were so detailed that communication breakdowns and negotiation for meaning were rendered highly unlikely.

Control (n = 7). It is widely accepted that taking part in a number of tests may provide a so-called *training* effect. The control group therefore received no treatment so that any gains or changes in performance could be compared to any gains or changes in other groups.

Procedure

Each test and treatment session lasted approximately 15–25 minutes. The study consisted of one session per day for 1 week, one session 1 week later, and a final session 3 weeks later. Both the treatments and the tests consisted of different examples of information-gap tasks, as can be seen in Table B7.4. Order of task presentation was counterbalanced. Working in NS–NNS dyads, participants were given three tasks to perform. In the test sessions, participants carried out 'spot the difference' tasks, in which each participant had a similar picture with 10 differences. The pictures were hidden from the view of the partner. The NNS was required to find the differences between the two pictures by asking questions. In the treatment sessions, participants

Table B7.4 Experimental procedure

Text B7.2
A. Mackey

Week	Day	Test/treatment	Activity	Examples
1	1	Pretest	Picture differences	3 examples
1	2	Treatment 1	Story completion	1 example
			Picture sequencing	1 example
			Picture drawing	1 example
1	3	Treatment 2	Story completion	1 example
			Picture sequencing	1 example
			Picture drawing	1 example
1	4	Treatment 3	Story completion	1 example
			Picture sequencing	1 example
			Picture drawing	1 example
1	5	Post-test 1	Picture differences	3 examples
2	5	Post-test 2	Picture differences	3 examples
5	5	Post-test 3	Picture differences	3 examples

performed three tasks. These were a picture-drawing task, a story-completion task, and a story-sequencing task. A variety of tasks was used to allow a range of contexts to occur for eliciting the targeted forms.

Coding

The pre- and post-tests were coded for the two measures of development: (a) developmental stages of participants, and (b) different stages of questions produced. Seventy-four hours of data were coded and used for this study. A selection (25%) of these transcriptions was coded by two other researchers (across all utterances). Interrater reliability was calculated using simple percentage agreement. Agreement for the coding of questions in the tests was 95%.

Task B7.16

In reports of studies like this one, a 'Coding' section is needed to show the readers that the data from which the conclusions are drawn are as objective as possible. In your opinion, has the author given enough information (a) to replicate this part of the study and (b) to convince the reader that the data on which conclusions are drawn is sufficiently objective?

Results

Text B7.2
A. Mackey

Developmental Stage Increase

Table B7.5 reflects sustained stage increase [which means that the learner is able to form a more complex question construction as reflected by Table B7.2] . As discussed above, in order to be designated as having increased in stage, a subject had to produce at least two different higher level question forms in at least two of the post-tests. This sustained stage increase analysis can be described in terms of individuals who changed as well as by percentages.

Table B7.5 Sustained stage increase by group

	Interactors	Controls	Interactor unreadies		Scripteds	Observers
Percent	71%	14%	86%		16%	57%
Ratio	(5/7)	(1/7)	(6/7)		(1/6)	(4/7)

The results for each group in terms of the number and percentage of participants who increased in developmental stage is summarized in Table B7.5. Figure B7.1 graphically represents this information. It can clearly be seen that the interactor groups developed the most. The Interactor and the Interactor Unready groups made large gains: 5 out of 7 Interactors (71%) and 6 out of 7 Interactor Unreadies (86%) increased in stage. The Observer group made some gains: 4 out of 7 (57%) showed an increase in stage. The Scripted group and the Control group made very little gains in stage: Only 1 person in each group increased in stage (14% and 16%, respectively).

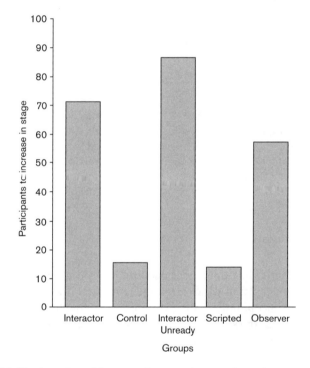

Figure B7.1 Number of participants to increase in stage in each group

 Task B7.17

➤ To carry out statistical testing, the number of subjects has to be large enough. The five groups separately had such small numbers that statistical testing could not be done. The author therefore merged the five separate groups into two groups. Based on the information above and keeping the main research question in mind, which groups do you feel could be logically combined?

Text B7.2
A. Mackey

In order to carry out statistical testing for the central prediction concerning development, a single group that took part in interaction was formed by combining the Interactor and the Interactor Unready groups. The groups that did not take part in interaction (the Observer, Scripted, and Control groups) were also combined. The two groups were compared using the chi-square test [a statistical technique to evaluate differences in frequencies]. Results showed that the group that took part in interaction was significantly more likely to demonstrate sustained stage increase than the group that did not take part in interaction ($\chi^2 = 7.77$, df = 1, p = .0053). Figure B7.2 illustrates this finding.

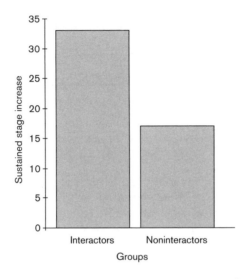

Figure B7.2 Summary of sustained stage increase for interactor and noninteractor groups

Task B7.18

➤ There is usually more than one way to look at data, and if different ways show the same result, the evidence is stronger. After you read the next section, try to answer the following questions. What is the difference between the analysis given above and below? Do they show the same general results?

Developmentally more advanced questions

Text B7.2
A. Mackey

Group and Test Comparison

Because second language development is a complex construct, both overall stage increase and specific question forms produced were analyzed in an effort to achieve a detailed picture of any interlanguage change or any development that took place. The analysis of developmental stage increase was reported above. The next analysis reported will focus on the production of higher level question forms.

The production of each of the groups for questions at stages 4 and 5 in each of the tests was also analyzed. Only questions at stages 4 and 5 are reported because the questions at stages 2 and 3 did not represent developmentally more advanced

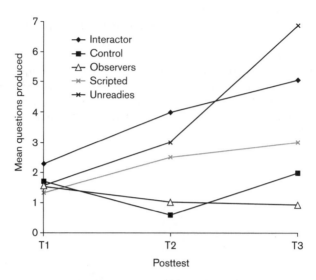

Figure B7.3 Increase in questions at stages 4 and 5 produced by each group in the post-tests

questions for any of the groups and were thus not a dependent variable in this study. Figure B7.3 shows the average number of questions (stages 4 and 5 combined) produced by each group at each test relative to initial pretest levels. To directly compare each group on the dimension of interest and change over time, difference scores were calculated by subtracting each participant's pretest scores from their post-test scores. Using difference scores minimizes initial group differences while providing a clear estimate of development, or change over time. The difference scores were analyzed using a 5 (Group) $\times$ 3 (Post-test) repeated-measures ANOVA. There was no main effect of Group, $F(4,29) = .786$, MSE = 42.5, $p = .5$; however, there was a marginally significant Group $\times$ Test interaction, $F(8, 58) = 1.99$, MSE= 5.89, $p = .080$. Examination of Figure B7.3 shows that, although all groups appear to slightly increase production of question forms during the first post-test, it is only the two interactor groups and the Scripted group that appear to maintain this increase during the subsequent tests. Although the Scripted group shows a very shallow rate of increase between post-test 2 and post-test 3, the two interactor groups appear to increase their rate of development across all tests.

Although the Control and Scripted groups do show some signs of increased production, the Observers, the only group not to actively participate in any form of interaction, have a flat or slightly negative trajectory of development. However, the fact that four of the five groups do show some increase in number of structures development is reflected in a significant main effect of Test, $F(2, 58) = 5.56$, MSE = 5.89, $p = .006$.

Group Analysis

To further explore these patterns of development, separate one-way repeated-measures ANOVAs were conducted for each group. These analyses examined the production of stage 4 and 5 question forms at each of the four test intervals. Significant differences in production of questions at stages 4 and 5 were only found for the groups that took part in interaction. These changes are described in more detail below.

Observer, scripted, and control groups

Text B7.2
A. Mackey

A one-way repeated-measures ANOVA was conducted for the Scripted group comparing their production of structures at stages 4 and 5 across the four tests. Despite the trends apparent in Figure B7.3, there was no evidence of significant change across the four testing periods, $F(3, 15) = 1.8$, MSE= 5.94, $p =19$. The same analysis was carried out for the Control group, $F(3, L8) = 1.3$, MSE=10.78, $p =32$, and the Observer group, $F(3, 18) = .236$, MSE= 5.85, $p = .87$, with neither showing any evidence of an increase in question-form production.

Interaction group: Questions at stages 4 and 5

A one-way repeated-measures ANOVA for the Interactor group, in contrast, provided clear evidence of change over time, $F(3,18) = 4.3$, MSE= 8.66, $p =.018$. As can be seen in Figure B7.4, this change took the form of a general tendency for production to increase at each time interval. This tendency is reflected in a significant linear trend, $F(1, 18) =12.07$, MSE= 8.66, $p =.002$. However, further analysis of this trend indicates that question-form production does not begin to significantly differ from pretest levels until post-test 2, $F(1, 18) = 8.44$, MSE= 8.66, $p = .009$. A very similar pattern of results emerged with the Interactor Unready group. Although this group produced a greater number of question forms than the Interactor group, their overall development was less systematic, which resulted in a significant, though somewhat weaker, main effect of test interval, $F(3,18) = 3.22$, MSE=11.39, $p =.048$. Again, there was a significant linear trend, $F(1, 18) = 9.49$, MSE=11.39, $p = .006$, but question-form production for this group did not significantly differ from pretest levels until the final post-test, $F(1, 18) = 9.06$. MSE =11.39. $p =.008$.

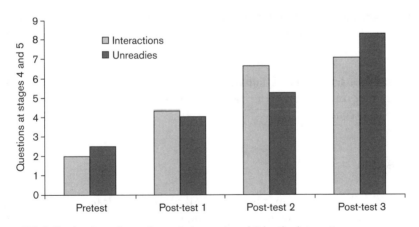

Figure B7.4 Production of questions at stages 4 and 5 by the interactor groups

Task B7.19

➤ The discussion section of an article usually gives in lay terms the main results of the experiment. Read the discussion below and see if you could summarise the findings in one sentence.

Text B7.2
A. Mackey

Discussion

To summarise, the results of this study show that the central prediction was confirmed. Conversational interaction did facilitate second language development. This can be seen in the finding that only the groups that actively participated in the interaction demonstrated clear-cut evidence of development. These interactor groups: (a) increased significantly in terms of developmental stage, as measured by the chi-square test, and (b) produced significantly more higher level structures, as shown by the one-way ANOVAs. Taken as a whole, both measures of development demonstrate unequivocally that the interactor groups developed.

The results also confirmed the related prediction that the extent of the increase would be related to the nature of the interaction and the role of the learner. Research on interaction reviewed in the introduction to this paper suggests that learners who actively participated in interaction would receive the most benefit and that learners who did not actively participate – for example, those who observed interaction without taking part in it, or who took part in scripted interaction – would receive less benefit. In the current study, it was useful to have measured development in terms of both movement of subjects between stages and numbers of higher level structures produced. The Observer group, who watched interaction but did not participate in it, did change somewhat on measure (a) in that four out of seven participants increased in developmental stage. However, when the Observer group was compared with the other groups, as shown in Figure B7.3, a slightly negative trajectory can be seen: Even the Control group was marginally higher than the Observers. Also, on measure (b) there was no significant increase in the amount of higher level structures produced by the Observers. The Scripted group, who participated in interaction but did not negotiate, showed no change on either measure (a), the developmental stage, or on measure (b), for higher level structures produced. To summarize, then, the Observer and Scripted groups behaved in a similar way to the Control group, who changed very little. None of the groups demonstrated unambiguous development except the Interactors.

In the original article some qualitative analyses of the types of questions used are provided here, but because we are focusing on the quantitative part here, we have omitted this section.

 ## Task B7.20

> In the following section it is clear that the interactive learners had developed even more between the first and second post-test. The author provides some possible reasons for this effect, but can you give another possible reason that has to do with the amount of variation from a DST perspective?

Text B7.2
A. Mackey

Effects over Time

It is interesting to note that the significant increase in production of questions for the interactor groups was found in delayed post-tests. As noted in the Method section, this study took place over the summer vacation and there was no instruction during the experimental period. There was an increase in production of questions at stages

4 and 5 in the second and final post-tests, which were 1 week and 1 month after treatment for the Interactor group; and in the final post-test for the Interactor Unreadies, there were no significant changes for the control group at any time. These findings suggest that an increase in developmentally more advanced structures was not an immediate effect of treatment but a more delayed one.

Why did the developmentally more advanced structures increase in the delayed post-tests and not immediately after treatment? Some researchers have noted that it is possible that effects of treatment on development may be delayed. Gass and Varonis (1994) cautioned that 'the absence of short term effects does not exclude the possibility of long term effects when the learner has had sufficient time to process and incorporate the feedback' (p. 286). Although the effects described as delayed in this study are in fact only delayed by 1 week and 1 month, the possibility that it may take time for processing and incorporation seems plausible. It is also possible that learners may hold features in memory until they are developmentally ready (Lightbown, 1994; 1998).

Conclusions

(. . .)

This study suggests that one of the features that best interacts with the learner-internal factors to facilitate subsequent language development is learner participation in interaction that offers opportunities for the negotiation of meaning to take place. This interaction is effectively obtained through the use of tasks.

As connections between interaction and SL development are being explored, problems concerning the cognitive processes that underlie both interaction and development are coming into focus. It has been known for some time now that taking part in interaction with opportunities for negotiation for meaning can provide comprehensible input, pushed output (Swain, 1985; 1995), and opportunities for noticing the gap (Schmidt and Frota, 1986), and that these are important parts of the language-learning process. It is known that interaction with these conditions can have a facilitative effect on SLA. Empirical research is now beginning to demonstrate that taking part in different types of interaction can have positive developmental effects. Researchers are beginning to isolate some of the particularly useful aspects of interaction and, equally important, some of the SL structures that are susceptible to interaction. However, exactly how these positive effects of interaction on language learning outcomes are achieved is still not known. The interactional processes that are claimed to promote noticing or attention to form are clearly worthy and important areas for future investigation.

As part of this exciting interactional research agenda, many questions can be addressed: How does development come about? What are the cognitive processes involved in recognizing and using feedback? How can insights and research designs from cognitive psychology and psycholinguistics be used to further fuel explorations of interactional processes? More finely grained analyses of the specific contribution of individual interactional features need to be carried out. For example, does the existence, quantity, quality, or nature of learner responses that are modified after feedback affect development? What is the contribution and role in development of positive and negative evidence in interaction? Do learners' perceptions about interaction affect their subsequent development? What is the role of learner–learner interaction in developmental processes? It seems that this area will continue to provide many challenges as well as potentially profitable avenues for future exploration of the interaction hypothesis in SLA.

 Task B7.21

➤ The author mentions several further research questions that can be addressed. Some of these questions have been partially addressed in this book; some have not. In your opinion, which of the questions are most useful for teachers in helping them determine the role of instruction?

Even though the study was not intended at all to test sociocultural theory (SCT) (see Unit A7), it could be argued that the methods used in the interactive groups do seem to reflect some of its practices. To what extent would you agree or disagree?

CONCLUDING REMARKS

In this unit, we have dealt with one article that closely examined the role of instruction. It showed that some instruction focusing on form or forms is useful, provided it is in addition to plenty of meaningful input. The second article demonstrated that interaction is useful in the acquisition of an L2. However, these articles do not provide straightforward answers to many remaining questions. We do not know which types of structures can best be taught either implicitly or explicitly, and which types of structures are better acquired without instruction. We do not know which type of learner at which specific level of proficiency is most likely to benefit from a specific focus on form. We do not know whether there is an optimal time to present certain structures and we do not know if a certain kind of feedback is more effective than another.

If we reason from a dynamic perspective, however, we have to accept that we will probably never know the exact answer to these questions. What we do know from previous research is that a great deal of meaningful input and interaction will help learners become proficient, but that some focus on form is necessary for accuracy. We also know that there are many differences among learners, and what works for one learner or group of learners may not apply to another group. Yet, this does not imply that studies like the ones included in this unit are useless. Although they cannot give the final answer to all our questions about the relationship between teaching and learning, they do provide small pieces of a complex and multidimensional puzzle.

SECTION C
Exploration

Unit C1
Introduction to Section C:
Doing SLA research

Most of the articles in Section B contained examples of empirical investigations into the nature or the development of second language acquisition. Reading about research that other people have conducted can be very instructive. However, learning about second language acquisition is best done by doing research yourself. Using this starting point, we have included several small-scale investigations related to each of the topics discussed in Section A. In this introduction, we will touch upon some methodological issues of SLA research that are crucial in setting up a study consistently and according to common research conventions. Within the scope of the current book, it is obvious that what we can explain is the very minimum one should know and that a more thorough introduction to SLA research methodology is highly recommended. In the 'further reading' relating to this section, we will make some suggestions on suitable texts for this purpose.

RESEARCH TYPES IN SECOND LANGUAGE ACQUISITION

A description of research types can take different starting points. We could distinguish longitudinal studies from cross-sectional studies, survey studies from experimental studies, and qualitative studies from quantitative studies. These terms are overlapping in different dimensions. The most important distinctions for our purpose are the one between qualitative research and quantitative research and the one between longitudinal and cross-sectional research.

Qualitative research focuses on a limited number of learners, often just one (a 'case study'), whose language or language behaviour is described in detail. Two major types of qualitative research can be distinguished: *observation* and *introspection*. In methods using observation, the participants are observed by researchers (or in the case of children often the parents), who produce detailed recordings of the learner's background and language behaviour. In introspective methods, learners are asked to reflect on their own language behaviour, often in so-called 'think aloud protocols'. Apart from direct recording sessions, learners (or people observing them) may also be asked to keep a diary, in which they reflect on their language use ('diary studies').

Quantitative research is different from qualitative research in two important ways. Firstly, the starting point is different: where qualitative research is largely exploratory, with a clear research question but without very strong expectation about the outcome, quantitative research is based on formulating very specific hypotheses in advance that are subsequently put to the test by systematically varying one or more variables. Secondly, quantitative research investigates the behaviour of a limited number of subjects (say 100) and then tries to generalise what is found to larger populations (all learners of French in Spain). The subjects in quantitative studies are therefore usually observed in groups that have one particular characteristic in common (like groups of learners with different L1 backgrounds, male versus female learners, etc.). To make the generalisations from the observed sample to the entire population, quantitative research normally makes use of 'inductive statistics'. This involves calculations that express the chance of making errors in accepting or rejecting hypotheses. That is why these investigations are also called 'statistical studies'. In the most typical type of statistical studies, subjects take part in an experiment in which one group that is given some kind of 'treatment' (like a particular method of instruction) is compared to a group that does not get this treatment. The label for this type of statistical research is 'experimental studies'.

A third type of research method that can be distinguished is called 'survey studies'. Information in survey research is gathered through interviews or through questionnaires. In SLA research, survey studies are set up to investigate people's opinions and personal experiences about language or language learning. We have seen examples of survey studies in our discussion of motivation and attitude. Since survey studies usually involve large groups of participants, we will regard survey studies as a type of quantitative research.

Another distinction that is commonly made in relation to research methods is the one between *longitudinal* and *cross-sectional* research. In longitudinal research, data are gathered about the same learners or groups of learners at different moments in time (often at regular intervals) to investigate their language development. This immediately shows the difficulty of administering a longitudinal study: it may take several take years to complete it. In cross-sectional research, different learners or groups of learners are examined at the same time. The different learners are then assumed to represent different stages of development. Both quantitative research and qualitative research can be longitudinal or cross-sectional. Labels that are also used for this distinction are 'real-time studies' versus 'apparent-time studies'.

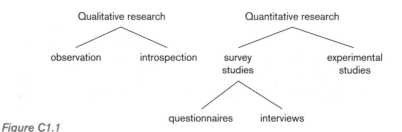

Figure C1.1

Task C1.1

➤ For the following research topics, think about the possible methods of investigation. Which method would be the best in each case? Try to anticipate possible complications in setting up investigations on these issues.

> ➤ The development of an individual's proficiency in a third language (including language acquisition and language loss) over a period of 20 years, to investigate the stability of L3 proficiency.
> ➤ An inventory of grammatical errors made in the written English of Vietnamese learners to investigate the role of the first language in SLA.
> ➤ The judgement about the correctness of verbal expressions in a second language to investigate learners' intuitions about second language idiomatic expressions.
> ➤ The relation between learners' motivation to learn a second language and their eventual attainment of L2 proficiency.

GENERALIZATION AND REPRESENTATIVENESS IN SLA RESEARCH

As we have seen in our discussion about investigating dynamic systems, in Unit A2, there have been heavy debates on the merits of qualitative and quantitative research in relation to language development. We do not want to open up that discussion here, but we do want to raise the reader's awareness of one of the crucial issues involved: to what extent can findings from a particular individual or group be generalised to other individuals or groups? Qualitative research is typically in-depth and small scale. An example is given in the article by Swain and Lapkin (1995), included in Unit B5. A carefully analysed set of data from a small number of informants is presented to prove a particular point. Whether these findings are relevant for other individuals is often unclear and therefore general claims based on such research should be viewed with caution.

In quantitative research, behaviour of groups and subjects is typically compared, for instance to show that a specific teaching method is more effective than another one. To test differences between groups various statistical methods are used. Most applied linguists are not statisticians, and that shows. As we mentioned in Unit B1, there is widespread misuse of even fairly simple statistical techniques such as analysis of variance (ANOVA). The availability of very user-friendly statistical packages such as SPSS has led to a somewhat unconstrained use of the most exotic statistical measures, and in particular the use of statistics that are not fit for the data analysed. Specific statistical procedures are based on specific assumptions with respect to the data. So even though the use of advanced statistics may be impressive, they may be overused and misused, and are not necessarily a sign of the quality of the research or data.

One basic assumption with respect to data concerns a comparison between groups: these groups should be as similar as possible except for the variable whose effect is measured. This is hardly ever the case in naturally occurring groups. A clear example is the last item in task C1.1: to draw decisive conclusions on the relationship between motivation and achieved L2 proficiency, all other variables will have to be kept constant. As we have seen in Unit A6, about learner characteristics, this is virtually impossible due to the large number of dynamically interacting factors. In addition, quantitative research is nearly always based on data from a sample (e.g. two secondary education schools in Shanghai) of the larger population (all people learning English in Chinese secondary education). It is very difficult, if not impossible, to assess whether a sample is really representative of the larger population.

 Task C1.2

> Assume you want to test a new method for teaching English intonation to adult learners of English in your country. Can you make a list of the characteristics of the whole group of adult learners in order to draw a representative sample? To help you get started: think about age, level of education, knowledge other languages and some of the individual differences discussed in Unit A6.

Concluding, we can say that generalisation and representativeness are very difficult to achieve. The best approach for most of us is to set up small-scale projects that aim at replicating what others have done or extend that within reasonable limits, i.e. in such a way that the findings can be compared directly with previous research but also add something new. To encourage beginning researchers to set up small-scale investigations, we have proposed several small-scale projects in relation to each of the topics discussed in sections A and B of this book.

REPORTING ON RESEARCH

As will have become apparent in the articles included in Section B, research reports are normally built up according to a conventional structure. This conventional structure has the advantage that research reports are transparent and complete. It is therefore best to conform to this structure, even in brief research reports. Although details may vary due to differences in topics, and in the scope of the investigation and research techniques used, the common structure is as follows:

1 *Introduction*: In this section, the topic is introduced and the *research question* is formulated. Normally a brief overview is given of what is to follow.
2 *Background*: This section positions the study in a more general framework: an overview of the most pertinent literature is given for the specific issue under investigation. This section provides a rationale for the research question and for the method section that follows. The contents of this literature section must be such that the method section follows logically.

3   *Method*: The method section describes and motivates the variables that are included and gives enough particularities of the study to enable replication by someone else.

    a   *Participants*: This section gives the details about the participants to the study: the number of participants (in each group) and everything else that might be relevant.

    b   *Materials*: The materials section describes and motivates the choices made in setting up tests and other types of elicitation methods and gives details about the data recorded.

    c   *Procedures*: The procedures section gives a detailed account of how the study was administered. What did the participants do exactly and where and how did they do that? This section gives all the details about the circumstances under which the study was conducted.

4   *Results*: The results section presents the most relevant outcomes of the study and gives details of the statistics used. The results are presented as objectively as possible, without further interpretation.

5   *Discussion*: In this section an interpretation of the results is given and the details of the study are evaluated.

6   *Conclusion*: The conclusion provides an overall evaluation of the study and links the results to the research question and the literature discussed previously. Normally, a conclusion also looks ahead at further steps required to investigate the topic.

7   *References*: A correct and appropriate documentation of all the sources used and referred to in the report is crucial. There are many different conventions of source documentation (APA, MLA, etc.). Always check which style must be used and apply it consistently.

8   *Appendices*: Scoring forms, surveys and other background material that may be required for replication must all be included in the appendix.

For reports on the small-scale projects proposed in the units that follow, it will not be necessary always to include all of the sections above. However, it is good practice to pursue completeness as long as this is feasible and functional. The best starting point to bear in mind would be that someone else should be able to replicate the project.

FURTHER READING

A very accessible text, especially geared towards second language learning is Brown (1988). The text is slightly dated, but provides a concise and clear introduction to understanding research statistics. The update of this book, Brown and Rodgers (2002), contains a detailed section on qualitative research techniques. It is a very accessible text that would be suitable for self-study. Other methodology books focusing on qualitative approaches to second language learning are Johnson (1992) and Gass and Mackay (2000). The first is a more general introduction; the second specifically focusses on introspective research. There are many general introductory textbooks on statistics. A reasonable trade-off between completeness and accessibility is, for instance, Moore and McCabe (2003).

Unit C2
Dynamic aspects of SLA explored

As we discussed in Unit A2, language proficiency is not something that simply develops and then remains stable. In fact, language proficiency is constantly changing. In this Exploration section, we want to make you 'experience' something of this dynamism by asking you to reflect on your own languages and language use, and to conduct some simple experiments.

Task C2.1

WHAT HAPPENED TO MY LANGUAGES?

Background

One of the authors of this volume acquired German as a foreign language in secondary education. He was taught according to the much-derided principles of the Grammar–Translation method (see Unit A7), so he only learned to translate from German to Dutch, and never spoke a word of German at school. As a university student, he had to read a few books on sociolinguistics in German, which was not easy, and he used some German on holidays; also, he got regular input from German television, both on German channels and on Dutch ones (with subtitling). Some years ago, his university started co-operating with German universities so he was in regular contact with German colleagues. He often felt embarrassed to have such limited speaking skills in German and decided to work on it on his own, by reading German fiction, watching German television without subtitles and by asking German colleagues to communicate in German only. He spent some time at a mainly German-speaking research institute and talked German regularly. Now he uses German for e-mails on a daily basis and feels comfortable speaking German, though his understanding and use of the German case-system stills leaves something to be desired. He feels his skills have declined after leaving the research institute, but they are still much better than they used to be some years ago. From this description it is clear that his foreign language has gone through phases of growth, but also decline.

Instructions

Now take one of your own second languages (if you do not belong to the minority of monolinguals) and question two or three other persons. Try to reconstruct the individual history of the second language in your case and that of this other person and try to indicate what factors played a role in changes in command of this language over time. In gathering your data, look back at your notes for task C1.1, above. In addition, you could consider the following points:

➤ Can you identify periods of acquisition?

➤ Can you identify periods of increased acquisition?

➤ Can you identify periods of increased attrition?

➤ Can you identify periods of attrition?

➤ Can you account for these different periods? You could think of factors like age, language contact, formal training, etc.?

➤ When was the highest level of L2 command?

➤ When was the highest amount of variation or fluctuation of L2 command?

➤ Do the language skills always decrease if nothing is done to maintain them?

➤ In DST terms, can you identify stages of stagnation? Do you think these can be regarded as 'attractor states'?

Write a brief report on the varying degrees of L2 proficiency and its possible causes. In your report, concentrate on the interaction between language proficiency and language contact. Compare the results of the different participants in your study. Comment on their similarities and differences, and try to generalise over the individual developments. For each person in your investigation, include a graph of the L2 proficiency in relation to time (see the figure taken from Van Dijk, 2003 in Unit A2). If you want to make a more sophisticated picture, you could make different graphs for speaking, listening, reading and writing. Make sure your report follows the conventions laid out in Unit C1 above.

 Task C2.2

ATTRITION AND RELEARNING

Background

It is a common observation that it is difficult to understand and speak a language that has not been used for some time. Is this because the words and the grammar of that language have simply disappeared? There is reason to believe that everything we once learned will stay in our memory system as long as we live, but that elements of a language that have not been used for some time will become very difficult to retrieve; they 'sink beyond reach', so to speak. Due to insights from the nineteenth-century German psychologist Ebbinghaus, we know that knowledge declines over time, but that there is always some knowledge left, which can be used for 'relearning'. A number of language learning experiments have indeed shown that relearning 'old' words, i.e. words that have been acquired at some point in the past, is easier than learning new words. This phenomenon has been referred to as the 'savings effect'.

The question is how the effect of residual knowledge on word learning can be investigated. Ideally, a group of people could be asked to relearn words they learned in the past and have forgotten and to learn some new words. It could then be tested which words are better retained, the relearned 'old' words, or the new words. However, the major problem in this type of research is that it is difficult, if not impossible, to determine if someone really knew those 'old' words in the past. The only possibility would be to conduct a longitudinal study in which the participants learn a set of words, forget these words and attempt to relearn the words after a number of years. Unfortunately, this approach is not realistic. An alternative is to find the teaching materials and wordlists that were used in the past and then to set up an experiment in which these words are relearned and compared to a set of 'new' words to be learned. The latter is what we are asking you to do in this task. We will make use of a list of French words, because a French word list exists that can be conveniently used for this purpose. Most of the teaching materials that were developed in the 1970s and 1980s were based on the 'Français Fondamental' (FF) word list, a list of French words that were selected on the basis of frequency and utility. This means that people who learned French at school for approximately four years probably acquired those words.

Instructions

The aim of this experiment is to compare the relearning of 'forgotten' words to the learning of new words. To make this comparison, two word lists are required. The starting point of this task is people who learned French at school and did not use French on a regular basis ever since. Of course, this experiment can be adjusted to other language situations.

Write or print the words from List A in the data section below on small note cards with the word to be translated on one side and the same word plus its translation in English (or your own L1) on the other side. Ask a small number of people (five to ten) to participate in your experiment. Make sure that these people once learned French – or any other language to which this task has been adjusted – and do not actively use it. Present the words from List A in the data section below to the participants one at a time and ask them if they know the word (ask them to translate each individual word). Present all the items of the list until you have a list of 15 words they did not know. Note that there will be separate lists for each individual participant, because people probably do not remember the same words.

The next step in this learning experiment makes use of these 15 words. Show each word and ask your subjects to translate it. If they cannot do it, show that word and its translation for 5 seconds. Go through the list and once a word has been translated correctly twice, remove it from the list. Keep presenting the words, and if necessary their translation, until all words are acquired. For each word, count the number of times it took your subjects to acquire it.

The next step is to repeat the learning experiment with the words in List B from the data section below. Present these words to your participants in the same way as the words from the List A: first go through the list to find 15 words they do not know. Then go through the same learning procedure as with the other words.

Compare the number of trials needed for the words in the two lists. If Ebbinghaus was right, the 'savings' effect should be found; the advantage of learning old over new. As in the experiment described in task C2.1, individual differences in level of proficiency, number of years of French in school, time elapsed since education and probably many more variables will play a role, but if the savings effect is strong enough, it should be visible in your data.

Write a brief report about this experiment. Make sure this report follows the conventions laid out in Unit C1. Although the report can be brief (especially on the 'background' of the experiment), it should contain all of the sections mentioned in Unit C1: an introduction explaining the purpose of the experiment and a hypothesis; information about the participants; a list of the materials used; a brief description of the procedure; a description of the results; the discussion of the results and a conclusion. In writing your report, you could consider the following points:

➤ In your results section, provide the mean number of trials needed for learning the words from the different lists. Compare these means and say whether you think the difference is big enough to be meaningful. If you can do statistics, test the difference on its significance.

➤ Try to create a graphical representation of the differences between the 'old' and the 'new' words: produce a graph for the average number of trials needed for the acquisition of the words from the two lists.

➤ In your conclusion, evaluate the experiment, considering the strong and the weak points of this approach. For instance, is there any information that is missing in the current experiment? Do the two word lists form a good basis for comparison?

➤ Towards the end of the conclusion, elaborate on the possibilities of applying the knowledge about relearning effects to teaching practice: if the relearning of old words turns out to be more efficient, how can language teaching benefit from this?

➤ What further research would you suggest to investigate this matter?

➤ What does this experiment tell you about the second language as a dynamic system?

Data

In the data section below, we have included two lists of French words that can be used for this experiment. Clearly, this experiment can also be adapted to other languages.

List A

The following is a list of frequent words from FF: A list of 'old'/frequent French words, their English translations and frequencies (source: Savard and Richards, 1970)

	French word	English translation	Frequency
1.	chose	thing	628
2.	main	hand	568
3.	rue	street	574
4.	pauvre	poor	574
5.	lit	bed	544
6.	oeil	eye	544
7.	gare	station	544
8.	fils	son	535
9.	chien	dog	535
10.	hier	yesterday	535
11.	bruit	noise	488
12.	canard	duck	488
13.	coiffeur	hairdresser	481
14.	chaleur	heat	481
15.	jaune	yellow	474
16.	lapin	rabbit	474
17.	pluie	rain	474
18.	toit	roof	471
19.	soulier	shoe	471
20.	bouche	mouth	460
21.	aile	wing	439

22.	seau	bucket	439
23.	goutte	drop	439
24.	cochon	pig	433
25.	ciel	sky/heaven	433
26.	cravate	tie	433
27.	coude	elbow	433
28.	roué	wheel	433
29.	tache	stain	433
30.	malle	suitcase	433
31.	orgueil	pride	433
32.	oreiller	pillow	433
33.	pierre	stone	417
34.	veau	calf	417
35.	rideau	curtain	417
36.	mairie	town-hall	417
37.	toile	cloth	417
38.	honte	shame	417
39.	soif	thirst	417
40.	cuiller	spoon	417

List B

List of 'new'/ low frequent French words, their English translations and frequencies (source: Savard and Richards, 1970).

	French word	English translation	frequency
1.	plaie	wound	296
2.	tissage	weaving	296
3.	houblon	hop	296
4.	cigogne	stork	297
5.	orge	barley	296
6.	boiteux	cripple	296
7.	houille	coal	296
8.	cheville	pin/ankle	296
9.	brouette	wheelbarrow	296
10.	navet	turnip	296
11.	bru	daughter in law	296
12.	cygne	swan	296
13.	grenouille	frog	296
14.	fente	gap	296
15.	maillet	hammer	296
16.	sanglier	wild boar	296
17.	coteau	slope	296
18.	cerf	stag	296

19.	lime	file	348
20.	grebe	bundle	348
21.	brin	blade	348
22.	ruche	beehive	348
23.	laid	ugly	348
24.	sourd	deaf	348
25.	boue	mud	348
26.	foin	hay	348
27.	charrue	plow	348
28.	paresse	laziness	348
29.	roseau	reed	348
30.	bouchon	traffic jam	390

Unit C3
Historical perspectives on SLA explored

In this unit, we will give some suggestions for several small-scale projects related to historical perspectives on SLA, based on the introduction in Unit A3 and the extension in Unit B3. The first task deals with syntactic creativity and addresses the debate about the possibility of language being innate. The second task focuses on error analysis: the best way to assess a theory of SLA is to experience its methods! The third task is a simplified replication of one of the experiments Eric Kellerman conducted in the late 1970s.

Task C3.1

EARLY SYNTACTIC CREATIVITY

Background

As we indicated in Unit A3, much of the linguistic debate of the last 50 years has been on the innate creativity in language use, and to account for such creativity, it has been hypothesised that a child must be endowed with some special language-learning device.

Although it is obvious that adults may be quite creative in their language use, not everyone agrees about the apparent creativity of children in acquiring their L1. According to Tomasello (2000: 77), quoted in Unit A3, children have a set expression available and so they simply retrieve that expression from their stored linguistic schemas and items that they have previously mastered (either in their own production or in their comprehension of other speakers) and then 'cut and paste' them together as necessary for the communicative situation at hand – what I have called 'usage-based syntactic operations'. Tomasello's conclusions are partially based on a study discussed in Lieven *et al.* (2003). They used a high-density database consisting of five hours of recordings per week for six weeks. They compared each utterance that contained a novel element (usually a noun) to any previous utterance that closely matched in structure. This task is intended to let you practise reading and interpreting data.

Instructions

Read the complete Tomasello quote again and then look at the data below very carefully. The general question is whether you agree with Tomasello's conclusions given below again.

> The general picture that emerges from my application of the usage-based view to problems of language acquisition is this: When young children have something they want to say, they sometimes have a set expression available and so they simply retrieve that expression from their stored linguistic schemas and items that they have previously mastered (either in their own production or in their comprehension of other speakers) and then 'cut and paste' them together as necessary for the communicative situation at hand – what I have called 'usage-based syntactic operations'. Perhaps the first choice in this creative process is an utterance schema which can be used to structure the communicative act as a whole, with other items being filled in or added on to this foundation. It is important that in doing their cutting and pasting, children coordinate not just the linguistic forms involved but also the conventional communicative functions of these forms – as otherwise they would be speaking creative nonsense. It is also important that the linguistic structures being cut and pasted in these acts of linguistic communication are a variegated lot, including everything from single words to abstract categories to partial abstract utterance or phrasal schemas.
>
> (Tomasello, 2000: 77)

Data

Table C3.1 is the result of 6 weeks of recordings (5 times a week for 1 hour) of a two-year-old child. The researchers are comparing the utterances made during the last recording (presented in the first column) with what the child has said during all the previous recordings in these six weeks. A 'matching schema or utterance' is a syntactic pattern. The 'W' stands for 'word'. For example, the first utterance the child made that day (utterance number 1), 'where's the bus-s?' had as its closest match 'Where's the W-s'. In other words, the child had said 9 times before 'where's the [word]', but this was the first time he had used 'bus' in this schema.

To help you answer the general question given in the instructions, you may want to look at the following sub-questions.

➤ Table C3.1 gives utterances the child made that day in one hour. Try to categorize these 48 utterances into more general schemas. (For example, there are 16 utterances with the schema 'where's the. . . .'). How many general schemas does the child use?

Table C3.1 Single-operation substitutions into 'noun' slots

Utterance and number		Closest match	Frequency of closest matching schema or utterance	Frequency of substituted item
1	Where's the bus-s?	Where's the W-s	9	0
9	Where's Mummy's plate?	Where's Mummy's cup+of+tea?	1	14
18	Where's Mummy's knife?	Where's Mummy's W?	2	11
73	Where's Mummy's car?	Where's Mummy's W?	3	27
10	Where's Annie's plate?	Where's Annie's W?	2	15
19	Where's Annie's knife?	Where's Annie's W?	3	12
11	Where's the butter?	Where's the W?	53	5
49	Where's the tape?	Where's the W?	54	1
64	Where's the box?	Where's the W?	57	9
80	Where's the hippo?	Where's the W?	58	1
81	Where's the elephant?	Where's the W?	59	2
87	Where's the dog?	Where's the W?	60	2
108	Where's the people?	Where's the W?	61	0
112	Where's the drawing?	Where's the W?	65	13
89	Where's sheep?	Where's W?	114	2
109	Where's my seat?	Where's the W?	52	3
2	Not a hat	Not a W	6	12
4	Hello toast	Hello W	25	28
5	I have some toast	I have some coke	1	29
6	Want a knife	Want a W	24	9
8	I want a toastie	I want a W	14	0
92	I want a paper	I want a W	16	15
22	Mummy wants butter	Mummy wants it	3	9
48	Want a football	Want a W	7	8
60	I want one+two ..... +six	I want W	44	58
63	I want one+two ..... + four	I want W	45	59
68	I want tissue	I want W	47	7
84	Want some water	Want some W	4	26
93	I want some water	I want some W	28	28
7	I got the butter	I got the door	1	3
20	I got no Puddleduck	I got no W	2	0
21	Got home	Got W	5	15
16	I don't like jam	I don't like W	2	5
17	Just butter	Just W	18	5
26	The toaster	The W	14	0
88	The sheep	The W	15	1
37	Dave's big	W's big	7	56
42	Cally's big	W's big	8	24
39	And baby smaller	And Annie smaller	1	97
43	Cally smaller	Baby smaller	1	11
45	Two penny-s	Two W-s	20	0
66	I need a tissue	I need a jacket	1	4
82	That's a big lion	That's a big step	1	1
91	That's a pig	That's a W	20	2
115	That's my bag	That's my W	30	23
85	And a chocolate	And a W	12	72
101	There's the rolling+pin	There's the W	7	2
Mean frequency and range			23.0 (1–114)	15.4 (0–97)

(Adapted from Lieven et al., 2003)

> Once you have categorised the utterances into a more general schema, look in Column 3 and add up the total number of times the child has uttered sentences according to the more general schema (for example, add the numbers of the closest matching schema of the sixteen 'where's the . . .' schema utterances).

> Find the five most frequently used words (see numbers in Column 4).

> Now look closely again at the Tomasello quote and try to apply it to the data. Do you agree with him? Does the child 'cut and paste' only a limited set of items? To what degree is there 'creativity'? If you were to give the child a 1 to 10 (with 10 being the highest) on creativity in language constructions, what grade would you give this child? Why?

Task C3.2

INTERLANGUAGE AND ERROR ANALYSIS

Background

Unit A3 showed that error analysis was an influential methodology to investigate data of second language learners. In the early 1960s, this method was initially used to try to predict learner errors in a contrastive analysis between the learner's L1 and L2. Later, studies applied the method to determine to what extent errors can be attributed to developmental factors and to what extent to L1 transfer. An example of a study that emphasised L2 developmental factors is the paper by Corder (1967), included in Unit B3. However, regardless of the underlying framework, a detailed analysis of learner errors can be helpful in revealing parts of the L2 learning process. Therefore, this task concentrates on doing an error analysis of L2 learner data. This task consists of two parts. In the first part, we have included some data for a guided analysis. In the second part, we are asking you gather and analyse your own EA data.

Instructions (1)

Each of the following sentences, written by Vietnamese first-year university students, contains, amongst other types, an error in the formation of an English adverb clause (adverb underlined). First, cluster the errors according to the type of error (put sentences with similar errors together – if there are sentences with more than one error, only categorise the first one) and then decide which of the types of errors is the most systematic. What type of L1 'rule' do you suspect might play a role?

Data

1 <u>Though</u> my hometown – Cantho – is not very large, <u>yet</u> there are many interesting places throughout the province.

2 <u>Because</u> they always teach their children to do good things <u>and</u> they don't want to hurt them.

3 <u>Because</u> the government wants to balance education, <u>so</u> the school should reduce school fee.

4 Another benefit I like to study abroad, <u>because</u> I want to know many about history and custom as culture of that country, <u>because</u> many countries have different cultures.

5 <u>Although</u> my family consists of many members <u>but</u> all of us love together.

6 <u>Because, when</u> we are married, our husband or wife will take care of us carefully or share the joys and problems in life and in contrast.

7 <u>Because</u> I am a youngest girl in my family <u>so</u> I was received special treatment from my family members.

8 <u>When</u> I was young, I like to go out, <u>although</u> I am a girl, the games of the boys.

9 Besides good things I have some problems <u>when a university student</u>.

10 I feel shocked, <u>because</u> I write or listen uncarefully <u>so</u>, I don't understand.

11 <u>Because</u> this is a first time I live far my family. <u>So</u> I must support and take care of myself.

12 It does not mean that other stages, I cannot learn, <u>however</u>, there is difference.

13 I must study hard <u>because a lot of knowledge which I must learn at the same time</u>, I also have pressure from the exam.

14 A low salary is not important, <u>but</u> it is very important <u>so that</u> looking for a good job, we should find a permanent job <u>although</u> the salary is low.

15 I loved him partly <u>because</u> he was rich partly <u>because</u> he was handsome.

16 Soc Trang is not large town, but it is a fascinating place. <u>Because there are many ethnic people and a lot of pagodas.</u>

17 Students will be friendlier <u>because</u> working together helps them to sympathize and understand.

18 I have not forgotten my childhood <u>because</u> having a lot of sad things.

Instructions (2)

The data above show that all the sentences above contained errors in adverb clauses. These were first found in essays that contained many different types of errors, but this was a type of error that was very conspicuous. Now conduct a similar study for your own context. Make sure you select one L1 and one common L2 for all participants in your study. You probably already have an idea of the types of constructions in which many errors are made (if nothing else, because you had trouble with a particular construction yourself). To conduct a similar study, proceed as follows:

1　Decide on a difficult construction for your group of students.
2　Ask a group of students to write a short essay, but make an effort to give a topic that elicits your 'target structure'. (For example, if your students have trouble using the English present perfect tense correctly, ask them to write about something that happened in the recent past, with relevance to the present.)
3　After you have collected your essays, underline all the incorrect uses of the targeted construction.
4　Write down all the incorrect uses of the targeted constructions by all the students.
5　Try to find some rhyme and reason to these constructions (as done in the previous task).

Task C3.3

TESTING THE 'KELLERMAN EFFECT'

Background

In Unit A3 we introduced the work of Eric Kellerman. In several studies, Kellerman found that learners are sometimes reluctant to use L2 words and expressions when these words are very similar to their L1. We have referred to this effect as the 'Kellerman effect'; Kellerman himself called it 'homoiophobia'. Kellerman's (2000) article included in Unit B3 exemplifies this approach. In this task, we are asking you to set up two simple experiments to investigate the effect of homoiophobia.

Instructions

This task focusses on polysemous words. These are forms that have several – related – meanings. For instance, a 'nugget' is literally a little lump of gold, but in expressions it is can also mean 'something precious' in a figurative sense. In designing an experiment investigating the 'Kellerman effect', go through the following steps:

Experiment 1

1　Explicitly formulate a hypothesis about the translatability of polysemous words.
2　Decide on the L1 and L2 you want to study.
3　Pick a commonly used verb (like *break*) or noun (like *house, heart*, or *stomach*) that is highly polysemous in the L2 (used with slightly different senses in many different expressions).

255

4 With the help of advanced dictionaries or native speakers, collect as many different expressions as you can. Construct complete sentences with these expressions.

5 Translate these sentences into L1.

6 Select those L2 sentences that can be translated rather literally (with the same noun or verb) into L1. (Be sure to have at least 12 of these to continue with the experiment.)

7 List these expressions randomly.

8 Ask about 20 L2 learners to judge whether the L2 expressions are acceptable expressions in L2. (According to Kellerman these do not necessarily have to be controlled for level of proficiency.)

9 Analyse the data and decide whether there are (significant) differences among the acceptability judgments of the L2 sentences.

10 If so, continue with experiment 2. If not, try to account for your findings. Why do think your findings are as they are?

After finishing Experiment 1, go on to Experiment 2. The purpose of Experiment 2 is to find out whether the acceptability judgements from Experiment 1 correlate with prototypicality judgements. For judging prototypicality you can use the 'piling the cards' system as explained by Kellerman (2000). If you are not a native speaker, apply the 'piling the cards' method to one or more native speakers. Another way of judging prototypicality would be to ask native speakers to judge sentences as indicated below.

Experiment 2

Prototypicality can be established as follows. Suppose you want to explain to someone who does not understand your language very well what 'break' means and you want to give some example sentences to illustrate the meaning; to what extent do you think the following sentences are suitable? Rate the sentences as follows:

4 = an excellent example
3 = a good example
2 = a somewhat poor example
1 = very poor example

1 A broken *man*
2 He broke his *leg*
3 He broke his *word*
4 His *fall* was broken by a tree
5 His *voice* broke when he was 13
6 She broke his *heart*
7 Some workers broke the *strike*
8 The *cup* broke

9 The enemy *resistance* was broken
10 The *waves* broke against the rocks
11 They broke the world *record*
12 Who broke the *ceasefire*?

Take the next steps to finish Experiment 2:

➤ Determine the prototypicality of the expressions from your own
Experiment 1 in the way described above.

➤ Compare the results of the acceptability test (Experiment 1) to the
prototypicality test.

➤ Try to draw conclusions about the differences and similarity between
acceptability and prototypicality as perceived by L2 learners.

Unit C4
The multilingual mind explored

In this exploration unit about the multilingual mind, you will be asked to be actively involved in thinking about the multilingual mental lexicon. After having carried out the three tasks worked out below, you will come to a fuller understanding of this subject matter, which may form the basis for future projects and papers.

 Task C4.1

WORD RETRIEVAL IN A SECOND LANGUAGE

Background

One of the crucial aspects of language production is retrieval of words. Even for very advanced learners of a foreign language it is still more difficult to find words in the foreign language than in the first language. We can show this by using a fairly simple (but sometimes highly frustrating!) test that is also widely used in research on aphasia. The so called 'verbal fluency' task goes as follows: the participant has to list as many words from a specific category as possible within one minute. There are basically two types of categories, phonological (e.g. words beginning with a 'd') or semantic ('Vegetables', 'Fruits', 'Girls' names'). This test appears to be very sensitive for word finding problems in aphasia, but it has also been used in language attrition research (e.g. Yagmur's (1997) study on the attrition of Turkish as a first language in Australia).

Instructions

You do not have to be fluent in the language you want to test; all you need is a good dictionary. Try to find 5 people with different levels of proficiency in the second language you want to test. Test them with two versions of each the phonological and the semantic verbal fluency task. Take one 'small' letter, i.e. with a small number of words beginning with that letter (e.g. 'K' in English) and one 'big' letter (e.g. 'S'). The number of pages devoted to it in dictionaries is a good and simple indication for size in this respect. Also take a large semantic category (e.g. 'furniture') and a small one (e.g. 'kitchen utensils'). You could try very specific one (e.g. 'birds' names'), but unless you hit the occasional bird-watcher, you should be prepared for some null-results here!

Write a brief report on your findings, in which you refer to the following points:

➤ What would be your predictions for this experiment with respect to level of proficiency, phonology vs. semantics and size of categories?

➤ Do you need control data from native speakers of L1 and L2?

➤ Evaluate the strong and the weak points of this test.

Task C4.2

EXPERIENCING L2 PROCESSING

Background

One of the most complex linguistic activities humans can do is to simultaneously interpret in a foreign language. The simultaneous interpreter must at the same time listen and understand what is being said and translate that and produce coherent speech. It is so difficult and demanding that even experienced interpreters can perform this task for no longer than 20 minutes when it is not routine text. For less experienced bilinguals, this task is therefore very difficult. This difficulty of this task is related to language processing. The purpose of this task is to experience simultaneous interpreting and to reflect on its difficulty with regard to language processing.

Instructions

Take a fairly simple text in your first language. Read it slowly and make a recording of your reading. Then, depending on whether you are working on your own or in a group do the following:

➤ when you're working on your own: take two tape recorders (or computers that have recording options). Start the tape with your reading of the text and at the same time start the other recorder to record your interpreting. Try to interpret the text in English or in another second language you master sufficiently.

➤ when you're working in a group: take someone else's reading to play on a recorder and make a recording of your interpreting.

Then transcribe your rendering and compare that with the original text. Analyse what went well and what went wrong. What made it so difficult, when did you feel as if you were losing control? You probably left out parts of the original text. What did you leave out and can you explain why? Can you relate the different sub-processes and the things you did to components of the Levelt model?

 Task C4.3

READING TEST

Background

In Unit A4, we addressed the processing of spoken and written language, as worked out in the Levelt model (Levelt, 1993). With regard to comprehension, we said that most word-finding problems can be interpreted as the difficulty of finding the lexeme belonging to a particular lemma, which can be seen as evidence for the separation of lemma and lexeme. We quoted evidence from tip-of-the-tongue phenomena that show that speakers normally do know the number of syllables and the stress pattern of a word but fail to fill in that skeleton with segmental information. This task is about the way we access words from the mental lexicon and about the relationship between form and meaning.

Data

The fragment below circulated in emails in 2003. Try to read this fragment.

> Aoccdrnig to rscheearch at Cmabrigde Uinervtisy, it deosn't mttaer in waht oredr the ltteers in a wrod are, the olny iprmoetnat tihng is taht the frist and lsat ltteer be at the rghit pclae. The rset can be a total mses and you can sitll raed it wouthit porbelm. Tihs is bcuseae the huamn mnid deos not raed ervey lteter by istlef, but the wrod as a wlohe. Amzanig huh?

Instructions

Set up a small-scale experiment in which you test lexical access in the multi-lingual mental lexicon:

➤ Create two similar texts as the one above (leaving the first and last letter in its place and randomising the in-between letters), one in the L1 of your subjects and one in the L2 of your subjects.

➤ Find subjects who are very proficient in the L2 and some that are not very proficient in the L2.

➤ Ask your subjects to read both the L1 and L2 texts aloud (in a 'random' order) and time the reading time.

In your experiment, try to answer the following questions:

➤ What does the experiment tell you about lexical access?

➤ How does language proficiency affect access, and how could you account for that?

If the same experiment were done with words in isolation, would you expect the same results? What does that tell you about the role of context for lexical access?

Unit C5
The developing system explored

 Task C5.1

IMPLICIT AND EXPLICIT LEARNING

Background

In Unit A5, we discussed the difference between explicit and implicit language knowledge. Most discussions on this topic are related to the possibility of an interface between explicit and implicit knowledge. The purpose of this task is to compare explicit and implicit knowledge. The subject we have chosen as an example is the use of 'apostrophe-s' possessives. For both native speakers and non-native speakers of English, the use of apostrophe ('s) for the possessive as in 'John's cat' is complicated, because it is formed somewhat differently with plural nouns (such as *kids* or *children*) and words ending in 's' (such as *Charles*).

Instructions

➤ First ask five learners of English to formulate a 'rule' of about the use of possessive 's' and from this, try to formulate a general 'learner's rule'.

➤ Then take some readily available text, such as an article from the CNN website, and try to find examples of the possessive 's' use.

➤ What rules can you deduct from those examples? Do the rules match the ones you previously formulated? If they do not, what does that tell you about the implicit learning of the possessive 's' rule?

➤ Now take another grammar construction and follow the steps above. Preferably, choose a construction with which L2 learners with your L1 background typically have problems. Of course, you do not have to stick to English as an L2.

➤ Report on your findings. In the conclusions of your report, address the difference between explicit and implicit knowledge and the possibility of going from implicit to explicit knowledge and vice versa.

Task C5.2

FREQUENCY AND ACQUISITION: THE USE OF CORPUS DATA

Background

Frequency turns out to be a very important factor in the acquisition of a second language. Many SLA studies have therefore included some measure of frequency. Before the computer age, the frequency of words could be looked up in books that contained lists of words and the frequency with which they occur. The Kucera–Francis word list (Kucera and Francis, 1967), for instance, was very often used as a source of information. Today, large computer corpora are used to come to reliable frequency counts. There are various computer corpora of spoken and written English that are widely available through university networks. In addition, computer analyses can be used to calculate frequencies of word combinations (collocations). The purpose of this task is to make you familiar with frequency data and to make you aware of the importance of frequency for language acquisition.

Instructions

Access a computer corpus that is available through your computer network. If no such corpus is available, you can make use of frequency lists that are widely available on the Internet. Using search terms such as 'English frequency list' in an academic search engine like Scirus (www.scirus.com) will yield many useful hits. Using the corpus or the frequency list, try to predict the order of acquisition of the following verbs on the basis of their frequency in the corpus:

1. Stay, 2. Undergo, 3. Attack, 4. Mourn, 5. Perpetrate

Now have a more detailed look at the occurrences of these verbs. Again using a computer corpus, find out in which contexts (i.e. the words surrounding them) they are used? Do they all occur with different words or are some co-occurring words ('collocations') more frequent then others? List the words that typically go with 'undergo' and 'attack'. What does that tell you about larger units in speech? If no computer corpus is available, newspaper archives can be used for this purpose. An extensive list of online newspapers can be found at www.kidon.com.

Write a brief report on your findings. In your report, address the questions above and pay special attention to the relationship between frequency (of words and collocations) and language acquisition.

Task C5.3

TRYING OUT THE COMPETITION MODEL

Background

In Unit A5, we briefly discussed MacWhinney's Competition model. The main point of this model is that it assumes a direct one-to-one mapping of functions (like 'agent' and 'object') and forms (see A5). It is fairly easy to test the model in different languages. What we are asking you to do in this task is to run the following experiment, based on the set-up developed by Bates and MacWhinney (1981).

Instructions

➤ Test the validity of three cues, Word order (WO), Animacy (AN) and Agreement (AG) in simple sentences consisting of two nouns and a verb ('The cow hits the wall').

➤ Use the following options:

■ Word order options: NVN, VNN, NNV
■ Animacy options: AA, AI, IA (A= Animate, I = Inanimate)
■ Agreement options: Ag0 (agreement with both nouns), Ag1 (agreement with the first noun) and Ag2 (agreement with the second noun).
■ In total there are $3 \times 3 \times 3 = 27$ combinations.

Here are some examples:

■ NVN, AI, Ag0: The zebra is hitting the wall
■ VNN, AA, Ag2: Are pushing the donkey the elephants
■ NNV, IA, Ag1: The cow the blocks is kissing

➤ Now make the full set of sentences using the following English nouns and verb (taken from Bates, Friederici, and Wulfeck, 1987) for your own language.

■ Animate nouns: Zebra, pig, cow, elephant, bear, donkey
■ Inanimate nouns: pencil, rock, block, ball
■ Verbs: eating, patting, kissing, licking, biting, hitting, pushing, grabbing, smelling

➤ Then present the sentences in a randomised order to speakers of your language who also speak at least some English (L2 condition) and give them the test in English and in your own language (L1 condition).

➤ The task for the subjects is to indicate for each sentence what the agent is. So the question to ask is: 'Who does the action?' For each sentence, you get either the first or second noun as a response.

➤ After you carried out the experiment, analyse the patterns of responses for your subjects in the L1 condition and the subjects in the L2 condition. How would you explain the different responses? (Note: we know from other research that for English as an L1, word order (WO) is the most important cue, then agreement (AG) and then animacy (AN)).

Unit C6
Learners' characteristics explored

 Task C6.1

WORKING MEMORY AND WORD LEARNING

Background

As we indicated in Unit A6, working memory is one of the important components of language aptitude, if not 'the' most important one. In this exploration, we propose a small experiment on the impact of working memory (WM) on word learning. By way of example, we will give words from French, but the experiment could easily be adapted to a different language.

➤ Before WM can be tested, it must be operationalised. In other words, a measure has to be formulated to represent WM. We propose using a simple and therefore not very sophisticated measure: recalling digits in reversed order. The learners have to recall increasingly longer list of digits, and they have to mention them in the reversed order of presentation. In the beginning, it is easy with 2 or 3 digits to be remembered, but with longer lists it tends to become more difficult and frustrating. Digits are presented orally. The test could look as follows:

Presentation	correct response
5, 4	4, 5
1,6	6,1
3,7,1	1,7,3
2,3,9	9,3,2
6,1,0,2	2,0,1,6
9,5,7,3	3,7,5,9

and so on.

➤ The number of digits remembered correctly is the indicator of WM capacity. So a learner who can recall both series of 5 digits backward has a score of 5.

Instructions

➤ Now we need a learning task. For this, you could use the lists of French words presented in Unit C2 on DST and SLA. In order to keep your learners motivated we suggest that you give a combination of easy words (such as cognate words in the two language: French 'prix', English 'price') and difficult words (the low frequency, non-cognate words from the list). Make a list of 20 words.

➤ Show each of the words and their translation for 5 seconds to the learners (you can do this either individually or in a group).

➤ Then show the French word and ask for the English translation (or the other way around if you want to make it more difficult). The number of words learnt is the measure to use.

➤ The final step is to compare the scores on the WM test and on the vocabulary test. The prediction is that there is a positive correlation between the two: higher scores on WM go with higher learning rates.

➤ Write a brief report on your findings, concentrating on the relation between the vocabulary test and the WM test.

Task C6.2

PHONOLOGY

Background

In Unit A6, we discussed the role of perception in the acquisition of an L2 phonological system. The difference between children and adults, we argued, is that children have not yet formed phonological categories. Once the phonological boundaries have been established, it will be difficult to distinguish sounds that are phonetically very similar to L1 sounds but not the same. This is what Flege (1993) labels 'equivalence classification'. At the level of categorical perception, L2 learners will not create a new phonetic category for sounds that are similar to L1 phonemes. However, for L1 sounds that do not exhibit a categorical overlap with L1 phonemes, no equivalence classification occurs, and a new category is created. Evidence for this hypothesis was found in, for instance, the difficulty for English learners to acquire French /u/ (as in *tous*) relative to the acquisition of /y/. French /u/ can be considered a 'similar' sound; French /y/ would be a 'new' sound. The data showed that learners had more difficulty in acquiring the 'similar' /u/ sound than the 'new' /y/ sound, because the /u/ sound was confused with the L1 sound and the /y/ was not. Flege thus argues that many of the speech production errors in non-native speech arise from an incorrect perceptual representation of the properties that specify L2 sounds. Here is an experiment to explore this phenomenon.

Instructions

➤ Make an inventory of sounds that are 'similar', 'identical' and 'new' for a language pair that you are familiar with. Dividing sound differences between languages in this way may not be obvious. Was it always easy to make a choice? Which of the categories was the most difficult to find examples of? Can you account for this?

➤ Now make a recording of a native speaker pronouncing one of the 'similar' sound differences (in minimal pairs) and one of the 'new' sound difference. For each of the sounds, record at least 10 minimal pairs.

➤ Mix the native speaker's words and ask ten L2 learners to assess your recording. To this end, ask the learners to identify the sounds. You can do this by asking them which word they perceived.

➤ How many times were each of the sounds identified correctly?

➤ Based on what you know about the relation between perception and production (see Unit A6), what does the outcome tell you about the *production* of that sound?

➤ How would this experiment have to be adjusted to test the hypothesis of 'equivalence classification' accurately?

 Task C6.3

SETTING UP ATTITUDE AND MOTIVATION SURVEYS

Background

Virtually all research investigating motivation and attitude consists of survey studies involving self-report. Setting up appropriate surveys and asking the right questions is not a simple assignment. The purpose of this task is to make you aware of the difficulties of setting up questionnaires, and this will help you to become more critical about research in this field. The context of this task is well illustrated in a fragment from a book on this issue by Dörnyei (2001):

Constructing motivation scales

Having seen some useful techniques to measure attitudes/beliefs/values, it may seem fairly easy to construct a L2 motivation scale: why not simply ask learners to respond to the following trigger sentence '*I am motivated to learn English*' by marking an agree/disagree response option? Although one can intuitively feel that there is something wrong with such a simplistic method, there are actually examples in the literature when such a single-item approach was used (e.g. in the Pimsleur

Language Aptitude Battery; Pimsleur, 1966). The main theoretical problem with simply asking learners how motivated they are is that this question will be interpreted by different learners in very different ways and many learners' interpretations will not coincide with the researcher's originally intended meaning. Because in self-report scales everything depends on how the trigger sentence is interpreted (since the scores will be based on the evaluative responses to these trigger statements), motivation test constructors need to do at least four things to ensure the reliability and validity of their items [we have included two of them]:

1. . . . researchers need to break up the umbrella term 'motivation' into a number of *subcomponents* and address each component as a separate item.
2. Instead of using single items to focus on a specific motivation aspect, researchers need to construct *summative scales*, that is, sets of several differently worded items focusing on the same target, (. . .) so that any idiosyncratic interpretation of an item will be averaged out during the summation of the item scores (. . .).

(1966: 201–202)

Now consider the following quote from a study that included a measure of attitude and motivation:

> For a survey on English proficiency in adolescents in different countries in Europe we set up a questionnaire to find out about their attitudes towards English. It was a long questionnaire and we were only allowed two questions:

■ Do you like the English language?

very much	☐
more like than dislike	☐
more dislike than like	☐
Not at all	☐

■ How important is it for you to know English?

very important	☐
rather important	☐
less important	☐
not at all important	☐

(Bonnet, 2002)

Instructions

1. Do you think attitudes were measured in a valid way through those questions?
2. If we were to hire you to improve this study and you could have six questions in the survey, what would be your questions?
3. Explain why you have selected these questions, keeping in mind what has been said in unit A6 and taking into account what Dörnyei said in the quote above.

Unit C7
The role of instruction explored

Task C7.1

DEVISING INSTRUCTION

Background

Applying knowledge from research into feasible teaching practice can be quite challenging. The purpose of this task is to let you experience setting up a set of instructions. Suppose someone asks you to help her learning to do oral presentations in a foreign language, say, English. Your advice could be to do an oral presentation every day, but that may not be enough. Doing an oral presentation consists of various activities that have to be combined. Therefore, one way to approach this is to analyse the activity and then attempt to practise each of the components separately.

Instructions

➤ Make a list of components of the task. Components you can think of are: setting up a clear structure, preparing slides of pages in PowerPoint in L2, making short notes with key words that may be difficult, and so on.

➤ Devise one training activity for each of these components. If you are doing the task in a group, present your ideas to the group and ask them for feedback.

➤ Report on the difficulties of each of the steps above, especially in relation to the usefulness of providing explicit training for oral presentations.

Task C7.2

THE EFFECT OF INTERACTION

Background

Mackey (1999) provides direct empirical support for the claims of the inter-action hypothesis. L2 learners who actively participated in conversation with native speakers made more progress in the targeted structure than the others.

Mackey chose to investigate question formation because a great deal of research had already been done on such constructions, their developmental patterns had already been established, and they are easily elicited in a controlled setting. However, Mackey implies on page 579 that active interaction and the nego-tiation of meaning may benefit other areas of language (such as pronunciation and vocabulary) as well because '[t]he learner in the Interactor group receives far more varied input and produces a great deal of pushed output'.

Instructions

To find out other potential beneficial effects of active interaction, conduct an in-depth explorative, qualitative study as follows:

➤ Find a beginning or low-intermediate L2 learner and a native speaker of the learner's L2.

➤ Devise a task similar to the one described in Mackey, one that is conducive to exchanging information, preferably one in which there is an 'information gap'.

➤ Ask your two subjects to solve the task.

➤ Tape (audio and/or video) their interaction.

➤ Make a detailed transcription of the interaction (see Mackey for examples).

➤ Analyse the transcription to find out possible beneficial effects to the L2 learner of the interaction.

➤ Decide which of these could possibly be tested in a more controlled study such as Mackey's.

Task C7.3

ANOTHER CASE STUDY IN INTERACTION

Background

In Units A5 and B2 we discussed the ZPD and in Unit B4 we have included two articles on the importance of interaction. According to Vygotsky, interaction helps L2 acquisition, because learners may fill gaps in each other's knowledge. The purpose of this task is to set up an experiment to test if creating knowledge gaps can create learning moments. In this task, we have provided an example of an experiment given in French, but it could be adapted to a different language if French is not the most suitable language in your own context.

Instructions

➤ Use the text below or create a text in an L2 with the first and the last section in the right place, and the order of the other sections in random order.

➤ Find two participants for your experiment, with different levels of proficiency in the L2.

➤ First, ask the less proficient participant to reconstruct the text you created in its original form. Ask him or her to think aloud. (If your subject has too much difficulty or no difficulty at all, adjust the material or find another subject who can barely do the text.)

➤ Then ask the more proficient participant to help. The more able student should help the less able one to find his or her way through the text, but not just give away the right order.

➤ Audio-tape the session and identify the learning moments. Categorise the learning moments according to grammar, vocabulary, etc.

➤ Write a brief report on your findings. In your report, say whether the data from your experiment provide support for the Vygotskyan idea that creating gaps in knowledge causes learning moments and that a peer can help fill those gaps.

Data

Dans l'enseignement bilingue, il y a les professeurs qui enseignent LE français et ceux qui enseignent EN français. La réflexion qui suit souligne l'importance – et la spécificité – du travail de ces enseignants, insuffisamment aidés et reconnus.

1. Enseigner *LE* français langue seconde dans les sections bilingues ? On voit sans peine de quoi il s'agit : on a des outils, des livres, des revues, des méthodes ; et puis on a appris, à l'université ou ailleurs, grâce aux cours de français langue étrangère . . .

2. Bien sûr, ces professeurs de « disciplines non linguistiques » (DNL) connaissent le français, à des degrés divers (études en pays francophone, apprentissage à l'école . . .) mais ils n'ont pas appris en langue française leur métier d'enseignant en biologie, en histoire ou en chimie . . .

3. **Pourquoi enseigner *EN* français ?**
   Il convient de toujours rappeler les (bonnes) raisons qui font qu'à côté d'un enseignement solidement structuré *DU* français, un enseignement *EN* français est particulièrement pertinent.

4. Mais enseigner dans ces sections la biologie, l'histoire, les maths, la chimie, etc. *EN* français, c'est tout de même un peu plus compliqué . . . quand on est espagnol travaillant en Espagne avec des enfants espagnols, ou bulgare travaillant en Bulgarie avec des enfants bulgares . . .

5. Utiliser le français comme langue d'enseignement, comme langue instrumentale, pour apprendre des contenus disciplinaires, est évidemment un excellent moyen de conforter ce français, de le tester, de le mettre à l'épreuve; c'est une mise en pratique fonctionnelle, opérationnelle, c'est une manière d'évaluation, une épreuve de vérité.

6. Et pourtant, toute la spécificité, l'originalité, la richesse, voire l'excellence des sections bilingues repose fondamentalement sur ces professeurs. Sans eux, sans ces « professeurs de DNL », pas de sections bilingues . . .

7. Et puis c'est aussi revisiter l'épistémologie de cette discipline et donc, au total, favoriser les constructions conceptuelles.

8. Mais il y a plus : utiliser la langue française, des documents et livres scolaires français – parallèlement aux outils didactiques ordinaires en langue première – pour enseigner/apprendre des contenus de telle ou telle discipline, c'est varier et diversifier les approches méthodologiques et didactiques, c'est favoriser l'abstraction et la conceptualisation (la langue seconde étant forcément plus abstraite que la première, lourdement chargée d'affectivité).

9. De plus, ils n'ont pas beaucoup de documents, de méthodes, pour les aider à accomplir ce travail particulier d'enseigner leur discipline *EN* français, dans leur pays, à des enfants de leur pays . . .

10. Enfin, comment ne pas voir que cette utilisation de deux codes linguistiques pour apprendre (au lieu d'un seul) est porteuse d'ouvertures culturelles, chaque langue, on le sait, « découpant le réel » à sa manière . . .

Further reading

Suggestions are included below for further reading on each of the topics covered in the book.

UNIT A1

There are quite a number of introductory books on SLA, and we will name only a few recent ones.

Cook (2002) is an edited volume presenting thirteen contributions on a wide range of aspects dealing with the L2 user. Topics range from neurological correlates of fluency, Neurolinguistics, Minimalism to Ecolinguistic treatments of learners' rights. The contributions differ considerably in depth and scope.

Lightbown and Spada (2003) is probably the most widely used introduction to language learning and covers a wide range of topics. Each chapter is combined with interesting activities for students. However, the psycholinguistic perspective is somewhat limited and little space is devoted to the acquisition of different aspects of the language system.

Mitchell and Myles (1998) is quite theoretical in nature and provides a thorough discussion of various theories on second language learning but it presents only some suggestions for application in teaching.

Schmitt (2002), an edited volume, aims at absolute beginners in SLA as its readership. There are basic introductions for aspects of language use (vocabulary, pragmatics), language skills (listening, writing), and a group of contributions that provide background information about related fields (sociolinguistics, psycho-linguistics). Each chapter ends with a 'hands-on' activity for students.

In addition to these introductory texts, there are several recent Handbooks and Encyclopaedias on SLA. These include Byram (2000), Kaplan (2002) and Davies and Elder (2004). They all have their own choice of topics, and for a first reading on a given topic the contributions to these books are very useful. Also, the indexes provide a useful means to get acquainted with the core ideas and readings on a given topic.

UNIT A2

Since this is a rather new approach to SLA, there are only a few publications that take this perspective. The only two we are aware of are Larsen Freeman (1997) and Herdina and Jessner (2002). The Larsen Freeman article was the first to explore the link between DST and SLA and is still a very useful article in that it explains DST rather well. The Herdina and Jessner book is more ambitious in that it tries to capture many aspects of SLA and multilingualism and Chomskian syntax from a DST perspective.

The literature on DST is typically written from a science perspective, and therefore even books that aim at a larger audience, like Waldrop (1994) are not so easy to read for non-scientists. Very useful introductions and more specialised articles can be found in Thelen and Smith (1994) and Port and Van Gelder (1995). One of the few researchers who has focused on (first) language development is van Geert. His 1991 article in *Psychological Review* is extremely rich, but fairly complex. His 1995 contribution to the Port and Van Gelder book is more accessible.

UNIT A3

Different books cover different phases of the recent history of language learning and teaching.

Lado (1964) is a landmark publication for behaviourism in SLA. It is a good overview of thinking about learning at that time. Chomsky (1959) is the famous review of *Verbal behavior* by B. F. Skinner, which marked the demise of behaviourism and the beginning of the generative revolution. An accessible book on nativism and universal grammar is *The Language Instinct* (1994) by Pinker.

How generativist ideas found their way in SLA is described in Gass and Schachter (1989) and in Flynn *et al.* (1998).

James's (1998) book marks the renewed interest in contrastive analysis and error analysis.

For connectionist approaches to language development Elman *et al.* (1996) is an excellent book, though parts of it are fairly technical.

Detailed descriptions of Krashen's theories can be found in several of his books (Krashen 1982, 1985; Krashen and Terrell 1983)

UNIT A4

The best resource for background information on Levelt's Speaking model is still Levelt's original book on speech processing: Levelt (1989). For more recent elaborations of the model, including the production side, Levelt (1993) is useful. A detailed account of Levelt's model worked out for lexical access in particular can be found in Levelt, Roelofs and Meyer (1999, 22: 1–38), which is a very thorough (and lengthy) article. Kees de Bot (De Bot 2003, 32: 92–103; De Bot 1992, 13: 1–24) has written several articles in which he proposes an adjustment of Levelt's blueprint for multilingual processing.

For a good overview of work done on the bilingual mental lexicon, two books can be recommended: Schreuder and Weltens (1995) is a slightly outdated collection of articles on the issue, but is very useful for a historical perspective. Singleton (1999) contains several useful chapters on the second language lexicon. A more recent account of the mental lexicon can be found in an article by de Groot (2002: 32–63). An update on work done on the BIA model can be found in Kroll and Dijkstra (2002: 301–321), which is included in the Exploration section.

UNIT A5

Mitchell and Miles (1998) is a well-written and well-organised overview of research on SLA in different learning traditions. In particular, the comparison between nativist, connectionist, information processing and sociocultural views on learning is informative.

Though the third edition of Brown's *Principles of Language Learning and Teaching* (1994) is becoming a bit outdated, the clarity of the style and the connection between learning theories and what the implications of the theories are for language teachers make this book unique.

For an introduction to sociocultural Theory, Lantolf (2000) with a number of papers by other researchers working in this approach is useful. The research reported on covers a wide range of languages and activities with a strong emphasis on cultural aspects of language learning. For a link between Vygotskian thinking and DST, the work by van Geert is essential reading, in particular his 1994 article in Human Development and his contribution to Port and Van Gelder (1995).

The articles in the section on second language learning in Kaplan (2002) deal with various approaches to learning.

UNIT A6

A very brief review with many further references can be found in Singleton (2001, 21: 77–89). An article that makes strong claims in favour of the critical period hypothesis for morphosyntax is DeKeyser (2000, 19: 499–533). For recent studies that provide some counter-evidence for the critical period, see Bongaerts et al. (1997, 19: 447–465).

A somewhat dated, but very well-known review of aptitude research is Carroll (1981: 83–117). A recent history of aptitude research including suggested directions for future research can be found in Skehan (2002: 69–94). An overview of recent developments in aptitude research is to be found in Sparks and Ganschow (1991, 75: 3–16), an excerpt of which has been included in the related extension chapter.

A detailed account of motivation, including the instructions and items of the Attitude/Motivation Test Battery can be found in Gardner (1985). A good discussion of recent work done on motivation can be found in Dörnyei (2001, 21: 43–59). The same author has written a book (Dörnyei 2001) that offers a very comprehensive and accessible overview of several aspects of motivation, including a detailed discussion of the methodologies; the book is strongly recommended for anyone who considers investigating motivation.

Many books have been devoted to individual differences, but two recent volumes are especially worth considering: Birdsong (1999) is primarily devoted to the age issue in second language learning. Robinson (2002) is an edited volume containing an interesting collection of articles on how individual differences affect instructed language learning.

UNIT A7

A thorough and convincing overview on the role of teaching in SLA is Norris and Ortega (2000). It is probably the best overview and meta-analysis available. Several aspects of language teaching are treated in the section on second language teaching in Kaplan (2002). For the link between SLA theories and practices, Lightbown and Spada (1999) continues to be a good and accessible source. Ellis (2003) presents an overview of research on task-based learning, while Johnson (1996) discusses language teaching and skill learning.

References

Adams, K. L. and Conklin, N. (1973). Toward a theory of natural classification. In C. Corum (Ed.), *Papers from the Ninth Regional Meeting, Chicago Linguistic Society* (pp. 1–10). Chicago: Chicago Linguistic Society.

Adams, M. J. (1990). *Beginning to read.* Cambridge, MA: MIT Press.

Allan, K. (1977). Classifiers. *Language, 53,* 284–310.

Ammerlaan, T. (1996). 'You get a bit wobbly . . .': exploring bilingual lexical retrieval processes in the context of first language attrition. Ph. D. thesis, University of Nijmegen.

Andersen, R. (1983). Transfer to somewhere. In S. Gass and L. Selinker (Eds), *Language Transfer in Language Learning* (pp. 177–201). Rowley, MA: Newbury House.

Anderson, J. R. (1976). *Language, memory and thought.* Mahwah, NJ: Erlbaum.

Anderson, J. R. (1983). *The architecture of cognition.* Cambridge, MA: Harvard University Press.

Anderson, J. R. (1990). *Cognitive psychology and its implications.* (3rd ed.) New York: Erlbaum.

Anderson, J. R. and Reder, L. M. (1979). An elaborative processing explanation of depth of processing. In L. S. Cermak and F. I. M. Craik (Eds), *Levels of processing in human memory* (pp. 385–403). Mahwah, NJ: Erlbaum.

Au, T. K. F., Knightly, L. M., Jun, S. A., and Oh, J. S. (2002). Overhearing a language during childhood. *Psychological Science, 13,* 238–243.

Bates, E., Friederici, A. D., and Wulfeck, B. (1987). Comprehension in aphasia: A cross-linguistic study. *Brain and Language, 32,* 19–67.

Bates, E. A. and MacWhinney, B. (1981). Second language acquisition from a functionalist perspective: pragmatic, semantic and perceptual strategies. In H. Winitz (Ed.), *Annals of the New York Academy of Sciences conference on native and foreign language acquisition* (pp. 190–214). New York: New York Academy of Sciences.

Beauvillain, C. and Grainger, J. (1987). Accessing interlexical homographs: some limitations of language-selective access. *Journal of Memory and Language, 26,* 658–672.

Beheydt, L. (1987). The semantization of vocabulary in foreign language learning. *System, 15,* 55–67.

Birdsong, D. (1992). Ultimate attainment in second language acquisition. *Language, 68,* 706–755.

Birdsong, D. (1999). *Second language acquisition and the critical period hypothesis.* Mahwah, NJ: Erlbaum.

Bley-Vroman, R. (1988). The fundamental character of second language learning. In W. S. S. M. Rutherford (Ed.), *Grammar and second language teaching: a book of readings* (pp. 19–30). Rowley, MA: Newbury House.

Bloomfield, L. (1933). *Language.* New York: Holt, Rinehart and Winston.

Bongaerts, T. (1999). Ultimate attainment in L2 pronunciation: the case of very advanced late L2 learners. In D. Birdsong (Ed.), *Second language acquisition and the critical period hypothesis* (pp. 133–159). Mahwah, NJ: Erlbaum.

Bongaerts, T., Mennen, S., and Van Der Slik, F. (2000). Authenticity of pronunciation in naturalistic second language acquisition: The case of very advanced late learners of Dutch as second language. *Studia Linguistica, 54*, 298–308.

Bongaerts, T., Van Summeren, C., Planken, B., and Schils, E. (1997). Age and ultimate attainment in the pronunciation of a foreign language. *Studies in Second Language Acquisition, 19*, 447–465.

Bonnet, G. *et al.* (2002). *The assessment of pupils' skills in English in eight European countries.* Paris: Ministery of Education.

Breen, M. and Candlin, C. (1980). The essentials of a communicative curriculum in language teaching. *Applied Linguistics, 1*, 89–112.

Briggs, J. and Peat, F. (1989). *Turbulent mirror: An illustrated guide to chaos theory and the science of wholeness.* New York: Harper & Row.

Brown, C. and Haagoord, P. E. (1999). *The neurocognition of language.* Oxford: Oxford University Press.

Brown, H. (1994). Principles of language learning and teaching. Englewood Cliffs, NJ: Prentice Hall.

Brown, J. D. (1988). *Understanding research in second language learning: a teachers guide to statistics and research design.* Cambridge: Cambridge University Press.

Brown, J. D. and Rodgers, T. S. (2002). *Doing second language research.* Oxford: Oxford University Press.

Brown, R. W. and Fraser, C. (1964). The acquisition of syntax. In U. Bellugi and R. Brown (Eds), *The Acquisition of Language Monograph of the Society for Research in Child Development, 29*, 43–79.

Brumfit, C. (1984). *Communicative methodology in language teaching: the roles of fluency and accuracy.* Cambridge: Cambridge University Press.

Brysbaert, M. (1998). Word recognition in bilinguals: Evidence against the existence of two separate lexicons. *Psychologica Belgica, 38*, 163–175.

Byram, M. (2000) (Ed.). *Routledge encyclopedia of language teaching and learning.* London: Routledge.

Carey, S. (1978). The child as word learner. In M. Halle, M. J. Bresnan, and G. A. Miller (Eds), *Linguistic theory and psychological reality.* Cambridge, MA: MIT Press.

Carroll, J. B. (1958). A factor analysis of two foreign language aptitude batteries. *Journal of General Psychology, 59*, 3–19.

Carroll, J. B. (1962). The prediction of success in intensive foreign language training. In R. Glaser (Ed.), *Training and Research in Education* (pp. 87–136). Pittsburgh, PA: University of Pittsburgh Press.

Carroll, J. B. (1966). Research in foreign language teaching: the last five years. In Report of the Northeast Conference 1966.

Carroll, J. B. (1981). Twenty-five years of research on foreign language aptitude. In K. C. Diller (Ed.), *Individual differences and universals in language learning aptitude* (pp. 83–117). Rowley, MA: Newbury House.

Carroll, J. B. and Sapon, S. M. (1959). *Modern language aptitude test.* New York: The Psychological Corporation/Harcourt Brace Jovanovich.

Chamot, A. U. (1994). A model for learning strategies instruction in the foreign language classroom. *Georgetown University Round Table on Languages and Linguistics*, 323–336.

Champagne-Muzar, C. (1996). The contribution of phonetic facts to the development of second-language auditory comprehension. *Canadian Modern Language Review-Revue Canadienne des Langues Vivantes, 52,* 386–415.

Chapelle, C. and Green, P. (1992). Field independence/dependence in second language acquisition research. *Language Learning, 42,* 47–83.

Chastain, K. (1969). The audiolingual habit theory versus cognitive code-learning theory: some theoretical considerations. *International Review of Applied Linguistics, 7,* 97–106.

Chaudron, C. (1988). *Second language classrooms: Research on teaching and learning.* Cambridge: Cambridge University Press.

Chen, H.-C. and Leung, Y.-S. (1989). Patterns of lexical processing in a nonnative language. *Journal of Experimental Psychology: Learning, Memory and Cognition, 15,* 316–325.

Chomsky, N. (1959). Review of *Verbal behavior* by B. F. Skinner. *Language, 35,* 26–58.

Chomsky, N. (1966a). *Cartesian linguistics.* New York: Harper Row.

Chomsky, N. (1966b). Research on language learning and linguistics. In Report of the Northeastern Conference 1966.

Chomsky, N. (1975). *Reflections on language.* New York: Pantheon.

Chomsky, N. (1980). *Rules and representations.* New York: Columbia University Press.

Chomsky, N. (1981). Principles and parameters in syntactic theory. In N. Hornstein and D. Lightfoot (Eds), *Explanations in linguistics: the logical problem of language acquisition* (pp. 123–146). London: Longman.

Chomsky, N. (1982). *Noam Chomsky on the generative enterprise.* Dordrecht: Foris.

Clark, H. H. (1996). *Using language.* Cambridge: Cambridge University Press.

Clément, R. (1980). Ethnicity, contact and communicative competence in a second language. In H. Giles, W. P. Robinson, and P. M. Smith (Eds), *Language: social psychological perspectives* (pp. 147–154). Oxford: Pergamon Press.

Clément, R., Dörnyei, Z., and Noels, K. A. (1994). Motivation, self-confidence and group cohesion in the foreign language classroom. *Language Learning, 44,* 417–448.

Clément, R., Gardner, R. C., and Smythe, P. C. (1977). Motivational variables in second language acquisition: A study of Francophones learning English. *Canadian Journal of Behavioural Science, 9,* 123–133.

Clément, R., Gardner, R. C., and Smythe, P. C. (1980). Social and individual factors in second language acquisition. *Canadian Journal of Behavioural Science, 12,* 293–302.

Clément, R. and Kruidenier, B. G. (1985). Aptitude, attitude and motivation in second language proficiency: A test of Clément's model. *Journal of Language and Social Psychology, 4,* 21–37.

Cohen, A. D. and Robbins, A. (1976). Toward assessing interlanguage performance: The relationship between selected errors, learners' characteristics, and learners' explanations. *Language Learning, 26,* 45–66.

Cook, V. (1995). Multi-competence and the learning of many languages. *Language, Culture and Curriculum, 8,* 93–98.

Cook, V. (2002) (Ed.). *Portrait of the language learner.* Clevedon: Multilingual Matters.

Cook, V. J. (1992). Evidence for multi-competence. *Language Learning, 42,* 557–591.

Coppetiers, R. (1987). Competence differences between natives and near-native speakers. *Language, 63,* 544–573.

Corder, S. P. (1967). The significance of learners' errors. *International Review of Applied Linguistics in Language Teaching, 5,* 161–169.

Corder, S. P. (1981). *Error analysis and interlanguage.* Oxford: Oxford University Press.

Craig, C. (1986). *Noun classes and categorization.* Amsterdam: John Benjamins.

Daneman, M. and Carpenter, P. A. (1980). Individual differences in working memory and reading. *Journal of Verbal Learning and Verbal Behaviour, 19,* 450–466.

Davies, A. and Elder, C. (2004) (Eds). *The handbook of applied linguistics.* Oxford: Blackwell.

Day, E. and Shapson, S. (1991). Integrating formal and functional approaches in language teaching in French immersion: an experimental study. *Language Learning, 41,* 25–58.

De Bot, K. (1992). A bilingual production model: Levelt's speaking model adapted. *Applied Linguistics, 13,* 1–24.

De Bot, K. (2002). Cognitive processing in bilinguals: language choice and code-switching. In R. B. Kaplan (Ed.), *The Oxford Handbook of Applied Linguistics* (pp. 287–300). Oxford: Oxford University Press.

De Bot, K. (2003). Bilingual speech: from concepts to articulation. *Fremdsprachen lehren und lernen (FLuL) 32,* 92–103.

De Bot, K. (2004). The multilingual lexicon: modeling selection and control. *International Journal of Multilingualism, 1,* 17–32.

De Bot, K. and Clyne, M. (1994). A 16-year longitudinal study of language attrition in Dutch immigrants in Australia. *Journal of Multilingual and Multicultural Development, 15,* 17–28.

De Bot, K. and Weltens, B. (1991). Recapitulation, regression, and language loss. In H. Seliger and R. Vago (Eds), *First language attrition* (pp. 31–52). Cambridge: Cambridge University Press.

De Bot, K. and Weltens, B. (1995). Foreign language attrition. *Annual Review of Applied Linguistics, 15,* 151–164.

De Groot, A. (2002). Lexical representation and lexical processing in the L2 user. In V. Cook (Ed.), *Portrait of the L2 user* (pp. 29–36). Clevedon: Multilingual Matters.

De Groot, A. M. B., Delmaar, P., and Lupker, S. J. (2000). The processing of interlexical homographs in translation recognition and lexical decision: Support for non-selective access to bilingual memory. *Quarterly Journal of Experimental Psychology Section A-Human Experimental Psychology, 53,* 397–428.

DeKeyser, R. M. (1994). How implicit can adult second language learning be? *AILA Review, 11,* 83–96.

DeKeyser, R. M. (1995). Learning L2 grammar rules: an experiment with a miniature linguistic system. *Studies in Second Language Acquisition, 17,* 379–410.

DeKeyser, R. M. (2000). The robustness of critical period effects in second language acquisition. *Studies in Second Language Acquisition 19,* 499–533.

Derwing, T. M. (1998). Evidence in favor of a broad framework for pronunciation instruction. *Language Learning, 48,* 393–410.

Dijkstra, A., De Bruijn, E., Schriefers, H., and Ten Brinke, S. (2000). More on interlingual homograph recognition: Language intermixing versus explicitness of instruction. *Bilingualism: Language and Cognition, 3,* 69–78.

Dijkstra, A., Van Jaarsveld, H., and Ten Brinke, S. (1998). Interlingual homograph recognition: Effects of task demands and language intermixing. *Bilingualism: Language and Cognition, 1,* 51–66.

Dijkstra, T., Grainger, J., and Van Heuven, W. J. B. (1999). Recognition of cognates and interlingual homographs: The neglected role of phonology. *Journal of Memory and Language, 41,* 496–518.

Dijkstra, T., Timmermans, M., and Schriefers, H. (2000). On being blinded by your other language: Effects of task demands on interlingual homograph recognition. *Journal of Memory and Language, 42,* 445–464.

Dijkstra, T., Van Heuven, W. J. B., and Grainger, J. (1998). Simulating cross-language competition with the Bilingual Interactive Activation model. *Psychologica Belgica, 38,* 177–197.

Dinklage, K. (1971). Inability to learn a foreign language. In G. B. Blaine and C. C. McArthur (Eds), *Emotional problems of the student* (pp. 185–206). New York: Appleton-Century.

Donato, R. (1994). Collective scaffolding in second language learning. In J. P. Lantolf and G. Appel (Eds), *Vygotskian approaches to second language research* (pp. 33–56). Norwood, NJ: Ablex.

Dörnyei, Z. (2001a). New themes and approaches in L2 motivation research. *Annual Review of Applied Linguistics, 21*, 43–59.

Dörnyei, Z. (2001b). *Teaching and researching motivation.* Harlow: Longman.

Dörnyei, Z. and Ottò, I. (1998). Motivation in action: a process model of L2 motivation. *Working Papers in Applied Linguistics, 4*, 43–69.

Doughty, C. (1991). Second language instruction does make a difference. *Studies in Second Language Acquisition, 13*, 431–469.

Downing, P. (1984). Japanese numeral classifiers: A syntactic, semantic, and functional profile. Unpublished Ph.D. dissertation, University of California, Berkeley.

Dussias, P. (2001). Sentence parsing in fluent Spanish–English bilinguals. In J. Nicol (Ed.), *Two languages: Bilingual language processing* (pp. 159–176). Cambridge, MA: Blackwell Publishers.

Edelman, G. M. (1989). *The remembered present. A biological theory of consciousness.* New York: Basic Books, Inc.

Ellis, N. (1993). Rules and instances in foreign language learning. Interactions of explicit and implicit knowledge. *European Journal of Cognitive Psychology, 5*, 289–318.

Ellis, N. C. (1994). Implicit and explicit language learning. An overview. In N. C. Ellis (Ed.), *Implicit and explicit learning of languages* (pp. 1–32). London: Academic Press.

Ellis, R. (1985). Sources of variability in interlanguage. *Applied Linguistics, 6*, 118–131.

Ellis, R. (1993). The structural syllabus and second language acquisition. *TESOL Quarterly, 27*, 91–113.

Ellis, R. (1994). *The study of second language acquisition.* Oxford: Oxford University Press.

Ellis, R. (2003). *Task-based language learning and teaching.* Oxford: Oxford University Press.

Ellis, R., Tanaka, Y., and Yamazaki, A. (1994). Classroom interaction, comprehension and the acquisition of L2 word meanings. *Language Learning, 44*, 449–491.

Elman, J. L., Bates, E. A., Johnson, M. H., Karmiliff-Smith, A., Parisi, D., and Plunkett, K. (1996). *Rethinking innateness : a connectionist perspective on development.* Cambridge, MA: MIT Press.

Ely, C. M. (1986). Language learning motivation: A descriptive and causal analysis. *Modern Language Journal, 70*, 28–35.

Ericsson, K. A. and Simon, H. A. (1993). *Protocol-analysis: Verbal reports as data.* Cambridge, MA: MIT Press.

Flege, J. E. (1987). The production of 'new' and 'similar' in a foreign language: evidence for the effect of equivalence classification. *Journal of Phonetics, 15*, 47–65.

Flege, J. E. (1993). Production and perception of a novel, 2nd-language phonetic contrast. *Journal of the Acoustical Society of America, 93*, 1589 1608.

Flege, J. E. (1995). Second language speech learning. Theory, findings and problems. In W. Strange (Ed.), *Speech perception and linguistic experience* (pp. 233–277). Timonium, MD: York Press.

Flege, J. E., Munro, M. J., and Mackay, I. R. A. (1995). Factors affecting strength of perceived foreign accent in a second language. *Journal of the Acoustical Society of America, 97*, 3125–3134.

Flege, J. E., Yeni-Komshian, G. H., and Liu, S. (1999). Age constraints on second-language acquisition. *Journal of Memory and Language, 41*, 78–104.

Flynn, S., G. Martohardjono, and W. O'Neill. (1998). *The generative study of second language acquisition.* Cambridge: Cambridge University Press.

Francis, W. S. (1999). Cognitive integration of language and memory in bilinguals: Semantic representation. *Psychological Bulletin, 125,* 193–222.

Francis, W. S. and Kucera, H. (1982). *Frequency analysis of English usage: lexicon and grammar.* Boston: Houghton Mifflin.

Frost, R. (1998). Toward a strong phonological theory of visual word recognition: True issues and false trails. *Psychological Bulletin, 123,* 71–99.

Ganschow, L., Sparks, R. L., Javorsky, J., Pohlman, J., and Bishop-Marbury, A. (1991). Identifying native language difficulties among foreign-language learners in college. A foreign-language learning-disability. *Journal of Learning Disabilities, 24,* 530–541.

Gardner, H. (1983). *Frames of mind: the theory of multiple intelligences.* New York: Basic Books.

Gardner, H. (1999). Are there additional intelligences? The case for naturalist, spritual and existential intelligences. In J. Kane (Ed.), *Education, information, and transformation* (pp. 111–131). Upper Saddle River, NJ: Prentice Hall.

Gardner, R. C. (1985). *Social psychology and second language learning : The role of attitudes and motivation.* London: Edward Arnold.

Gardner, R. C. and Lambert, W. (1972). *Attitudes and motivation in second language learning.* Rowley, MA: Newbury House.

Gardner, R. C. and Macintyre, P. D. (1991). An instrumental motivation in language study: who says it isn't effective? *Studies in Second Language Acquisition, 13,* 57–72.

Gardner, R. C. and Macintyre, P. D. (1993). On the measurement of affective variables in 2nd-language learning. *Language Learning, 43,* 157–194.

Gardner, R. C. and Smythe, P. C. (1975). Motivation and second language acquisition. *Canadian Modern Language Review-Revue Canadienne des Langues Vivantes, 31,* 218–230.

Gardner, R. C., Tremblay, P. F., and Masgoret, A.-M. (1997). Towards a full model of second language learning: An empirical investigation. *Modern Language Journal, 81,* 344–362.

Gary, J. D. and Gary, N. (1981). Talking may be dangerous to your linguistic health: The case for a much greater emphasis on listening comprehension in foreign language instruction. *International Review of Applied Linguistics, 19,* 1–14.

Gass, S. M. (1988). Integrating research areas: A framework for second language studies. *Applied Linguistics, 9,* 198–217.

Gass, S. M. (1997). *Input, interaction and the second language learner.* Mahwah, NJ: Erlbaum.

Gass, S. M. and Mackay, A. (2000). *Stimulated recall methodology in second langauge research.* Mahwah, NJ: Erlbaum.

Gass, S. M., Mackey, A., and Pica, T. (1998). The role of input and interaction in second language acquisition – Introduction to the special issue. *Modern Language Journal, 82,* 299–307.

Gass, S. M. and J. Schachter. (1989). *Linguistic perspectives on second language acquisition.* Cambridge: Cambridge University Press.

Gass, S. M. and Selinker, L. (1983) (Eds). *Language transfer in language learning.* Rowley, MA: Newbury House.

Gass, S. M. and Varonis, E. M. (1994). Input, interaction, and second language production. *Studies in Second Language Acquisition, 16,* 283–302.

Gatbonton, E. (1978). Patterned phonetic variability in second language speech: a gradual diffusion model. *Canadian Modern Language Review, 34,* 335–347.

Genesee, F. and Hamayan, E. (1980). Individual differences in second language learning. *Applied Psycholinguistics, 1,* 95–110.

Gentner, D. and Medina, J. (1998). Similarity and the development of rules. *Cognition, 65*, 263–297.

Gottlob, L. R., Goldinger, S. D., Stone, G. O., and Van Orden, G. C. (1999). Reading homographs: Orthographic, phonologic, and semantic dynamics. *Journal of Experimental Psychology-Human Perception and Performance, 25*, 561–574.

Green, D. W. (1986). Control, activation, and resource: a framework and a model for the control of speech in bilinguals. *Brain and Language, 27*, 210–223.

Green, J. M. and Oxford, R. L. (1995). A closer look at learning strategies, L2 proficiency and gender. *TESOL Quarterly, 29*, 261–297.

Gregg, K. R. (1984). Krashen's Monitor and Occam's Razor. *Applied Linguistics, 5*, 79–100.

Grevisse, M. (1980). *Le Bon Usage*. Onzieme edition revue. Paris: Duculot.

Grosjean, F. (1988). Exploring the recognition of guest words in bilingual speech. *Language and Cognitive Processes, 3*, 233–274.

Grosjean, F. (1998). Studying bilinguals: Methodological and conceptual issues. *Bilingualism: Language and Cognition, 1*, 131–149.

Guiora, A. (1990). A psychological theory of second language production. *Toegepaste Taalwetenschap in Artikelen, 37*, 15–23.

Guiora, A. (1991). The two faces of language ego. *Toegepaste Taalwetenschap in Artikelen, 41*, 5–14.

Habermas, J. (1987). *Theory of communicative action, Vol 1. Reason and the rationalization of society*. Boston, MA: Beacon Press.

Hakuta, K., Bialystok, E., and Wiley, E. (2003). Critical evidence: A test of the critical-period hypothesis for second-language acquisition. *Psychological Science, 14*, 31–38.

Hammond, R. (1995). Foreign accent and phonetic interference: The application of linguistic research to the teaching of second language pronunciation. In F. Eckman, D. Highland, P. Lee, J. Mileham, and R. Rutkowski Weber (Eds), *Second language acquisition theory and pedagogy* (pp. 293–303). Mahwah, NJ: Erlbaum.

Hanks, W. F. (1996). *Language and communicative practices*. Boulder, CO: Westview Press.

Hansen, J. and Stansfield, C. W. (1981). The relationship of field dependent-independent cognitive styles to foreign language achievement. *Language Learning, 31*, 349–367.

Hansen, L. (2000a) Language attrition in contexts of Japanese bilingualism. In M. Nogushi and S. Fotos (Eds), *Studies in Japanese bilingualism* (pp. 353–372). London: Multilingual Matters.

Hansen, L. (2000b). Language attrition research archive (LARA). http://byuh.edu. academics/lang/attritionbiblio/main.htm.

Hansen, L. and Chen, Y.-L. (2002). What counts in the acquisition and attrition of numeral classifiers? *JALT Journal, 23*, 90–110.

Hansen, L. and Reetz-Kurashige (1999). The study of second language attrition: An introduction. In L. Hansen (Ed.), *Second language attrition in Japanese contexts*. Oxford: Oxford University Press.

Harley, B. (1989). Functional grammar in French immersion: a classroom experiment. *Applied Linguistics, 10*, 331–359.

Harley, B. (1993). Instructional strategies and SLA in early French immersion. *Studies in Second Language Acquisition, 15*, 245–260.

Harley, B., Allen, P., Cummins, J., and Swain, M. (1990). *The development of bilingual proficiency*. Cambridge: Cambridge University Press.

Harley, B. and Swain, M. (1984). The interlanguage of immersion students and its implications for second language teaching. In A. Davies, C. Criper, and A. P. R. Howatt (Eds), *Interlanguage* (pp. 291–311). Edinburgh: Edinburgh University Press.

Harwood, N. (forthcoming). Citation analysis: A multidisciplinary perspective on academic literacy. In M. Baynham (Ed.), *Applied linguistics at the interface*. London: Equinox.

Hatch, E. (1978). Acquisition of syntax in a second language. In J. Richards (Ed.), *Understanding second and foreign language learning* (pp. 34–70). Rowley, MA: Newbury House.

Hatch, E. and Wagner-Gough, J. (1976). Explaining sequence and variation in second language acquisition. *Language Learning, 4*, 39–47.

Herdina, P. and Jessner, U. (2002). *A dynamic model of multilingualism. Perspective of change in psycholinguistics*. Clevedon: Multilingual Matters.

Holliday, L. (1995). NS syntactic modifications in NS–NNS negotiations as input data for second language acquisition of syntax. Unpublished doctoral dissertation, University of Pennsylvania, Philadelphia.

Horwitz, E. K., Horwitz, M. B., and Cope, J. (1986). Foreign language classroom anxiety. *Modern Language Journal, 70*, 125–132.

Howatt, A. P. R. (1984). *A history of English language teaching*. Oxford: Oxford University Press.

Hulstijn, J. H. (2000). Intentional and incidental second-language vocabulary learning: A reappraisal of elaboration, rehearsal and automaticity. In P. Robinson (Ed.), *Cognition and second language instruction*. Cambridge: Cambridge University Press.

Hulstijn, Y. and De Graaff, R. (1994). Under what conditions does explicit knowledge of a second language facilitate the acquisition of implicit knowledge? A research proposal. In J. Hulstijn and R. Schmidt (Eds), *AILA Review* (pp. 97–112).

Ioup, G. (1995). Evaluating the need for input enhancement in post-critical period language acquisition. In D. Singleton and Z. Lengyel (Eds), *The age factor in second language acquisition* (pp. 95–123). Clevedon: Multilingual Matters.

Jakobson, R. (1968). The role of phonic elements in speech perception. *Zeitschrift für Phonetik, Sprachwissenschaft und Kommunikationsforschung, 21*, 9–20.

James, C. (1998). *Errors in language learning and use: exploring error analysis*. London: Longman.

James, C. T. (1975). Role of semantic information in lexical decisions. *Journal of Experimental Psychology–Human Perception and Performance, 104*, 130–136.

Johnson, D. M. (1992). *Approaches to research in second language learning*. New York: Longman.

Johnson, K. (1982). *Communicative syllabus design and methodology*. Oxford: Pergamon Press.

Johnson, K. (1996). *Language teaching and skills learning*. Oxford: Blackwell.

Johnson, L. and Newport, E. (1989). Critical period effects in second language learning: the influence of maturational state on the acquisition of English as a second language. *Cognitive Psychology, 21*, 60–99.

Kaplan, R. (2002) (Ed.). *The Oxford handbook of applied linguistics*. Oxford: Oxford University Press.

Kawamoto, A. H. and Zemblidge, J. H. (1992). Pronunciation of homographs. *Journal of Memory and Language, 31*, 349–374.

Kellerman, E. (1977). Towards a characterisation of the strategy of transfer in second language learning. *Interlanguage Studies Bulletin, 2*, 138–145.

Kellerman, E. (1979). Transfer and non-transfer: Where are we now? *Studies in Second Language Acquisition, 2*, 37–57.

Kellerman, E. (1995). Age before beauty: Johnson and Newport revisited. In L. Eubank, L. Selinker, and M. Sharwood Smith (Eds), *The current state of interlanguage: Studies in the honour of William E. Rutherford* (pp. 219–231). Amsterdam: John Benjamins.

Kellerman, E. (2000). Lo que la fruta puede decirnos acerca de la transferencia léxico-sémantica: una dimensión no estructural de las percepciones que tiene el aprendiz sobre las relaciones lingüísticas [What fruit can tell us about lexicosemantic transfer: A non-structural dimension to learners' perceptions of linguistic relations]. In C. Muñoz (Ed.), *Segundas lenguas. Adquisición en la aula* (pp. 21–37). Barcelona: Ariel.

Kellerman, E. and Sharwood Smith, M. (1986) (Eds). *Cross-linguistic influence in second language acquisition.* Oxford: Pergamon Press.

Klein, W. (1995). Language acquisition at different ages. In D. Magnusson (Ed.), *The lifespan development of individuals: Behavioral, neurobiological and psychosocial perspectives. A synthesis* (pp. 244–264). Cambridge: Cambridge University Press.

Knudsen, E. (1998). Capacity for plasticity in the adult owl auditory system expanded by juvenile experience. *Science, 279,* 1531–1533.

Kowal, M. and Swain, M. (1994). From semantic to syntactic processing: How can we promote it in the immersion classroom? In R. K. Johnson and M. Swain (Eds), *Immersion education: International perspectives.* Cambridge: Cambridge University Press.

Krashen, S. D. (1973). Lateralization, language learning and the critical period: some new evidence. *Language Learning, 23,* 63–74.

Krashen, S. D. (1981). *Second language acquisition and second language learning.* New York: Pergamon Press.

Krashen, S. D. (1982). *Principles and practice in second language acquisition.* Oxford: Pergamon Press.

Krashen, S. D. (1985). *The input hypothesis: Issues and implications.* London: Longman.

Krashen, S. D. (1987). *Principles and practice in second language acquisition.* Englewood Cliffs, NJ: Prentice-Hall.

Krashen, S. D. and Terrell, T. (1983). *The natural approach: Language acquisition in the classroom.* Oxford: Pergamon.

Kroll, J. F. and Curley, J. (1986). Picture naming and bilingual translation. Unpublished manuscript. South Hadley, MA: Mount Holyoke College.

Kroll, J. F. and Curley, J. (1988). Lexical memory in novice bilinguals: The role of concepts in retrieving second language words. In M. Gruneberg, P. Morris, and R. Sykes (Eds), *Practical aspects of memory* (pp. 389–395). London: John Wiley & Sons.

Kroll, J. F. and Dijkstra, T. (2002). The bilingual lexicon. In R. Kaplan (Ed.), *The Oxford handbook of applied linguistics* (pp. 301–321). Oxford: Oxford University Press.

Kroll, J. F. and Sholl, A. (1991). Lexical and conceptual determinants of translation performance. *Paper presented at the 16th Annual Boston University Conference on Language Development, Boston, MA.*

Kroll, J. F. and Sholl, A. (1992). Lexical and conceptual memory in fluent and nonfluent bilinguals. In R. Harris (Ed.), *Cognitive processing in bilinguals* (pp. 191–204). Amsterdam: Elsevier.

Kroll, J. F. and Stewart, E. (1989). Translating from one language to another: The role of words and concepts in making the connection. Paper presented at the Meeting of the Dutch Psychonomic Society, Noordwijkerhout, The Netherlands.

Kroll, J. F. and Stewart, E. (1990). Concept mediation in bilingual translation. Paper presented at the Thirty-First Annual Meeting of the Psychonomic Society, New Orleans, LA.

Kroll, J. F. and Stewart, E. (1994). Category interference in translation and picture naming – evidence for asymmetric connections between bilingual memory representations. *Journal of Memory and Language, 33,* 149–174.

Kucera, H. and Francis, W. S. (1967). *Computational analysis of present-day American English.* Providence, RI: Brown University Press.

Lado, R. (1964). *Language teaching: A scientific approach*. New York: McGraw-Hill.

Lambert, W. E. (1966). *Some observations on first language acquisition and second language learning*. (Mimeograph).

Langacker, R. W. (1972). *Fundamentals of linguistic analysis*. New York: Harcourt Brace Jovanovich.

Lantolf, J. (2002). Sociocultural theory and second language acquisition. In R. Kaplan (Ed.), *The Oxford handbook of applied linguistics* (pp. 104–114). Oxford: Oxford University Press.

Lantolf, J. P. (1994). Sociocultural theory and 2nd-language learning – Introduction to the special issue. *Modern Language Journal, 78*, 418–420.

LaPierre, D. (1994). Language output in a cooperative learning setting: Determining its effects on second language learning. Unpublished master's thesis, University of Toronto (OISE), Toronto, Canada.

Larsen-Freeman, D. (1976). An explanation for the morpheme accuracy order of learners of English as a second language. *Language Learning, 26*, 125–135.

Larsen-Freeman, D. (1997). Chaos/complexity science and second language acquisition. *Applied Linguistics, 18*, 141–165.

Larsen-Freeman, D. and Long, M. H. (1991). *An introduction to second language acquisition research*. London: Longman.

Lefebvre, R. C. (1984). A psychological consultation program for learning disabled students. *College Student Personnel, 7*, 361–362.

Lefrancois, G. R. (1994). *Psychology for Teaching*. Belmont, CA: Wadsworth Publishing Company.

Lenneberg, E. (1967). *Biological foundations of language*. New York: John Wiley & Sons.

Lenneberg, E. H. (1966). The natural history of language. In F. Smith and G. A. Miller (Eds), *The genesis of language*. Cambridge, MA: MIT Press.

Levelt, W. J. M. (1989). *Speaking: From intention to articulation*. Cambridge, MA: MIT Press.

Levelt, W. J. M. (1993). The architecture of normal spoken language use. In G. Blanken *et al.* (Eds), *Linguistic disorders and pathologies: an international handbook*, pp. 1–15. Berlin, New York: Walter de Gruyter.

Levelt, W. J. M, A. Roelofs, and A. S. Meyer. (1999). A theory of lexical access in speech production. *Behavioural and Brain Sciences, 22*, 1–38.

Li, P. (1996). Spoken word recognition of code-switched words by Chinese–English bilinguals. *Journal of Memory and Language, 35*, 757–774.

Lieven, E., Behrens, H., Spears, J., *et al.* (2003). Early syntactic creativity: a usage-based approach. *Journal of Child Language, 30*, 333–370.

Lightbown, P. M. (1991). What have we here? Some observations on the role of instruction in second language acquisition. In R. Phillipson, E. Kellerman, L. Selinker, M. Sharwood Smith, and M. Swain (Eds), *Foreign/second language pedagogy research: a commemorative volume for Claus Faerch* (pp. 197–212). Clevedon: Multilingual Matters.

Lightbown, P. M. (1994). The importance of timing in focus on form. Paper presented at the Second Language Research Forum, McGill University, Montreal.

Lightbown, P. M. (1998). The importance of timing in focus on form. In C. Doughty and J. Williams (Eds), *Focus on form in classroom second language acquisition* (pp. 177–196). New York: Cambridge University Press.

Lightbown, P. M. (2000). Classroom SLA research and second language teaching. *Applied Linguistics, 21*, 431–462.

Lightbown, P. M. and Spada, N. (1990). Focus on form and corrective feedback in communicative language teaching. *Studies in Second Language Acquisition, 12*, 429–448.

Lightbown, P. M. and Spada, N. (2003). *How languages are learned.* Oxford: Oxford University Press.

Lightfoot, D. (1982). *The language lottery: toward a biology of grammars.* Cambridge, MA: MIT Press.

Linnell, J. (1995). Negotiation as a context for learning syntax in a second language. Unpublished doctoral dissertation, University of Pennsylvania, Philadelphia.

Littlewood, W. T. (1981). *Communicative language teaching: an introduction.* Cambridge: Cambridge University Press.

Lokerson, J. (1992). Glossary of some important terms. Learning Disabilities Online (Retrieved 21.02.2005 from http://www.ldonline.org/ld_indepth/glossaries/glossary_of_terms.html)

Long, M. H. (1980a). Input, interaction, and second language acquisition. Unpublished doctoral dissertation, University of California, Los Angeles.

Long, M. H. (1980b). Inside the 'black box': methodological issues in classroom research on language learning. *Language Learning, 30,* 1–42.

Long, M. H. (1983a). Linguistic and conversational adjustments to non-native speakers. *Studies in Second Language Acquisition, 5,* 177–194.

Long, M. H. (1983b). Native speaker/non-native speaker conversation and the negotiation of comprehensible input. *Applied Linguistics, 4,* 126–141.

Long, M. H. (1985). Input and second language acquisition theory. In S. M. Gass and C. G. Madden (Eds), *Input in second language acquisition* (pp. 377–393). Rowley, MA: Newbury House.

Long, M. H. (1991). Focus on form: a design feature in language teaching methodology. In K. De Bot, R. Ginsberg, and C. Kramsch (Eds), *Foreign language research in cross-cultural perspective* (pp. 40–52). Amsterdam: John Benjamins.

Long, M. H. (1993). Second language acquisition as a function of age: Research findings and methodological issues. In K. Hyltenstam and A. Viberg (Eds), *Progression and regression in language: Sociocultural, neuropsychological and linguistic perspectives* (pp. 196–221). Cambridge: Cambridge University Press.

Long, M. H. (1996). The role of the linguistic environment in second language acquisition. In W. C. Ritchie and T. K. Bhatia (Eds), *Handbook of language acquisition: Vol. 2. Second language acquisition* (pp. 413–468). New York: Academic Press.

Long, M. H., Inagaki, S., and Ortega, L. (1998). The role of implicit negative feedback in SLA: Models and recasts in Japanese and Spanish. *Modern Language Journal, 82,* 357–371.

Loschky, L. C. (1994). Comprehensible input and second language acquisition: What is the relationship? *Studies in Second Language Acquisition, 16,* 303–325.

Lowie, W. M. (2000). Cross-linguistic influence on morphology in the bilingual mental lexicon. *Studia Linguistica, 54,* 175–185.

Lupker, S. J. (1984). Semantic priming without association: A second look. *Journal of Verbal Learning and Verbal Behavior, 23,* 709–733.

Lyster, R. (1987). Speaking immersion. *Canadian Modern Language Review-Revue Canadienne des Langues Vivantes, 43,* 701–717.

Lyster, R. (1994). The effect of functional-analytic teaching on aspects of French immersion students' sociolinguistic competence. *Applied Linguistics, 15,* 263–287.

MacIntyre, P. D. (1995). How does anxiety affect second language learning? A reply to Sparks and Ganschow. *Modern Language Journal, 79,* 90–99.

MacIntyre, P. D. and Gardner, R. C. (1989). Anxiety and second language learning: Toward a theoretical clarification. *Language Learning, 39,* 251–275.

MacIntyre, P. D. and Gardner, R. C. (1991). Language anxiety: Its relation to other anxieties and to processing in native and second languages. *Language Learning, 41,* 513–534.

Mackey, A. (1994a). Targeting morpho-syntax in children's ESL: An empirical study of the use of interactive goal-based tasks. *Working Papers in Educational Linguistics, 10,* 67–88.

Mackey, A. (1994b). *Using communicative tasks to target grammatical structures. A handbook of tasks and instructions for their use.* Sydney: Language Acquisition Research Centre, University of Sydney.

Mackey, A. (1995). Stepping up the pace: Input, interaction and interlanguage development. An empirical study of questions in ESL. Unpublished doctoral dissertation, University of Sydney, Australia.

Mackey, A. (1997). Stepping up the pace: Input, interaction and second language development. Unpublished manuscript, Michigan State University, East Lansing.

Mackey, A. (1999). Input, interaction, and second language development: an empirical study of question formation in ESL. *Studies in Second Language Acquisition, 21,* 557–587.

Mackey, A. and Philp, J. (1998). Conversational interaction and second language development: Recasts, responses, and red herrings? *Modern Language Journal, 82,* 338–356.

MacWhinney, B. (1989). Competition and connectionism. In MacWhinney and E. Bates (Eds), *The crosslinguistic study of sentence processing* (pp. 422–457). Cambridge: Cambridge University Press.

MacWhinney, B. (1997). Second language acquisition and the competition model. In A. de Groot and J. Kroll (Eds), *Tutorials in bilingualism: Psycholinguistic perspectives* (pp. 113–142). Mahwah, NJ: Erlbaum.

Marchman, V. A. (1997). Models of language development: An 'emergentist' perspective. *Mental Retardation and Developmental Disabilities Research Reviews, 3,* 293–299.

Marsh, D., Maljers, A., and Hartiala, A. (2001). *Profiling European CLIL classrooms: Languages open doors.* Jyväskylä: University of Jyväskylä.

Martohardjono, G. and Flynn, S. (1995). Is there an age factor for universal grammar? In D. Singleton and Z. Lengyel (Eds), *The age factor in second language acquisition* (pp. 135–153). Clevedon: Multilingual Matters.

Maury, F. (1995). Les mécanismes intrapsychiques de l'adoption internationale et interraciale. l'adoption des enfants coréens en france. PhD thesis, Université de Paris VIII, Paris.

McClelland, J. L. and Rumelhart, D. E. (1981). An interactive activation model of context effects in letter perception, Part 1: An account of basic findings. *Psychological Review, 88,* 375–405.

McLaughlin, B. (1978). The Monitor model: some methodological considerations. *Language Learning, 28,* 309–332.

McLaughlin, B. (1987). *Theories of second language learning.* London: Edward Arnold.

McNeill, D. (1966). Developmental psycholinguistics. In F. Smith and G. A. Miller (Eds), *The genesis of language* (pp. 1–84). Cambridge, MA: The MIT Press.

Meisel, J., Clahsen, H., and Pienemann, M. (1981). On determining developmental stages in natural second language acquisition. *Studies in Second Language Acquisition, 3,* 109–135.

Miller, G. A. (1964). On the new scientists of language. *Encounter, 23,* 29–37.

Miller, G. A. (1966). Language and psychology. In E. H. Lenneberg (Ed.), *New directions in the study of language* (pp. 89–107). Cambridge, MA: MIT Press.

Mitchell, R. and Myles, F. (1998). *Second language teaching theories.* London: Edward Arnold.

Mohanan, K. P. (1992). Emergence of complexity in phonological development. In C. Ferguson, L. Menn, and C. Stoel-Gammon (Eds), *Phonological development* (pp. 635–662). Timonium, MD: York Press, Inc.

Mondria, J. A. (1996). Vocabulaireverwerving in het vreemde-talenonderwijs: De effecten van context en raden op retentie [Vocabulary acquisition in foreign language instruction: The effects of context and guessing on retention]. Unpublished doctoral dissertation, University of Groningen.

Moore, D. S. and McCabe, G. P. (2003). *Introduction to the practice of statistics.* (4th ed.) New York: Freeman.

Naiman, N., Frölich, M., Stern, H. H., and Todesco, A. (1978). *The good language learner.* Toronto, ON: Ontario Institute for Studies in Education.

Nobuyoshi, J. and Ellis, R. (1993). Focused communication tasks and second language acquisition. *English Language Teaching Journal, 47,* 203–210.

Norris, J. M. and Ortega, L. (2000). Effectiveness of L2 instruction: A research synthesis and quantitative meta-analysis. *Language Learning, 50,* 417–528.

Obler, L. K. (1982). The parsimonious bilingual. In L. K. Obler and L. Menn (Eds), *Exceptional language and linguistics* (pp. 339–346). New York: Academic Press.

Oller, J. and Perkins, K. (1978). Intelligence and language proficiency as sources of variance in self-reported affective variables. *Language Learning, 28,* 85–97.

Oltman, P. K., Raskin, E., and Witkin, H. A. (1971). *Group embedded figures test.* Palo Alto, CA: Consulting Psychologists.

Oxford, R. L. (1986). Development of a new survey and taxonomy for second language learning. Paper presented at the Learning Strategy Symposium, New York.

Oxford, R. L. (1990). *Language learning strategies: What every teacher should know.* Boston, MA: Heinle & Heinle.

Oxford, R. L. and Burry-Stock, J. A. (1995). Assessing the use of language learning strategies worldwide with the ESL/EFL version of the Strategy Inventory for Language Learning (SILL), *System, 23,* 1–23.

Oxford, R. L., Nyikos, M., and Crookall, D. (1987). *Learning strategies of university foreign language students: A large-scale factor-analytic study.* Washington, DC: Center for Applied Linguistics.

Oxford, R. L., Park-Oh, Y., Ito, S., and Sumrall, M. (1993). Japanese by satellite: Effects of motivation, language learning styles and strategies, gender, course level and previous language learning experience on Japanese language achievement. *Foreign Language Annals, 26,* 359–371.

Pallier, C., Dehaene, S., Poline, J. B., LeBihan, D., Argenti, A.-M., Dupoux, E. *et al.* (2003). Brain imaging of language plasticity in adopted adults: Can a second language replace the first? *Cerebral Cortex, 13,* 155–161.

Palmer, H. E. (1917). The scientific study and teaching of languages. Harrap: London.

Paradis, M. (1994). Neurolinguistic aspects of implicit and explicit memory: Implications for bilingualism and SLA. In N. Ellis (Ed.), *Implicit and explicit learning of languages* (pp. 393–420). London: Academic Press.

Paradis, M. (2004). *A neurolinguistic theory of bililngualism.* Amsterdam: John Benjamins.

Patkowski, M. (1994). The critical age hypothesis and interlanguage phonology. In Yavas, M. (Ed.), *First and second language phonology* (pp. 209–221), San Diego: Singular.

Pavlenko, A. (1999). New approaches to concepts in bilingual memory. *Bilingualism: Language and Cognition, 2,* 209–230.

Pavlenko, A. and Lantolf, J. P. (2000). Second language learning as participation and the (re)construction of selves. In J. P. Lantolf (Ed.), *Sociocultural theory and second language learning* (pp. 155–177). Oxford: Oxford University Press.

Peal, E. and Lambert, W. E. (1962). The relation of bilingualism to intelligence. *Psychological Monographs, 76,* 1–23.

Perani, D., Paulesu, E., Galles, N. S., Dupoux, E., Dehaene, S., Bettinardi, V. *et al.* (1998). The bilingual brain – Proficiency and age of acquisition of the second language. *Brain, 121*, 1841–1852.

Piaget, J. (1970). *Epistémologie génétique.* Paris: Presses universitaires de France.

Pica, T. (1992). The textual outcomes of native speaker–nonnative speaker negotiation: What do they reveal about second language learning? In C. Kramsch and S. McConnell-Ginet (Eds), *Text and context: Cross-disciplinary perspectives on language study* (pp. 198–237). Lexington, MA: D.C. Heath & Co.

Pica, T. (1994). Research on negotiation: What does it reveal about second-language learning conditions, processes, and outcomes? *Language Learning, 44*, 493–527.

Pica, T. (1996). Second language learning through interaction: Multiple perspectives. *Working Papers in Educational Linguistics, 12*, 1–22.

Pica, T., Young, R., and Doughty, C. (1987). The impact of interaction on comprehension. *TESOL Quarterly, 21*, 737–758.

Pienemann, M. (1984). Psychological constraints on the teachability of languages. *Studies in Second Language Acquisition, 6*, 186–214.

Pienemann, M. (1985). Learnability and syllabus construction. In K. Hyltenstam and M. Pienemann (Eds), *Modelling and assessing second language development* (pp. 23–76). Clevedon: Multilingual Matters.

Pienemann, M. (1989). Is language teachable? psycholinguistic experiments and hypotheses. *Applied Linguistics, 10*, 217–244.

Pienemann, M. and Johnston, M. (1987). Factors influencing the development of language proficiency. In D. Nunan (Ed.), *Applying second language acquisition research* (pp. 45–141). Adelaide, Australia: National Curriculum Resource Centre, AMEP.

Pienemann, M. and Mackey, A. (1993). An empirical study of children's ESL development. In P. McKay (Ed.), *ESL development: Language and literacy in schools. Vol. 2: Documents on bandscale development and language acquisition* (pp. 115–259). Canberra: National Languages & Literacy Institute of Australia and Commonwealth of Australia.

Pimsleur, P. (1966a). *Language Aptitude Battery.* New York: Harcourt Brace.

Pimsleur, P. (1966b). *Pimsleur Language Aptitude Battery.* New York: Harcourt Brace.

Pimsleur, P. (1968). Language aptitude testing. In A. Davies (Ed.), *Language testing symposium: A linguistic approach* (pp. 98–106). New York: Oxford University Press.

Pinker, S. (1994). *The language instinct.* New York: William Morrow.

Pinker, S. and Prince, A. (1988). On language and connectionism: analysis of a parallel distributed processing model of language acquisition. *Cognition, 28*, 73–193.

Politzer, R. L. (1983). An exploratory study of self-reported language learning behaviors and their relation to achievement. *Studies in Second Language Acquisition, 6*, 54–68.

Politzer, R. L. and McGroarty, M. (1985). An exploratory study of learning behaviors and their relationship to gains in linguistic and communicative competence. *TESOL Quarterly, 19*, 103–124.

Pompian, N. and Thum, C. (1988). Dyslexic/Learning disabled students at Dartmouth College. *Annals of Dyslexia, 38*, 278–284.

Port, R. and T. van Gelder. (1995) (Eds). *Mind as motion: Exploration in the dynamics of cognition.* Cambridge, MA: Bradford.

Potter, M. C., Kroll, J. F., Yachzel, B., Carpenter, E., and Sherman, I. (1986). Pictures in sentences: Understanding without words. *Journal of Experimental Psychology: General, 115*, 281–294.

Potter, M. C., So, K. F., Von Eckhart, B., and Feldman, L. B. (1984). Lexical and conceptual representation in beginning and more proficient bilinguals. *Journal of Verbal Learning and Verbal Behavior, 23*, 23–38.

Ransdell, S. and Fischler, I. (1987). Memory in a monolingual mode: When are bilinguals in a disadvantage? *Journal of Memory and Language, 26,* 392–405.

Ranta, L. (2004). Focus on form from the inside: The relationship between grammatical sensitivity and L2 acquisition in communicative ESL programs. PhD dissertation, Concordia University, Montreal, Canada.

Robinson, P. (1996). Learning simple and complex second language rules under implicit, incidental, rule-search, and instructed conditions. *Studies in Second Language Acquisition, 18,* 27–67.

Robinson, P. (2002). *Individual differences and instructed language learning. Language learning and language teaching.* Amsterdam: John Benjamins.

Roeper, T., Lapointe, S., Bing, J. and Tavakolian, S. (1981). A lexical approach to language acquisition. In S. Tavakolian (ed.) *Language acquisition and linguistic theory* (pp. 35–58). Cambridge, MA: MIT Press.

Rosenshine, B. and Furst, N. (1973). The use of direct observation to study teaching. In R. M. W. Travers (Ed.), *Second handbook of research on teaching* (pp. 122–183). Chicago: Rand McNally.

Saporta, S. (1966). Applied linguistics and generative grammar. In A. Valdman (Ed.), *Trends in modern language teaching* (pp. 81–92). New York: McGraw-Hill.

Sato, C. J. (1985). The syntax of conversation in interlanguage development. Unpublished doctoral dissertation, University of California, Los Angeles.

Sato, C. J. (1986). Conversation and interlanguage development: Rethinking the connection. In R. R. Day (Ed.), *Talking to learn: Conversation in second language acquisition* (pp. 5–22). Rowley, MA: Newbury House.

Savard, J.-G. and Richards, J. (1970). *Les indices d'utilité du vocabulaire fondamental français.* Québec: Les Presses d'Université Laval.

Savignon, S. (1972). *Communicative competence: an experiment in foreign-language teaching.* Philadelphia: Centre for Curriculum Development.

Scardamalia, M. and Paris, P. (1985). The function of explicit discourse knowledge in the development of text representations and composing strategies. *Cognition and Instruction, 2,* 1–39.

Schachter, J. (1974). An error in error analysis. *Language Learning, 24,* 205–214.

Scherer, G. and Wertheimer, F. (1964). *A psycholinguistic experiment in foreign-language teaching.* New York: McGraw Hill.

Schmid, M. and De Bot, K. (2003). Language attrition. In A. Davies and C. Elder (Eds), *The handbook of applied linguistics,* pp. 210–234. Oxford: Blackwell.

Schmidt, R. W. (1990). The role of consciousness in second language learning. *Applied Linguistics, 11,* 127–158.

Schmidt, R. W. (1994). Deconstructing consciousness in search of useful definitions for applied linguistics. *AILA Review, 11,* 11–26.

Schmidt, R. W. and Frota, S. N. (1986). Developing basic conversational ability in a second language: A case study of an adult learner of Portuguese. In R. R. Day (Ed.), *Talking to Learn: Conversation in second language acquisition* (pp. 237–326). Rowley, MA: Newbury House.

Schmitt, N. (2002) (Ed.). *An introduction to applied linguistics.* London: Edward Arnold.

Schreuder, R. and B. Weltens. (1995) (Eds). *The bilingual lexicon.* Amsterdam: John Benjamins.

Schumann, J. (1975). Affective factors and the problem of age in second language acquisition. *Language Learning, 25,* 209–225.

Scovel, T. (1978). The effect of affect on foreign language learning: A review of the anxiety research. *Language Learning, 28,* 129–142.

Scovel, T. (1988). *A time to speak: a psycholinguistic inquiry into the critical period for human speech*. Rowley, MA: Newbury House.

Selinker, L. (1972). Interlanguage. *International Review of Applied Linguistics, 10*, 209–231.

Selinker, L., Swain, M., and Dumas, G. (1975). The interlanguage hypothesis extended to children. *Language Learning, 75*, 139–152.

Sfard, A. (1998). On two metaphors for learning and the dangers of choosing just one. *Educational Researcher, 27*, 4–13.

Sharwood Smith, M. (1986). Comprehension vs. acquisition: two ways of processing input. *Applied Linguistics, 7*, 118–132.

Simpson, G. B. (1984). Lexical ambiguity and its role in models of word recognition. *Psychological Bulletin, 96*, 316–340.

Singleton, D. (2001). Age and second language acquisition. *Annual Review of Applied Linguistics 21*, 77–89.

Singleton, D. M. (1999). *Exploring the second language mental lexicon. The Cambridge applied linguistics series*. Cambridge: Cambridge University Press.

Skehan, P. (1989). *Individual differences in second language learning*. London: Edward Arnold.

Skehan, P. (1991). Individual differences in second language learning. *Studies in Second Language Acquisition, 13*, 275–298.

Skehan, P. (2002). Theorising and updating aptitude. In P. Robinson (Ed.), *Individual differences and instructed language learning*, Amsterdam: John Benjamins.

Skinner, B. F. (1957). *Verbal behavior*. Englewood Cliffs, NJ: Prentice-Hall.

Smith, P. D. (1969). The Pennsylvania foreign language research project: teaching proficiency and class achievement in two modern languages. *Foreign Language Annals, 3*, 194–207.

Sorace, A. (1993). Incomplete vs. divergent representations of accusativity in non-native grammars of Italian. *Second Language Research, 9*, 22–47.

Spada, N. (1987). Relationships between instructional differences and learning outcomes: a process-product study of communicative language teaching. *Applied Linguistics, 8*, 137–161.

Spada, N. (1997). Form-focussed instruction and second language acquisition: A review of classroom and laboratory research. *Language Teaching, 30*, 73–87.

Spada, N. and Lightbown, P. M. (1989). Intensive ESL programs in Quebec primary schools. *TESL Canada Journal, 7*, 11–32.

Spada, N. and Lightbown, P. M. (1993). Instruction and the development of questions in L2 classrooms. *Studies in Second Language Acquisition, 15*, 205–224.

Sparks, R. L. and Ganschow, L. (1991). Foreign language learning differences: Affective or native language aptitude differences? *Modern Language Journal, 75*, 3–16.

Sparks, R. L. and Ganschow, L. (2001). Aptitude for learning a foreign language. *Annual Review of Applied Linguistics, 21*, 90–111.

Sparks, R. L., Ganschow, L., and Pohlman, J. (1989). Linguistic coding deficits in foreign language learners. *Annals of Dyslexia, 39*, 179–195.

Spivey, M. J. and Marian, V. (1999). Cross talk between native and second languages: Partial activation of an irrelevant lexicon. *Psychological Science, 10*, 281–284.

Spolsky, B. (1966). A psycholinguistic critique of programmed foreign language Instruction. *IRAL, 4*, 119–129.

Spolsky, B. (1989). *Conditions for second language learning*. Oxford: Oxford University Press.

Stern, H. H. (1983). *Fundamental concepts of language teaching*. Oxford: Oxford University Press.

Sternberg, R. J. (2002). The theory of successful intelligence and its implications for language-aptitude testing. In P. Robinson (Ed.), *Individual differences and instructed language learning* (pp. 13–44). Amsterdam: John Benjamins.

Stevick, E. W. (1980). *Teaching languages. A way and ways.* Rowley, MA: Newbury House.

Swain, M. (1985). Communicative competence: Some roles of comprehensible input and comprehensible output in its development. In S. M. Gass and C. G. Madden (Eds), *Input in Second language Acquisition* (pp. 235–253). Rowley, MA: Newbury House.

Swain, M. (1988). Manipulating and complementing content teaching to maximize second language learning. *TESL Canada Journal, 6,* 68–83.

Swain, M. (1993). The output hypothesis: Just speaking and writing aren't enough. *Canadian Modern Language Review–Revue Canadienne des Langues Vivantes, 50,* 158–164.

Swain, M. (1995). Three functions of output in second language learning. In G. Cook and B. Seidlhofer (Eds), *Principle and practice in applied linguistics: Studies in Honour of H. G. Widdowson* (pp. 125–144). Oxford: Oxford University Press.

Swain, M. and Lapkin, S. (1982). *Evaluating bilingual education: A Canadian case study.* Clevedon: Multilingual Matters.

Swain, M. and Lapkin, S. (1995). Problems in output and the cognitive processes they generate: A step towards second language learning. *Applied Linguistics, 16,* 371–391.

Swain, M. and Lapkin, S. (1998). Interaction and second language learning. Two adolescent French immersion students working together. *Modern Language Journal, 82,* 320–337.

Tees, R. C. and Werker, J. F. (1984). Perceptual flexibility: Maintenance or recovery of the ability to discriminate non-native speech sounds. *Canadian Journal of Psychology, 38,* 579–590.

Terrell, T. (1991). The role of grammar in a communicative approach. *Modern Language Journal, 75,* 52–63.

Thelen, E. and Smith, L. B. (1994). *A dynamic systems approach to the development of cognition and action.* Cambridge, MA: MIT Press.

Tomasello, M. (2000). First steps toward a usage-based theory of language acquisition. *Cognitive Linguistics, 11,* 61–82.

Tomlin, R. and Vilia, V. (1994). Attention in cognitive science and second language acquisition. *Studies in Second Language Acquisition, 16,* 183–204.

Tremblay, P. F. and Gardner, R. C. (1995). Expanding the motivation construct in language learning. *Modern Language Journal, 79,* 505–518.

Van Baalen, B. (1983). Giving learners rules: A study into the effect of grammatical instruction with varying degrees of explicitness. *Interlanguage Studies Bulletin, 7,* 71–100.

Van Dijk, M. (2003). *Child language cuts capers. Variability and ambiguity in early child development.* Groningen: University of Groningen.

Van Dijk, T. A. and Kintsch, W. (1983). *Strategies of discourse comprehension.* New York: Academic Press.

Van Geert, P. (1994a). *Dynamic systems of development: Change between complexity and chaos.* New York: Harvester Wheatsheaf.

Van Geert, P. (1994b). Vygotskian dynamics of development. *Human Development, 37,* 346–365.

Van Geert, P. (1998). A dynamic systems model of basic developmental mechanisms: Piaget, Vygotsky and beyond. *Psychological Review, 5,* 634–677.

Van Geert, P. and Van Dijk, M. (2002). Focus on variability, new tools to study intra-individual variability in developmental data. *Infant Behavior and Development, 25,* 340–374.

Van Hell, J. G. and Dijkstra, T. (2002). Foreign language knowledge can influence native language performance in exclusively native contexts. *Psychonomic Bulletin & Review, 9,* 780–789.

Van Heuven, W. J. B., Dijkstra, T., and Grainger, J. (1998). Orthographic neighborhood effects in bilingual word recognition. *Journal of Memory and Language, 39*, 458–483.

Van Wuijtswinkel, K. (1994). Critical period effects on the acquisition of grammatical competence in a second language. MA Thesis, Dept of Applied Linguistics, University of Nijmegen.

VanPatten, B. (1993). Grammar teaching for the acquisition-rich classroom. *Foreign Language Annals, 26*, 435–450.

VanPatten, B. (1994). Evaluating the role of consciousness in second language acquisition: terms, linguistic features and research methodology. *AILA Review, 11*, 27–36.

VanPatten, B. and Cadierno, T. (1993a). Explicit instruction and input processing. *Studies in Second Language Acquisition, 15*, 225–241.

VanPatten, B. and Cadierno, T. (1993b). Input processing and second language acquisition: a role for instruction. *The Modern Language Journal, 77*, 45–57.

VanPatten, B. and Sanz, C. (1995). From input to output: Processing instruction and communicative tasks. In D. Eckman, D. Highland, P. Lee, J. Mileham, and R. Weber (Eds), *SLA theory and pedagogy*. Mahwah, NJ: Erlbaum.

Vargha-Khadem, F., Carr, L. J., Isaacs, E., Brett, E., Adams, C., and Mishkin, M. (1997). Onset of speech after left hemispherectomy in a nine-year-old boy. *Brain, 120*, 159–182.

Varonis, E. M. and Gass, S. M. (1985). Miscommunication in native/non-native conversation. *Language in Society, 14*, 327–343.

Vellutino, F. and Scanlon, D. (1986). Linguistic coding and metalinguistic awareness: Their relationship to verbal and code acquisition in poor and normal readers. In D. Yaden and S. Templeton (Eds), *Metalinguistic awareness and beginning literacy* (pp. 115–141). Portsmouth, NH: Heinemann.

Verspoor, M. and Lowie, W. (2003). Making sense of polysemous words. *Language Learning, 53*, 547–586.

Von Studnitz, R. and Green, D. (2002). Interlingual homograph interference in German-English bilinguals: Its modulation and locus of control. *Bilingualism: Language and Control, 5*, 1–23.

Vygotsky, L. S. (1978). *Mind in society: the development of higher psychological processes*. Cambridge MA: Harvard University Press.

Waldrop, M. (1992). *Complexity: The emerging science at the edge of order and chaos*. New York: Simon and Schuster.

Weinreich, U. (1953). *Languages in contact: findings and problems*. New York: Linguistic Circle of New York. Reprinted in 1974 by Mouton, The Hague.

Wesche, M. (1981). Language aptitude measures in streaming matching students with methods, and diagnosis of learning problems. In K. C. Diller (Ed.), *Individual differences and universals in language learning aptitude*. Rowley, MA: Newbury House

White, L. (1985). Is there a 'logical problem' of second language acquisition? *TESL Canada Journal, 2*, 29–42.

White, L. (1987). Against comprehensible input: The input hypothesis and the development of L2 competence. *Applied Linguistics, 8*, 95–110.

White, L. (1989). Processing strategies: Are they sufficient to explain adult second language acquisition? Paper presented at the 9th Second Language Research Forum, UCLA, Los Angeles, February 23–4.

White, L. (1991). Adverb placement in second language acquisition: some effects of positive and negative evidence in the classroom. *Second Language Research, 7*, 133–161.

White, L. and Genesee, F. (1996). How native is near-native? The issue of ultimate attainment in adult second language acquisition. *Second Language Research, 12*, 238–265.

White, L., Spada, N., Lightbown, P. M., and Ranta, L. (1991). Input enhancement and L2 question formation. *Applied Linguistics, 12*, 416–432.

Widdowson, H. (1978). *Teaching language as communication.* Oxford: Oxford University Press.

Williams, J. N. (2003). Implicit learning of form-meaning connections in vocabulary and grammar. Paper presented at Erurosla conference, Edinburgh.

Witkin, H., Goodenough, D., and Oltman, P. K. (1979). Psychological differentiation: Current status. *Journal of Personality and Social Psychology, 37*, 1,127–1,145.

Wode, H. (1994). Nature, nurture, and age in second language acquisition: the case of speech perception. *Studies in Second Language Acquisition, 16*, 325–345.

Woutersen, M. (1997). Bilingual word perception. Ph.D. University of Nijmegen.

Yagmur, K. (1997). *First language attrition among Turkish speakers in Sydney.* Tilburg: Tilburg University Press.

Index